Ariosto and Boiardo

Ariosto and Boiardo

The Origins of *Orlando Furioso*

Peter V. Marinelli

University of Missouri Press
Columbia, 1987

Library of Congress Cataloging-in-Publication Data

Marinelli, Peter V.
   Ariosto and Boiardo: the origins of Orlando furioso.

   1. Ariosto, Lodovico, 1474-1533. Orlando furioso—Sources. 2. Boiardo, Matteo Maria, 1440 or
41-1494—Influence—Ariosto. 3. Boiardo, Matteo, Maria, 1440 or 41-1494. Orlando innamorato.
I. Title.
ISBN 0-8262-0636-0 (alk. paper)

∞™ This paper meets the minimum requirements of the American National Standard for
Permanence of Paper for Printed Library Materials, Z39.48, 1984.

Illustrations by Jean-Honoré Fragonard courtesy of The Rosenbach Museum & Library,
Philadelphia. Frontispiece, *Ruggiero and Alcina Confess their Mutual Passion*; Part I, *Eager to
Embrace Angelica, Ruggiero Divests Himself of his Armor*; Part II, *Ruggiero Despairs at Having Lost
Angelica.*

To the memory of
Lena Leone Marinelli and Viola-Yolanda Leone

Acknowledgments

Needless to say, I have accumulated numerous debts in the many years during which this study assumed its final shape. Here I wish to record my sense of deep gratitude to the astonishingly knowledgeable, perpetually helpful personnel of the libraries of the various institutions where I did research for this book: Princeton University, the New York Public Library, Harvard University, the Newberry Library, and the Henry E. Huntington Library. Five scholars read various versions of the manuscript and returned them to me with long, invaluable commentary and a host of suggestions for the improvement of its infelicities and errors (all those that remain are ineradicably mine). I owe special thanks for this labor to Hugh MacCallum, my colleague at the University of Toronto; Giuseppe Mazzotta of Yale University; D. W. Robertson, Jr., upon whose retirement I intruded, for which I beg forgiveness; Raymond Waddington of the University of California at Davis; and Professor Martin Wine of the University of Illinois at Chicago. Over many years Raymond Waddington has demonstrated a very moving interest in my work and a cheering solicitude in helping to see it placed; I thank him once again, as I do Professors Mazzotta and Robert J. Rodini for their advice and counsel in the same matter. Next, I wish to record my thanks to two old friends, Elizabeth Dipple and Albert R. Cirillo, both of Northwestern University, for encouragement and support over the years; to my own university, my college, and my department at Toronto; and to my many excellent students, both graduate and undergraduate. I take great pleasure in thanking my former student, Mr. Wayne Daniels, now associated with University of Toronto Press, for compiling the index. Finally, my deepest thanks must go to Rea Wilmshurst, who not only typed various versions of the manuscript but also constantly clarified difficulties, solved problems, and swept away obstacles. To really extraordinary intellectual gifts of organization and analysis she added inexhaustible resources of imagination, tact, and taste, and, in ways too numerous to record, this is her book as well as mine.

P. V. M.
April 1987

Contents

Introduction

Ariosto was irreverent, or what comes to the same thing, indifferent; his spirit was
areligious as it was aphilosophical, untormented with doubts, not concerned with human
destiny, incurious as to the meaning and value of this world, which he saw and touched,
and in which he loved and suffered.
    Benedetto Croce, *Ariosto, Shakespeare and Corneille*

This must be one of few examples of a work that is a great achievement in its own right
existing merely as a sequel to another. . . . Such a procedure must necessarily sacrifice
integrity and completeness of design; it is most likely to seek its effects by a brilliant
elaboration of episodes and a harmony of atmosphere rather than structure.
    Graham Hough, *A Preface to "The Faerie Queene"*

Brimming with life and movement, the chivalric poems of the Italian Renaissance
are a literary landmark and more than a literary phenomenon. In the grand spaces of
Pulci, Boiardo, Ariosto, and Tasso, artists as various as Berni, Monteverdi, Spenser,
Poussin, and Byron repeatedly found inspiration, and the impact on European life of
these fertile narratives is recorded not only in dozens of translations but also in
quantities of dramas, ballets, operas, and in art ranging from designs on majolica to
frescoes on the walls of palaces. The twentieth century still preserves a powerful
memory of their beauty and delight, and poems that interpenetrated the imagination of our forebears maintain a certain claim on our modern attention. Curiously,
nonetheless, they often appear to have blurred into the same furious, featureless
thing, one and all acquiring the same characteristics of high coloration and boisterous, unthinking vivacity—modified only in the always difficult case of Tasso by a
dubious pietism. About the honey on the rim of the cup we are not very much in
doubt; there is sweetness in plenty, but we go elsewhere for cordials and bitters.
Here time has intervened decisively in the transformation of taste. The rise of the
novel, offering a more proximate reality and immediately sympathetic personnel
than those of the senior tradition, has forever altered our sense of narrative. Uncom-
fortably errant in woodlands with viragoes and magicians, we are in a landscape
without a geography; our desperation in naming—is this the country of chivalric
romance, of romantic epic, or epic-romance?—betrays an elementary confusion.
    In remarkably intensified form the fortunes of *Orlando Furioso* repeat the history
common to the group of which it is really a very uncommon member. It was immediately and indisputably the poem of its age, challenged only by *Gerusalemme Liberata,* and then only after a crisis in European thought. It ran through well over one
hundred and fifty separate editions in the sixteenth century alone[1] and, singular
among Renaissance epics of any nation, spoke in every major and many a minor
European tongue. Till roughly a century ago it was a staple in the formation of an
educated western sensibility, its prime importance lying in its pivotal role in the

1

transmission of the epic tradition. As the first of the vernacular epics of the Renaissance, it threw a bridge across the chasm between the three classical epics of Homer and Vergil and the succeeding epics of Italy itself, and then of France, Portugal, and England. Tasso's *Gerusalemme Liberata*, Ronsard's *La Franciade*, Camoens's *Os Lusíadas*, Spenser's *The Faerie Queene*, even Milton's *Paradise Lost* profited from Ariosto's example and reveal its impact, sometimes directly, sometimes indirectly, but always with undiminished intensity over the course of time. Apart from epic, dramatic literature in France, Spain, and England soon gave evidence of the poem's fertilizing influence, and the sister arts of painting and music directed the poem's vitality into another series of still potent artistic reincarnations.[2] In the late twentieth century it remains possible, without ever having read a word of Ariosto, to encounter him in a variety of manifestations. In the world of painting his text inspired artists as different as Dosso Dossi, Tiepolo, Fragonard, Ingres, and Doré; in music his octaves were set by Giaches de Wert in Ferrara, Lully in France, and William Byrd in England. Best of all, perhaps, at present he is available in many a recording of baroque opera—Vivaldi's "Orlando Furioso," Haydn's "Orlando Paladino," Handel's "Orlando," "Alcina," and "Ariodante"—whose libretti, however much violence they do the poem from which they were carved, constantly remind us of the great original, reverberating still in the gleaming tessitura of Joan Sutherland or in the haunting expressiveness of Alfred Deller descending into Stygian madness.[3] And lest this be thought of as merely a matter of *castrati, fioriture,* and feather-headdresses, absurdly charming, the knowledge should be better diffused that such brainy, unsentimental readers as Voltaire and Charles James Fox were among the *Furioso*'s chief admirers.[4] The Enlightenment marked a zenith in the poem's fame. Soon after came decline into amused admiration, its fortunes an allegory of vanishings and losses, its meaning an Angelica ungraspable and forever in flight, perhaps not really worth having at all. Concurrently the poet's portrait underwent a drastic overpainting: where his great humanist contemporary, Celio Calcagnini, had invoked the Horatian formula and asserted clearly that the *Furioso*'s author, alone of all his group, had mixed the useful and the sweet,[5] Fragonard, with French complaisance, could depict an "Ariosto Inspired by Love and Folly,"[6] while Dr. Johnson, with British phlegm, would declare flatly, "Ariosto's pravity is generally known."[7]

There is no need to belabor the point, either of the *Furioso*'s pedigree as a very great work of art, or of its popular reputation as a basically structureless and negligibly serious poem whose essence lies in some brief, coruscating episodes of pure fantasy and in its kaleidoscopic sweep, movement, and style. The epigraphs with which I preface this Introduction and the chapters of Part II testify to fairly continuous, widespread misunderstanding or devaluation occurring since the nineteenth century, and this in spite of renewed critical interest in the poem and the problems it presents, an interest that, most often displayed in studies of particular episodes or thematic strands of the *Furioso,* allows us to imagine an Ariosto of deeper sensibilities and shaping intellect, at least on a fairly limited scale.[8] Nevertheless, the *Furioso* as something like an artistic whole remains a mirage on the horizon, alluring but unreal. The following chapters attempt to establish the basis for a more comprehensive interpretation of this ungraspable Angelica of a poem.

The interpretation of the poem has proved an inordinately difficult affair for several reasons: sheer length, variety of inherited and original material, complex mode of narration, labile and elusive style, and ignorance of the tradition in which the work originates. One of the greatest stumbling-blocks to more informed reading must assuredly lie in the fact that the *Furioso* is a poem that from first to last grows out of a torso of sixty-nine cantos, Boiardo's *Orlando Innamorato,* the two *Orlando*s comprising a total (if most certainly not a unit) of one hundred and fifteen cantos and over 70,000 lines. The *Furioso* distinguishes itself from its chief source by beginning in medias res and from other European epics by continually utilizing the *materia* of a relatively unfamiliar work as long as itself. Throughout and paradoxically, it establishes an almost obsessive but highly independent relationship with its parent. Ariosto's dominance of Boiardo's text is total, his assertion of that dominance ubiquitous. At every point we are confronted (if we hold the two poems simultaneously to the lens) with the most elaborate discrepancies, testifying to the wide range of techniques Ariosto employed for the piecemeal absorption and transformation of Boiardo's truncated poem—techniques of suppression, compression, conjunction, expansion, outright contradiction and reversal, transference, and termination. Italian Carolingian poetry is an artistic continuum in which deliberate rivalry and supercession is the norm.[9] Since the *Furioso* is part of the continuum that crystallizes in Boiardo, in reading the poem we are constantly forced back (or should be) to the *Innamorato,* to find out how any action, characterization, train of ideas, or association of ideas and images got started at all; and this scrutiny should operate most particularly in the poem's opening cantos, where Ariosto is simultaneously concerned to hinge his own work onto Boiardo's and to declare his own individuality in the most tacitly forceful manner.[10] It is not too much to say that never do the narrative joins fit without the purposefully jagged edges showing, that in no instance do the superimposed characterizations, events, and images overlap without abundant evidence of quite provocative incongruency.[11] In a word, Ariosto's sense of rivalry, his sense of "overgoing" in creating deeper intellectual and moral content and a superior sense of form, places considerable stress on our knowledge of the details of the *Innamorato,* and of what Ariosto has done to thrust across them. Bland acceptance of what we see before us in the *Furioso* emasculates the complex, competitive nature of Ariosto's art and effaces the unique relationship (in time it was to be Oedipal) it sets up with its poetic foil. Differentiation becomes the first and greatest prerequisite for interpretation.

This is a matter that was very obviously intended to engage the attention of the society for which the two poems were written, and that, inevitably, must have been clearest when the memory of the two poems was fresh in the minds of its courtly readers. Equally inevitably, the ascendancy of the one over the other, together with the tempestuous cultural shifts of the sixteenth century, worked to eclipse the unique alliance, tearing the *Furioso,* in the process, from its cultural, social, intellectual, and artistic moorings.[12]

Not only did the *Innamorato,* after 1544, cease to be printed for almost three hundred years,[13] but the Aristotelian triumph in the fourth decade of the century also brought about the first serious encroachment on the essential nature and method of the *Furioso,* while the simultaneous establishment of the Inquisition sometimes made difficulties for it in other areas. What happened to Ariosto's epic in the ensuing thirty or forty years is an object lesson, first, on the fragility of a poem's original conception, and second, of its protean adaptability to the requirements of new generations and new conditions.[14] Only a very short while intervened between the poet's death in 1533 and the "rediscovery" of the *Poetics*; the debate about the relative merits of Ariosto and Tasso in the last decades of the sixteenth century took place against this new critical background and provided the focus both for the charge against the *Furioso* of failing in unity and for its defense as a poem not meant to adhere to standards of which its author had had no knowledge. Nevertheless, the Aristotelian revival soon came to function as the conventional starting-point for criticism of the *Furioso,* habitually usurping the artistic standards of the society for which it was created. The application of the Aristotelian yardstick rapidly became the fashion—Tasso himself employed it against Ariosto—and the repercussions have lasted well into the modern period. Say "unity," and a linear, Aristotelian conception of the term comes instantly, perhaps inevitably, to mind. But, by the supposed standards of Aristotle, the *Furioso,* with its elaborate pattern of interlacing multiple actions, had neither unity nor form, and no amount of cramping or cutting could resolve the difficulty. The tedium of the documents in the Great Debate arises precisely from the prolonged, pointless pursuit of this arid question.[15] Indeed, the individual texts of the controversy often have the appearance of pedantic tactical maneuvers, opportunistic and improvisatory, with a strong ad hominem component, rather than of deeply considered broad strategy. In the long run, the Ariostans' responses, launched from ground chosen by the antagonists, are less effective than the attacks, which concern themselves with the form, content, and unity of true epic, but do so prescriptively, with little or no attention to the wellsprings of Ariosto's art and the special circumstances of its creation. The debate, in brief, was ultimately more illuminative of the literary world of late sixteenth-century Italy than of the first three decades of that century, decades in which Ariosto published, corrected, and expanded his poem with his own particular society and audience in mind. Thanks to its supporters' mistaken desire to assert its adherence to Aristotelian regularity,[16] the *Furioso,* born to one law, was now to another procrusteanly bound.

From the critical wars, Ariosto emerged as a displaced person, Boiardo as something of a *desaparecido*. For, if the controversy had the effect of substituting Aristotle for Plato as an artistic influence in the composition of the *Furioso,* it likewise, by way of by-product and in the same spirit of anachronism, presented Tasso in place of Boiardo as the conventional standard of measurement against Ariosto. In after times this gives us, inappropriately standing in for an outmoded great poet of the fifteenth century, a great modern talent of the sixteenth century. Even more appealingly, apparently, it produces a more sensational contrast than that offered by Boiardo to Ariosto. Against the latter, cast as the unfettered free spirit of a more relaxed and opulent High Renaissance, there is now poised the mad, sad celebrator of post-Reformation orthodoxy, obsessed with the rules of Aristotle and composing not a *Furioso* with its turbulent Carolingian whirlwind of fantastic event but a true poem of history, based on the events of the first Crusade: a complacent and far too highly colored diptych.

Well into our own century the Boiardo-Ariosto relationship seemed to have simply evaporated from the notoriously impermanent faculty of human memory, which Ariosto might wryly, were he alive, have assigned to some jug in the moon's wasteland of lost things. Consequently, and particularly in the English-speaking world, Ariosto is often supposed to be little more than a more "artistic" Boiardo, and the *Furioso* is generally held to be not essentially dissimilar, either in content or form, from the jesting, endearingly chaotic *Innamorato*. In fact, the differences are both of degree and kind, with important implications for the study of the development of vernacular Renaissance epic, a line in which the *Furioso* stands out as the first true exemplar. The enduring fascination of the *Furioso* is that it is a Renaissance comic epic that is not produced ex nihilo; it applies itself steadily and continuously to eliciting from a comic romance with tardily introduced epic elements every undeveloped hint, no matter how slender, that it can utilize to its own higher artistic purposes. In so doing, the poem offers a unique opportunity to determine what a Renaissance poet, at length and over a long period of time, aimed to create in his confrontation with a single perpetually fascinating work—a work that acted as a receptacle for almost everything else he knew and absorbed in a lifetime of study, and a work to whose re-creation he directed a quarter-century of writing, correction, and expansion. Hence the *Innamorato* as "palimpsest."

This book, then, is intended to fill the need for a fuller and more precise account of the Ariosto-Boiardo relationship than it has yet been accorded.[17] The question to be addressed is whether it is possible to establish a pattern in Ariosto's method of composition in his remanipulation of Boiardo's text, whether we can speak of an Ariostan aesthetic rather than a series of ad hoc maneuvers and random scatter-shots. Aiming to situate the *Furioso* as far as possible in its original cultural context, this study inevitably attempts to illuminate the poet's ambition to accumulate strengths of structure and meaning as his poem grows, moment by moment and with visible power and control, out of the source it both feeds upon and re-creates.

The nature of the problem addressed dictates the two-part form of this book. Part I attempts to set in relief some of the signal features of the *Innamorato*, as constituting a kind of poetic capital that proved especially profitable for Ariosto when he combined it with a wide variety of interrelated Neoplatonic resources. This represents a very selective treatment of the *Innamorato*.[18] For purposes of clarifying a complicated and often confusing narrative, I have divided the discussion into two parts, one treating the Orlando-world of manic passion and the other treating the world of the future dynasts, Bradamante and Ruggiero. In both, the critical approach is often proleptic, looking ahead from a characterization, an incident, or scene in Boiardo to one concluded many cantos away in Ariosto, thus providing at the very start a few crucial instances of Ariosto's method of "continuation."[19] This part terminates with an intensive analysis of the crucial first meeting of Bradamante and Ruggiero in 3.5,[20] four cantos away from the *Innamorato*'s abruptly truncated ending: the sine qua non of the *Furioso,* which itself terminates with the dynasts' marriage feast.[21] This is possibly the richest and most fruitful area for a view into Ariosto's eagle-eyed way of seeing poetic possibilities in Boiardo's text; and if for no other reason than that it is also one of the most splendidly powerful examples of Boiardo's art, it forms the climax of Part I of this study, as it does, cliff-hanger fashion, of the *Innamorato* itself, mutely crying out for completion.

Ten years intervened between the breaking off of the *Innamorato* in 1494 and the beginning of the *Furioso*; approximately thirty years intervene between the beginning of the *Innamorato* in 1476 and the beginning of the *Furioso*; over fifty years separate the beginning of the *Innamorato* from the third and final edition of the *Furioso* in 1532. The poems proceed from two different eras and are accommodated to two different societies.

To aid in differentiating, Part II concerns itself with events and issues that intervened massively between the *Innamorato* and the *Furioso*—political changes, Vergilian scholarship, Neoplatonic love-lore, the impact of Lucianistic writing—and that are essential for understanding its content and structure. For purposes of immediate contrast, Part II opens with an interpretation of the *Furioso* as a work reflective of history and contemporary society in a way utterly distinct from the *Innamorato*. Thereafter, it gradually draws into focus the various elements, Neoplatonic in origin, orientation, or affinity, that provided the material for the classical overlay of the Boiardan text. Necessarily, the reading of the *Furioso* is paradigmatic rather than sequential or chronological, but it will be obvious that I attempt to go beyond partial readings and strive to present the poem as an organic whole with a particular, complex form arising from its distinctive mode of narration.[22] A basic triadic organization, tied to the adventures of three of the poem's main characters, is at the heart of Ariosto's rich multiplicity of actions and his orchestration of diversities. It springs from the literary Platonism fashionable during the poet's formative years, when interest in the varieties of love, usually expressed in triadic terms, was a constant in the courtly circles of the period. It is reflected in works with revealing titles (*De generibus amoris* by Petrus Haedus, *I tre libri d'amore* by Francesco da Diacetto), and it underlies the swirling complexities of his narrative, giving substantial intellectual force to the interlace technique of storytelling he had inherited as a matter of course from the romantic-chivalric tradition. To speak for a moment as if they were really divisible instead of being reflections of each other, the Neoplatonism of the *Furioso* is manifested as clearly in its form as in its content.

Neoplatonism flowed in on the *Furioso* from a variety of sources. In its rudimentary contrast of two loves and two contrasted pairs of lovers, one manic, one decidedly more human, the *Innamorato* already gave evidence of Neoplatonic influence in distinguishing between loves and lives, a characteristic that could only be reinforced by Ariosto's contact with Bembo. In aiming to conclude and to surpass the poem, Ariosto immediately took up the *genus unde* motif Boiardo associated with Ruggiero and Bradamante and expanded its Vergilian resonances, evoking, in the process, a universally diffused tradition of Neoplatonic allegorization of the *Aeneid* that was still being augmented by scholars in his own time and city. Finally, in bringing the dynastic themes of Vergil and Boiardo under the scrutiny of sublunary activity visible in classical models like Lucian's Menippean dialogues, Macrobius's *Somnium Scipionis,* and Boethius's *Consolation,* he invoked a Platonic vision of reality on two levels, material and eternal, to complicate the praises of an earthly glory. Neoplatonism thus comprehends and subsumes both the Vergilianism and the Lucianism of the *Furioso,* in the sense, in the latter case, of its comically contemplating the antlike earthly perturbation of the Many from a distanced speculative perspective on high of the One. Not for nothing, then, does the poet repeatedly refer to himself as a weaver of multiple strands (2.30; 13.8; 20.3), and, as a musician evoking different harmonies (8.29), he reveals a real discrimination among sonorities. Plato, Vergil, and Lucian are the main elements harmonized in the *Furioso,* which is a poem of harmony in ways rather different from those the followers of Croce imagined.[23]

The fusion of Boiardo and Neoplatonism in various phases (Vergil being always one of the main considerations subsumed in the latter) reflects two of the ascertainable passions of Ariosto's young manhood. When, around 1505, he first began to compose, Aristotelianism and Counter-Reformation lay far in the future, and if the spirit of a Greek philosopher presided over the arts, it was that of the Christianized Plato. If the *Furioso* is ever to be truly "placed," there are some essential biographical facts with which we should begin.[24] One of them, embarrassing to anachronism, is that the first letter Ariosto is ever recorded as having written, on January 5, 1498, when he was twenty-three and attending the humanists' lectures at the Studio di Ferrara, reveals him in direct contact with Neoplatonic tradition, both Florentine and Boethian. As Edmund Gardner long ago noted,[25]

The only extant letter of Ariosto's that belongs to this epoch in his life is also written, like the poetry, in Latin. It is addressed to Aldo Manuzio, and is an appeal to the great Venetian publisher to send for sale what books he has printed of Marsilio Ficino and other translators of Platonic literature to Ferrara, where Sebastiano dell'Aquila, who is teaching both medicine and philosophy at the Studio, "readeth Plato on the *Timaeus* on feast-days with a very great audience." The writer knows that Aldo can supply him and his friends with what they want, from Alberto Pio [lord of Carpi, Ariosto's fellow-pupil in the Augustinian friar Gregorio da Spoleto's classes] "who, when he returned from thee to us some days ago, brought amongst others a volume in which certain works of some Platonists were collected."

This was, we should note, four years after the death of Boiardo and the truncation of the *Innamorato,* less than seven years before composition of the *Furioso* commenced, and exactly contemporaneous with the arrival in Ferrara, for the first of two extended periods (1497–1499 and 1502–1503), of one of the major Neoplatonists of his time, the youthful Pietro Bembo, Ariosto's friend for life.[26]

In spite of Croce's curious postulation of Ariosto's resistance to any system of thought, there is no need to make heavy weather of Ariosto's Neoplatonism, which is not, in any case, the abstruse and densely philosophical one of Ficino and Pico, but rather one deriving from the literary and "social" Platonism of a generation that had absorbed and popularized the Florentine philosophers. Ariosto falls naturally here into the company of writers like Pietro Bembo, Mario Equicola, and Baldassare Castiglione, his friends and familiars throughout his life, all of them students of Neoplatonist love-philosophy and compositors of love-treatises dealing with a spectrum of loves that is most often arranged in triads. From this tradition Ariosto, intensely practical, took merely an organizing principle of elegant simplicity, one commonly found in the writing of his contemporaries and friends. His genius consisted in his giving vivid dramatic life to abstract conceptions, in three central cases choosing particular Boiardan characters to play the roles of different kinds of lovers: interleaving their lives in a welter of chivalric incidents, he reveals the profound differences in their inclinations and ambitions and the particular qualities of their loves. What they love and desire reveals, at any given moment, where they stand on a vertical ladder of values, marked by animalistic, human, and transcendent stages. They provide the spine of his richly pullulating narrative, framing and strengthening its vagaries.

A modern critic has declared, "Neo-Platonism leaves very little mark on the *Furioso,*" arguing that the poem is "anything but an academic treatise on love."[27] But why the poem's appeal to ideas and images commonly found also in the love-treatises by which it may have been influenced should render it a treatise remains unclear. Ariosto's art is utterly different from the static, descriptive procedure of the writer of the Neoplatonic love-treatise: having chosen various Boiardan characters to play particular roles, he propels them into action progressing toward the exemplification of various states of life and love (bestial, active, transcendent) that the treatises describe from the outside, as it were. One of his chief claims to originality as a poet consists in his continuous differentiation between and among these characters as they move to their various fates. The process is unremittingly dynamic, filled with as much regression as progression, jagged and dramatic in the unceasing motion of love in evolving its various capacities. The poem's principle of unity is therefore to be sought not in a linear Aristotelian narrative but in a kaleidoscopically changing Neoplatonic one, in which the various component elements of a triad are constantly being contrastingly rearranged against one another, dramatized in marvelous fictions of controlled errancy and directed deviation; they are the constants in a multitudinous swarm of characters. So Orlando degenerates into a beast, Ruggiero (after many struggles) achieves a wife and a crown, and Astolfo surveys earth from the moon—an abstracted "loony," in quite a different way from the mad Orlando. Put another way, Ruggiero works the Orlando aspect out of his nature, and Astolfo (always represented as being in advance of the other two warriors) rises (temporarily, at least) above both the Orlando and Ruggiero aspects in himself.

The various chapters of Part II, then, exploit the ways in which Ariosto utilized and transformed Boiardo's Orlando and Ruggiero, lovers both, as exemplars of two very different kinds of lives, the feral and the active, that respectively make up the lowest and middle elements in the typically tripartite arrangement of lives familiar in Renaissance Neoplatonism. That arrangement was available in Fulgentius's allegorization of the Choice of Paris, in Macrobius's *Somnium Scipionis*, in Landino's allegorization of the *Aeneid*, the *Disputationes Camaldulenses*, and in Erasmus's *Praise of Folly*—to say nothing of Ficino and Bembo. Ariosto's originality and inventive powers are prominently on view as he amplifies Boiardo's legacy by imagining continuous, extended moral careers for the two warrior-lovers, one doomed to erotic madness at the poem's midpoint, the other fated to achieve a ruler's position by the poem's end, though only after a protracted set of errors and downfalls culminating in an inability to achieve any victory on his own, which is a lesson clearly imparted to Astolfo and cheerily acknowledged. However much the arc of Ruggiero's individual story is intercepted and broken into segments by the exuberant interposition of other romance narratives in Ariosto's *entrelacement*, taken as a whole it falls distinctly into hierarchical component parts and presents a remarkably clear outline of programmatic movement.[28] The poet drives clear lines of incremental meaning through complicating overgrowths of parallel and subsidiary tales.

Ariosto criticism has long resisted any kind of protracted thematic treatment with regard to the *Furioso*'s main characters, especially if the treatment threatened to assume the aspect of moral advance: a residual Burckhardtian view of Italian Renaissance poetry often comes into play. Nevertheless, if Ruggiero's progress to princely and husbandly status is marked into clear stages, so too is Astolfo's very different progress, one in which he escapes (in two senses) the gravity of earth. In this instance, Ariosto was working in almost total independence of Boiardo, in contrast to his development of Orlando's real *furia* out of Boiardo's comic *pazzia,* or his development of Ruggiero's prolonged career out of strong hints at a program of action hinted at in some of Boiardo's last cantos. For Astolfo, Ariosto had no such hints at all. Astolfo plays a very negligible part indeed in the *Innamorato,* but in a powerfully assertive gesture, Ariosto selects Astolfo, one of the least likely candidates, for an unimaginably important part in the *Furioso*. He appears first as repentant sensualist, soon begins to operate as righter of wrongs and dispenser of justice in a tour of the monster-ridden chivalric world, and next triumphs (for a brief while at least) as blithe moon-voyager and laughing Lucianic contemplator of the manic sublunary world: a surrogate for the poet in the end, and hence the only one who, of all those passion-blinded denizens of the *Furioso*'s landscapes, shares something of the poet's perspective over the stir and bustle below. Here again there is programmatic progression and continuity of movement through constantly intervening narratives, which require the reader's immediate attention and consequently distract from the purely linear movement of any one of the three main stories. Ariosto's mode of narration requires readers to widen the span of their critical attention to accommodate both the leisurely ambages of romance as well as the linear progression of the three main champions as they move to various destinies. My reading therefore seeks to present Ariosto in a new light, as both strategist and tactician, as climatologist as well as weatherman.

A good part of the *Furioso* is shaped by the contrast developed at length between the interwoven careers of Ruggiero and Astolfo. Mediated by Neoplatonist criticism, the *Aeneid* came to Ariosto as a poem of indispensable moral growth in a mythical dynast who is projected as a kind of Everyman, journeying through physical and spiritual obstacles to his ultimate destiny. While, in Ruggiero's story, Ariosto's emphasis falls quite as much as Vergil's on the vicissitudes suffered by an ancestor before he can found his city, his conception of that movement varies greatly, almost necessarily, from that of Vergil. It is no longer an end in itself, with a moral imperative, "parcere subiectis, et debellare superbos." Once he sets his Astolfo on the moon amid those tumid exploded bladders that represent ancient failed empires, Ariosto transcends the theme of glory he had out of Vergil. As a poet working at a court that sought to present itself as Christian, sometimes by conviction but certainly by policy, Ariosto filters the Vergilian vision through the lenses of Neoplatonic mutability and transcendence, adopting the celestial distancing of Boethius and Macrobius on human activity and blending it with the laughing lunar perspectives of Lucian's Menippus. The view from the moon puts Ferrara (toward whose founding and glorification the whole poem has been working) into true perspective *sub specie aeternitatis*. The episode places centrally what is an intrinsically brief element in the celebration of all epic enterprise, the warning against human pride, familiar in Priam's warning to Achilles, in Evander's instruction of Aeneas in humility, in the Old Man of Belem's outcry against Vasco da Gama's expedition. In a poem where so many lunatics lose their wits, the moon is appropriately the highest boundary of its vertical movement, but Ariosto's Ptolemaic-Christian universe recognizes another city higher up than Ferrara, one into which the decorum of the comic Charlemagnic poem and the monopoly of Dante forbid entrance. Although he has his (very complex) joke with the saintly author of the Heavenly Jerusalem, and though there are some merited shots at the cardinal whom chance made

Ariosto's employer, it is possible that the poem's values are not annihilated in a momentary flash on the moon; more especially, Cardinal Ippolito's failings did not undermine for Ariosto the great achievements in history of his entire family. Ariosto wrote comic, not mock, epic; there is a profound difference. The following pages investigate the possibility that, far from being satirical or deconstructive of the genre, the comic epic is the obverse of the "sober" or "earnest" epic, and that it offers parallel, not antagonistic, values to its illustrious Latin parent.[29] In relation to "solemn" epic the *Furioso* may stand as a prolonged litotes, a comic understatement affirming values in a different mode of expression.

In the readings of Part II, then, the principle behind the construction of the *Furioso* is represented as fugal—"horizontal" in its progression in time as we turn the pages to follow the tale, but "vertical" in the sense that its component elements are kept in constant interaction against each other on a hierarchical scale and are under the supervision of a directing, organizing mind. Astolfo's downward glance from the moon on all the fury and passion of the Boiardan-Ariostan landscape provides overt confirmation of the epic verticality Ariosto deliberately builds into his poem's structure through his manipulation of the time scheme. In a word, the poet repeatedly scrambles time, disrupts sequence, disjoins cause from result to produce a higher reality than the one that immediately catches the reader's eye. Human actions are viewed from the perspective of an ideal time, an All-time or No-time, which is, in essence, God's time: past, present, and future seen *in ictu oculis*. A Neoplatonic perspective on the wide theater of human activity is therefore built into the poem's very structure, into its mode of narration, and it is complex, laborious, and difficult to comprehend. Indeed, though this aspect of the *Furioso* seems to have passed largely unnoticed and unappreciated, it provides the most powerful contrast with Boiardo's relatively simple conception of his poet's role and his mode of telling and is one of the chief principles of organization and unification operating behind the poem's many-mindedness. Quite simply, it forces the reader to reassemble the deliberately disarranged and scattered segments of the poem in his mind and to recognize that he is in the control of an awesomely attentive craftsman and constructor.

There is a pattern discernible in this procedure that points to a new view of the poet's role in the *Furioso,* one that, considering how deeply it is embedded and manifested in the poet's conception of his own art, and what immense ramifications it has in the structure of his masterwork, argues against a view of his poetry as skeptic, at odds with its society, alienated. Unless Ariosto was deeply schizophrenic, his Neoplatonism, woven into the very tissues of his poetry and functioning as the source of its form, evinces a lifelong fascination with its central ideas. Concerned with the growth of civilizations in time, his epic shows how carefully he had stored his imagination with significant resonances of ancient, medieval, and contemporary history, how adroitly he had learned to leap back and forth from past to present to future because to him, as God-like poet to his own creation, the multitudinous moments of time were, Neoplatonically, one. There are, as a consequence, no historical "digressions" in the *Furioso,* no passages of dynastic praise falling into the category of "non poesia" that Ariosto barely thought worthy of writing and that bored readers may skip or relegate to the realm of satirical undermining. The poem is radically concerned with the shifting of time and with the panoramas of human passion in both romance and history. Ariosto's awareness is witnessed by the immense geographical extension of his poem, by its broad recall of vast areas of human history, and especially by the action on two levels that takes place concurrently on his mental map of both the actual and the fantastic worlds: the hurly-burly of events in the time of Charlemagne, and the perpetually shifting, repercussive, deadly politics of ancient, medieval, and contemporary Europe. Some of the most influential events of his time were set in motion by the poet's contemporaries and familiars, and he interleaves them meaningfully with the quests and the errancies of the *donne e cavalier* of romance. We shift alternately between the fictional worlds of Bradamante and Ruggiero in the era of Charlemagne and another imperial world of the sixteenth century, where Charles V rules as Holy Roman Emperor, and where the dynasts' descendants play roles of power and influence on the great stage of the world. Hence, as we are to see later, we experience the *Furioso* on a level very like that of the *Aeneid,* where creatures of fiction like Aeneas, Ascanius, and Lavinia share the narrative with historical figures like Julius Caesar, Caesar Augustus, and Marcellus. History and legend cohabit and establish a series of mutually reflecting mirrors.

The *Furioso* demonstrably attempts to be the record of its civilization, often achieving its end by a proleptic movement of considerable force, by constantly incorporating or alluding to or transforming the cultural achievements of Ferrara's intellectual energies in both past and present. In so doing, it functions as a vast treasure-house or repository of the city's achievements over the centuries, offering testimony to the magnificence of its House and utilizing the accomplishments of its civilization to enhance the telling of the tale of its origins in the time of Bradamante and Ruggiero. From the time scheme of the Carolingian narrative, those cultural triumphs are still far in the uncertain future; from the perspective of the poet and his audience, they are now ineluctably part of the society the two lovers once founded and can be drawn on to magnify their story. Conceived as a social work of art from the very beginning, and manifesting an increasing awareness of that dimension in its third and last edition, the *Furioso* is the product of a diplomatic intelligence, skilled in subtly meaningful gestures and in points established by minimal means for maximum effectiveness with aristocrats who understood. On this level, the poem represents a ceaseless quest for poetic opportunities for festive celebration, functioning as an epic should, as the most comprehensive epideictic memorial of its civilization, the separate elements of which it magnifies by unifying and preserving them in a massively comprehensive poetic frame. Frequently it achieves this end by the gesture of silently transforming works of literature known to, written for, or even dedicated to munificent members of the Este court. Just as often, it breaks from its preoccupation with romantic fantasy to render homage by outright recall of reverberative events or distinguished actions set afoot by members of that relatively small society. The poet continually demonstrates an up-to-the-minute attentiveness to the literature, art, and politics of his day, and he writes with an eye alerted to the practicability of both the old and new. He remembers, for instance, the recently recovered Lucian as well as Vergil, and thereby silently pays tribute to the great educator, Guarino da Verona, who, after his discovery of the Menippean satirist in the libraries of Constantinople, became the founder of the Studio di Ferrara and the tutor to the Marquis Leonello.[30]

Nevertheless, the first and greatest of Ariosto's gestures to his society is one that simply presents itself, with utmost quietness and wholly without drawing attention to itself. This gesture involves the bold, decisive resumption of the *Innamorato,* a masterstroke of courtly grace on Ariosto's part as an obeisance to a dead aristocrat, Matteo Maria Boiardo, the Count of Scandiano, the favorite poet of Duke Ercole I and his young daughter, Isabella. Boiardo is the source that Ariosto, in the first and greatest of his ironies, never once mentions or credits. The choice reveals a characteristic courtier's gesture mingled with an unyielding independence of mind. Ariosto's genius was not only to resume the beloved *Innamorato*—and he must have loved it very deeply to have mastered it so completely—but also to rehearse its matter in conformity with a new standard of learning and sophistication, for a new court in a newer and more brilliant phase of its history. When Ariosto began to write, the Este scions were no longer the children and young adolescents whom Boiardo had delighted in delighting with tales of an oafish Orlando in love. Now Alfonso was Duke of Ferrara; his brother, the Cardinal Ippolito, was Ariosto's patron; their sister, Beatrice Sforza (d. 1497), had been Duchess of Milan and the patroness of Leonardo; while Isabella, by marriage with Francesco Gonzaga, had become Marchioness of Mantua, a fact that invites attention to the Vergilian overlay that Ariosto gave the whole *Innamorato.* Ferrara itself, already substantially enlarged under Ercole by the "addizione erculea," grew ever more architecturally splendid as it moved from the late Quattrocento into the splendors of the Cinquecento, when its poets as well as its rulers felt the need for more elaborate constructions. In the case of Renaissance architecture, a new building incorporates but obliterates the original, whose shape, structure, and size can often only be guessed. In the case of the two *Orlandos,* by virtue of the special magic attached to the written word, we are privileged to see the original still standing beside the more splendid reconstruction. It seems time that we had a more accurate measure of their respective ground plans and elevations.

I

Orlando Innamorato

The Palimpsest

1

"Furore" and "Dismisura"

The Orlando-World of Immoderate Passion

He was playing there at the palla.
Parisina—two doves for an altar—at the window,
"E'l Marchese
Stava per divenir pazzo
after it all." And that was when Troy was down
And they came here and cut holes in rock,
Down Rome way, and put up the timbers;
And came here, condit Atesten . . .
    "Peace! keep the peace, Borso."
And he said: Some bitch has sold us
    (that was Ganelon)
"They wont get another such ivory" . . .
(Este, Nic Este speaking)
    Ezra Pound, *The Cantos*

Brilliant in their compression and their evocation of an historical moment, Pound's verses provide a peculiarly fitting introduction to the poetry of Boiardo. All the agonies and the pleasures of a lifetime are jumbled together in Niccolò d'Este's deathbed delirium—his heir Ugo's execution for incest with his stepmother, Parisina, the maddened father in torment "after it all," the dynastic crisis thereafter, the illegitimate Leonello's and Borso's succession, Roland dying at Roncesvalles, Troy down and Rome up and, as an offshoot of Empire, the rise of ancestral Ateste. Shot through with recollections of Niccolò's favorite literature and urgent with fear for the state under illegitimate new rulers, the passage strikingly captures the Ferrara of its mid-century crisis, its atmosphere of blood, chivalry, and classicism, its obsession with several literatures and mythologies. The synopsis prepares us for the poetry of Boiardo in the next generation, a poetry that, celebrating the reign of Duke Ercole I, the rightly restored legitimate successor to Borso, is at once Carolingian, classical, and dynastic, optimistic in all its opening gestures and supremely comic in temper and treatment. Begun in 1476, the *Innamorato* is truly a poem of delightful new beginnings, immediately promising (in its second line) "cose dilettose e nove," of which Orlando as a parody of the Arthurian lover is the glaring first.

A project so bold and flaringly initiated inevitably throws the poet's figure into high relief, inviting scrutiny of the author's progressive realization of a literary self in the tale he tells.[1] As an innovator who first conceives of re-creating the vital but disheveled matter of the plebeians in the piazza for the courtly audiences of the Este castle, Boiardo hovers constantly between the popular and the aristocratic, the gro-

17

tesque and the idealized, the comic-satiric and the abundantly lyrical, between knockabout Carolingian and magical Arthurian. The clearest demonstration of the alternating attractions of these popular and courtly elements is visible in his proems, in his dramatizations of his poet's role and his relation to his real or imaginary audience. Ariosto will later determine for a set of personae at once, but Boiardo gives clear evidence of a gradually evolving conception of his role *after* his poem is already under way. This can easily be illustrated. Book 1 begins with an address to the "Signori e cavallieri" who have assembled to hear "cose dilettose e nove," but within that entire book this address forms only one of two acknowledgments of the courtly nature of the audience. In all but one other instance of the book's twenty-nine cantos (the exception occurs at 1.19.1), Boiardo's proems are amusingly businesslike and abrupt, imitations of the rough openings used by popular storytellers who, after a brief salute, commonly proceeded at once to the narrative. Though Boiardo's audience is obviously no marketplace mixture of rabble and bourgeoisie, it is similarly and unceremoniously bidden to be quiet ("State attenti e quieti"; "Stati ad odir").

Book 2 provides an electrifying change. Here only, abruptly and gratifyingly in the poem's mid-career, does the narrator finally clarify his role and characterize his audience. The change in mode of address seems to herald and to accompany the introduction of a new and greater hero, Ruggiero, whose appearance represents yet another "new thing." The new proems offer repeated opportunities for some of the most radiant and characteristic poetry of the *Innamorato,* and they form part of the general heightening of tone apparent from book 2 onward. Now the narrator is no brusque minstrel but instead a gracious courtier singing his stanzas to an audience of damsels and gallants in appropriate courtly settings. On thirteen separate occasions thereafter, all through books 2 and 3, the proems touch gracefully on this idyllic situation, the poet imaginatively re-creating a lovelier and long-vanished past, a time "quando virtù fioriva" and youths and maidens had free scope for the exercise of martial bravery and virtuous love. Though it is clear, of course, from recurring internal references that the poem was always intended to be read, the poetic fiction of the proems reveals that Boiardo has suddenly fleshed out the single unprecedented address to the "Segnori e cavallieri innamorati / Cortese damiselle e graziose" of 1.19.1 and produced an imaginative situation in which singer and auditors are harmoniously assembled together like figures in a manuscript illumination. Amusingly, because they are being called on to listen to tales of unbridled passion and berserk irascible fury in the popular mode, the attentive audience emerges in the round as a group of "legiadri amanti e damigelle" who carry love within their gentle hearts ("Che dentro ai cor gentili avete amore," 2.31.50), as nobles who imitate the "valor" of ancient exemplars and whose "animo gentile" rejoices at every "atto degno e signorile" (2.24.1). With great charm and nobility, wishing them "Vita zoiosa, e non finisca mai" (2.5.1), the poet-minstrel gives unstintingly to his hearers, establishing an unchangingly perfect rapport:

Ed io pur chieggio a voi che sete intorno
Che ciascun ponga ogni sua noia in cassa,
Ed ogni affanno ed ogni pensier grave
Dentro vi chiuda, e poi perda la chiave. (2.31.1)

And I beseech you, as you sit round me, that each of you will put his sorrows in a chest, and lock it up with every grief and graver thought, and lose the key.

The sense of withdrawal is intense—in time as in place. We should not be surprised if this poet were suddenly to sing "Avete 'n voi li fiori e la verdura" or "Al cor gentil ripara sempre Amore," for the high idealism and nostalgia of his invocations and addresses, his emphasis on love and the gentle heart, repeatedly invoke the medieval love-poetry of the two Guidos, Cavalcanti and Guinizelli.[2] Again, the proems, in their pictorial freshness and bright clear colors, have their closest literary affinity with the enameled May-time lyrics of Angelo Poliziano.[3] This is evident when, idealizing the poet as well as his audience, Boiardo imagines himself in distinctive postures, coming to his recital from a summer world of nightingale's music (2.8.1), from a seaside rose garden trembling with light and echoing to a maiden's love song (2.19.1), or from a solitary summer garden blazing with flowers (3.3.1), which he forsakes for the greater delights of youthful company. The only inhabitants of this world are nobles in the flower of their age unvisited by any of the changes of time or fortune, and its manners are those of aristocrats moving to feudal codes of elaborate courtesy. There is nothing with the stamp of mortality on it; nothing mean, vulgar, or inharmonious intrudes in the picture, and the darkest aspects of the human spirit, passions with which the *Furioso* is throughout concerned, find no place in this secure enclosure.

Not only does the poet associate himself with the green vigor of youth in gardens and the lush renewal of the natural world, but in an important image his poem also is overtly conceived as a garden and his work as a poet is approximated to that of a gardener—a gardener who "plants" his two subjects of love and war, concord and discord:

. . . diversamente il mio verziero
De amore e de battaglia ho già piantato:
Piace la guerra a l'animo più fiero,
Lo amore al cor gentile e delicato.
        (3.5.1–2)

I have planted my garden diversely with Love and with Battle: war pleases the fiercer soul, but love the gentle and the delicate heart.

A garden is a world apart, delimited and enclosed. This conception of poetry offers immediate room for a challenge from Ariosto, who conceives of his poem as a wild forest, a mighty Broceliande, mirroring the intricate darknesses of life. And this is to consider, centrally, what it is that the *Innamorato* exiles from its poetic world and what the *Furioso*, by way of deliberate contrast, imports for the closest of scrutiny. Composed intermittently over approximately eighteen eventful years, from 1476 to 1494, the *Innamorato* prescinds with remarkable deliberateness from the world of historical action and event, firmly banishing the world of politics to a very remote, indeed unapproachable, distance. The grim moments of contemporary history are presented as painful interruptions of the poet's art and the audience's pleasure. Boiardo shrinks from displaying such moments in all their fury, and only glancingly do we catch glimpses of the larger world beyond the castle halls and gardens of the proems. A few lines at the beginning of book 2 refer in very romanticized terms ("un inverno," "a winter-time") to the frightening war from 1478 to 1480, during which Ferrara found herself threatened by a shifting combination of hostile Italian powers. The penultimate stanza of book 2 alone records, in language equally allusive, the dark days of Ferrara's struggle from 1482 to 1484 against a rapacious Venice in league with Pope Sixtus IV. Only a brief mention at the beginning of book 3 indicates that the "infernal tempesta" had passed. History is held at bay throughout. Yet the frame (and the poem) is finally shattered forever by the poem's last stanza, stunningly and passionately recording the greatest historical disaster of all, the descent of the "Gauls" under Charles VIII into Italy in 1494, which revealed an Italy ripe for conquest and open for devastation by all comers. Though Boiardo was perforce, by birth and position, fully engaged in the life of his times—courtier to Ercole from 1471 on, governor of Modena from 1480 to 1483, governor of Reggio from 1487 to his death in 1494—the world of daily reality was at the furthest edges of his artistic vision, and his poem represents an unyielding retreat to romance. Ariosto was especially aware, as every reader inevitably must be, that the *Innamorato* breaks apart under the pressure of an unwithstandable historical reality, and that only an external force terminates the poem's interminable adventures. He himself chose another and more rigorous path. His eye was not merely on the idealized past but also on a menacing present in relation to the terrifying past and to the ominous future, none of which offered cause for jubilation or self-congratulation. In over thirty years of composition and revision, as opposed to Boiardo's nearly twenty years, his eye missed little of the human furies passing on the great stage of Europe and of two other nearby continents, and the record is incorporated into the very fibers of his poem, as evidenced in canto 33. Ariosto's "stati attenti" is delivered to his own audience in terms that neither the minstrels nor Boiardo could have imagined.

The "furia" and "furore" of the *Furioso* is opposed to the parodic and burlesquing "pazzia" of the *Innamorato,* an insanity delighted and contented with its state, all serious issues held in abeyance by a kind of intellectual compact between the poet and his enchanted audience. The love-madness of Orlando, which opens the poem and confers on that mysterious, eighth-century Hruodlandus, Count of the Marches, his penultimate and (till then) most unimaginable metamorphosis, is a stylized madness: it touches its peak at the very beginning, and thereafter the poet's job is to maintain it in motion.

In the *Innamorato*'s opening canto, two traditions come together at once. Courtly and learned, popular and outrageous merge with the suddenness of great inspiration in the first and greatest of the *Innamorato*'s innovative moments, the headlong and instantaneous capitulation to love, at first sight and within moments of the poem's opening, by the previously chaste Orlando. Popular literature had been verging on making Orlando a romantic lover throughout the fourteenth century by making him the ever-chaste focus of maidenly love, but it was Boiardo who clinched all these tentative gestures. He makes good his promise to provide "cose dilettose e nove" (1.1.1), and the startling novelty and delight of the situation are brought before us immediately, all the essential characteristics of the poem emerging at once and in concert: stylization, reversal of reverend tradition, the clash of two worlds of literature meeting in comic confrontation. Mingling Breton and Carolingian motifs, Boiardo begins his poem with the Whitsuntide feast of *Charlemagne* (not Arthur) in *Paris* (not Winchester). Here, where twenty-two thousand and thirty kings, pagan and Christian, are banqueting in hyperbolical splendor, the enchantress Angelica, newly come with mischief in her heart from her eastern realm, enters the stage of literary history for the first time. Her appearance is memorable, for (in the distant future) she is to be Armida and Florimell too. With that phantasmagoric, cartoonlike rapidity that characterizes events and actions in Boiardo, everyone, not excepting the weepy old dotard Charlemagne, falls immediately and helplessly in love with the Cathayan princess. Orlando first and foremost is stricken with the dart of love, and his first speech is a revealing assessment of his "inner" condition:

"Ahi paccio Orlando!" nel suo cor dicia
"Come te lasci a voglia trasportare!
Non vedi tu lo error che te desvia,
E tanto contro a Dio te fa fallare?
Dove mi mena la fortuna mia?
Vedome preso e non mi posso aitare;
Io, che stimavo tutto il mondo nulla,
Senza arme vinto son da una fanciulla.

Io non mi posso dal cor dipartire
La dolce vista del viso sereno,
Perch'io mi sento senza lei morire,
E il spirto a poco a poco venir meno.
Or non mi val la forza, né lo ardire
Contra d'Amor, che m'ha già posto il freno;
Né mi giova saper, né altrui consiglio,
Ch'io vedo il meglio ed al peggior m'appiglio."
        (1.1.30–31)

"Ah, loony Orlando!" he said in his heart, "how you let your will carry you away! Don't you see the error that makes you go astray and causes you to sin so greatly against God? Where is my fortune leading me? I see myself captured and cannot help myself. I, who set the world at nought, am overcome, without arms, by a damsel. I cannot sunder the sweet sight of that lovely face from my heart, because I feel myself die for lack of her, and my spirit, little by little, fainting within me. Neither force nor courage avail me against Love, who has already set his bridle upon me. Neither knowledge nor counsel will profit, for I see the better and yet cling to the worse."

Orlando's monologue provides a double shock. Not only had the paladin never before spoken in lover's accents, but no Orlando had previously spoken, so lengthily and with such comic comprehensiveness, in so clearly learned and humanistic a rhetoric, defining his love as a madness. This Orlando is immediately familiar with the authoritative love-treatises of past ages reaching back to Greek medicine, which first defined the bodily disturbance that made for the malady of love;[4] his speech is top-heavy with references to a particular literary tradition, and to mythographic and iconographic traditions as well. The fine comic excess provides us at once with an indication of how the moralized classics were to affect the situations of chivalric romance, and its comic juxtaposition of the ridiculous and vulgar with the aristocratic and learned will later produce important repercussions. Most important of all, the comic excess supplies a necessary context for the craziness to ensue in the *Innamorato,* as well as for the insanity in the *Furioso.* We are now, Boiardo announces with palpable delight, in a world where the banalities of the *cantastorie* are being wondrously fused with the poetry of the humanist tradition; and the poet's warm humor and intelligence appear in making Orlando speak not merely in the ludicrous, self-pitying voice of a lover *bouleversé* by Cupid but also in a profusely classical strain. A whole complex of Platonic ideas resides in Boiardo's creating a crazy Orlando who, *transported* by his *will,* allows *Amor* to fasten a *bridle* on him, attributes the process to his bad *Fortune,* and sees the *good* but persists in pursuing the *worse.*

This picture is amusingly relentless. To an audience trained in the classics and nurtured on Petrarch, the last four lines, culminating in the "meglio-peggior" antithesis, especially would have carried its own meaning. It was Ovid's Medea who first stated that she perceived the better yet clung to the worse ("Probo meliora, deteriora sequor"), and her story since medieval times has been a chief monitory emblem of the destructiveness of love-passion.[5] In the immediate Italian literary past, Boccaccio himself retold her story to this end,[6] and the emphasis on the transports of the will derive from Petrarch's canzone in the *Rime,* itself alluding to Medea:

Ma io incauto dolente
corro sempre al mio male, et so ben quanto
n'ò sofferto et n'aspetto; ma l'engordo
voler ch'è cieco e sordo
sì mi trasporta.

But I, incautious, miserable, keep running toward my own undoing, and I know well how much I have suffered from it and expect to still; but my greedy desire, which is blind and deaf, so transports me.[7]

Finally, of course, the final line of Orlando's lament is not original with Boiardo: it is a quotation from another Petrarchan canzone (264) lamenting the wastefulness of his still unregenerate passion for Laura.[8] The line of literary and mythographic tradition extends, therefore, from Ovid through Boccaccio and Petrarch to Boiardo, and both the *De claris mulieribus* and the *Rime* are laid under contribution, connecting the story of Orlando's passion with other literary manifestations of the same defection from rationality. Perhaps Ferrara could even furnish a humanist or two to spot an allusion in Orlando's lament to the traditional thought and imagery of Boethius:

Qui se uolet esse potentem
Animos demet ille feroces
Nec uicta libidino colla
Foedis submittat habenis.
    (*Cons. Phil.* 3.met.5.1–4)

Who would be powerful, must / His own affections check, / Nor let foul reins of lust / Subdue his conquered neck.[9]

A complicated joke is being made over the paladin's head, and Orlando is a mouthpiece living well beyond his intellectual means. Another way of putting this is that Boiardo thinks of him not as a "character" but as a rhetorical mechanism. This was a mechanism that prepared the way for the Ariostan Orlando to assume various successive guises, including lyric *tenorino* (8), knightly stalwart in missions of mercy (9–10), savage wildman (23), and finally noble captain (29)—each endowed with a corresponding rhetorical utterance: not only the cold artificialities of the Petrarchist lover, the tempered courtesies of the savior-knight, the frightening illogicalities of the madman, but also (in a remarkable funeral oration over the bier of Brandimarte) in the rounded classical periods of the "senator romano," Orlando is at last restored to being (43.170ff.).

As so often happens in reading the *Innamorato,* we are aware of Ariosto as a reader of Boiardo, and we must await his profounder artistry to depict the consequences inherent but deliberately left unexplored in Orlando's *innamoramento*; and it is of the utmost significance that he will fasten immediately on Orlando's imagery of horses and bridles to reveal the depth of meaning implicit in the paladin's first cry, "Ahi, *paccio* Orlando." By introducing the figure of the bridle into Orlando's speech, Boiardo invokes an ancient iconographic tradition deriving from Plato, and no one in his audience would miss the Neoplatonic imagery of the horse of passion in its various configurations. Representations of humans caught, horselike, by a bridle of profane love are one of the omnipresent iconographic traditions of the Middle Ages and the Renaissance, as we shall see later in Ariosto's thoroughgoing exploitation of

the ancient motif first employed here by Boiardo. One of the most familiar represen-
tations of the cardinal virtue of temperance, common (to name no others) to
Orcagna, Raphael, and Veronese, is a female figure either carrying a bridle or wear-
ing one passed through her mouth.[10] The flesh is bridled either by Amor or by
Temperance, and in Orlando's case it is clearly the first who has triumphed. Now
Orlando is not merely a lover but also a lover in a particular tradition of profane and
cupidinous love attended by disaster. In this he is "chivalric" blood-brother to
Sidney's Astrophel, who sadly recognizes, like Orlando, his helpless moral status:

I on my horse, and *Love* on me doth trie
Our horsemanships, while by strange worke I prove
A horseman to my horse, a horse to *Love*;
He sits me fast, how ever I do sturre
And now hath made me to his hand so right
That in the Manage myself takes delight.[11]

In its first canto, then, the *Innamorato,* by fusing a fabulous romance world with a
profounder one of classical learning, offers a hold for the grappling irons with which
Ariosto later accosts it. Hence it is intriguing to find Ariosto himself "excusing" his
own delinquent Orlando and then applying to his own persona of manic lover the
very lines that Boiardo had previously applied to *his* Orlando:

ch'anch' io sono al mio ben languido et egro,
sano e gagliardo a seguitare il male.
          (9.2.3–4)

For I too am sick and slow in pursuing the good, but hale and hearty on the tracks of evil.

With good reason, therefore, did Lodovico Dolce claim that Boiardo had, by showing Orlando in love, clearly shown the way for him to go mad ("*impazzire*");[12]
indeed, Bembo had said the same thing before Ariosto: "Ma tutto dì vegiammo
mille uomini, e quelle per aventura che più costanti sono e per più saggi reputati,
quando ad amar si conducono, palesamente *impazzire*"[13]—words directly and pointedly recalled in the proem to canto 9 of the *Furioso,* in overt allusion and compliment.

The first canto of the *Innamorato* wittily sets up a static situation that endures
until the very end: Orlando's is a passion trembling forever on the burning knife-
edge of nonachievement. This avoids conclusions and throws the major emphasis on
the poet's inventiveness in casting a gullible blockhead, driven (paradoxically) by
obsessive appetite and unswerving sentimental fidelity into one absurd dilemma
after another. Orlando may be a comic vulgarization of the cupidinous heroes of the
Arthurian cycles, but he has none of the courtly graces of Lancelot or Tristan, none
of their inclination to sensual enjoyment when the occasion offers; indeed, the contrast is repeatedly drawn between his great strength of sinew and his feeble resource
of intellect. The willing victim of Pandemian passion is presented throughout in
terms of loving burlesque, as a dolt in matters of love, a lumpen maladroit in matters

of problem-solving—a conception probably meant to appeal to an informed juvenile taste, like that of the young Isabella d'Este, which was formed by acquaintance with both classical and chivalric literatures.

Boiardo suspends, Ariosto invites, conclusions. The degenerative process inherent and inevitable in Orlando's sudden infatuation is Ariosto's significant departure from Boiardo. Nevertheless, it implies a link with, a development of, a challenge to, something essential in Boiardo's telling of his tale. Already in Boiardo there is an initial and implicit moral judgment of Orlando's love; Ariosto renders it overt, thereby distinguishing his own kind of comedy from Boiardo's relatively simpler one. Ariosto does this with two gestures. The first is turning "paccio" into "furioso," invoking the "furens" aspect of classical heroes like Hercules. The second involves indicating meaning through the use of allegory. In both the 1516 and 1521 editions, Orlando no sooner deserts Paris at midnight to seek Angelica than he falls, ineluctably, into the gilded trap of Atlante's Palace of Illusion, where he is "housed" with a number of other mad Boiardan desirers like himself, and where one and all, intent solely on the objects of their desires, fail to recognize any of their fellow prisoners in their self-created prison. By such devices does Ariosto "place" utter single-mindedness, the monopolistic nature of human craving. The episode provides immediate demonstration of his method—dependence on his source, but great independence of treatment, conclusively rendering the implications of the text he adapts. Matters have grown more serious in the generic move from comic romance to comic epic. Orlando is now being consistently measured against other heroes, and he represents what they could potentially become—Ruggiero, for instance, who is embarked on a heroic career, often comes close to becoming what Orlando truly becomes, mere animal, his intellect drowned in surges of passion.

Even before Ariosto sends him definitively over the edge into madness, Boiardo's Orlando reveals on occasion after occasion that his deficiencies involve his mind. His ultimate weapon is brawn, not brains, and seeking an efficient, elegant solution to problems is not his forte. This involves a decided disadvantage in the situations Boiardo invents for the display of his hero in action. Invoking famous episodes from the Matter of Rome, in which problems abound and demand solutions that involve the application of human intelligence, Boiardo relishes sending his strongman into landscapes populated with parodic versions of the monsters and the felons of classical myth to devastate the lot with unparalleled, often sumptuous outlays of physical force. The use of classical mythology is an area in which Ariosto sought most particularly to challenge his predecessor. As we shall see later, he observed carefully these episodes, imitating but definitively altering them; in several cases he concluded the episodes when Boiardo left them unfinished, assigning them, significantly, to Astolfo, who utilizes well the magical devices that Orlando casts away in favor of his muscle and sinew. Here again we see two kinds of comedy in confrontation: burlesque and parody on the one hand, and a serious playing on the other hand.

The relatively simple burlesque and parody are in evidence at the *Innamorato*'s

beginning. Two cantos after Boiardo had initiated Orlando into romantic love, we
find the paladin reduplicating the adventures of various Greek and Roman heroes in
the third "Matière." In his very first adventure Orlando emerges as a new Oedipus
confronting a wonderfully revivified sphinx who poses her eternal question and
foolishly threatens his passage (1.5.68ff.). In total contrast to the Theban hero who
triumphed by the exercise of his wit, Orlando takes the easy way out, making short
work of the problem by a characteristically violent massacre and devastation of the
monster. Only afterward does he recall that he could have spared himself the trouble
by consulting a magic book, given him by a palmer:

Tornagli a mente il libro del palmiero,
E fra sé disse: Io fui ben smemorato!
Senza battaglia potea satisfare.
Ma così piacque a Dio che avesse andare.
          (1.5.76)

Suddenly he remembered the book the palmer had given him and said: "That was
thoughtless of me! I could have won without fighting. But so it pleased God that it should
go."

Deprived of mystery, the sphinx turns out to be, like Lady Bracknell, a monster
without a myth. This initial folly provides the opportunity for the *prodezze* of
Orlando to crowd one after another, wonderfully and repeatedly burlesquing their
classical models. For the first time, Carolingian landscapes begin to fill up with
familiar figures imported from the dark places of classical epic. Shortly after disjoint-
ing the sphinx, Orlando is called on to annihilate a Cyclopean giant (1.6.34). This he
does in the classic Homeric manner by thrusting a lance into its single eye, but with
a gusto in violent activity ("con flagello") peculiar to the popular imagination.
Immediately thereafter, in a parody of Hercules at the crossroads, he arrives at a
complex of not merely two, but *four* roads running together (1.6.39), a fine instance
of farcical doubling with even greater opportunities for confounding his limited
mental capacity for choice and decision making. His next encounter is with the
enchantress Circella, who bears a cup of oblivion in her hand, from which he all too
deeply drinks at once (1.6.44ff.), forgetting not only his duty to Charlemagne but
also his love for Angelica, and giving hard evidence, if any were needed, that he is
indeed no wily Homeric hero. He is always spoken of as "il franco Orlando," which
usually signifies "sincere," "open," "frank," but which in this case suggests someone unprovided, idiotically trusting and guileless: the opposite of crafty Ulysses,
polytropon, meaning crafty, agile in mind, provided with multiple resources.

Though the contrast is repeatedly drawn with classical exemplars who penetrated
mysteries, made prudent choices, resisted enchantments, Orlando's failures of perception, heavily underscored by laughter, are utterly without consequence,
repetitive but without increment. At 1.24 of the *Innamorato,* Orlando is once again
enveloped in the aura of classical heroism with a visually charming but wonderfully

deflating effect. Two classical heroes provide the exemplar against which the paladin is measured and found wanting. Meeting with one of those endlessly proliferating Fays ("Fate") with whom his path is strewn, Orlando is given a magic horn and a magic book and instructed, rather superfluously, that if he wishes to enjoy unheard-of adventures he need merely blow three successive blasts on the horn and three times consult his book for help. The horn blasts introduce two vigorous comic reworkings of Ovidian materials: Jason's struggles with the fire-breathing bulls and with the dragon whose teeth he must sow (*Met.* 7.100–58), and Cadmus's encounter with the Serpent of Mars (*Met.* 3.1–137). To a society bred on both the classics and the romances, Boiardo's delightful contamination, not only of two literary worlds but also of Ovid's two stories, would have proved especially piquant. For, in contrast to the graceful triumphs of the great heroes of the Theban line, Orlando must struggle sweatily indeed, suffering repeated tossings and thudding, bone-crushing falls ("con grave percossa," "gli fe' doler le polpe e l'ossa") from which his magic book, unfortunately, in no way preserves him. He takes his revenge in the usual manner, utterly annihilating the field of armed men that springs up from the dragon's teeth, devastating the new seed as thoroughly as his creator devastates the high mystery of Ovid's prophecy of fraternal strife and civil conflict in Thebes. In passages like these, Boiardo takes comic disparity to its furthest limits.

Books and reading serve only to bring Orlando into distress. So too does the application of breath to horns, for horns do not in any way disperse or vanquish evil but merely bring forth monster after monster. Ariosto (more economical and pointed) will improve the situation at once, and Astolfo (to whom such weapons are transferred) will know precisely how to employ both book and horn to good effect against the outlaws and monsters in the landscape of the *Furioso*. By then, of course, Ariosto will have restored their original allegorical power. In the *Furioso* the romance paraphernalia of book and horn, as the "allegorizers" recognized at once, reassumed the value of moral concepts that was wittily and purely for comic effect stripped from them by Boiardo:[14] they are the gifts to Astolfo, not of an occasional enchant-ress, nameless and encountered by pure chance, but of Logistilla, Reason herself, and they symbolize two of the cardinal virtues, prudence and justice. Boiardo knew as well as Ariosto that the consultation of a book symbolizes a moment of prudence and provision; he says so very clearly:

Ben si ricorda di quella scrittura
Che gli mostrava il suo libretto aponto,
Però provede prima che sia gionto.
    (2.4.48)

Well he remembers the writing that his book showed him clearly, and so he provides before he arrives.

Yet, while deliberately recalling the learned association of books with the virtue of

prudence and with intellectual activity, Boiardo veers delightedly away from humanistic concerns, purposing novelty and pleasure primarily, and providing them in
plenty. If Orlando fails to consult his "libro" to take action against the sphinx, his
use of both "libro" and "corno" in his conflict with bulls and dragon avails him not
a whit either, and the outcome is exactly the same in both cases. He wins, as usual,
by lumbering, laborious brute force, in an atmosphere of massive comic inconsequentiality. This is typical of the poet's comic strategy: he constantly places Orlando
in situations that, in detail and structure, have all the panoply of deeply considered
allegory—a reader can now look with profit at Michael Murrin's analysis of the
allegorical content of the paladin's encounter with Falerina[15]—but from which, by a
kind of constitutional lack of brains, he remains utterly remote. Put simply, allegory
involves challenge and growth; and growth is not even a minor consideration in the
depiction of Boiardo's Orlando.

Orlando's exploits in Falerina's garden (2.4.4ff.) achieve a ne plus ultra of drop-
sical classicism. Here again his triumph over evil forces apparently (but only apparently) depends on his use of a book, a magic "libretto" provided by yet another
chance damsel, as the paladin re-enacts romantically and comically the Odyssean
conquest of the Siren as well as the Herculean triumph over the Harpies. He distinguishes himself, however, by the nature of his precautions in the first case and by
his unprecedented final success in the second. This is no Odysseus avid for knowledge and bound to a mast while his rowers stop their ears with wax. Charmingly
daft and wonderfully silly, apparently in obedience to the directive of his "libretto,"
he fills his helmet with roses—roses, of all things—to shut out the music of the
Sirens, whose trilling he terminates by a swift decapitation (2.4.39); he treats the
Harpy, characterized hilariously in plebeian terms as an "occellaccio" or "mega-
bird," to a neat partition with his sword ("da l'un a l'altro lo divise") that effectively ends its terrors forever (2.4.52). This kind of movie-cartoon annihilation
seems possible only in comic romance; in allegory the enemy is coextensive with
human nature, and the victory is as momentary as the struggle is continuous. So
Boiardo's Harpy and Siren are finished off with a blow, the Alcinas and Duessas
survive and reappear in multiple guises.

Ariosto, more conservative than his predecessor, never employs the classics in the
Boiardan manner, that is, for purely parodic or decorative purposes. He always
implies some moral dimension. His conscious use of mythology in the humanistic
manner is one of his chief strengths in taking a stride beyond the gains achieved by
Boiardo and constitutes one of his chief challenges to the art of the *Innamorato.* The
re-creation of classical myth in strange and original forms is a major vehicle for the
creation of meaning in the *Furioso,* and Ariosto infiltrates classicism into medieval
poetry in more thorough and profound a manner than does Boiardo. Theirs is,
fundamentally, a difference in classicisms, one genial and amusing, the other pointed
and profound: delightful in the first instance, both delightful and fruitful in the
second. Nevertheless, Boiardo provides the necessary breakthrough. His Orlando,
an eternally laboring but essentially dim-witted version of Oedipus, Ulysses, Her-

cules, Jason, and Cadmus, provides, in his very limitation, the precedent for a greater and more positive development, for Ariosto's Ruggiero as a new Aeneas, for Astolfo as a witty Hercules, for Rodomonte as Turnus *redivivus* as Saracen warrior.

Many of the same motifs and devices that Boiardo uses for Orlando are picked out and utilized by Ariosto for his two greater heroes, in situations of greater import and greater moral consequence. Orlando's triumph by brute strength is what Ariosto directly challenges in his Logistilla episode, in which (like Boiardo) he sets Ruggiero and Astolfo down into a brimmingly allegorical atmosphere, and from which (unlike Boiardo) he expects them both to profit. One does not, one does, and the poet therefore puts the former through a vigorous course of re-education in the hardships of the world he must inevitably face. Ariosto transfers Orlando's book and horn to Astolfo, who learns from Logistilla to achieve moral victories with ease and expedition, not through grunting expenditures of mere physical energy. Again, he transfers to Ruggiero in the episode of the runaway hippogriff Orlando's exactly similar Petrarchan penchant for being "transported by love" ("sì mi trasporta"). In addition, he early re-creates for Ruggiero the Hercules at the Crossroads motif of Orlando, positioning the young dynast at the first of his forking roads and presenting him with the first of his moral dilemmas. The hero's choice of Alcina over Logistilla brings him, exactly like Boiardo's Orlando at 1.6.44, into the toils of a new Circe, and the outcome in their parallel oblivion of a great love is pointed and deepened, for whereas Orlando merely forgets Angelica—

Angelica la bella gli è fuggita
Fuor della mente, e lo infinito amore
Che tanto ha travagliata la sua vita
          (1.6.46)

Beautiful Angelica is fled from his mind, and the infinite love that so troubled his life

—Ruggiero forgets Bradamante, the mother of his race:

La bella donna, che cotanto amava,
Novellamente gli è dal cor partita;
Che per incanto Alcina gli lo lava
D'ogni antica amorosa sua ferita.
          (7.18.1–4)

The beautiful lady whom he loved so much is now fled from his heart; for Alcina by enchantment washed him clean of every one of his old amorous wounds.

Here, certainly, is clear evidence of how carefully Ariosto courted comparison with Boiardo in his more penetrative classicism.

He courted comparison, not only in the areas of classicism and comedy but also in his conception of allegory—what it does, what it can be used for. There is more allegory in Ariosto, and of a deeper and more continuous kind, because the use of allegory for commenting is already ingrained in Boiardo; here also Ariosto perceived an opportunity to cast himself in the role of challenger and improver. To the disgust of Pio Rajna, who saw it as a noxious weed that had "gained territory" in the *Furioso*,[16] there is repeated but discontinuous allegory in the *Innamorato,* particularly in several places in the narrative populated by personifications that are often without preparation whatever, and without continuance. In the deployment of these "allegorical pools" (as C. S. Lewis called them in Spenser), suddenly concentrated passages presided over by figures whose names represent abstractions and whose actions are manifestations of their natures, Boiardo is once again, as in so much else, the great innovator and model for his successor. Yet nowhere is the employment of similar techniques to different ends more clearly marked than in their distinctive uses of allegory. For Boiardo (however ironically) writes an allegory of Fortune that Ariosto counters with one of Reason: Morgana is the heroine of the first, Logistilla (Ariosto's own invention) is the heroine of the second.

   Boiardo's allegory of Morgana is the abrupt epiphany of tendencies visible in his satirical treatment of the inopportunistic, stupidly idealistic Orlando, whose lack of sexual initiative draws down the sneering description, "mal scorto e sozzo amante" (2.3.66). The allegory voices, as in an emblem come vividly to life, the carpe diem strain of philosophy to which the poem repeatedly, if humorously and satirically, gives rise. The brevity of the sun's shining and the swift fall of the rose's bloom are Catullan and Horatian motifs that Boiardo invokes throughout, most comically when mocking his hero's inability to participate in offered moments of carnal joyfulness. Yet the theme of mutability is not always put in so light-hearted a way, and perhaps the idealized "vita zoiosa" of the proems is the clearest and most poignant expression of the wish that youth and joy could flourish forever: "e non finisca mai." The sentiment may suddenly flower in a single haunting line when Boiardo's own voice breaks through in one of Orlando's laments, mourning that human life is mere dust on the wind ("La nostra vita è un polvere al vento," 2.12.18). Or it may appear in one of Boiardo's perfect stanzas, intensely reminiscent of Poliziano's lyrics and Boiardo's own sonnet sequence, and overshadowed by a melancholy sense of the fugacity of life:

Questa età giovenil che è sì zoiosa,
Tutto in diletto consumar si deve,
Perché quasi in un ponte ce è nascosa,
Come dissolve il sol la bianca neve,
Come in un giorno la vermiglia rosa
Perde il vago colore in tempo breve,
Così fugge la età come un baleno,
E non se può tenir, ché non ha freno.
      (1.12.15)

This time of youth, so filled with joy, entirely we should consume in delight, for it is hidden away from us in a trice. As the sun dissolves the white snow, as in a day the crimson rose loses its lovely hue of a brief hour, so youth flies off in a lightning flash, not to be held, not having any leash.

This lyrical sentiment is precisely what solidifies into an extended allegory begun at 2.8.42 and continued into the next canto, turning evanescent arpeggios into a dominant chord. The allegory of Morgana-Fortuna is very carefully prepared and is quite deliberately linked to an earlier moment in the narrative involving Orlando's absurd abstention from sensual enjoyment. We begin with the earlier episode and progress to the more important later one. In Orlando's very early pursuit of Angelica (1.3.71), he happened on the enchantress vulnerably asleep under a tree but, in innocence of heart, forbore to grasp what fortune had so obviously placed in his way, and what his rivals would instantly have seized:

Così mirando quella si diletta
Il franco conte, ragionando in vano.
Oh quanto sé a battaglia meglio assetta
Che d'amar donne quel baron soprano!
Perché qualunque ha tempo, e tempo aspetta,
Spesso se trova vota aver la mano:
Come al presente a lui venne a incontrare,
Che perse un gran piacer per aspettare.
    (1.3.71)

The Count is delighted with mere looking, talking vainly to himself. Oh, how much more suited he is to battling than to loving women! Because, whoever has the opportunity and yet bides his time, often find himself with empty hands; as now befell him, who lost a great pleasure by waiting too long.

Here the narrator initiates his practice of jeering at his hero, and at the same time introducing a series of interrelated ideas about the brief nature of "diletto" and the swiftness of time that are developed like a leitmotif in the course of the poem. The goddesses that Orlando repeatedly outrages by his silly purity are, we suspect here but know definitely in retrospect, Occasion, Opportunity, and Fortune. For it is these goddesses, combined into one allegorical form and called by Boiardo either "Ventura" ("Fortune") or Morgana, who suddenly take shape in the long allegory of book 2 and teach Orlando a needed lesson.

The allegory begins when Orlando is sent to rescue a captive from the fairy Morgana's power and learns from other prisoners in her submarine realm, where she presides over a garden full of the most wonderful treasures and riches, that if he is to succeed in his quest he must first seize Morgana-Ventura by her forelock. Boiardo presents his Fortune-figure in the traditional iconographic terms familiar both from emblem books and from Machiavelli's little poem, "L'Occasione":[17]

Lei tutti e crini avea sopra la fronte,

E faccia lieta, mobile e ridente;
Atta a fuggire avea le membre pronte,
Poca trezza di dietro, anzi niente;
Il vestimento candido e vermiglio,
Che sempre scappa a cui li da de piglio.
          (2.8.43)

She wore all the hair she possessed upon her brow, and she had a happy face, mobile and smiling; her limbs were always girded for flight; she had few tresses behind, indeed none at all; and her dress was white and red, forever out of the grasp of the man that reached for it.

Penetrating her garden, Orlando finds the fairy asleep by a well, but he delays his capture to admire her and thereby misses his opportunity. Suddenly waking and sensing her danger, she dances enticingly before him, fleeing him at every step but luring him onward with a tantalizing song. In light of Morgana's reappearance as an allegorical figure in the *Furioso,* her song is worth quoting:

Qualunche cerca al mondo aver tesoro,
O ver diletto, o segue onore e stato,
Ponga la mano a questa chioma d'oro
Ch'io porto in fronte, e qual farò beato;
Ma quando ha il destro a far cotal lavoro,
Non prenda indugia, ché il tempo passato
Più non ritorna e non se ariva mai,
Ed io mi volto, e lui lascio con guai.
          (2.8.58)

Whoever in the world wishes to have treasure or delight, or seeks honor or power, let him set hands to this golden tress of hair that I wear on my brow, and that will make him blessed; but once he has set his hand to the work, let him not delay, for time past never returns again, and I turn away and leave him with his woes.

A hideous storm bursts over the scene as Orlando vainly pursues the creature, baffled in his exertions and whipped by the ghastly figure of "Penitenza" because he has let the occasion slip. Finally, after punishingly exerting himself, he takes Morgana-Ventura by the forelock, the weather suddenly clears, Penitence ceases to beat him, and the prisoners Orlando has come for are released into his hands.

The episode deserves more than casual attention, and for several reasons. In the first place, it is wholly characteristic of Boiardo's wonderfully independent way with traditional materials: at one point the suffering Orlando indignantly turns and aims a buffet at Penitence, not idly suffering her belaboring. Again, it is wholly characteristic of the *Innamorato*'s ironic inculcation of the carpe diem philosophy. Reaching backward over many cantos, this scene forms a retrospective commentary on Orlando's earlier conduct when confronted with the vulnerable Angelica, and the symmetry of the two passages, both of which involve a sleeping woman and center on the paladin's inopportune hesitancy on two very similar occasions, reinforces the sense, established early and at once, of the hero's bumbling. Yet the allegory does a good deal more. Both Morgana's song and the proem to canto 9 are fraught with irony, and we have only to listen to the fairy's singing to realize that Boiardo had read his Boethius very attentively. The "tesoro" and "diletto," the "onore" and "stato" that Morgana says only she can confer are unmistakable in their origins, for they are obvious translations of Lady Philosophy's enumeration in book 3, prosa 2, of the *Consolation,* of the slippery forms of human felicity confided to the power of Fortune: "opes, honores, potentiam, gloriam, voluptates."[18] The Morgana allegory suddenly universalizes a particular situation and becomes concerned with all human grasping after material gain or physical pleasure. Even while ostensibly belaboring Orlando for his hesitancy the poet, always satirical about court life (2.21.38), grows insistently and openly scornful as he urges the courtier, in the proem attached to canto 9, to grasp and seize time:

Odete ed ascoltati il mio consiglio,
Voi che di corte seguite la traccia;
Se alla Ventura non dati de piglio,
Ella se turba e voltavi la faccia. . . .

A che da voi la Fortuna è biastemata,
Che la colpa è da lei, ma il danno è vostro?
Il tempo viene a noi solo una fiata,
Come al presente nel mio dir vi mostro;
Perché, essendo Morgana adormentata
Presso alla fonte nel fiorito chiostro,
Non seppe Orlando al zuffo dar di mano,
Ed or la segue nel diserto in vano.
        (2.9.1–2)

Listen and take my advice, you hangers-on at court; if you do not reach out and seize Fortune, she grows disturbed and turns her face. . . . Why do you curse Fortune, when (though the fault is hers) the loss is yours? Opportunity comes only once, as the story before you plainly tells. For when Morgana was sleeping by the fountainside, Orlando did not grasp the forelock and so he vainly follows her now in the desert.

Boiardo is scarcely urging readers to surrender to the power of slippery Fortune. Here Boiardo's idealistic spirit manifests itself in a transparent irony in carpe diem encouragement of the devotees of Fortuna: injunctions to seize the day, laughingly applied to Orlando within the harmless world of romantic fiction, turn sour when applied to the cutthroat grasping of ambitious courtiers. The aristocratic scorn in "Voi che di corte seguite la traccia" is almost palpable; the poet's tone is that of a teacher, protective of his charges and wary of shadows falling on their lives, turning to confront the sinister figures that any Renaissance court could supply. Boiardo knew all about the gifts of Fortune, how unstable she is, "fleeting, ruinous, and more untrustworthy than any other thing," and his true voice, not brittle with irony, is heard in the proem at 1.16.1:

Tutte le cose sotto della luna,
L'alta richezza, e' regni della terra,
Son sottoposti a voglia di Fortuna.

All things below the moon, lofty riches and the kingdoms of the earth, are submitted to the willfulness of Fortune.

Orlando is not given credit for much in the *Innamorato,* but if he is a booby for having fallen irremediably in love in the first place, and for failing to take advantage of sleeping Angelica in the second, his disturbances of appetite remain lustful merely and praiseworthily have nothing whatever to do with avarice for worldly goods like treasure, honor, power, or titles of glory. Boiardo makes him reject, with great courtliness and self-possession, the temptations of treasure and power offered by Morgana on three separate occasions in the *Innamorato* (1.22.59, 1.25.13–15, 2.8.26), and in this at least he recovers some of the original dignity associated with the chief of the paladins. One senses his creator's idealism in the paladin's stalwart refusals of lunatic treasure. This is the one situation in which Orlando is wise and provides a fine contrast with Ariosto's Ruggiero, who will thirst for riches and power.

The allegory of Morgana is a poetic moment as evanescent as the goddess's favors, and it has no further echo or development in the *Innamorato.* But the allegory has a resounding one in the *Furioso* and repays attention for that reason alone. Boiardo's allegory provides essential materials for the understanding of Ariosto's allegory of Alcina, Morgana, and Logistilla, too long considered to have sprung up from nowhere, too long misunderstood when not actively despised or roundly dismissed. Boiardo's Morgana-Ventura ("Questa Morgana è fata del Tesoro," 2.12.24) becomes one of the major figures of the prominent humanist allegory that Ariosto writes in cantos 6 through 10 of the *Furioso.* Morgana remains there what she was previously in Boiardo, a fairy associated with avarice and worldly grasping, as well as a sister of the fairy Alcina ("Alcina fu sorella di Morgana," 2.13.55). In Boiardo Morgana and Alcina lead quite separate lives, and Orlando encounters them one by one, at random and with long spaces between. In Ariosto, however, they are joined in deadlier and more sinister proximity, working together in strict conjunction (as was manifestly not the case in Boiardo) to achieve the overthrow of a third, elder sister (unheard of in Boiardo) whom they seek to usurp and to destroy.

The creation and introduction of this third sister, Logistilla, is a deliberate innovation and invention of Ariosto. For her name, character, and operations there is no precedent whatever in the *Innamorato.* She is the virtuous sister of the triad, but with insufficient power to master them, and they have succeeded in chasing her into her northern dominions where she barely resists their incursions and maintains a threatened existence. By contrast the two sisters have overspread the island and flourished. Alcina, in both the *Innamorato* and the *Furioso,* is an enchantress of Circean nature capable of transforming men to beasts by the offer of sensual indulgence: her mythological equivalent is Venus. As we have already noted, Morgana presides over a garden of riches and tempts with the glories of the world: her mythological equivalent is Juno. Both sisters are subject (or would be, if things were ordered justly) to a virgin sister by the name of Reason (*to logistikon* in Plato's *Republic*) who lives restrictedly in the northern territories separated from the large domains of her usurping and imperializing sisters and who presides with diminished power but still with some authority and moral splendor. As chaste governess of a castle in whose lucent walls a man may Socratically look deep into himself and learn wisdom by knowing himself ("se stesso conoscendosi," 10.59), her mythological equivalent is Minerva. Hence the island onto which Ruggiero descends is an emblem of the entire world in the choices it offers among approaches to life: it functions as the island-world that the hero sees from the heavens in Cicero's *Dream of Scipio,* a major source for the concept of the three lives and three loves.[19]

Two of the elements for Ariosto's full-panoplied allegory of the Choice of Paris are, therefore, already in place in Boiardo's line, "Alcina fu sorella di Morgana," which Ariosto faithfully repeats in his line, "Con la fata Morgana Alcina nacque" (7.38). Boiardo's Alcina may capture Astolfo with temptations of the flesh and draw him to her island to be enslaved by sensual passion, and that is where we find him, degenerated into the form of a tree, when the *Furioso* recalls him into the narrative after a long absence. Morgana may lure Orlando with temptations of avarice and worldly dominion and be thrice rejected. But there is no figure like Logistilla anywhere in all the *Innamorato,* for it is a world from which rationality is almost totally exiled. That is the element Ariosto overtly and decisively elected to supply in his rehandling of a story of madness, his own figure for "misura" confronting the "dismisura" of Boiardo. In setting his own allegory of Logistilla-Reason against Boiardo's allegory of Morgana-Ventura, he deliberately set a threatened and insufficient Reason against Fortune, to the diminishing of the latter. By this one action he unambiguously placed himself in a humanist framework in which, pictorially and literarily, such a central opposition of values was of very common occurrence.[20] In Ariosto's hands, the allegory is not merely comic or ironic. It involves an island platonically divided in tripartite manner between the forces of appetite and those of reason, and it is now reserved for the life choice of the dynastic hero, Orlando being demoted to a lesser place and a more wretched destiny. Here Ariosto fully indulges his characteristic technique of transferring themes, devices, and symbols from Orlando to worthier heroes, and of returning allegory, turned inside out by his witty predecessor for purely comical purposes, to its traditional dignity. For where Orlando has been the central character in a confrontation with Fortune, Ariosto brings both Ruggiero and Astolfo under the tutelage of Reason. Boiardo's Orlando may have loftily and nobly rejected Morgana on three separate occasions, but Ariosto's Ruggiero will repeatedly succumb not only to Alcina's sensual love but also to profound avarice for honor, treasure, and power. Raised high by Morgana-Fortuna he will succumb also to the final great lure of pride, exploring one by one the entire range of human deviations into evil and revealing the mind's capacity for perversion as well. The mere love-madness of Boiardo's Orlando expands into other madnesses of desire for power and perverse complacency of intellect, and they are graver in a dynast than in Boiardo's love-stricken paladin of pitifully limited intellectual capacities.

This Ariostan technique of challenging and converting what (in a very real sense) he chooses to misrepresent by denying its irony, feigning to take it seriously and then offering to go beyond it, is visible in the cases of several other madmen in the poem. In Orlando, Boiardo concentrates the main features of his narrative. The paladin is distinctive only in being the paragon of fools, and the melody of madness established on his single string is soon passed over to the entire orchestra. Madness of all kinds proliferates wildly about Orlando, indistinguishable from his own, engrossing and engulfing the territory, and no attempt whatever is made to relieve the delightful condition. Instantaneous combustion at the sight of Angelica is thus the rubric for an entire poem. Here the poet's hyperbole is that of the fairy tale rather than that of the martial Carolingian poem, and the delight he proffers so prodigally is cunningly adjusted to the intelligences of children learning to be wise and adults wise enough to turn children at need. From the beginning Boiardo creates a world of instantaneous and extravagant attraction to some elusive good, a good pursued with unflagging energy and violence. The field of vision narrows irremediably to some unobtainable object; the motion of pursuit, though frequently checked and frustrated, is, within episodes and segments of episodes, unyielding and headlong; and the emotional dropsy of the poem is at once endemic, chronic, and universal. Needless to say, nothing proceeds in a straight line; there are no direct flights or express conveyances through the boscage, and the *Innamorato*'s characters, for all their impetuous haste, are the least demanding and impatient of tourists. Hence, characters are not so much errant (which presupposes a point of departure and return) as erratic. Delays and diversions, the intervention of chance adventures and importunate enchantresses at steadily proliferating magical bridges or entrapments in a poetic archipelago of islands—all these ensure side-trips to unintended destinations and a fine complication of the original plan, whose beautiful simplicity was to chase after, to seize, and to enjoy for one's self alone. One begins to see something of the *Furioso* already in these vanishings and forgettings of the thing pursued, in the multiple heads rearing up to disturb the sight-lines. For it is sight, precisely, physical and mental vision, that is continually being baffled in the *Innamorato,* and merely by twisting her magic ring—a device with direct origins in Plato's fable of Gyges's ring (*Republic* 2.359)—Angelica can elude and delude.

Boiardo's avoidance of a clear narrative line wound perceptibly through looping complication has its effects on character portrayal, his personages being no more clearly differentiated than his Paris or his Albracca. In contradistinction to the *Furioso,* the *Innamorato* absolutely rejoices in its fixed and undeveloping set of characters. In Ariosto they change their attitudes dynamically or exemplify varying moral postures according to the nature of the locales they inhabit: in dream and reality Orlando travels regularly to terrestrial paradises and pastoral havens, Ruggiero twice and very significantly visits islands (Alcina's and a hermit's), and Astolfo twice visits elevations on the earth and on the moon. But though the *Innamorato* swarms with vital characters, religion, nationality, age, and sex do not create discrimination in bizarre appetite or contrast in thrust toward fulfillment. Not one of the paladins is untouched by caprice or rabidity. Pervasive inflammation is the order of the day, and the poet repeatedly casts his puppets in towering, insistent adherences to passion, where they gigantize delightfully. In tracing these swollen ambitions, Boiardo's poetry is very often visually tremendous, aurally deafening. *Amans, amens.* Again, the *Innamorato* has directions rather than places, and while to go either east or west is to be somehow retrograde to, or tardily conscious of, the claims of "Christianitate," the two directions are complementary rather than antithetical. The poem's comic annihilation of real issues and values assures that the *perpetuum mobile* of its characters is movement without advance or regression. Indeed, the *Innamorato* is committed brilliantly and joyously to momentum alone, and it lives by shuttling.

The poem projects itself at once as an extravagant comic work of immense, unquenchable, impossible desiring—and this even before Orlando has his first disastrous glimpse of Angelica. At the beginning we hear that Gradasso of Sericana, somewhere "di là da l'India," intends to invade France, and the sole cause is that, having heard tell of Durindana and Bayard, he lives in a rapture of desire for the sword and the horse (1.1.4–5). The plain statement is not allowed to stand without emphasis. On two other occasions the poet tells us, insinuatingly and with ironic relish, that Gradasso is not at all impelled by ambition for territory, for causes of state or zeal for religion (1.7.41–43, 1.10.14); he has assembled his hordes and put his kingdom in peril only because of desire. The cause is in his will; he *will* come on, and the poet allows us to overhear an exceptional but important meditation:

E sì come egli avviene a' gran signori
Che pur quel *voglion* che non ponno avere,
E quanto son difficultà maggiori
La desiata cosa ad ottenere,
Pongono il regno spesso in grandi errori,
Né posson quel che *voglion* possedere;
Così *bramava* quel pagan gagliardo
Sol Durindana e'l bon destrier Baiardo.
       (1.1.5; italics mine)

And, as often befalls great lords who, *craving* what they cannot have, no matter how great the obstacles, put their realms into the greatest tribulations to obtain some *desired* thing and find it still eludes them, so that gallant pagan *hungered* only for the sword, Durindana, and the great steed, Bayard.

Hence Gradasso's "voglia" and "brama" for horse and sword frames the story of

Orlando's craving for Angelica; in similar fashion, it is throughout detained from coming to any conclusion. And here again, as with Orlando, Ariosto elicits the moral that Boiardo held in abeyance—that Gradasso is the victim of his appetites, that his craving has a cost: when he first appears in the *Furioso,* he is a prisoner in Atlante's Palace of Illusion, and "housed" with the paladin; their conditions are morally equated by their co-tenancy in the empty chambers of hope and desire. Boiardo's bare representation of romantic excess has hardened into an Ariostan allegory of chase and pursuit before our very eyes.

In this instance, Ariosto clearly found verbal instigation in Boiardo for his independent creation of allegory. But the *Furioso* is later so determinedly allegorical because several of Boiardo's prominent characters are clearly if momentarily enveloped in allegory—for example, Orlando's two cousins, Rinaldo and Astolfo. Boiardo was all too happy to avail himself of the tradition of Astolfo's impudent buffoonery and irrepressibility, craven lack of courage, and bad horsemanship—a bequest from the extensive Carolingian tradition that the poet was in process of concentrating. One stanza at the very beginning of the *Innamorato* catches the handsome rapscallion at the peak of his development previous to Boiardo, epitomizing his most notable and most endearing characteristics:

> Segnor, sappiate ch'Astolfo lo Inglese
> Non ebbe di bellezze il simigliante;
> Molto fu ricco, ma più fu cortese,
> Leggiadro e nel vestire e nel sembiante.
> La forza sua non vedo assai palese,
> Che molte fiate cadde del ferrante.
> Lui solea dir che gli era per sciagura,
> E tornava a cader senza paura.
>   (1.1.60)

My lords, you know that Astolfo the Englishman had no peer for good looks; he was very rich, but he was even more courteous, and as graceful in his dress as in his mien. I don't find that he was famous for his strength, for many was the time that he fell from his horse. He used to say it was no fault of his, and fell to falling fearlessly again.

True to his madcap nature, Astolfo flies out of his saddle head-over-heels at his very first encounter in Boiardo: "Ma come Astolfo fu tocco primero, / Volto le gambe al loco del cimero" (1.1.64.7–8). The action is the hallmark of his character, and the querulous speech he addresses to Fortune as he lies sprawled on the ground is wholly characteristic:

> Fortuna fella,
> Tu me e' nemica contra a ogni ragione;
> Questo fu per diffetto della sella.
>   (1.1.65.2–4)

Cruel fortune, you oppose me against all reason. This happened because there's something wrong with the saddle!

From the very beginning of the *Innamorato,* the paladin lives with a new and even more vivacious life than in his previous incarnations. A lover of practical jokes, provocative and insulting to make himself even more endearing when the joke is over, he challenges Charlemagne himself in a scene overflowing with confidence in his own great powers (1.3.27ff.) and, in an amusing encounter with spiritual rather than regal authority, jauntily addresses Archbishop Turpin with the less than honorific "Pritone" ("Priestie" or "Blackrobe"), scandalously pretending a solemn conversion to Muhammadanism (1.7.63ff.). In later episodes he gives demotic excess a new dimension: at 1.12.51 he threatens to kick King Monodante so hard that his shoe will stick in his stomach; at 1.19.28 he threatens to wheel an enemy around his head and hurl him so high that he will take three days to descend. Madcap and buffoon, the Astolfo of Boiardo stands at the very pinnacle of a long tradition.

From the passages cited, it becomes evident that Astolfo passes lightly in and out of the narrative. Boiardo found him an endearing presence, but he was not studious to give the paladin's adventures a continuity or curve of their own, and hence his appearances are intermittent and rather undeveloped. One signal addition to his portrait is crucial to his development in the *Furioso*: to make him even more outrageous than usual, Boiardo equips him with a magical golden lance, formerly owned by Angelica's brother, that makes him invulnerable and confers on him the ability to unhorse all comers. This piece of romantic paraphernalia bestows on the cowardly buffoon a wholly original comic supremacy, prelude to his moral supremacy in Ariosto, where the lance is challengingly endowed with other than merely laughter-provoking powers and (because Bradamante fights with it too) functions as a sign of providential protection, "magic" in quite another sense.

Typically, critics see Ariosto's severely altered paladin as something of a loss, failing to recognize what has been clearly substituted in place of the old and familiar. But, however one appreciates the vivacity and boldness of Boiardo's creation, one must have an inordinate appetite for homespun horseplay and practical joking to prefer this endearing lunatic to the luminously mild Astolfo imagined by Ariosto, a character morally reoriented in a way that Boiardo might have had difficulty in imagining. Still, Ariosto's transformations always occur with the warrant of some suggestion at least from Boiardo, and the remaking of Astolfo testifies to the intermediate position Boiardo occupies in the movement from romance to epic. As with Orlando, the *Innamorato* takes the unprecedented and indispensable first step in involving Astolfo (of all people) in humanistic allegory. In Astolfo's last appearance in the *Innamorato* (2.13.54–66), Boiardo delivers him into Alcina's power, an episode that Ariosto read with narrowed eyes, retelling it at length and with remarkable emphasis in canto 6 of the *Furioso,* and eliciting from its allegorical suggestiveness and latent allusiveness the elements of his own central allegory. Impetuous and ungovernable to the end, Astolfo is riding westward from Albracca to Paris in company with Rinaldo and Dudone when, by the shores of the sea, they come on a whale that Alcina has sent to entrap them. The whale (only its back protruding from the waves) does not reveal itself until it is too late, but Astolfo's companions recognize the possibility of danger and warn Astolfo against riding onto it. Nevertheless, in an access of inquisitive curiosity, he rides heedlessly onto the "island," and the enchantress herself, significantly represented as fishing by the sea-shore ("la fata pescava"), watching delightedly as her prey is entrapped, leaps up behind him as the whale moves into the deeps and steers them both into some mysterious future that Boiardo never lived to write:

Quella balena andava lenta lenta,
Ché molto è grande e de natura grave;
De giongerla Ranaldo se argumenta,
Natando il suo destrier come una nave.
Ma io già, bei segnor, la voce ho spenta,
Né ormai risponde al mio canto suave,
Onde convien far ponto in questo loco.
Poi cantarò, ch'io sia posato un poco.
        (2.13.66)

Slowly, slowly that whale went on its way, enormous in size and grave in demeanor. Rinaldo tried to reach it by swimming his horse like a boat. But, my dear lords, my voice is gone and will no longer obey my sweet song. Here I shall stop and, after I have rested a while, I shall sing again.

Boiardo was to sing for many cantos more, but never again about Astolfo; the paladin disappears forever. The episode, like many others in Boiardo that Ariosto later completed, has an incipient allegorism that is teasingly unmistakable, for here at least we see the beginning of Boiardo's commentary on Astolfo's rash nature that he never developed. Alcina's whale, showing only its back above the waters and giving the impression of solid permanence rather than of slippery mobility, seems "un isoletta posta a mezo il mare." If we hear echoes of an equally beguiling Miltonic whale that draws men to their destruction ("Deeming some island, oft, as Seamen tell"), it is because Boiardo as well as Milton had read *Physiologus* and knew that "Balena" incarnates satanic evil, alluring with shows of false security.[21] Again, obviously, he knew the old tradition of the Venereal delights promised by fisherwomen by the sea, fishers of men in quite another sense than biblical. Tasso after him continued the tradition in Armida's piscatorial habits after Alciati had already represented it in a famous emblem ("Meretrix"), and Donne had made it supremely satirical in "The Bait," after Shakespeare had contrived an equally emblematic fishing for Cleopatra.[22] All of these elements, already suggestively present in Boiardo, Ariosto employed in his more explicit allegory of Reason and Passion, which is at once a commentary on the past career of Astolfo and on the initial stage of his new life of conversion. Astolfo vanishes from the pages of the *Innamorato* at this fairly early point, when the *Innamorato* has twenty-six cantos yet to run; when we next see the paladin, a full *thirty-one* cantos later, in canto 6 of the *Furioso*, Ariosto demonstrates a long memory and a very extensive reach, and he pictures Astolfo in the wholly surprising form of a repentant tree. For his improvident lechery he has degenerated into an embodiment of the sentient life merely, and, repentant, he has learned his lesson well. Hence in the *Furioso* he rehearses at length this very lapse in the *Innamorato,* counsels Ruggiero (who is now on the verge of repeating Astolfo's experience) to avoid lechery and captivity to Alcina, and points out the path to Logistilla's domains. A turnabout indeed, for he is now the central figure in a literary revolution and is about to play, shockingly and in wholly unprecedented a fashion, a central, not a subordinate, part in a Carolingian narrative. In his first appearance in the *Furioso,* Astolfo is already, by his fall and by his remorse, a moral step ahead of the dynastic hero, and he will maintain that advantage throughout.

Accorded the star turn in two or three brilliant scenes of comedy, Astolfo passes lightly in and out of the *Innamorato,* leaving the stage, as usual, to personalities of greater glamour and staying power. Rinaldo is the great rival of Orlando for Angelica's affections and consequently the paladin's rival for pride of place. But whereas the droll booby is fixedly and undeviatingly enamored, Rinaldo, not at all sentimental, provides an interesting variation on the pattern, constantly negotiating the distance between love and hate and illustrating yet another aspect of romantic love, its tendency toward mutually exclusive extremes. For Rinaldo, as only for Orlando, Astolfo, and Ruggiero, among all his other personages, Boiardo provides strong mythic elements and an allegorical center; they signal the importance of elements widely diffused in the poem by contracting and crystallizing them in allegory.

A brilliant piece of Ovidian classicism, the particular allegory reserved for Rinaldo begins at 2.15.42 and represents him in one of those moments when he is suffering revulsion for Angelica at the same time that she, reversing her role, is maddened by love of him. The cause is in two fountains, early introduced by the poet, that alternatively provoke and repel love. At this moment, newly arrived in the forest of Ardennes, Rinaldo is suddenly greeted by the vision of a naked boy singing delightfully while three naked damsels dance lightly about him. Interrupted by his approach, they hail the intruder with cries of "ecco il traditore, ecco il villano," and then, in a scene of superlatively lovely romantic fantasy, proceed to scourge him with flowers: "Chi getta rose, chi getta viole, / Chi zigli e chi iacinti a più non posso." Leaving him half dead from this tender punishment (Rinaldo wonders how he has been vanquished by naked spirits and by leaves and flowers) they spread their wings and fly off, that is, all but one, who reveals that her companions are Cupid and two other Graces. She herself is Pasitea, and he has been punished, she announces, for his treason to the laws of love; in correction of which she delivers a lyric sermon on reciprocity:

Amore ha questa legge, e tal statuto,
Che ciascun che non ama, essendo amato,
Ama po' lui, né gli è l'amor creduto,
Acciò che'l provi il mal ch'egli ha donato.
Né questo oltraggio che te è intravenuto,
Né tutto il mal che puote esser pensato,
Se può pesar con questo alla bilancia,
Ché quel cordoglio ogni martìre avancia.
          (2.15.54)

Love has this law, Love has this statute, that whoever is beloved and does not love, if he loves thereafter, has no success in love until he experiences the pain that he himself has given. Neither this beating that has befallen you, nor all the evil that can ever be thought can be weighed in the balance with that, for that grief of the heart surpasses all other suffering.

Rinaldo is thus instructed and promises "repentance." After another drink from the Fountain of Love he is again enamored of Angelica, again free to threaten his rivals with battle and havoc. The whole passage is in the carpe diem vein of Orlando's allegorical encounter with Morgana-Ventura, and it reveals the same delightful ambiguity about the poet's stance, mingling lyricism and satire. Does the allegory truly represent the poet's serious views on love? Not at all. On another occasion not far off, he will tell us in lines of witty irony that while Orlando in his total previous inexperience might be forgiven for falling in love, Rinaldo should have known better, for he had been in the dance before (2.21.13).

Romantic infatuation and romantic disaffection are like two sides of a knife, and the *Innamorato*'s characters are often torn by conflicting passions of attraction and repulsion, contrarious pulls on their simple natures. Alternatively counseling his characters to fall in love and to serve Cupid, then swiftly berating them for having so foolishly plunged into the whirlpool, Boiardo nevertheless wittily preserves them from blame by representing them as victims of magic. In the case of Orlando and others, they are victims of Cupid and his arrows. In the case of Rinaldo and Angelica, they are victims of a very pretty mechanical device, mythical in origin and a source of the most delightful confusion. Unable to resist the inundations of desire or to control the upsurge of fury and revulsion, their lack of equipoise is attributed to unfortunate, chance, recurrent sips from two fountains deep in the wood of Ardennes, alternatively provocative of either love or hate:

Il Fonte de Merlino era in quel bosco,
Sì come un'altra volta vi contai,
Che era a gli amanti un velenoso tosco,
Ché, ivi bevendo, non amavan mai;
Benche lì presso a quel loco fosco
Passava una acqua che è megliore assai:
Meglior de vista e de effetto peggiore;

Chiunque ne gusta, in tutto arde d'amore.
        (2.15.26)

As I told you earlier, the Fountain of Merlin was in that wood—bitter poison to lovers, for if they ever drank from it, they ceased to love; nevertheless, near that shadowy place, there ran another source of much better nature; better at least to sight, though worse in effect: whoever tasted of it, burned wholly with love.

Here is the Catullan "odi et amo" romantically revived in the burning attraction and freezing aversion fed by two magic sources. In dull, unmythologized reality, every reader of earlier literature knows that the two fountains constitute two aspects of a single kind of love, sensual in origin, having no fixed center of constancy and order, and hence subject to the revolutionary whims of the soul's perturbations. "Non s'adorna di riposo mai," said Guido Cavalcanti of this kind of love in his famous canzone: "poco soggiorna."[23] And as Petrarch well knew, it finds no peace.[24] Located deep in the forest, the Fountain of Love is rooted in the sensible part of the soul, near neighbor to the other passion of "Sdegno," or wrath. Hatred is never far from this kind of love, attraction never far from antagonism, and for that reason the two fountains are clearly stated to be not far distant from each other, and also very similar in appearance. Hence the ease with which they are often mistaken.

Between the two fountains, if one shuttles only laterally between them, there is not much to choose. For if the one temporarily annuls excessive love, the other gives (in the famous pun on "amare-amaro" that Petrarch and then Bembo made much of) only bittersweets: "di amore amaro il core accende / A chi gusta l'acqua delicata," 2.15.59. In the two waters Boiardo symbolizes the discordant Mars and raging Venus that animate his characters, irascible strength seduced downward by concupiscible appetite and alternating with it, instead of setting its powers at the service of intellect to regulate firmly the lowest but most ambitious member of the soul's hierarchy. Rinaldo drinks and so passes from revulsion to attraction again with such remarkable haste because Cupid and the Graces appear to him in the neighborhood of the two fountains, and he submits to their counsel to drink of the better-seeming but worse one. Though the drink "cures" him of lovelessness, it merely marks another stage, and he is still firmly strapped on the wheel. Yet both he and Angelica have been in the neighborhood before and should recognize the fountains' natures; they are blinkered, however, and do not.

The twin waters have already made an early and crucial appearance in the poem. In his first pursuit of Angelica in 1.3.32, Rinaldo had already come by chance on the Fountain of Hate, unwarily imbibed, and fled the princess in aversion; hard on his heels the fleeing Angelica had come to the same spot, imbibed of the Fountain of Love, and pursued the lover she had wildly fled before. Now here, at 2.15.60–61, instructed by Pasitea, Rinaldo drinks again, and again grows inflamed with love; but Angelica at 2.20.45–46 will likewise drink again, again feel aversion, and again take to flight. No clearer illustration could be given of the whimsicality of disordered appetite and the volte-face of the will. The lovely symmetries mimic those intricate ballets of confusion choreographed by a cross-eyed Cupid in many romantic situations, where A loves B, who loves C instead, who loves D, ad infinitum.

"Accidental" draughts at these convenient taprooms in the forest merely confirm, humorously, what had previously happened without the intervention of such magical beverages. Just as Demetrius requires no mistake by Puck to fall out of love with Helena and in love with Hermia before *A Midsummer Night's Dream* opens, so no one required the Fountain of Love to fall in love at Angelica's first appearance; only an inclination of the will was then sufficient. What seems the purely chanceful maneuvering of characters to drink now from one, now from the other is really a purely traditional outlook on "amor soperchio," for the fountains are not merely decorative but allegorical in nature. They declare their ultimate origins clearly as lovely transfigurations of the five golden and five leaden arrows that Belaceuil carries in the *Roman de la Rose,* a book much in favor at the court of Ferrara;[25] these equally awaken and extinguish love, and the love on which they operate is the same disturbed one we find in such comic flagrancy in Boiardo. Not lacking precedents, Boiardo also had his waters from Petrarch's canzone 135, where two fountains in the Fortunate Isles bring either laughter or death, and after him Tasso remembered the first fountain for his "Fonte del Riso," which he then passed on to Spenser.[26] Nevertheless, the clearest analogue to Boiardo is in Shakespeare's comedy. In his delight in the mere mechanics of sudden infatuation and equally sudden disaffection, Boiardo is as content as the English poet to throw the responsibility on external causes, two fountains instead of two flowers, and not fear being misunderstood. This kind of comedy amusingly shifts blame for disorder onto shoulders other than those of erring romantic lovers—to Cupid's winged ones preferably.

Ariosto all but suppresses the Fountains, and the sense of human responsibility makes itself apparent, even in the passages where he minimally acknowledges them.[27] Nevertheless they assume an important role in an allegory at the end of the *Furioso,* where he is finally about to bring Rinaldo to an understanding of the passion in which he has so long languished. As he had supplied an allegorical conclusion to the Astolfo whale allegory, so Ariosto once again, in full command of the ramifying intricacies of the *Innamorato* and continually aware of its possibilities for elaboration and deepening, remembered the Fountains in the allegory of canto 42: we are now at a distance of *fifty-eight* cantos from Rinaldo's flower-beating by Pasitea. As usual, Ariosto operates to close off the endless succession of adventures and to indicate a moral progression in his own characters. The *Furioso* is only four cantos from its ending when Rinaldo, soldierly and faithful to Charlemagne till the pagan debacle, hears finally that Angelica has yielded herself to Medoro. The old passion stirs him, jealousy inflames him for a last time, and, pretending a need to search for his lost horse, he rushes madly away from Paris. Soon he is in the kind of desolate landscape far from human habitation ("da ville e da castella allontanato") traditionally associated with allegories of uncultivated passion and moral peril. Predictably, an allegorical monster, woman-faced and serpent-tailed, with a thousand watchful eyes, the very incarnation of wakeful Jealousy, leaps out upon him. Entangled in her embraces, Rinaldo is on the point of succumbing utterly when yet another allegorical figure, identifiable from his crest of a broken yoke ("giogo rotto"), beats her down and drives the monster back to her cave to gnaw at herself. Then, as the rescuer and the paladin ride away together, Ariosto suddenly juxtaposes this arid landscape with the lush one of Boiardo's Ardennes: Wrath and Rinaldo are suddenly in the neighborhood of the two Fountains and the heat is oppressive. For a last time the paladin drinks of the Fountain of Hate, banishing love, jealousy, and passion in a trice, and the helpful knight reveals himself (late as always in Ariosto) as Indignation itself ("Sdegno"), its martial power aiding the reason and operating virtuously against the concupiscible appetite.[28] The moment he is identified he vanishes, interiorized in Rinaldo's new outlook and return to martial activity. Four cantos away from the end of the *Furioso,* the appearance of an energetic and effective allegorical figure signals the conclusive reestablishment of a moral hierarchy in Rinaldo himself, as the irascible power in his heart cooperates with reason to subject, rather than to reinforce, the desiring power of the loins. As a consequence of that action Rinaldo, now decisively putting his love for Angelica to the side, determines to go in quest of his runaway horse: a horse indeed this time, and not a runaway woman:

Per Baiardo riaver tutta fiata
verso India in Sericana andar disegna.
        (42.67.7–8)

To recover Bayard he still proposed to travel toward India into Sericana.

Here it is worth noting that Simone Fornari was the first to suggest the implication of determining to recover and control the chief Neoplatonic symbol for passion.[29] By canto 42 only the most ingenuous reader should be confused about the nature and the meaning of Ariosto's horses and the metaphorical values he attributes to bridling, or about the importance of Boiardo's allegorical beginnings to his successor.

Again, as these two examples concerning Astolfo and Rinaldo indicate, there is more allegory in the *Furioso* than is usually perceived or acknowledged because there is more in the *Innamorato* that remains uninvestigated and unanalyzed. The introduction of humanistic allegory into Carolingian romance, even for purely comic purposes, was unheard of before Boiardo, whose originality appears in this as in so much else. He provides the basis and prepares the way for Ariosto's more continuous and more deeply serious advances in this mode, for the characteristic, central allegories of the *Innamorato*—Orlando's encounter with Fortuna-Morgana, Astolfo's voyage on Alcina's whale, Rinaldo's punishment by Cupid and the Graces—provoke a greatly deepened allegorical response in the *Furioso,* and on another moral level entirely. In choosing to ignore Boiardo's irony about cheerful submission to passion, by pretending to take his poem "au sérieux," and by rendering the moral overt rather than implicit, Ariosto pretends to "convert" the elusive *Innamorato* to orthodoxy. He himself was to suffer the same fate at Spenser's hands. Hence, just as the English poet demoted Ariosto's "Tuscan fountain" and elevated his own "Nepenthe" (see *The Fairie Queene* 4.3.45)—so Ariosto pretended to misunderstand Boiardo and "overwent" Boiardo's Fortune and her ironic carpe diem philosophy in his allegory of beleaguered but beneficent Reason, subjecting Alcina and Morgana to Logistilla. Again, he contrived that Boiardo's improvident Astolfo, sailing off on a whale, should arrive—shockingly—on a wholly Ariostan island, slip into a lecherous life, suffer a punishment, and undergo a hard-won repentance. Finally, losing sight of nothing, he closed off the tale of Boiardo's twin liquors by devising Rinaldo's encounter with Wrath and reorienting him in the paths of martial honor. Rescuing and redeeming Boiardo's heroes, Ariosto in effect reclaims romance and allegory for the epic.

However deep an impression Ovidian lyricism leaves on the pages of the *Innamorato,* the poem often proceeds under the shadow of Vergilian epic. From the final stanzas of book 1, where a "cosa nuova" involving the appearance of the dynastic hero Ruggiero is promised, the reader of Boiardo becomes aware of the continual pressure exerted on the comic romance by the *Aeneid,* reminiscences of whose language in the form of lines and half-lines permeate the *Innamorato*'s pages from beginning to end.[30] Considering the place of the *Aeneid* in the education of the Este scions, Boiardo's introduction of its diction into their other favorite literature, romance (cross-fertilizing the two), is a stroke of genius. The continual pressure of a Latin vocabulary in even the most farcical moments reveals the poet looking beyond the popular model he is manipulating toward a more classical and courtly art, which remains the true but unachievable ideal; toward the poem's end, the poet, with a certain pathos, will confess this *in propria voce* (2.22.2–3). Engaged in tentative transfusions of classical myth into a resistant but yielding comic demotic model, he writes with an imagination permeated by the verbal splendors and moral dignity of Latin epic; and with a firm sense of the chasm between them, he is obsessed with building verbal bridges. Boiardo's are first steps, relatively simple and baldly humorous, in trying to make the Italian language do what the parent Latin had done on an exalted level; on its humbler level it repeatedly coasts within the orbit of the greater form to veer away into the knockabout Punch and Judy humor of the Carolingian poems and the exquisite lyricism of Ovidian fancifulness. Boiardo is the first to take the measure of this particular literary world originating in medieval France, preparing the way for Ariosto to reduce its immoderateness more fully to measure and form.

That element of epic immoderateness that Boiardo translated by using the Italian equivalent of a word from medieval French romance ("desmesuré," "dismisurato"), is one of the strongest and most powerful characteristics of the *Innamorato,* deeply impressed in every scene of terrific slaughter or ungovernable love. Appearing in hundreds of variations, and in every possible context, "dismisura" and the "dismisurato" are the unmistakable means by which Boiardo, harping assiduously on an implied negation of form, harmony, symmetry, measure, temperance, proportion, and equilibrium, continually raises an easy laugh while putting his reader in mind of those very qualities. In the mid-sixteenth century, Simone Fornari cunningly revealed his attention to this strain in the *Innamorato* by characterizing Orlando's love as "smisurato," and indeed no reader familiar with the poem can, except by utmost inattention, ignore its presence. *Smisurato* is Boiardo's favorite adjectival and adverbial qualification, comprehending a great variety of meanings, from "huge" or "monstrous" to "numberless" or "unrestrained" or "irrational," in any case, meaning beyond the mind's imagining. This constant element of hyperbole is the verbal objectification of the amorous and belligerent furies of the romance poem, as well as of that poetry's straining toward the illimitable. The *Innamorato*'s very first stanza sets the stage for what is to follow, promising "gesti smisurati," and the word occurs on five other occasions in canto I alone: "valore ismesurato," "amava oltra misura," "Argesto smisurato," "salto smisurato," "forza oltra misura." It is one of Boiardo's favorite rhyme words, occupying a position where its appearance can often be predicted. For the skeptic this necessitates a brief "dismisura" of documentation. Choosing with utmost selectivity over as wide an area as possible in book I, we find representative instances everywhere: "un gigante troppo ismisurato" (1.6.2); "trombe, tamburi, e cridi ismisurati" (1.7.5); "smisurato Radamante" (1.10.10); "lancie grosse e smisurate" (1.11.8); "zuffa smisurata" (1.11.20); "veloce a dismisura" (1.13.4); "colpo feroce e smisurato" (1.15.29); "il ronzone suo fu il più dismisurato / Che giamai producesse la natura" (1.18.6); "color smisurato" (1.21.42); "ira smisurata" (1.26.28); "fuoco smisurato" (1.28.39). The notion of "dismisura" affects every aspect of life in the poem: giants, war cries, heroes, lances, battles, motion, blows, war steeds, and the passions of grief, wrath, and love; and when we hear that Gradasso's ship is of a "quantità fuor di ragione" (1.7.71) we recognize the fundamental irrationality of being "fuor di mesura" and its link to being "fuor d'intelletto." Book 2 has at least as many instances to offer, and book 3 shows the still undiminished frequency of its use after almost twenty years of composition: "quel dismisurato" (3.1.59); "il saettar fuor di misura" (3.4.32); "un colpo tanto orrendo e smisurato" (3.6.3); "le Naiade allegre oltra misura" (3.7.9); "Orlando se avampò fuor di misura" (3.7.49). Certain passages are a veritable heaping up of Pelion on Ossa. The pagan Marfisa, already as an Amazon suggestive of natural disorder, is, within three stanzas describing her accoutrements, removed even further into hyperbolical unreality: her lance is "troppo smisurata," her steed is the most "dismisurato" ever seen and is "fiero oltra misura" to boot (1.18.4–6). Here, doubtless, the dyer's hands seems subdued to its colors; it becomes too easy a manner, the repetition over long stretches often rendering it monotonous. Perhaps the parody or satire of a literary manner, to avoid becoming itself what it parodies or mocks, must necessarily be brief. Yet for the original audience, reading or hearing the individual cantos as they were composed over a very long period and with many intervals in between, the monotony must have been considerably moderated. A modern reader with the entire poem before him senses all the more keenly, in this very repetitiveness of immoderation, an essential aspect of the poem's nature and the poet's perspective, though he pays the price of sensing its limited rhetoric and limited comedy as well.

Still, considering that Pulci, for example, employs "dismisurato" only on the very rarest occasions, and quite properly and unsurprisingly to characterize giants, who by their nature are given to a certain disproportion, Boiardo's humorous addiction to the concept must be accounted an unusual though characteristic gesture, clamoring for attention and representative of a certain disengagement. In a society simultaneously drawn to the romances and to Vergil, this Boiardan mannerism may not have gone unnoted as a vernacular parody of Vergil's exactly similar reliance on the monstrous or outsized—"ingens." Every schoolboy has found something faintly comic in "ingens Sarpedon," "bellum ingens," "ingens ara," "ingens truncus," "ingens tellus," "ingens laetitia," "ingens sus," "dolor ingens," "corpus ingens," "ingens Aeneas," "ingens fragor," "telum ingens," "ingens Turnus"— nearly one hundred and forty instances in the whole,[31] applied (as in Boiardo) to a whole range of things: to personages, passions, emotions, weapons, war gear, and animals. With no strain on the imagination we may picture some clever pupil in the ducal schools, Isabella herself perhaps, giving Vergil's repetitive "ingens" the romantic translation of "dismisurato" and savoring Boiardo's jest. For the sober epic is quite as full of the "informe" and "ingens" as Boiardo's romance, quite as "lumen ademptum" in its blind, outsized passions, though they proceed from extraordinary rather than trifling or fantastic circumstances and are both explicitly and implicitly reprehended, not temporarily rejoiced in. Unlike the *Innamorato* and its heroes, the *Aeneid* and its titular hero work amidst all this excess and turbulence toward a condition of measure and peace, a state of repose in the mean embodied in many lapidary classical phrases: "meden agan," "modum serva," "medium tenere," "ne quid nimis."

In harping so delightedly and at such length on "dismisura," Boiardo gives evidence of knowing something about the "mensura" represented by those Greek and Latin phrases. "Dismisura" repeatedly brings to the fore an aristocrat's sense of aesthetic disproportion and moral disequilibrium in romantic excess—points, in fact, to a standard of which the poet renders only the comic negatives. In the one instance that "dismisura" passes over into the negative, Boiardo employs it (significantly in a proem addressed to his courtly auditors in the ideal "frame") in its more philosophic sense of "disproportionate," informing his audience that the delight *he* hopes to give is a proportionate one, and one *not* out of measure (2.4.86).

E io diletto a tutti vi vo' dare
Tanto che basta, e *non* fuor di misura.
       (2.4.86; italics mine)

And I wish to give delight to all, as much as is fitting, and *not* out of measure.

Gentle criticism and warm affection, commingled and inseparable, always produce strange ironies. In so clearly distinguishing his own aims and that of his audience from the world of the poem, the poet holds himself decisively apart from his beloved creatures who, in a wildly tangled tale of recurring disproportions, splendidly abandon themselves to unreason of language, action, and reaction. Writing chivalric romance, Boiardo throughout assumes the stance of Renaissance courtier, aristocratic poet, translator of classical literature, admirer of Vergil, and entertainer of the aristocratic young. He very mildly deprecates the inordinate, gargantuan quality informing his own narrative, its six-hundred-pound warriors (1.17.24), its slapstick horses stolen out from under sleeping warriors (2.5.40); and though he supplies one droll "dismisura" after another, tripling and quadrupling his romantic motifs, providing pages teeming with essentially indistinguishable magical sites ("Ponte delle Rose," "Ponte della Morte," "Ponte Periglioso," "Isola d'Amanzone," "Isola del Foco," "Isola del Lago"), superfluously multiplying enchantresses into Circella, Dragontina, Falerina, Morgana, Alcina, the Fata Bianca, the Fata Nera, and the various Fate del Castello, del Tesoro, and del Lago, it is licensed irregularity in which he deals, curbed by irony and laughter. None of his society's values is at all threatened by his laughter, for poetry of the kind he writes is possible only when a tradition, long established, penetrates every level of a society. Reduction to formula courts the audience's delighted anticipation, encouraging participation in the act of writing. Constantly expected and graciously provided, formulaic "furia" and "dismisura" fall regularly and with rhythmic recurrence in scenes whose outcome the audience can predict, and whose turns of phrase and very rhymes it can supply in delighted chorus at the appropriate moments.

The *Innamorato*'s passions are an irregularity grown regular and so rendered harmless; their depiction assumes a common standard of thought and conduct. The boundary-breaking of the narrative deliberately and hilariously runs counter to the sense of "misura" of a courtly audience, inculcated from other, more dignified sources and directed to another ideal of deportment. That audience, we might well recall, was heir to four distinct literary traditions: not only the courtly French and demotic Italian chivalric traditions but also the classical one centering on Vergil, Horace, and Ovid, and the vernacular one as well, still only two hundred years old but already numbering the poets of the "dolce stil nuovo," Dante, Petrarch, Boccaccio, and Poliziano. "Mensura" and "Misura" are enshrined as ideals in the latter two, and perhaps the *Innamorato*'s audience heard repeated overtones of that other music in Boiardo's holiday verses: heard Dante, for instance, asserting, through Vergil's lips, that human love requires measure ("Mentre ch'egli è ne' primi ben diretto, / e ne' secondi se stesso misura, / esser non può cagion di mal diletto"); or heard Cavalcanti philosophically describing the "esser," the quiddity of profane love, as a state in which "lo voler è tanto / ch'oltra misura di natura torna"); or heard Petrarch (knowing the inefficacy of praying to Cupid) praying nevertheless that his heart should burn temperately ("che mesuratamente il mio cor arda"), even while continuing to measure only his paces in wild deserts of love ("i più deserti campi / vo mesurando").[32] All this was the common property of Boiardo and his audience; it was also the common property of Ariosto and *his* audience, when the example of the older poets was reinforced by Bembo's instructions, in the *Asolani,* to guard against things desired "oltra misura," to avoid the dangers involved in "amare oltre modo," and to desire "mezzanamente"—"middlingly" or "according to the mean."[33]

The *Innamorato* succeeds in staving off the intrusion of that adult world, with its responsibilities and cares, its sense of struggle and need for regulation, for as long as it possibly can. In the interim a particular tempest of intemperance and restlessness triumphs in the landscapes created by Boiardo's overflowing imagination. This is the fiery empire of emotion, impulse, and whim, of thoughtless movement in unbridled, choleric haste or, alternatively, the moist world of crystalline palaces in marvelous underwater gardens where naiads and warriors are locked in leisure for a while. Boiardo's rampaging Mars and raging Venus remind us that the lower two-thirds of the tripartite soul is a wonderfully rich and remarkably funny place indeed; and there is much to be said for a literary world where both black and white horses have seized the bridle and driven the chariot into the ditch; or, if we prefer the imagery of the *Republic* to that of the *Phaedrus,* where insubordinate rabble instinct has run amok, the soldiery has gone crazy and revolted, and the philosopher kings are nowhere to be seen. *Mind,* in fact, has simply been neatly snipped from the picture and dementia overruns the entire territory: Orlando is "paccio," Rinaldo "fuor d'intelletto," and even in Angelica "ragion non trova loco." There is room enough for a Logistilla, and the badly shrunken kingdom Ariosto gives her finds a ready explanation in the proliferating madness in Boiardo's pages.

The Renaissance writer of epic, traditionally an allegorist, will put a Logistilla or a Medina, a St. John or an Alma, into the panoramas of passion to signify the presence of "Ratio" or "Mensura" or "Modus" on the one hand and "Grace" on the other; and the standards being outraged by the main characters will then be both visible and clear, a beacon toward which to strive. Boiardo, as he himself knew well, made no pretension to writing epic poetry and he deliberately withheld characters like Ariosto's Astolfo or Spenser's Guyon, who quiet Furies, fight excess, demonstrate deliberation, seek Measure and Mean. For sixty-five of the sixty-nine cantos of the *Innamorato* nothing distinctively human—that is to say, rational—is allowed to appear, and as a consequence characters seem little more than carriages of a particular chafe, puppets acting (if we may so put it) with the lower two-thirds of their bodies only, passionately and wilfully. They reveal that perceptibly inhuman quality that we associate with the phantasmagorical world of elemental passions, and they are repeatedly caught in emblematic postures: Grandonio gnashing his teeth and shaking his head ("battendo i denti e crollando la testa," 1.3.2); Rinaldo clashing his teeth together but with a funny twist in his eyes rather than with a metronomic shake in his head ("Dente con dente batte con gran furore, / L'uno e l'altro occhio nella fronte ha torto," 1.4.58); Agricane biting his hands for rage ("Per la grande ira morde ambe le mane," 1.10.52).

Not allegorical in themselves, Boiardo's depictions of passion continually put us in mind of allegory, for to be perpetually "infiammato" and "furioso" in the unrestrainably wild and terrific manner of popular romance is to possess, ultimately, valid passports for the four separate but adjacent territories of romance, comedy, epic, and allegory. In importing into comic romance its insistent concern with concupiscible and irascible fires and passions of so inordinate and sudden a kind, the *Innamorato* employs emblematic techniques of graphic representation used by all those various modes. All those teeth-gnashings, head-shakings, eye-twistings, and hand-bitings remind us inevitably of the representation of wrath in Seneca's *De ira*; they become, by sheer accumulation, not so much a realistic Aristotelian imitation as a Platonic idea of wrath. If there were, then, a single knight in Boiardo who, attempting to remain unaffected by desire or rage, undertook to extinguish or at least abate their fires, we should almost think we were in book 2 of *The Faerie Queene*, with its neat balance of characters like Furor, Pyrochles, and Atin, who are martial and fiery, and others like Phaedria, Cymochles, and Acrasia, who are limited to Venereal and watery elements of love-in-idleness. Only thin partitions divide the absurdly comic and the intrinsically serious, and the burning excesses passed on to Orlando and his companions from Turnus and Dido can quickly be transferred to the pyrotechnical furies of Spenserian fire-breathers: all can cry with Atin, "I burn, I burn," for Spenser consciously turns epic and romance furies into unmistakable allegory, and Carolingian characters and allegorical personages, sharing descent from a common branch, share also a fundamentally comic nature.

Passion, finally, is grotesque and indecorous in its unrestraint, and the business of princes, courtiers, and gentlemen is decorum and mannerliness.[34] The manic world attends inevitably on another world, one with a more human physiognomy, and in the long-deferred appearance of Bradamante and Ruggiero, Boiardo, writing another kind of poetry altogether, tardily but splendidly furnishes it. Now comic romance makes gestures in the direction of comic epic, evoking dynastic ancestors to challenge Orlando and Angelica. With them come also the first glimmerings of that Providence which Ariosto, fully engaged for epic, developed into so great and over-ruling a power. Here in Boiardo, in two young archetypes of the Estensi princes, Providence finally has fit material to work on and so can demonstrate both its reach and its grasp.

2

"Con atto umano"

The World of Bradamante and Ruggiero

Love not that Love that is a child and blynde
But that Heroicke, honorable Love
Which first the fightinge Elements combinde,
And taught the world in harmony to move:
  That God of Love, whose sweet attractive power
  First founded cityes, and societyes . . .
    Sir John Davies, "Epithalamium for the
    Marriage of Lady Elizabeth Vere and William
    Stanley, Earl of Derby"

The thing, they here call Love, is blinde Desire,
  Arm'd with bow, shafts, and fire;
Inconstant, like the sea, of whence 'tis borne,
  Rough, swelling, like a storme:
With whom who sailes, rides on the surge of feare,
  And boyles, as if he were
In a continual tempest. Now, true Love
  No such effects doth prove . . .
    This beares no brands, nor darts,
  To murder different hearts,
But, in a calme, and god-like unitie,
  Preserves communitie.
    Ben Jonson, "Epode"

For its first thirty-one cantos, *Orlando Innamorato* pursues a course of pure and unshadowed delight, wholly humorous in its exploration of crazed impulse and robust thwacking and slamming, and according the feral aspects of the human microcosm, centered in Orlando, the large stage their tyrannical and imperious nature demands. In its dense concentration of motifs of love and war, book 1 is already a singular rehabilitation of Carolingian romance, conceived primarily for a youthful courtly audience, and, if at first for its members' delight, eventually and increasingly for their delight in their children's delight. From its beginning the poem bespeaks a warm and generous relationship between the poet and the ducal family. Boiardo's relationship to Ercole was brotherly, to his children avuncular, and his work gives a sense of a dynasty in formation. Thus, at the close of book 1, there is another even more singular and unimaginably influential "cosa nuova" at hand, and book 2 reveals the poet's relationship to his patrons suddenly intensified by the openly epideictic materials that Boiardo begins to introduce at this point. The object is not merely to please and to charm, but also to praise; to create models for admiration for the young, to flatter the older generation with dreams of their House's antiquity. Where book 1 is steadfastly comical and outrageous in its treatment of standard Carolingian personages and happenings (qualities, indeed, that persist in strength in the following books), book 2 begins on a distinctly "epic" note, if by epic we mean a narrative of Alexandrian charm rather than of Homeric or Vergilian solemnity. The introduction of a previously unmentioned Ruggiero into the swarm is the occasion for making repeated reference to Este history and the appeal, in many of its proems, to a higher, more human love than Orlando's, one that (in Jonson's phrase) "preserves communitie" rather than wrecks it.

Fittingly, the dynastic archetype arrives on the scene with all the epic panoply of a true hero; he is not at all subject to satire, and he is therefore in studied contrast to the nominal hero, so often diminished by epic comparisons. With this abrupt appearance of a more dignified Ruggiero and Bradamante, the *Innamorato* introduces epic themes of dynastic praise *directly* into romance, thereby altering its nature. Boiardo's innovation has tremendous impact on the development of romantic epic in the courts of the European Renaissance: Ariosto, Tasso, Camoens, Ronsard, and Spenser all profit from this first example. For Ariosto particularly, Boiardo's juxtaposition of "amore insano" and "amore umano" is intensely provocative and fruitful; the duality of loves is imported into and reinforced in the *Furioso*.

If only because he had taken "Amor vincit omnia" as his *impresa*,[1] and because he was not only the contemporary of Ficino but also the cousin of Pico della Mirandola (whose mother was Julia Boiardo),[2] Boiardo was well aware of the "due Venere" of Italian mythographic tradition and of their renewed importance in the Neoplatonic tradition.[3] But the two loves do not make a simultaneous appearance in the *Innamorato*: the poem moves according to an evolving rather than a predetermined design, and there is a strong sense of shift of purpose—or better, of expanding purpose—in mid-poem, a sense of a previously unthought-of opportunity for panegyric having tardily presented itself, so that the two major narratives, Orlando's and Ruggiero's, are presented in successive rather than simultaneous phases. Hence the *Innamorato* repeatedly struggles to join two lines of narrative, one romantic and comic, the other erratically "epic." In the closing stanzas of book 1, then, bidding farewell to his audience, the poet suddenly takes his hearers into his confidence and announces that the tale of Orlando's love must give way for a while. Now he proposes to tell of a "cosa maggiore," and the final stanzas of book 1 close on a grave and portentous rhythm, "epically" announcing the advent of Ruggiero (29.55–56).

Ruggiero becomes domesticated as a Ferrarese hero in three separate stages. Tito Vespasiano Strozzi, a classicizing poet at Duke Ercole's newly stabilized court, reworked old romantic materials in the popular storyteller Andrea da Barberino, and in a Latin poem of his own he appropriated the half-Saracen, half-Christian Ruggiero as the ancestor of the Estensi, single-handedly inserting him as a descendant into the line of Hector of Troy and furnishing him with a bride in the person of

Bradamante, sister of the paladin Rinaldo.[4] Strozzi's Vergilianizing attempt to imitate the descent of the Julian House from the survivors of Ilion and to cross the matter of romance with epic panegyric soon provoked the attention of his nephew—Boiardo himself—who, with his relationship to Pico, was one of the most fortunately connected of all poets: Vergil and Plato come to him almost as a family inheritance.

He appears also to have been fully aware of significant alterations of the Vergilian tradition: first, the *Aeneid*'s transformation into romance in the twelfth-century *Eneas,* in which the hero loves Dido with "amour desmesuré," and in which Lavinia indulges in the elaborate self-analysis of girls in Ovidian poetry;[5] and, secondly, Maphaeus Vegius's recent provision of the *Aeneid* with a thirteenth book, in which the truncated poem was rounded off with a marriage ceremony.[6] In both, the barely perceptible love interest of the Latin original is magnified at length, allowing for the rich interaction of male and female that is the basis of romance.

Boiardo's choice of Ruggiero as a hero in the *Innamorato* is in the nature of a compliment and a challenge to his uncle's initiatives, and a bow to both the literary and political interests of the court. His elaboration of his source, producing young dynasts of flesh and blood, with distinct, vivacious personalities, out of the mere names of his uncle's poem, once again witnesses the fertility of his poetic imagination. In the story of Ruggiero's birth, all the elements for a great personal struggle are present: a motive for revenge, a mysterious heritage torn between conflicts of religion and nationality, rich opportunities for false attachments and labyrinthine self-discovery, and, in the end, conversion. Ruggiero's "Saracen-ness" is an extreme representation of a condition common to all who have not yet been moved to conversion by grace. Obviously no Este ever believed he had a demi-Saracen among his ancestors. However, all of them knew about having to work the "infidel" out of their natures; and that, in essence, is what the story of Ruggiero begins to record. The grand, complex elaboration of this story was the work of Ariosto in the third and last stage, but Boiardo provided the crucial incentives. Bequeathed the bare fact of an orphaned Ruggiero, Boiardo begins to wrap him in a mythological framework worthy of a hero, endowing him with characteristics reminiscent of great exemplars in antiquity. No one had ever claimed a Greek or Trojan ancestry for Tristan, Lancelot, Roland, or Oliver, but for Ruggiero Boiardo reaches beyond the chivalric to the classical past, to Hector and Achilles, thus providing the example by which Ariosto, more specifically Vergilian, reaches continually to Aeneas.

Book 2, in which Ruggiero finally appears, is notable for a fitful classical stir in the poetry, an attempt at epic pomp and panoply visible in war councils, genealogies, Homeric similes, invocations, and two separate catalogues or roll calls, one of land forces, one of ships, in the Homeric manner. Boiardo launches this "epic" section with the fervor and the swiftness he always brings to new beginnings and "cose nove." The scene opens in Bizerte, where King Agramante of Africa determines war on Charlemagne and calls his council to debate the issue.

The epic council of thirty-two kings is convoked by the twenty-two-year-old king to array their banners for war, and Agramante proposes an immediate embarkation for France. In this superlatively managed scene (2.1.31–56), remarkable for its anticipation of Milton's council of demons, one elderly king, Branzardo, counsels the cancellation of the preparations, alleging the past misfortunes of pagan invaders of Europe; another king, the aged Sobrino, makes a more personal appeal to the same effect, vowing his concern for his lord and noting the present strength of the paladins; and a third king, the young, brash, and wonderfully tempestuous Rodomonte, denounces their dotard caution and urges the glory of the enterprise. The crisis is resolved by a soothsayer. A priest of "Apollino" rises to inform Agramante that his invasion is indeed bound for destruction but that "per astrologia" he has learned that if he carries along with him a certain fated youth, his long-lost cousin, he will at least often triumph over Charlemagne and acquire "pregio ed onore." The youth, orphaned by his mother's death, has been brought up in strict seclusion in the Atlas mountains, in a magic garden built by his savior and protector, the sorcerer Atlante. With this cheering news, all objections are overridden, the search for Ruggiero begins, and the canto comes to a close, a great enterprise afoot. Since the very next canto returns us to the crazy romantic world of Orlando, Rinaldo, and company, Boiardo appears to be aiming belatedly at the kind of *entrelacement* of major actions that Ariosto more triumphantly adopts in his first stanzas. Yet the search for Ruggiero provides a thread of only minimal strength for fifteen cantos more, and the foreground is immediately usurped by personalities, new and startling, that erupt in the poet's imagination. It is Rodomonte, "superbo e orgoglioso" (2.1.52), impatiently starting off for France alone, who engages his attention and evokes a vital and prodigious page of poetry. Defiantly embarking for France in the teeth of a tempest (2.6.1–15), giving his challenge to the winds, and deliberately driving his vessel to shipwreck at Monaco, he gives, in *rodomontade,* a word for vainglorious and hyperbolical speech to the English language. The individual is again greater than the concerted action, and the King of Sarza, errant as any Arthurian knight, augments the manic qualities of the European theater he now enters. Already he reveals that breakaway assertiveness and egocentric independence of will that bodes ill in epic.

Rodomonte and Ruggiero are, much altered, to be ranged against each other as the great antagonists of the *Furioso,* and their final, titanic struggle will end the poem in the simultaneous death of the one and triumph of the other. Their mutual opposition is implicit from the first, most prominently in the epic qualities and genealogy Boiardo assigns to each. Rodomonte is of the race of Nimrod and the Titans who warred on Jove, because (by a curiously synoptic view of myth):

Nembroto il fier gigante, che in Tesaglia
Sfidò già Dio con seco a la battaglia.
    (2.14.32)

Nimrod, the fierce giant, once defied God in battle in Thessaly.

The association with superlatively overweening types who warred on heaven and found only disaster is carried out at length. Not only is Rodomonte born of the breed of Nimrod ("Re Rodomonte nacque di sua gesta," 2.14.34), but the very sword he carries was forged at the command of the enemy of God (2.14.32); and the biblical reference is invoked once again for his helmet, said to have been cast for his biblical ancestor ("Nembroto il fece fare, il fier gigante," 2.15.5). In addition, there is the curious similarity of his name to that of Rhadamanthus, the infernal judge of Greek myth; and also to that of the fallen angel in Wolfram von Eschenbach's *Parzival,* "Radamant."[7] It is probably in memory of this ancestry of the damned and the infernal that, at the council in Bizerte, Rodomonte swears (2.1.64) he will seek no repose until he has conquered "la gente battizata" but will abandon his heart to the subjugation of the earth, and when that falls before his power, will make war even on paradise itself. Rodomonte suggests demonic possibilities without overtly becoming a demon in form. He retains his human form and name throughout, as he will, though in superlatively darkened a form, in Ariosto, who models him on Turnus as seen through the eyes of Fulgentius, Petrarch, and Maphaeus Vegius.

The ominous biblical genealogy Boiardo assigns to Rodomonte throws into even greater relief the heroic, classical one he imagines for Ruggiero, wholly positive and enhancing in effect. Agramante learns that his cousin is being hidden from view by his fearful protector, Atlante, who, knowing his future, interposes himself between his charge and his destiny. Agramante at once seeks to entice the youth by staging a mock combat at the foot of his secret mountain haunt, thereby hoping, Agamemnon-like, to allure the boy by awakening his martial instincts. According to his usual romantic refashioning of classical myth, Boiardo re-creates Ruggiero in the mold of Achilles, an Achilles educated by the centaur Chiron and withdrawn into effeminizing security by the fond protectiveness of his sea-nymph mother. Like Achilles, Ruggiero is brought into the war by a trick: the joust of arms organized for his benefit is successful in drawing him first to watch, then to join daringly in the spectacle (2.16.15ff.), and soon to participate in Agramante's expedition. The magician in vain asserts the peril to his life, but his hold over the youth is loosened; loosened, not broken, for though Boiardo represents him as a pathetic, fond old man, the male equivalent of Homer's Thetis or Spenser's Cymoent, he continues to intervene in Ruggiero's life in France (2.31.33), and he appears determined in his mission of circumventing his destiny as Christian and dynast. Ariosto reinforces the classicism of his characterization: whereas Atlante had previously withheld Ruggiero from the real world of arms, in the *Furioso* he not only sequesters him in a castle in the Pyrenees but also, in successive, linked, and deepening moral intrusions, actively propels him away from Bradamante into the lustful embraces of Didonian Alcina, then into the Palace of Illusion.

All this lies far ahead. Yet, like Achilles or Hercules, Ruggiero chooses the life of activity rather than of love-in-idleness—short life and long glory—though that will have its perils and temptations as well. In choosing the world of heroic action,

Boiardo's Ruggiero is propelled into initially parallel, increasingly divergent courses of epic action in comparison with Rodomonte, if only because his own course of life is dynamic and developing, and Rodomonte's is fixed and firm. The youth's acceptance of Agramante's invitation to cross over to France is portentous with fate, all the Estensi of history, by a charming poetic fiction, hanging dependent on his marriage to the heiress of Chiaramonte. His appearance is the signal for the delayed invasion to proceed, and the epic machinery of book 2 rather tardily begins to operate in earnest. The two parts of the *Innamorato,* it appears, are finally to be drawn into a semblance of unity, for Gradasso is deploying in the East, Marsilio in the West, and Agramante is ready to sail from Africa: the two epic catalogs of cantos 22 and 29 reinforce the gathering epic movement. The pagans land in France, and the larger part of the remainder is given over to the great clash of Saracens and Franks at Montalbano, a battle that results in staggering defeat for Charlemagne, who withdraws to Paris, which is soon beleaguered. The *Innamorato* continues for the nine further cantos of the truncated book 3, but it is with this dramatic moment of crushing rout that Ariosto chooses to inaugurate his own poem and effect the joining of his own art to that of Boiardo. In so doing he chooses to begin with a disaster and ends, forty-six cantos later, with a triumph. A *discordia-concors* is implicit from the beginning.

The rout at Montalbano serves Ariosto well, because in Boiardo it is already intermingled with historical matter that looks beyond the immediate disaster to a glorious future: concord begins dimly to emerge from the heart of discord. Well before Ruggiero meets Bradamante in book 3, a series of four separate prophetic visions brings the distant glories of the Estensi into play. These celebratory passages revive a technique original to Vergilian epic art, but romantically rehandled. Atlante initiates these glimpses into the future, heralding the unimaginable fruit of the lovers' relationship and (by representing it as having already occurred) giving to their marriage a quality of prophetic inevitability no earthly power can withstand. Pleading before Agramante (2.2.53ff.), he ambivalently rehearses not only the youth's past misfortunes but also his glorious posterity.

The wheel of destiny turns, the fleet embarks, and Ruggiero has barely arrived on the soil of France when the mark of history begins ever more strongly to be impressed on the poem's pages, strangely commingled with its continuing romantic extravagances. A passage of praise for the Aragonese dynasty of Naples occurs at 2.23.6–7, in obvious compliment to Duke Ercole's consort, Eleanora, whom Boiardo had himself escorted north to Ferrara. A more extended passage in the same vein occurs at 2.27.52–61, comprising ten octaves of eulogy for the twelve Alfonsos of the same royal House, a House not only linked by marriage to the Estensi but also, in 1483, allied to Ferrara in her struggle with Venice: and here Eleanora's own son, the future Alfonso I, is praised in the language reserved for small children, precious in their parents' eyes, as a "piccolino Febo, dio d'amore." Vergilian in its prophetic quality, the passage is Vergilian also in its rendering the future as a subject for art. The difference is that whereas Vergil represents the Roman future as a series of scenes embossed on Aeneas's shield, Boiardo pictures the Spanish kings in embroideries on a magic pavilion, giving impetus, certainly, to Ariosto's pavilion of canto 42, which illustrates episodes in the life of his patron, Ippolito. Much the same pictorial quality animates the representation of future Este glory in 2.25.41–56, when the knight Brandimarte comes upon, deep in the woods, a mysterious gallery frescoed with four scenes, two recording the past glory of the Estensi (Guelfic antecedents engaged in combat with Ezzelino and Frederick II, enemies to "la santa Chiesa") and two depicting the present splendor (Ercole I and his son and successor, Alfonso). Again, Ariosto adopts and deepens the technique when Bradamante (whom the visions concern more nearly than they do a stray wanderer like Brandimarte) scrutinizes the wondrous historical frescoes of the Castle of Tristan, which detail the wars of the French in Italy (canto 33).

In these and similar passages, Boiardo predicts in a Vergilian manner the phantom future, which is his own very real historical present, thereby occasionally anticipating Ariosto by looking forward from the past with a full awareness of the time to come, and by contemplating from the fulfillment of the present the unbroken link of greatness to the past, achieved, nevertheless, always with struggle. When, therefore, Boiardo finally brings Bradamante and Ruggiero together for the first time, they meet as a pair of young lovers over whom an atmosphere of dynastic fatality already presides. The issue now is not whether they will love, but how. The manner in which they respond to the obstacles in their path—and there will be many, as Boiardo begins to suggest by their immediate separation after their first meeting—is the soul of their story.

Before we examine this tantalizing one and only meeting of the lovers, we should observe that Ariosto recalled it at the beginning of the *Furioso* in notably brief terms:

La donna amata fu da un cavalliero
che d'Africa passò col re Agramante,
che partorí del seme di Ruggiero
la disperata figlia d'Agolante:
e costei, che né d'orso né di fiero
leone uscí, non sdegnò tal amante;
ben che concesso, fuor che vedersi una
volta e parlarsi, non ha lor Fortuna.
   (2.32)

The lady was beloved by a knight who had crossed over from Africa with Agramante: he was sprung from the seed of Ruggiero, and the desperate daughter of Agolante had given birth to him. The lady herself, being born of neither a bear nor a savage lion, in no way disdained such a lover, even though Fortune had not conceded more to them than to meet and speak only one time.

Ariosto is particularly worth watching whenever he lapses into this kind of suave litotes, for what he is summarizing is nothing less than the single most memorable meeting in all the *Innamorato,* providing the climax of Boiardo's action and the beginning of another poem born from its ruins. It is an extended passage, dense with meaning, and it deserves very close scrutiny.

The lovers meet, significantly, amid a burst of warfare, with a destructive Mars in the ascendant, though a Venus who promotes generation is soon to subdue him. Military strife and its potential solution in Love converge in an emblem of Empedoclean discord and concord. Amid the stormy clashes of the rout of Montalbano, with its presage of impending ruin for Charlemagne, Ruggiero, riding around the devastated battlefield, climbs to the top of a high hill and sees, below him, Rodomonte and a Christian adversary (Bradamante, her sex concealed by her male armor) locked in a fiery duel. Riding swiftly down, he interrupts the combatants with news of the Emperor's retreat to Paris, now itself to be threatened with destruction. In the poem-long oscillation of love and strife, the latter, it seems, is poised to triumph. Yet even as one Christian civilization trembles on the verge of ruin, another, in the loins of Bradamante and her husband-to-be, is on the verge of beginning. In the flush of the Saracen triumph, Ruggiero generously requests that Rodomonte allow his unnamed antagonist to withdraw and follow the retreating Emperor, but Rodomonte furiously demurs. Inflamed by Rodomonte's discourteous refusal, Ruggiero (already mannerly with his beloved, though she is encased in armor and appears to be male) intervenes in the combat and takes the battle on himself, giving the Christian "knight" leave to depart. Thwarted, Rodomonte turns on him in choler, and the two pagan heroes break into a great struggle, the first prophecy of their last grim battle in the *Furioso,* which then pits a *Christian* hero against the greatest of the infidels.

Ruggiero gives an early earnest of his superior moral traits (and therefore of his eventual capacity to be a true Christian). After Rodomonte has angrily refused Bradamante permission to break off the fight, Ruggiero, in the manner of a tenor in a trio with a soprano and an evil baritone, introduces a melodic strain that will resonate through the entire canto. Gravely reproving Rodomonte for his discourtesy, he initiates the theme of courtesy with becoming moderation of speech and behavior:

Esser non può ch'io non me doglia,
Se io trovo gentil omo discortese,
Però che bene è un ramo senza foglia,
Fiume senza onda e casa senza via
La gentilezza senza cortesia.
      (3.4.58)

It cannot but grieve me to find a gentleman discourteous, for a branch without a leaf, a river without a wave, a house without a path, is gentle blood when lacking courtesy.[8]

Among the driven puppets that have so long occupied our attention, Boiardo's Ruggiero and Bradamante are the first humans, and they are recognizably so in courteous gesture and speech. They speak in terms that recall both the commonplaces of the Renaissance courtesy book and the apothegms of the rhetorical manual, and we may, perhaps, imagine that Boiardo found it pleasant to dramatize a pattern of ideal conduct to the Este children by this brilliant imaginative means. For it is not only the male ancestor who is mindful of courtesy. Bradamante has departed from the scene and is proceeding on her way when she suddenly turns aside to reflect on the discourtesy of letting another assume her battle. "Ben discortese," she imagines, echoingly, "ben discortese," that youth can rightly call her for leaving him to fight alone a battle that was hers and that she has so swiftly deserted (3.5.6). She therefore returns to resume her place in the fight, though her motives, as she confesses to herself, are not at all chivalric; she wishes only to see that courteous youth again ("Sol per vedere il cavallier cortese," 3.5.7). She returns just in time to see Ruggiero fail to seize a dishonorable advantage when Rodomonte is temporarily stunned by a blow on the head, and she rejoices to see that she has rightly praised him for courtesy ("Ben drittamente aggio io lodato / Di cortesia costui nel mio pensiero," 3.5.9). She breaks in on him with a humane gesture—"con atto umano"—of excuse and apology (3.5.10), while even Rodomonte, rousing from his stupor, recognizes the courtesy of Ruggiero and pays tribute to it: "Non sono io vinto già di cortesia?" (3.5.13). Then, cursing and furious at being vanquished in both arms and courtesy, the desperate Rodomonte rides off so swiftly "che sembra un diavolo," leaving the young Saracen and the young Christian "youth" together. In a few swift strokes Boiardo presents a first emblematic encounter of three great principals. This is the first and only time they are together in the same place in the *Innamorato,* and it provides a long foreshadowing of the final moments of their second and last encounter at the *Furioso*'s end when the dark presence, heightened in ominousness by Ariosto's masterstroke of art, again functions as an implacably disruptive element in the meeting of lovers, this time at their marriage-feast.

With Rodomonte's departure, calm descends swiftly. In a scene of unusual tranquillity, a lyrical stasis at the center of abounding turbulence, the two young people are left abruptly alone, the focus of romance, of history and providence, and of some intensely focused poetry rich with sustained irony and humor. Immediately and momentously their story becomes (without the knowledge of one of the participants) a love-story, projected against the background of human destiny that transcends them as individuals and makes their little lives a mere link in a long chain, agents of renewal and replenishment. On a disastrous battlefield contested by Christians and Saracens, two antagonistic powers of which they are each adherents, it now becomes their destiny, by love, to order chaos and to subdue hate and strife. Courtesy opens the way to that love, and it is evidence of a "misura" heretofore invisible and unknown. Enemies by every standard of religious or national attachment, they nevertheless fall easily into the ways of courtliness, and an air of quiet gentility pervades the passage. In one swift movement the idealized, aloof world of the proems finds an embodiment in these two figures in the narrative, and the "cortesia" of that lovely world is at last accorded an equivalent in the mild action of the story itself. Bradamante lingeringly makes to depart, but Ruggiero, "il giovane cortese" (3.5.16), gravely asserts his superior manhood and refuses to let his younger companion ride off alone, alleging (remarkably) that the country is full of barbarian hordes, amusingly unaware that as one of the African invaders he is logically her enemy, and appearing to forget her courage in fighting Rodomonte, just tested in his very sight. Nevertheless, pleased with the *humanity* of his gesture, his "proferir umano" (3.5.17) in offering to accompany an enemy, she assents without revealing herself, and he escorts her gently away, discoursing the while. There is evidence of blood in the considerateness of his manner, but there is also, more wittily, a potential vanity and desire for supremacy that Ariosto will exploit fully in Ruggiero's passion for honor.

The situation is ripe with bewitching irony, playing lightly over the dialogue and hovering in the narrator's interjections. Bradamante's face is concealed and her sex and identity remain unknown to her escort, so that she retains the advantage throughout. Boiardo himself, tenderly ironic about the two lovers, ensures that the whole scene is viewed from her perspective rather than Ruggiero's, allowing an appealing wit to light this first encounter. The poet's choice of language is unusually resonant with implied metaphor. When, at 3.5.16, Ruggiero offers to accompany his young friend through the dangerous territory, he speaks a line with stunning resonance: "Ma sempre sarò teco in compagnia," the "sempre" giving the immediate, light-hearted offer of companionship on a hard road the resonance of a longer and more profound relationship. The line's effect is reinforced by the gravely allusive effect of the poet's narration of their turning their horses into the same path, "E così insieme presero il camino" (3.5.17). This latter line is heavy with overtones and vibrates with significance, giving to the simple action of taking the same literal path the resonance of a longer and more metaphorical journey through existence. This ironic effect appears a third time in a line applied to Bradamante. Seeking (without revealing herself or her purpose) to find a way to lead Ruggiero into revealing something of himself and his background, and fearing to appear forward and yet anxious to know, she is described by Boiardo as taking the long way round, leading him from mountain to plain, and arriving finally at her destination: "gionse ultimamente al destino" (3.5.17). But the simple "destination" of her immediate aim is also a revelation of her "destino" indeed, her destiny in the long, event-ridden future that lies before her, heavy with vicissitude and crowned, as Boiardo will soon intimate, by the tragedy of Ruggiero's eventual murder by treachery.

The sheer wonder of human history: begot by a mere itch of adolescent emotion and requiring all heaven's prompting and careful provision. Out of sight for so long, the two lovers-to-be are caught immediately in swift, sure strokes of affectionate portraiture, two beings vividly cast in particular postures of boyish gravity and superior girlish intelligence: he totally unaware of her identity or sex, she (in the concealment of disguise) highly aware and at once attracted and amused. In this, their first conversation, Boiardo envelops them in a mood of naive and awkward gravity perfectly suited to the unwitting instruments of Providence; and the canto's peculiar charm results precisely from the paradoxicality of the situation, a fatal burden of history, so wholly unlooked for, descending abruptly onto their slight romantic figures. They might pass for young scions of the House in Boiardo's own day, rather than distant, immemorial ancestors, and surely that is the effect intended. The *Innamorato* was begun in 1476, when Isabella, the eldest of Ercole's children, was only two years old and her siblings either newborn infants or yet unborn. The last cantos were produced in the decade 1484–1494 when the children were in their teens. The past is renewed in the delightful heirs of the present, the present is dignified by ancestral memory.

Their rich common destiny throws long shadows into the future, which every word and gesture in their chance meeting is unconsciously and implacably bringing on. Present already, in tiniest germ, is the Ariostan concept that humans act apparently by and for themselves without awareness of the immense consequences to follow from even the most trivial and unconsidered of their actions. In a scene composed with notable care, Boiardo demonstrates vividly that the best kind of human love is always accompanied by both decorum and laughter. Bradamante apologizes for her discourtesy with "atto umano," and Ruggiero offers companionship with "proferir umano"; their first encounter is marked heavily both with a sense of *humanity* and a sense of civility—a distance further enhanced by the mischievous disguise of one participant. Echoing each other in the repeated gestures of chivalric ceremony, creating a chime of courtesies in a very small compass of exigent time, their relationship, whatever difficulties are inevitably to ensue, is pitched immediately on a level of its own, worlds apart from that of crazed paladins and disturbing enchantresses. Here, for the first time, is a countermovement to the madness of the impassioned moment, a sense (with the hovering of Providence) of long time and eventual design. For at their first meeting the pair does not sink down in convenient meadows or grapple wildly in chance pavilions. They talk genealogy.

Nevertheless, Providence works through the convolutions of the particular human will, and Boiardo delineates it craftily. Feminine in spite of her doughtiness, by nature more sophisticated and clever in adolescence than her escort, Bradamante begins to live in an oxymoronic state, proximately remote beside her attractive gallant, responsive to her feelings but still reserved and apart, independently Amazonian but tenderly inclined and submissive to his masculine attention. Nevertheless she has a definite end, a "destino" in view. As they take their ambling way together, she, with a specific purpose kept firmly in mind, very distantly and only by degrees ("ben da lontano") leads him to the object of her circuitous conversation; and her request, irretrievable once proffered and portentous with destiny, finally leaps out: let him "dolcemente e in cortesia" tell her his lineage ("de che gente sia").

The subjunctive phrase translates merely into a polite inquiry into his family history, one warrior to another, in the approved manner of epic heroes. But from her point of view (and the unusual circumstances necessitate her acting swiftly and for herself) the question is one more often put to prospective sons-in-law, in either bolder or more subtle ways, by alert and interested parents: "Who are you, and what are your prospects?" At this point, Ruggiero is only his past, and not even all of that: Ariosto will give him a fuller knowledge of his birth, and provide him with a future as well. In the familiar manner of heroes boastful of their lineage, Ruggiero obliges unhesitatingly and launches into a long account of his ancestry, tracing it from remotest antiquity in the fall of Troy through the Rogers of Sicily to the comparatively unpromising present. He concludes his narrative of twenty octaves with a ringing assertion that links his end to his beginning, "Rugier son io; da Troia è la mia gesta" (3.5.37; "Roger am I, my line descends from Troy"). Here the House of Ferrara suddenly acquires a genealogy parallel and alternative to that of the House of the Julians, the line of Trojan Hector replacing that of Trojan Aeneas. Astyanax, it turns out in Ruggiero's tale, was saved by stratagem, and another child was slaughtered in his place; and from this little scion (his descendants moving ever westward) grows the whole ancestral tree.

The tale of civilization in transit that Boiardo so expertly puts into the mouth of Ruggiero is a welter of motifs in one of the poet's favorite modes, classical myth regenerated in astonishing romantic forms. Delicately allusive symbols of death and renewal, the tomb and the sea, figure importantly throughout Ruggiero's narrative: Astyanax evades capture by hiding in a sepulcher under a great and ancient stone in a forest, and then he emerges to cross the waters, making his way to Sicily. His destiny establishes a mythic pattern of disaster and renewal that courses rhythmically through the tale that Ruggiero tells, a tale that is (unbeknownst to him) a prophecy about his own life. In Boiardo's hands, popular romantic history becomes part of a cyclical movement, and the disasters that fall on all the children of Hector's line not only recall the death by treachery of Aeneas, the widowhood of Lavinia, the orphaning of Ascanius, but also shadow the lives of those descendants as far as Bradamante—who will, herself, providentially survive a fall arranged by murderous Pinabello to extinguish her race and emerge from a stony cavern, like Astyanax from a tomb, to pursue her destiny (*OF* cantos 2–3). Under the jumble of fantastic and fanciful details is a distinct pattern of recurrence and a wholly unsentimental view of history, one in which evil is deeply rooted and long-enduring, springing, moreover, in utterly mysterious a manner, from the same source as goodness: in Boiardo's genealogy, two brothers (as in Genesis) are repeatedly poised against each other as representatives of opposing inclinations in the human spirit.

In a word, then, Ruggiero's Trojan inheritance is emblematic, an inheritance of passion. Repeated lusts, hatreds, and betrayals impend over his own destiny. The final part of the tale he now narrates to Bradamante effects the join. In the generation preceding their own, the Saracens under Agolante, Agramante's father, had invaded Southern Italy, and the ruler at the time, Duke Rambaldo, with his two sons, Ruggiero II and Beltramo, had undertaken the defense. Love produced strong and divergent effects in the two brothers, leading Ruggiero to fall in love with and secretly marry the Saracen princess Galaciella; and leading his brother Beltramo, inflamed by jealousy and lust, to betray the city and his family to Saracen slaughter. Amid fire and storm the city fell into ruin, Ruggiero II was killed, and the Saracens temporarily triumphed. Now the history Ruggiero III is recounting to Bradamante resumes its thematic harmonies but with a profounder emphasis, for Ruggiero is describing the murder of his own father, the travails of his own mother, his own birth amid chaos and strife. Her husband murdered, the pregnant Galaciella is punished by her father and brothers by being set adrift in a fragile skiff, and her cruel fate recapitulates that of her immemorial ancestors.[9] Committed helmless in frail barks to the uncertain sea, the very realm of Fortune, they have been traditionally watched by the eye of Providence and protected by its power, steered to safe shores and worldly renewals in the lives of their heirs. Likewise, borne unerringly to Libya, Galaciella gives birth to her child on the shore and dies; and by good fortune the child is found and reared by the magician, Atlante.

This is the point at which the reader of the *Furioso* must be particularly alert. An "enfant" of popular romance, by strange insertion into the line of Troy, recapitulates the destiny of his epic forefathers. As his innocently boastful words to Bradamante make clear, Ruggiero is youthfully proud of his education amid the savage landscapes of the Atlas mountains. Yet for one destined to be a founding father of a civilization, he is accorded an especially uncivilized and primitive beginning, one that mirrors, Petrarchanly perhaps, a delight in solitariness, a rejoicing in pathless and unfrequented "loci selvaggi," haunted by strange "bestie" and "fere" of all kinds. Atlante (Ruggiero narrates) fed him on the brains and sinews of lions, and his childhood playmates were serpents and dragons carefully deprived of their teeth. His youth, more adventurous, was sportfully devoted to tracking wild animals and hunting gryphons and pegasean beasts ("grifoni et pegasei"). This is an amusingly and vividly feral beginning in which Ariosto sees wonderful possibilities. Ruggiero is, though unaware, a Christian by birth and heritage, an African pagan and a *jeune sauvage* by rearing and education: he will be a long time working out the beast within himself in the pages of the *Furioso*.

At the end of this remarkable recital Ruggiero, suddenly abashed at his own ready flow of language and at his own delight in his wild beginnings, catches himself up short by protesting that he must be boring his companion, but not before he utters his final, simple, all-encompassing cry, "Ruggier son io; da Troia è la mia gesta." His fears appear to be motivated by a sudden awareness that his companion's attention is wandering. And therein lie all the difficulties, all the ironies. For what, in essence, does Ruggiero narrate if not the present and future as well as the past? The tale of Andromache, of Galaciella, is to be Bradamante's as well: widowhood and exile with her infant son; and the vicissitudes of Ruggiero's male ancestors, so blithely narrated here in a spirit of youth, are to be exactly his own in the not distant future. Yet he is unaware of their resonance, treating them as past and external; and he is right to be solicitous about boring his companion, for she does indeed miss it all—the aura of providential care presiding over widows and orphans in the long declensions of human passion, the repeated uprootings and displacements of civilization, the inheritance of evil passed ineluctably from generation to generation. In two equally valid senses Ruggiero's narrative should *involve* Bradamante: wind her (even as an apparently external auditor) into sympathetic fascination in its intricate movements; and (beyond her power fully to perceive) draw her as a participant relentlessly into its patterns, as wife of Ruggiero III and mother of his infant son, Ruggierino. But it does not. The gap between providential foresight and human vision is very wide, and Boiardo's poetry acts as a mediator to fix youth's wandering attention and narrow the distance. For however set apart by Providence Bradamante and Ruggiero may be, neither of them is conceived by Boiardo as an embodiment of plaster perfection. As Ariosto later makes plain that he has understood, Bradamante, smitten and surrendering at once, has simply lost herself in admiring the love-creating sight of her young companion, with attendant loss to her ears, "more busying her quick eyes his face to view" than hearing the overtones in his tale:

Non avea tratto Bradamante un fiato,
Mentre che ragionava lei Rugiero,
E mille volte lo avea riguardato
Giù dalle staffe fin suso al cimero;
E tanto gli parea bene intagliato,
Che ad altra cosa non avea il pensiero:
Ma disiava più vederli il viso
Che di vedere aperto il paradiso.
    (3.5.38)

Bradamante had not even drawn a breath while Ruggiero was speaking to her, and a thousand times she looked him up and down from his spurs to his helmet; and he seemed so well made to her that she had thought for no other thing; more she wanted to see his face than to see paradise open before her.

Her inattention here has a decided impact on her initial appearance in the *Furioso*, when, consumed by love, she stands at a mental crossroads of her own, torn between love and duty (2.65), rejects a plea from defeated Charlemagne to come to his aid to seek Ruggiero, and, then, after a brush with death at Pinabello's hands, must have her destiny a second time—and now, more Vergilianly and sternly— communicated to her by Merlin. Ariosto renders the role of Providence in her affairs more startlingly overt, its commands more peremptory.

To fall in love is inevitably to fall into the irregularities, some laughable, some not, attendant upon passion. If Bradamante and Ruggiero meet first on a level of humanity and courtesy, if they are fenced from fleshliness by wit and distanced by disguise, they soon begin to demonstrate inherent weaknesses of sentiment. Hushed into silence by the comeliness of his figure rather than by his long dynastic recital, Bradamante is alive and young at one particular moment of time, and she has a very immediate end in view, not the long ones of providential history. Ruggiero's speech makes him eminently desirable in her eyes, his boast of Trojan ancestry makes him eminently marriageable. Still secure in the fortress of her disguise, she makes daring sallies of double-edged language, averring her utter willingness to please him and to reveal her origins:

Così vedestù il cor, che tu non vedi,
Come io ti mostrarò quel che mi chiedi.
        (3.5.39)

Would that you could see my heart, that you do not see, as clearly as I shall reveal what you request of me.

Her tale is simple but pointed. She is of the family of Chiaramonte (Clairmont) and Mongrana, clans to which his own (as he must realize) are related. She is the sister of Rinaldo, the famous paladin. Then, passing from language to action, suddenly, ostensibly to give him proof of her statement but in reality to play the trump card of beauty, she draws her helmet from her head, loosening her golden tresses and revealing her face. The result of that decisive and unforgettable gesture is one of those transcendent revelations that Ariosto and Spenser employed so often for their own heroines:

Nel trar del l'elmo si sciolse la treccia,
Che era de color d'oro allo splendore.
Avea il suo viso una delicateccia
Mescolata di ardire e de vigore;
E labri, il naso, e cigli e ogni fateccia
Parean depenti per la man de Amore,
Ma gli occhi aveano un dolce tanto vivo,
Che dir non posso, ed io non lo descrivo.

Ne lo apparir dello angelico aspetto
Rugier rimase vinto e sbigotito,
E sentissi tremare il core in petto,
Parendo a lui di foco esser ferito.
Non sa pur che si fare il giovanetto:
Non era apena di parlare ardito.
Con l'elmo in testa non l'avea temuta,
Smarito è mo che in faccia l'ha veduta.
        (3.5.41–42)

In lifting her helmet she loosened her tresses, and they were the color of gold in their splendor. Her face had delicacy mingled with spirit and strength; lips, nose, brows, every feature seemed painted by the hand of Love; but her eyes especially possessed so lively a sweetness that they were indescribable, and so I forbear to describe them. At the revelation of that angelic aspect, Ruggiero was overcome and stunned; he felt his heart tremble in his breast as if it were assaulted by fire. The youth stood quite helpless, he was not even bold enough to speak. With her helmet on her head he would not at all have feared her, but now he is vanquished merely by looking on her face.

The effect of her gesture on Ruggiero heralds a problem for both: they may fall short of their greatness by proposing simpler, less laborious solutions in immediate felicity. Hence Bradamante assumes the lead at once. Hers is the motive power of the genteel and well-bred huntress, and she is never to lose it till her wedding day, fifty cantos away. Her conduct at this urgent but difficult moment suggests the prompting of a nursemaid to her headstrong charge, "Be bold, be bold, be not too bold." Marriage is in her mind and, like Juliet curbing an alarmingly transported Romeo, she subtly seizes the initiative and with a deft, glancing speech, an inquiry hidden in a request, by asking to see his face asks in effect if he is already taken by another or (in another sense) "taken" by her:

> Deh bel segnore!
> Piacciavi compiacermi solo in questo,
> Se a dama alcuna mai portasti amore,
> Ch'io veda il vostro viso manifesto.
>   (3.5.43)

Sweet lord, be pleased to please me in this one thing only, if ever you bore love to a lady, let me see your face clearly.

We are at the climactic moment. Ruggiero is about to oblige her by removing his own helmet when, with astonishing suddenness, the world, held for a moment at bay, intrudes again. The quiet idyll of love is over and a band of Saracens erupts frightfully on the scene. Fires of rage put out for a brief while again break out in the "ira accesa" with which the pagans ride down upon the Christian knight, striking her on her unhelmeted head, in spite of Ruggiero's cry of self-identification. In a confused melee of hacking and hewing, his injured outburst, "Gente discortese"— the last recall of a great theme—is totally submerged. Yet for all the accelerated violence and noise, an important event has occurred, propitious of a great later development. Bradamante's wound reveals her as vulnerable, and Ruggiero assumes a posture protective of a maiden, not (as he thought before) of a younger boy. When she revives from the stunning blow, they find themselves together in attacking Saracens: a good earnest of things to come as the youth passes even momentarily from fealty to a pagan cause to adherence, because of love, to the Christian faith. Concern for Bradamante's well-being already begins to move him away from his early attachments, and though their tenacity will be proved again and again by Ariosto, love is already beginning to order a society almost undone by strife.

At this point the lovers, at the beginning of a warm, witty, and passionate courtship, are separated in the melee of warriors, never to be reunited in the few remaining cantos of the *Innamorato.* Boiardo leaves them in two separate and distinct positions. Ruggiero is "transported" by the sight of his beloved's face, and Bradamante is in a fever of suspense, having heard Ruggiero's voice but never having had sight of his visage. She is in pursuit of an image. Ruggiero's is the worse case, figured by a volatile flying-off or "transport," from which his beloved will have to rescue him. It should be of interest therefore that Ariosto's crucial first approaches to this material hinge on the power of *sight*: Bradamante and Ruggiero's love has begun—traditionally enough according to Renaissance love-doctrine—with love breeding images in their eyes. As a result, and with nothing more than this to guide him, Ariosto at once represents his own transfigured Atlante beginning to operate against lovers with a magic shield whose brilliance has power to stun and disarm; along with Ariosto's bequest to him of a hippogriff and a castle of idleness, the new Atlante now has (exactly like Petrarch's Amor, identified by a great burst of light: beauty that blinds the senses)[10] a blinding light to identify him as the sorcerer Amor. He is twice quibblingly and cleverly identified in this new role by Pinabello in his narrative to Bradamante of the magician's attributes and power ("Presi la via che mi mostrava Amore," 2.40; "Or giudicate s'altra pena ria, / Che causi Amor, può pareggiar la mia," 2.57). Bradamante herself is repeatedly warned against his power over human sight, instructed to guard her eyes.

This, then, is the fulcrum between the *Innamorato* and the *Furioso.* Separated on the disastrous battlefield of Montalbano by unlucky chance, the lovers are fully equal to their station, not yet worthy of their destiny. Rightly are they called to be founders of cities and makers of manners: they are, even without a court of their own as yet, fountainheads of the virtue to which courts give a name. Nevertheless, the dynasts demonstrate a potential for growth into their roles, which Ariosto will remorselessly interpret as the ability to undergo great stress from within and without. A relative innocence is about to be severely tried in the *Furioso,* where, because values and ideas harden and grow more imperative, the generous, intelligent youngsters about whom Boiardo is so lovingly ironic become almost symbolic figures in a movement to dynastic responsibility. Two gallant juveniles are re-characterized and emerge as a young man and a young woman, freighted with awesome historical responsibility. One of the greatest of Ariosto's transformations is to make Bradamante an irresistible force in pursuing her beloved, the flawed vehicle of an overriding spiritual power in whose service she often blindly moves to her destiny. Another is to make Ruggiero a headstrong, impassioned warrior whose evasion of Providence through a sequence of concatenated temptations will delay his marriage for forty-six cantos. Ariosto's unidentified Bradamante first appears in complete silence, clad in white armor, to overthrow Angelica's would-be rapist, Sacripante, then, in total self-possession, she passes silently on her solitary way. In these images, the poet conveys a virgin strength and a confident purpose that carry Bradamante on her poem-long voyage. In the languid imprisonment in which Ruggiero, captive to

Atlante, first appears in the *Furioso,* the poet provides an exact recall of his mental and moral situation at the end of the *Innamorato.* The emblematic postures are wholly faithful to the source.

Barely four cantos from the end of his poem, Boiardo achieves the sine qua non of the *Furioso,* Bradamante "innamorata," Ruggiero "innamorato," achieving, in the process, a Neoplatonic humanization of love and a breakthrough into quasi-Vergilian epic, rife with the forces of human history overshadowed by watchful Providence. How Boiardo would have pursued the story of this new and delightful pair must remain forever unknown. But there was much latent in this one encounter that attracted Ariosto's eagle eye, much that accounts for his immediate singling out of the lovers' story in the *Furioso*'s opening cantos. This first, cruel separation sets a pattern for the future: Ariosto sees it as emblematic, witness to Ruggiero's youthful unreadiness to win his love and embark on rule; there are oats to sow. Nevertheless, he takes Ruggiero's future marriage as a given, written immutably in the decrees of Providence, and so he takes a cue from Boiardo for the length of the path between the moment and its eventual fulfillment; a fulfillment involving a return, with greater and more painfully acquired knowledge, to another kind of innocence than the fragile one established here in the beginning. In the *Furioso* the hero will need to be rescued repeatedly from the encroachments of evil, which are arranged with programmatic precision in triadic form.

In the first of these three stages of temptation, a stage with three separate aspects of its own, dramatizing the familiar concept of "amore-amaro," "fel in melle," or "love sweet in beginning, sour at its end," Ruggiero is a light-headed young man being wafted romantically about ("against his will" we are ironically told) on a fanciful hippogriff (see Petrarch, "Lasso, Amor mi trasporta ov'ir non voglio," *Rime* 235). In the grip of amorous infatuation, he will need to be rescued successively from Atlante's castle of idleness in the Pyrenees, a kind of entrance hall into the world of pleasure, filled with enticements to lust; from Alcina's palace of sensual consummations, to which Atlante, intensifying his powers, sends him next; and finally from Atlante's palace of disillusion and frustration, when acquaintance with fleshly indulgence goads his appetite with delusive hungers. Ariosto himself points the triple progression of this first stage, when Atlante prepares his third palace:

Dopo il castel d'acciar, che nulla giova,
E dopo Alcina, Atlante ancor fa pruova.
   (12.21)

After the steel castle, which proves unavailing, and after Alcina, Atlante tries yet another stratagem.

In a second and more serious stage of his Ariostan existence, Ruggiero is no longer a fantastical young man with a magical beast but a hard-headed, aggressive young man in search of honor. This is a stage heralded already in Boiardo by Ruggiero's pride of ancestry and attachment to self. In this second stage he will have to be separated, with great difficulty, from Agramante's camp with its devotion to worldly honor and false heroism, which is embodied in imperial eagle ensigns and blazons of martial glory. In the third and most perilous stage of all, Ruggiero, consumed with ambition and desire, will have to be won from Leo's dungeons with their temptation to prideful despair and suicide. It is a long, hard journey, and we are allowed to see the first faint glimmers of its beginning at the very end of the *Innamorato.*

What still remains to be demonstrated in Ariosto criticism is the way in which Boiardo provided hints for an outline of Ruggiero's future course of life in its carefully graduated stages, and how Ariosto, alert to every possible opportunity, developed them at length, inventing incident after incident to depict the traditional hierarchical design of the temptations of flesh, world, and devil.[11] Here particularly we need to scrutinize the *Innamorato*'s final cantos. When Boiardo mentions Ruggiero for the last time, a hermit in the forest is confiding news of him to the bereaved Bradamante: he has (she learns) been rapt away from France, from baptism and marriage, by a band of aerial spirits (3.8.55–59). Questing and rescue are already in the air. Though Boiardo does not say so specifically, Ruggiero's "rapture" appears to be a stratagem of Atlante's, destined to save him from conversion and death: his "transport" is what keeps the two lovers apart. Certainly Ariosto interprets the matter in this metaphorical way, attaching silken cords to these snapped strings of suggestion. He accords Atlante's invention of gilded prisons the most prominent place in the first twelve cantos. As the cunning narrative links he forges to Boiardo's text make clear, Ariosto sees the essential struggle for Ruggiero's soul as already begun in this first aerial transportation of the youth to some mysterious unnamed place, and he sees forces hostile to Ruggiero's destiny already at work. Demonstrating great and original powers of invention, he names the place as a castle in the Pyrenees and clearly makes Atlante its creator and maintainer. He makes the palace a place of pleasure and indolence, traditional first steps into profane love; and by so doing he makes Ruggiero an active rather than merely passive participant in his own destiny. Internal as well as external obstacles begin to stand in his way, and when he is borne away on a hippogriff, we are dealing not in marvelous fables for Mother Goose enthusiasts but in meaningful images that have a Neoplatonic context in Bembo's *Asolani,* in Bembo's own Neoplatonic medal, to say nothing of Petrarch's *Rime* and *Trionfi.*[12] The Estensi were a talented clan, and they assembled a rich collection of treasures and curiosities, but the chronicles record no winged horses in their stables and no ability in their scions to take to the air in intercontinental flight. The histories, of course, do tell of many other kinds of transport, violent and passionate; in the hippogriff-flight of their poetic "ancestor," his "descendants" might have recognized a newly reimagined Platonic metaphor for the vertiginous impulses of unbridled human sexuality—one to which even Bradamante, much further on in the poem, gives clearest voice.[13]

For Ariosto, therefore, the question is whether Ruggiero will sink into the idle occupations of the sensualist, for all his fair beginnings and good intentions, in resistance to the path marked out by Providence, by increasingly refractory stages, or whether he will strike out on the voyage of heroic destiny, laborious and finally tragic, but glorious. More simply, what will the puny, pugnacious human will ("voglia") do to attempt to confound the Will of heaven ("voler")? Another question hinges on the first: shall Ferrara be founded or not, and how will the chosen dynast learn to make the difficult Herculean choice, so that the Estensi may break into history? The questions are both explicit and implicit in Boiardo; Ariosto gives it greater moral, intellectual, and artistic intensity, elaborating on it immediately in his opening cantos, in contrast to its very late appearance in the *Innamorato*. From one point of view (the historian's, perhaps) the whole issue is childish nonsense, since the Estensi were highly visible, often in sensational ways, and the fiction of how they came to be is merely wearisome. This misses the point. Every generation of the family must pose for itself an essential question: what happens to the House, to Ferrara and its citizenry, to the course of history in the peninsula and in Europe itself, if the scions of that House, furnished with opportunities and privileges of every kind, should succumb to some vicious mole of nature and be less than themselves? The laughable aspect of civilization is that it can be undone so quickly by one mere human will. The problem occasionally perturbs the citizens of even democratic societies, but the most autocratic courts of the Renaissance had the advantage in counseling order by being provided with universal intellectual patterns that took shape in pleasing myths. By virtue of being limited creatures, men and women will inevitably fall, succumbing to concupiscence, wrath, and pride. The myth, by illustrating what inevitably lies ahead and marking out the clear stages in which temptations would appear, provides a partial defense against that inevitability, inculcating the need for awareness at least. For both the pattern and the myth of Ruggiero's future weaknesses, Ariosto was, as for so much before, indebted to Boiardo.

It is as supreme mythmaker and creator of thoughtful images that Boiardo finally triumphs. The *Innamorato* proved the most tractable of fables for Ariosto precisely because it was a treasure-house of poetic riches, splendid in both their rounded fullness and their unfinished suggestiveness, and the later poet's task of instructing through appealing fictions was made easier by virtue of Boiardo's grand bequest. Riotously colorful though the *Innamorato* is throughout, in its last nine cantos it is fertile, allusive, and symbolic in the extreme, as if the creator's imagination were working with even greater intensity and concentration than before. Book 3 furnishes Ariosto with some of his most fruitful pictorial concepts, and the grand nexus for all these is the "Fonte del Riso" (3.7.7ff.), a reservoir of "hilaritas mundi" elaborated from several earlier appearances and revised and deepened for Ruggiero in the *Furioso*. The text gives every indication that Ruggiero is to be the subject of an appropriate allegory, as Orlando, Rinaldo, and Astolfo, the other principals, were before him, and he is introduced into a setting that represents a very unmartial indolence, an appropriately watery place where laughter and hilarity drown reason and consideration. The Fountain of Laughter is described as a great pool in whose depths are glistening gardens and dazzling palaces of gold and crystal, ruled by lovely naiads, and filled with dancing, feasting, and song; a place where unwary knights, accidentally falling or willingly plunging into the waters, live thoughtlessly for love alone and suffer oblivion of purpose and self ("Scordando tutte le passate cose"). Echoes of Hylas, lured to the depths by water-nymphs as the Argonauts sail on, bubble up from Boiardo's waters, and shadows of Narcissus's pool hang about the environs: Orlando, trapped here earlier (2.31.43–48), still spends his days in self-admiration ("A l'onde chiare specchiandosi il viso," 3.7.9). In its "mala arte" the pool functions clearly as a watery, Venerean trap for warriors over-inflamed with martial heat.

Only two cantos after meeting Bradamante, Ruggiero is lured into this allegorical landscape (3.7.3ff.). He does not enter without sufficient warning. At the entrance to the great magical wood that encloses the fountain he is greeted by a maiden holding a scroll, which contains a mysterious but suggestive message that Ariosto gives evidence of having scrutinized with deep interest:

"Desio di chiara fama, isdegno e amore
Trovano aperta a sua voglia la via."
Questi duo versi avea scritti di fuore,
Poi dentro in cotal modo se leggia:
"Amore, isdegno e il desiare onore
Quando hanno preso l'animo in balìa,
Lo sospingon avanti a tal fraccasso,
Che poi non trova a ritornare il passo."
           (3.7.13)

"Desire of bright fame, disdain and love find pathways open to their will": these two verses were written on the outside; but within, the following were to be read: "Love, disdain, and the desire for honor, once they have taken the soul into their power, drive it before them with such an uproar that it cannot find the way back."

Here then, neatly ordered, clearly recognizable, and accompanied by a clear reference to Neoplatonic imagery of the soul's chariot driven by concupiscence and wrath, is the paradigm for Ruggiero's allegorical career in the *Furioso,* when "amore" and "il desiare onore," in clearly demarcated stages, will indeed possess his soul and drive it crashingly before them, rendering the wood denser and more impassable. As Ariosto himself exclaims at a crucial juncture in Ruggiero's career,

Oh gran contrasto in giovenil pensiero,
desir di laude et impeto d'amore.
           (25.1.1–2)

Oh, the great struggle in youthful minds, between desire for praise and the impulse to love!

Here also in Boiardo is the basis for Ariosto's Vergilian overlay of the *Innamorato,* attributing to Ruggiero errors not only of the concupiscible but also of the irascible passions: love and honor. In a word, Boiardo forecasts what he could not accomplish and what Ariosto, who almost certainly knew him and had as one of the closest friends of his youth the poet's nephew, Ercole Strozzi, faithful to this incipient program, accomplished at length and with virtuosity. Young love, its feet broaching the first copses, breeds attraction and cupidinous love, but wrathful scorn ("isdegno") and desire for glory are hidden deeper in the "selva oscura," lurking to do their mischief.

This increasing constriction of the wood of life for those who enter it unwarily, in the confusedness of their love, should strike the memory with echoes of a passage from Bembo's *Asolani,* whose Horatian source we shall see later; "for just as at the entrance of some forest we seem to have a beaten path, but the further we penetrate, the narrower that track becomes, so when the desire for some object first arouses us, we seem to be able to attain it with the greatest ease, but the further we go, the smaller and the more difficult our road becomes at every step."[14] Ten years after Boiardo wrote his stanza about the message on the maiden's scroll, Bembo phrased the very same concept in Ciceronian prose. Under the influence of two masters, Ariosto proved faithful to both in giving Ruggiero's career of temptations the exact shape of "amore" and "desio di gloria" that Boiardo had so clearly delineated and that Bembo's prose statement so clearly reinforced. The *Furioso*'s Ruggiero, with his intricate concatenation of worldly passions, his ever-lengthening, ever-narrowing track of desire, is the poet's prolonged piety to a familiar Platonic idea ingrained in the literature of his society, and his greatness lies in his invention of passionate, compelling fictions to dramatize that idea: not, one would think, a task of consummate facility.

For both Boiardo and Ariosto, Ruggiero is involved in testing; testing implies struggle and growth; growth implies direction toward an end. Nevertheless, the imagery of the two poets is significantly different, witness to the independence of each. Here, in a magical Boiardan forest that heralds the more "realistic" but equally symbolic ones of Ariosto, Ruggiero strikes at a tree root, wondrously releasing a maiden, a "falsa dama" by whom he is cunningly led to the fountain, into which he plunges with glee, joining Orlando, Sacripante, and many others. The youth is already demonstrating a tendency to fall into unholy loves. This maiden is unnamed, but she is clearly a descendant of Oiseuse ("Idleness"), usher to the garden of love, for she initiates the first steps of a prolonged and painful progress through the stages of sensual passion. The "ballo," "danze," "giochi," and "canto" that greet Ruggiero's eyes and ears in this submarine paradise are the very elements that Ariosto selects to continue this allegory of the hero's entrance, in clearly marked stages, into the joys and miseries of love. The first of Atlante's prisons, the castle in the Pyrenees, is utterly symphonic with music and dance, with feasting and change of clothing, and all the relaxation listed in Boccaccio's Temple of Venus in the *Teseide.* There is no physical consummation here, only the preparation for it—what the modern world calls "atmosphere."

To Boiardo's fountain Ariosto thus closely joins his own castle, preferring a different kind of image but preserving the same meaning. The ambiguous joys of this Fountain of Laughter, laughter that soon turns to tears ("Qual nome ha Riso, e veramente è un pianto," 3.6.55), provide the basis for Ruggiero's allegory of profane love in the first quarter of the *Furioso:* the threshold formed by the indolent amusements of Atlante's castle, titillating but still relatively innocent; the full entrance, after music and dance, into sensual satisfaction in Alcina's palace, when desire hardens into habit; and the bitter dramatization of "amore-amaro" in the inevitable sequel of empty disillusion and complaint in Atlante's Palace of Illusion. If Ruggiero later begins to live out the tripartite career in love of a sonnet hero in successive stages of idleness and infatuation, total surrender, and final frustration, it is because Boiardo marked out the way and supplied the basis for the imagery. Forests unexpectedly providing maidens announcing choices among ruling passions of love, hate, or glory; appropriately watery places of feasting and forgetfulness—these Boiardan creations reappear transformed in the forests, castles, and islands of pleasures of Ariosto's opening cantos, but they are linked by the hero's continuous, progressive descent into a life of fleshly enjoyment and glory-seeking. They are unified, particularly, by being unwaveringly focused on a hero for whom the wrong choice of life is supremely portentous. Ariosto's *selection* of Ruggiero for this important destiny represents a real advance in art and meaning over the *Innamorato,* for in Boiardo Ruggiero is only one of many who fall into the pool, and no great consequences ensue. In Ariosto the fall marks a first stage in a parabola of gathering speed and increasingly darkening consequence: as Ariosto could have learned, if only from Boiardo's monitory maiden, "amore" and "desio di chiara fama" do indeed crowd in on the chariot of the soul, rendering the forest an ever-narrowing wood of no return.

Boiardo's wood and fountain are splendors enough, but canto 7 of book 3 is important for yet another of his commanding images, providing a crucial element in Ariosto's allegory. Here Boiardo furnishes the strangest and most wonderful of all his creations, a flying horse. Two cantos before the *Innamorato's* truncation, this magical beast, ancestor of the more dazzling hippogriff that later transports Astolfo to hell and to heaven, springs splendidly into existence from a cleft tree in the Magic Wood. It is created specifically to delude ("per inganno"), and Gradasso, who releases its life by smiting a tree root like Ruggiero before him, is not the man to avoid delusion. In Boiardo's Enchanted Forest, predecessor to Tasso's more famous one, two heroes find, imprisoned in bark, symbolic representations of things that attract them: an aerial horse leaps out for Gradasso, who lusts after the uncapturable courser Bayard, and a maiden for Ruggiero, who has just fallen wildly in love with Bradamante. Jumping delightedly into the horse's saddle, Gradasso is borne swiftly into the air and dropped from on high into the "Fonte del Riso," and the horse returns to take up its home in the wood. After this one, swift, fugitive action, it appears no more, but its action says something crucial about its nature, establishing links among cooperative horses that transport warriors to places of idle pleasure filled with yielding maidens, both the "acqua amorosa" and "foresta incantata." Boiardo's horse is wingless, bounding by its own strength into the upper sky, but Ariosto will furnish it with great multicolored vans like those most often seen on the shoulders of Cupid. He will also, single-handedly, make it the creation and property of Atlante, now endowed with the traditional characteristics of Amor. He will, finally, make Ruggiero the first of its only two human riders, both students of Logistilla, who teaches them the art of bridling and who represents the involvements of neither "amore" nor "desio di gloria," but something more rationally aloof. Again, the taut links between Boiardo's last cantos and Ariosto's beginning ones allow us to see something essential about the allegorical maneuvers of the later poem.

More than any other that precedes and follows, canto 7 of book 3 of the *Innamorato* possesses the indefinable but unmistakable allegorical density of a fairy tale. In clear, bold primary colors, and in a prodigal outpouring of allusive pictorialism, it provides a complex of images of haunted places and unnatural creatures, all entangled in a mysterious but inevitable relationship, all suggesting the power of human passion and human love. The surface of the narrative is itself so strong and satisfying, so freshly vital and rounded in contour, that we go to it not for strength of structure or complex continuity of theme and idea but for images and episodes rendered with sculptural solidity, always brimming with incipient allegorism, verging always on the typical and universal, but never decisively passing over into allegory. There is indeed enough overt allegory in Boiardo, as in the gardens of Morgana and the beating Penitenza administers to Orlando. But the Fountain of Laughter in canto 7, its Magic Wood and Soaring Horse live with another life altogether. Who or what is controlling them we do not know. The emphasis is on causeless mystery rather than on the enlightenment or on the moral progress of Ruggiero. Coasting ever closer to traditional allegory, Boiardo's poetry, original and unprecedented, most often has something of the astonishing singularity and wild weird inventiveness of Celtic narrative. The central mysteriousness of the *matière de Bretagne* repeatedly colors and conquers the poem, and the *Innamorato* persists in being its own forest, turning ever inward on its own mystery and wonder and never leading outward to a conclusion as on several occasions it promises (perhaps threatens is the better word) to do.

The *Innamorato* simply does not represent a sustained creative effort moving to a clearly demarcated end, and the two remaining cantos of the poem give no sign of developing this richly symbolic material. The search for novelty, which provides (sometimes very superfluously, as in the case of Mandricardo) a new hero for each book, finally becomes an end in itself. The poem as a whole has the air of a series of improvisations around a few regularly recurring motifs rather than of an elaborated construction with a central objective. Part of the work's essential character seems dictated by external circumstances, Boiardo being, as governor of Modena and Reggio, a working aristocrat at the center of power. That the twenty-nine cantos of book 1 were completed in two or three years, and that the thirty-one cantos of book 2 were completed between 1478 and 1482 are inescapable facts. Two years of silence intervened while the war with Venice was in progress, and the ten years between the poem's resumption in 1484 and truncation in 1494 produced only the nine cantos of book 3.[15] Yet external difficulties are only a part of the problem; some of the difficulty must have originated within. There is no question of Boiardo's awareness of the desirability of unifying his tale and completing it. On one occasion he claims to be attempting to collect its "istorie sparte" into a unity (2.17.38); on another, he announces the planned conclusion of many promised actions, chiefly the triumph of Charlemagne, and the marriage and death of Ruggiero (3.1.3). Here the wish seems father to the thought, involving a serious miscalculation of the poem's nature or the powers needed to arrive at completion. The truth is that the *Innamorato* resists, as a matter of principle and in a manner extraordinary in Renaissance fiction, the closing off of any action. It lives by escaping conclusions, connections, developments, and its temporary solutions to "problems" like enchantments and imprisonments are splendidly arbitrary. There is, for instance, no reason why Brandimarte is the one chosen to rescue Ruggiero and his companions from their submarine pleasures. Indeed, once the rescue is effected, the poem proceeds as if the imprisonment had never occurred, sending Ruggiero off into the air in another novel adventure. The imprisonment marks no stage, gives evidence of no interior disposition, only barely suggests that characters are the "dungeon of themselves," scarcely points at all to Ruggiero's great future. The episode lives in and for itself alone, contrasting utterly with Ariosto's clearly escalating imprisonments of Ruggiero and his repeated rescues by Bradamante until she herself, at the demonstrated limits of her power, needs to be rescued.[16]

Compelling in the originality of its fictions, in the novelty of its characters, situations, and settings, the *Innamorato* presents a challenge to an artist of altogether more traditional and classical instincts. Ariosto's task was to anchor Boiardo's errant fancies and to deepen or overlay them with other, mythographic values derived from a long tradition of classical humanism. He gives his narrative coherence and direction by singling out a hero whom a deviation from responsibility most profoundly concerns. He pierces behind the mystery of magic and refers all those curious lures to dereliction—horses, enchantresses, fountains, palaces of pleasure—to a single source, Atlante the sorcerer, who now clearly creates and controls them. He both unifies and directs the narrative forward, letting it curl in on itself, but only in order to gather strength for a bound forward. Boiardo's unruly riches of content are ordered into a form of complementary richness. In this unprecedented labor of reconstruction, two things are clear. First, Ariosto submitted the last dozen or so cantos of the *Innamorato* to an especially patient scrutiny. Second, motivated as he was by an intense ambition to supersede, he descried, especially in those final cantos, opportunities enough to provoke the attempt. If the problem of "continuation" was to be resolved, it had to be resolved there, for the last cantos of Boiardo are a truly indispensable prelude. They contain the source of all those major actions—the rout of Montalbano, the siege and battle for Paris, the meeting and separation of dynasts, the proposed duel of Rinaldo and Orlando for Angelica, the flight of the enchantress from Charlemagne's tent—with which Ariosto opens his own poem. As the chapters to ensue will seek to demonstrate, Ariosto chained it to its predecessor with consummate art and palpable economy, creating from the elements of an older poetic entity a wholly new and original one.

The focus keeps sliding, repeatedly and ungratefully, over to Ariosto. Yet it does not always remain there, and we keep returning to Boiardo's irresistible art, a true forge of creativity. The cornucopia that poured forth Orlando, Angelica, Agramante, Atlante, and Rodomonte continued, undiminished to the very end and with an actual increment of poetic power, to yield original treasures like Ruggiero, Bradamante, and Mandricardo, all of them leaping unforgettably to life in a few swift strokes and finding a magical soil of circumstance in which to flourish and flower. All the elements necessary for Ariosto's ordination of their complexities are already present in germ, requiring only the piercing insight and laborious patience peculiar to poetic genius to elicit their hidden strengths. Were it not for Boiardo, we should never, it seems safe to say, have had Ariosto; as, were it not for Ariosto, we should not have had *The Faerie Queene,* at least as we now possess it. The invention of dynastic mythic protagonists, the invocation of a classical demigod's history for the legend of the hero, the rich eclecticism of the mythology, the halls storied with deeds of future generations and portentous with fate, the curious alliterative genealogies, even those sudden, unhelmeted revelations of the heroine's face, touched with visionary beauty and spirituality of feeling—all these may be traced back from Spenser through Ariosto to their beginning in Boiardo. Achillean Marinell, Herculean Arthegall, energetic Britomart, evasive Florimell, even those amorous forefathers, Rinaldo and Francus, are all, in a very real sense, the late progeny of the *Innamorato.* Rarely, perhaps never, has that influence been traced to its source. Yet the honor is the Count of Scandiano's of having first, at a specific time, in specific historical circumstances, invented a poetic vehicle for the glorification of a race of princes, and to have sounded something like the Vergilian note after a silence of fifteen hundred years, in the neighborhood of Mantua itself. That it sounded in the midst of a comic romance of chivalry makes its music all the more truly wonderful, "nuovo e dilettoso" indeed.

Near the end, Boiardo, in an unwonted confessional mood, professed himself disenchanted with the mixture, lamenting the lowered heroic tone of the age and its artistic correlative in a poetry whose subject was merely "antichi amori" and "battaglie de' giganti." The contrast of a vanished age of epic energy and epic poetry with a degenerate one of lovers and giants is clear in the contrast of the verb "canti" for the former with the altogether more prosaic "dir" and "narrar" for the latter. The poet complains that the road to Parnassus is lost ("de salirvi ormai perso è il camino"), and fame is invoked to chant in a lower strain ("al basso") the epic story of Agramante's invasion: even as the epic material begins tardily to infiltrate the action of romance, the poet evinces a sense of lowered or failing objectives (2.22.1–3).

Only an external event could have brought the poem to a kind of close. Surely no reader comes on the *Innamorato*'s last stanza, confided to the poem almost as to a diary in foreboding and distress, without a corresponding shock of his own. We have grown used to hearing the poet's voice breaking into the narrative, but this is unprecedented:

Mentre che io canto, o Iddio redentore,
Vedo la Italia tutta a fiama e foco
Per questi Galli, che con gran valore
Vengon per disertar non so che loco;
Però vi lascio in questo vano amore
De Fiordespina ardente a poco a poco,
Un' altra fiata, se mi fia concesso,
Racontarovi il tutto per espresso.
        (3.9.26)

Even as I sing—O God, Redeemer!—I see all Italy afire and aflame for these Gauls who, with great valor, come down to make a desert of I know not what place; and therefore I leave you in the midst of this vain love of Fiordespina, burning by little and little; another time, if it be allowed, I shall tell you the whole affair directly.

It was not to be. In the end, in mid-December of 1494, the poet lay worn out by the exigencies of the time, filled with grim apprehensions for the future.[17] There is no more desolating end in poetry, or, to those familiar with Italian history in the next century, none more alive with ironies. For the invader was no romantic Gradasso, no infatuated Agricane, no glory-seeking Agramante, puppets of the poet's imagination who had no care for "regno o stato" moving their hordes in the idealistic cause of love and honor alone. The stanza marks the first descent into Italy (herald of many more) of an alien army under that evil gnome, Charles VIII of France, father, ironically, of a son called Charles-Orland, after his favorite hero. Ironies accumulate. He came down at the invitation of Ludovico il Moro of Milan, husband to Beatrice d'Este, who, in an attempt at his own aggrandizement, urged the French attack on the Neapolitan kingdom of his wife's Aragonese relatives; and who, in the intricate politics of the era, found himself ranged against the Marquis Federigo Gonzaga of Mantua, husband of his sister-in-law, Isabella d'Este. A new age had dawned indeed, and with it a need for a new poetry, witnessing that history must, after all, be steadily accommodated in epic. And at this point, speeding past some minor poet-aster-competitors taking the low road of simple continuation, Ariosto steps in.

II

Orlando Furioso

The Overwriting

3

Homage to the House

A Poem of Love, History, and Society

Siamo nel regno della pura arte, assistiamo a' miracoli dell'imaginazione. Il poeta volge le spalle all'Italia, al secolo, al reale e al presente.

We are in the world of pure art, we witness the miracles of the imagination. The poet turns his shoulders on Italy, on his century, on the real, on the present.
    Francesco de Sanctis, *Storia della letteratura italiana*

If Boiardo conceived of himself as a courtly minstrel of bygone times, Ariosto totally reconceived the role of the poet in the Charlemagnic poem, and one of the chief witnesses of that reconception is his steadily increasing admission of history in its ancient, medieval, and contemporary phases into his fabulous narrative of Carolingian times. Since this is so peculiarly prominent a feature of the *Furioso*'s Vergilianism and must inevitably have been conceived from the first as the point of the wedge for the essential contrast between himself and his predecessors, it is difficult, now, to recapture the frame of mind that once depicted him as having no interest whatever, or only a very minimal one, in anything but the vagaries of romance. Frances Yates, Barbara Reynolds, and Giorgio Padoan have recently begun to reveal the essential absurdity of this neo-romantic critical posture,[1] but the matter goes much deeper than hitherto imagined, and Professor Wiggins's commentary, in his translation of the *Satires,* has a resonance as yet unexplored in the *Furioso.* Throughout, he gives us a moving account of Ariosto's efficiency and compassion as a man of both action and thought, in the trying circumstances of his term as governor of the bandit-ridden Garfagnana. Certainly Ariosto's letters, contemporaneous with the poem, reveal him throughout as a man living in a world of men amid a daily hard reality.[2] As a contemplative comic artist thrust brutally into the theater of political action as ambassador and administrator for the Estensi, the poet was, if not unique, far from the indolent voluptuary of romantic criticism. What other Renaissance poet-diplomat was threatened with a ducking in the Tiber by an enraged Julius II, or stood as ambassador for the Estensi at the cradle of the newly orphaned Caterina de' Medici and meditated on her future?[3] Ariosto lived at the center of the great events of his time, and he observed them unflinchingly with a clear sense of both their meaning and their mutability. The *Furioso* contains the fruit of that observation, transfigured; which is, we should be clear at once, not to say that he wrote historical allegory but rather to say that he addressed the events of history by incorporating them into the fictions of dynastic romance. In undertaking to write of Orlando's madness, he also projects himself vividly in the consciously public gesture of a new

83

Maro to a new Augustus (3.56), and the audience whose presence he continually assumes is, as we shall see, precisely the kind of audience he says he writes for in the proem to canto 7, an aristocratic and learned one, distinguished for its adherence to the mental life and fitted to appreciate the "frutto" of his labors. Appearing in the guise of the latest poet in the Carolingian tradition, he is also the conscious memorializer of his time, its ideas, its great events and major personalities; these are seen, steadily and throughout, against the complicated fabric of ancient and medieval European history, new elements accommodated to an old pattern perpetually in process of reforming.

The encompassing action of the *Furioso*—the action deliberately selected out of Boiardo's narrative to begin the new work in a prominently different way—is the love-quest of Bradamante for Ruggiero. The work begins with the young Saracen inveigled by enchantment from his great destiny, and it concludes with the converted and chastened young Christian sitting at his marriage feast, soon to begin the dynasty whose successive generations in history the *Furioso* has glorified from the beginning. The Bradamante-Ruggiero love-story encloses the action and marks the *Furioso* as a poem of dynasty and dynastic fatality. As a poem concerned with dynasty, it is inevitably a poem informed by a consciousness of history: past and contemporary, European and, more particularly, Italian, pagan and Christian. Regularly and consistently, historical allusions cast their shadow over Ariosto's narrative, either by way of the so-called digressions in the body of the tale or by way of reflective proems at the beginnings of cantos.[4]

History first begins to permeate the poem in Bradamante's Aeneas-like vision of her descendants, an extended roll call of the males of the Este line in canto 3.23–62, which proceeds, in Vergilian fashion, from the obscurity of legend to the bright blaze of glory in the present. The passage on the males is matched later by a long one on the females of the House in 13.56–73, celebrating the great women of the dynasty and providing yet another incentive for Bradamante to act with similar courage, to rescue and redeem her suitor from paganism, and to initiate the apparently stalled processes of history. Bradamante and Ruggiero's common destiny is to be Ferrara, that city of palaces with long ties to the Empire that Ariosto perceives, Vergil-like, as the fulfillment of a long, laborious historical movement, the unimaginable result of a few hovels huddled ages ago in a marshland. Surely no one could quarrel with his appraisal of its success or with his realization of the cost of civilization in terms of human effort. Ariosto's two young dynasts, even while the fathering Empire of Charlemagne is suffering assault and destruction, are themselves to plant the first slips of that glorious growth that is eventually to be Ferrara. Their progress to chastened and tempered love in the long-ago past, beset by all kinds of passions that they finally subdue and by temptations that they endure and overcome, is a mirror for their descendants in the here and now of the sixteenth century. For the present is clearly no less full of stresses and trials than the past: no less than the Empire of Charlemagne, the Christian world of Ariosto's day is threatened with dissolution by

internal dissension and by external infidel fury. Ariosto repeatedly represents Bradamante's and Ruggiero's descendants as princes and captains who are defenders of the
Empire and protectors of the Church, and it is clearly with an eye on them, their
courtiers and their fellow European rulers, that he repeatedly surveys the European
scene, focusing on the current mangled state of Italy in his own times.

A first powerful meditation on the matter occurs in the proem to canto 17.1–5,
where the poet interrupts his description of the crucial Saracen attack on Paris to
meditate fiercely on the travails of his own country, seeking to find some mysterious
providential justice in the chastisement of his own nation by others even more cor-
rupt and evil, though professedly Christian. The same sense of personal anguish is
revealed in the great and terrible outburst of the narrator at 17.73–79, a passage in
which the romance fabric of a tournament in Syria is shockingly torn apart by the
poet's sudden recall of a horrifying contemporary reality. This produces a ferocious
outcry against the "Most Christian" French and the "Catholic" Spanish killing
fellow Christians in Italy and elsewhere, while the holy places in the Near East yet
remain to be wrested from the infidel. The passage typically holds the present and
the past in tension, measuring the squalor of internecine Christian strife against the
splendor embodied in the old French kingdoms in the Near East, when Europeans
were custodians of the very places where "Almighty God dwelt in human flesh"
("dove in carne abitò Dio onnipotente," 17.73.6). On yet a third occasion, much the
same anger informs the proem to canto 34.1–3, where the poet, writing in imitation
of Vergil about an attack by Harpies, cries out against the Harpies infesting the
fruitful table of Italy, wreaking divine vengeance on her for her sins, and calls for
some princely savior to rid the world of their stench. What we have yet to realize is
that the passing from the airy fantasy of the fiction to the direct experience of the
moment is an Ariostan technique with profound resonances. These intermittent
reflections arise from and are bonded to the Carolingian tale, interacting with it to
form a unified poetic vision. The passage concerning the Harpies particularly has a
certain sinister resonance: it was Ludovico Sforza, Il Moro, husband of Beatrice
d'Este, sister of Alfonso, Ippolito, and Isabella, who first opened the gates to the
foreign invaders under Charles VIII of France, Harpies who ravaged and laid waste
and who provided the initial example for the devastation of the peninsula thereafter.
Il Moro's horrendous error and tragic ensuing history are part of Este family history,
a monitory emblem of evil with grave and unforeseeable consequences; and the family aspect is intensified by the fact that it was against his wife's own relatives, the
Aragonese rulers of Naples, that he had directed his wrath and ambition. Allusions
to that disastrous ruler, the very brother-in-law with whom Cardinal Ippolito had
spent part of his youth (46.94), the means by whom disaster came upon all Italy
("grave di tutta Italia danno," 13.63.6), occur repeatedly in the poem, especially in
the great vision of the French invasions of Italy that Bradamante sees prophetically
pictured on the walls of a palace in canto 33.31–34.

The importance of the atemporal nature of Ariosto's narrative, central to some of its profoundest moments, still goes unnoted. All three passages referred to above demonstrate the same tendency to break masterfully from the vagaries of the Carolingian tale to a meditation on actual contemporary history. The practice intensifies toward the end of the poem. There is a sudden, disturbing glance at the children and the mothers raped and killed under cover of the Christian assault on Bizerte in canto 40, an action that provokes the terse authorial comment: "Dei quali Orlando una gran parte intese, / Né lo poté vietar, né'l Duca inglese" (40.34.7–8; "which Orlando and Astolfo in great part knew about, but which neither could prevent")— an astounding, easily missed aside, where the poet's dark tone reveals that he is looking penetratingly at the inescapable side effects of human action, even the well-intentioned and sometimes necessary ones, like war. But the poet who glances at the incidental horrors generated in the interstices of an imaginary assault on Bizerte had previously, as the poetic historian of his own times, decried the thieving Christians who, at the gory battle of Ravenna in 1512, had violated "nuns and monks and wives and daughters and mothers, and had thrown Christ in the Sacrament onto the floor in order to steal a silver tabernacle" (14.8.5–8): even a battle in a just cause generates horror and sacrilege, good and evil being inextricably entangled in a postlapsarian world, where human powers are weak against evil. Yet another striking instance of Ariosto's deep sense of working on two levels, the historical and the fantastic, occurs when Sobrino, the aged counselor to the defeated pagan king, Agramante, dissuades him from suicide and urges him to call on his allies, fearfully conscious the while of the dangers to any prince who submits himself, in need, to the power of another outwardly friendly power: this (says Ariosto immediately, his imagination leaping from the distant world of Charlemagne backward to ancient Rome and forward to contemporary Italy) was the case for Hannibal and Jugurtha and Lodovico Il Moro, all of whom, trusting in aid from others, had their power wrested from them as a result (40.40–41). However unsettling for his readers, Ariosto thinks nothing of breaking the spell of his narrative for these abrupt ruminations on universal history. The dislocation in the story, the swift arrest of the action, the association of an idea in the fiction with a contemporary or ancient reality, all reveal a mind easily and deliberately negotiating the distance between the daily present and an imaginative world where reality is transfigured and made emblematic.

Forcefully juxtaposed and yoked together, particular phenomena, not only from different ages of history but also from fiction as well as history, assume the shape of an idea. By moving his readers away from a comfortable and lulling linear progression in time, Ariosto creates another time altogether, and the whole of history grows into a perceptible pattern in which the present is prefigured by the past. In perceiving recurrent patterns in the great pageant of history, in his constant joining of events and personages from the present and the past, Ariosto in effect telescopes and unifies all time, distancing change and impermanence under the aspect of eternity. The technique will be most evident in his simultaneous management of the multiple movements of his Carolingian narrative as well, where we are continually submitted to a characteristic Ariostan manipulation of time present, time past, and time future. We shall return to this matter later; here it is sufficient to note that Ariosto early reveals himself as the great mover of his own poetic world, viewing time from above, and fully in control of its manifold arenas of action. The perspective he assumes is that of the Vergilian poet; the multiple-time technique is that of the poem of history and dynasty, and it has no precedent whatever in the *Innamorato*.

The authoritative voice of Ariosto as the dynastic poet is epideictic, hortatory, moral. Speaking openly and forthrightly, he judges the European scene in some of its most momentous aspects, and there is no mistaking his power to apprehend both the contemporary realities of ambition, war, invasion, conquest, vengeance, punishment, misrule, and the regularly recurring falls of princes and the ways in which they conform to a universal pattern on the vast loom of human history. That is why, in his proem on the uses that Providence makes of human scourges, the poet can link Nero and Domitian with Attila and Ezzelino, and with the savage hordes of northern barbarians currently let loose on Italy (17.1–5); and why, *in his fiction*, Charlemagne prays fervently that the Saracenic hordes may not have been let loose on France for the same providential purpose (14.69–72). The fictional and meditative portions of the poem constantly reinforce each other and are, in the end, inseparable. Both "digressions" and proems are anything but scraps and patches of fortuitous, unassimilated material thrown out to whet our appetite for the suspended narrative. The poet who, after one such historical excursus, represents himself as scrambling to get back on his path ("Ma d'un parlar ne l'altro, ove sono ito / sì lungi dal camin ch'io faceva ora?" 17.80.1–2) is really tempting our complacency and inviting further scrutiny. His warriors constantly take the wrong turn in the road, but he himself never does; and he immediately assures us that no matter how much he appears to have lost his way, he knows how to find his way back again: "Non lo credo pero sì aver smarrito, / ch'io non lo sappia ritrovare ancora" (17.80.3–4).

This is especially true when the link between the historical commentary and the fiction is not immediately apparent. Ariosto's real ambush lies here precisely, in the tangles of his romantic tale, where he works by indirection and subtle allusion and studiously preserves a deceptively unengaged demeanor; a modern reader not particularly familiar with Renaissance history will especially fall victim to a bifurcated vision. A single crucial instance will suffice. In the meditation on mutability that opens canto 45, Ariosto comments on the dramatic shifts of fortune suffered by rulers like Louis XII of France and King Matthias Corvinus of Hungary, both plucked from the shadow of death in prison in order to rule in prosperity. With that last reference, the poet brings the matter very close to home, joining history and fiction in a not untypical manner, and in a way that his Ferrarese audience could not possibly have missed. Matthias Corvinus was the husband of Beatrice of Aragon, sister of Eleanor of Aragon, and therefore the uncle by marriage of the Este scions, Ariosto's patrons. It was through Corvinus that Ariosto's first employer, Cardinal Ippolito, became Bishop of Esztergom in Hungary (where Ariosto refused to accompany him, losing his favor as a consequence).[5] This meditation on Corvinus's change of fortune comes at a climactic point, when Ruggiero, the mythical fore-father of the Estensi, is similarly imprisoned and in danger of death for presumption and vainglory, his heroic strength having just won him a kingdom but his arrogance having been punished with a fall:

Si vede per gli essempii di che piene
sono l'antiche e le moderne istorie,
che'l ben va dietro al male, e'l male al bene,
e fin son l'un de l'altro e biasmi e glorie;
e che fidarsi a l'uom non si conviene
in suo tesor, suo regno e sue vittorie,
né disperarsi per Fortuna avversa,
che sempre la sua ruota in giro versa.
        (45.4)

Ancient and modern history are full of examples showing that good comes after bad, and bad after good, and that obloquy and glory tread on each other's heels; and that no man should trust to his treasure, his kingdom, his victories, nor despair when Fortune turns harsh, for her wheel keeps turning always.

Fiction "anticipates" history; or, put another way, history confirms the universal patterns exemplified in the fictional career of the mythical ancestor of the Estensi. The sudden confluence of historical exemplum and "mere" Carolingian fiction reveals that we had better bend a more attentive glance on Ariosto's story and realize, perhaps, that he is not a two-headed monster, psychologically fascinating but artistically impure, a moralist in his digressions and proems and a sophisticated trifler subversive in his narrative, but rather an artist who writes out of a single vision and reconciles the particular and the general, the timely and the timeless. Certainly he knew the power of Fortune. In undertaking to praise a great House, he committed himself to the long view and the assertion of some fundamental values by which the members of that House might still be guided in their actions. The Estensi were, especially in the sixteenth century, no trifling ménage. Oldest and most pres-tigious of the rulers of Italy, they had links to Spain, Naples, and Hungary, to Milan, Mantua, Rome, and Urbino, and they were allied culturally to France and politically to both the Church and the Empire.[6] Ariosto has the family history (and with it a large part of European history) by heart, and he puts it to excellent uses, often with a particular pointedness, as when recalling the emblematic careers of Ippolito's two relatives, Ludovico and Matthias. In his explicit commentary on historical events he is concerned to represent a current political reality in general, universal terms; in his Carolingian fiction he addresses the eternal moral values by which those realities are supported. History and literature interact at the level of myth.

Fantastic in appearance, the myth has a solid core of historical truth. The story of Bradamante and Ruggiero coming from France to found a dynasty in Ferrara memorializes the transfer of power in the great Italian centers from Lombard to Frank in the ninth century and the rise of duchies connected with the Empire.[7] But Ariosto's use of history is employed for poetic, not historical, ends. The great Muratori's disgust at the poet's use of these fabulous myths of Trojan descent—"it is an old sickness"[8]—represents the historian's view and the historian's failure to appreciate the poet's subtler purposes. The value of this mythology lies not in its literal assertion of relationship and descent but in the poetic truth elicited from it, the assertion of the continuity in time of enduring principles of human action in the progress toward civilization and order. Had Ariosto thought of Bradamante and Ruggiero as "real" historical personages, he might not have played quite so freely with them, especially when writing under the eye of their contemporary descendants. Their very lack of historicity, their *typicality* instead, allows him a large measure of imaginative freedom and the opportunity to order their adventures according to schematic patterns of growing temptation and advancing success. Bradamante and Ruggiero are important, finally, not in themselves but for what they represent as often (but not always) amusing and thoroughly tribulated rulers-in-training. Their adventures reveal an incremental pattern, and they stumble from difficulty to difficulty in successful preparation for their exalted roles as the first rulers of the Este domains and the prototypes of their long line. Only when the assertion of fabulous descent is static and inert does it offend as mindless flattery. But Ariosto's portrayal of Bradamante and Ruggiero is wholly and unremittingly dynamic. At no time are they represented as anything but deeply imperfect and developing creatures. Ariosto's awareness of the paradox of these obstreperous Carolingian creatures as vehicles of great ideas irradiates them with an unfailing wise laughter.

On the face of it, of course, it looks absurd that Boiardo's comic poem on the intemperately ardent love-madness of Orlando should accommodate a serious consideration of human love engaged in working out the program of providential history. Yet a moment's reflection will reveal the peculiar rightness of just such a juxtaposition of loves: Ruggiero and Orlando represent, respectively, what civilizations are and are not based on, the one striving blindly for some exit from his problems, the other succumbing without resistance to his appetitive fury. Ariosto's attention to that harder, more real issue (in contrast, that is, to Boiardo's altogether more fantastic concerns) is accompanied, almost necessarily, by a transformation of the stylized oriental locales and glorious inattention to time that characterize the earlier Carolingian romance. What Ariosto manifests, unlike any of his predecessors in the tradition, is an insistent concern for the concrete and the actual in choosing the various theaters of action for his story; his narrative is informed by a vivid sense of symbolic or allusive place.

This tendency is notable throughout as the setting for the poem ranges from Scotland to the Near East, but it becomes especially striking toward the end. Why, for example, should Ruggiero, in his last, climactic exploit, in cantos 44 and 45, find himself a captive, imprisoned in a dungeon in Eastern Europe—in, of all places,

Belgrade first, and later a town near Zagreb? These locations are unusual in Carolingian poetry. Yet a glance at the map will illuminate the relevance of the eastern locale for the Ferrarese poet and bring the realization that only twenty-one years separated the fall of Constantinople from his birth in 1474, and that the Italy he lived in was in perpetual danger of Ottoman invasion from the east and south.

Civilization, embodied in the Empire, and the threat to that civilization, embodied in the thrust of the infidel, are two of the dominant concerns of the *Furioso,* and Ariosto works in full awareness of what had been achieved and what was at risk in the Europe of his time. Since the fall of Constantinople to Sultan Mehmet II in 1453, the Islamic world had advanced a claim to world domination, strengthened by its prestigious possession of the imperial city itself. A triple drive followed: first, to break out beyond the Danube into central Europe; second, to establish Turkish power in North Africa; third, to dominate the Near East.[9] The first and second of these objectives kept Christian Europe in turmoil for over a century. Bulgaria had fallen in 1396, after the disaster of Nicopolis.[10] Greece was in Ottoman hands by 1460, Albania fell in 1478, and by the end of the century and to a steady rhythm, the Turks were in control of Herzegovina, Bosnia, Croatia, and Montenegro. Events like these brought the enemy to the confines of western Europe and to the very doorstep of Italy, with only the narrow stretch of the Adriatic lying between. Even today the Orlando-column in the Stradun at Dubrovnik, never overrun but constantly threatened, allusively honors the Christian fight against the infidel. States with which Ferrara had a certain connection early found themselves in a frontier position: Hungary from 1383, when Serbia and Bulgaria definitively passed under Ottoman control, and Venice from the mid-fifteenth century, when her commercial interests in the east were threatened by Muslim expansion. Upheavals in relatively distant political spheres had powerful repercussions near at hand. Thus, Matthias Corvinus, whose reign (1458–1490) was one long defensive movement against pressures exerted from the east, unsuccessfully attacked the Ottomans in 1476, and his opponents had then turned on Venice to gain power in the Adriatic and in Albania, their success there further emboldening them to gain the first toe-hold in Italy, at Otranto in the south in 1480. The closing off of the Adriatic at its southern end meant that Venice was effectively trapped in her own waters, without access to her spheres of influence.[11] This alarming state of affairs was only temporary, but it was an indication of what lay ahead. By the end of the fifteenth century, then, just before Ariosto began to write, the situation was perilous enough. It was to grow worse in the remaining thirty-three years of his life.

Sixteenth-century terrors of a resurgent Islam are understandable perhaps even today. Suleiman the Magnificent assumed power in 1520, exactly one year before the second edition of the *Furioso* appeared, and in the ensuing year of his reign his objective was nothing less than world domination and control over all Europe. Throughout the first third of the sixteenth century, which exactly coincided with the most creative years of Ariosto's life and his continual perfection of his masterpiece, the Turks struck from both an eastern and a southerly direction, from the Balkans and from Africa, where from 1499 to 1503 they had succeeded in establishing themselves as a considerable naval power in the Mediterranean.[12] The years between 1520 and 1532 were especially crucial, and they came to a climax with the publication, in 1532, of the amplified and restructured *Furioso*. Belgrade—the very city to which Ariosto decided, in the third edition, to send his dynastic hero on a mission of conquest—repeatedly attacked by Mehmet II in 1456, 1464, and 1490, finally succumbed to Suleiman in 1520, an event that breached the Danube defense line of Christian Europe. Hungary—the nation to which Ippolito had been sent as a child, where his uncle and aunt were once king and queen, and where he held the Bishopric of Eger near Budapest—now became the Sultan's primary objective and the subject of three separate campaigns.[13] The first, in 1526, brought the Ottomans into direct conflict with the House of Hapsburg and the Holy Roman Emperor, Charles V, whose very own sister, the recent Queen of Hungary, was driven from her throne when her husband was murdered by the invading Turks in the battle of Mohács. The second campaign, between 1527 and 1529, brought on the occupation of Buda and Pest, the first Ottoman siege of Vienna, Turkish raiders in southern Germany, and panic throughout Europe. The third campaign, in 1532, aimed directly at Vienna and Austria, fortunately failed of its effect, but gave Europe another frisson of horror. These were the very years when Hapsburg and Valois, Charles V and Francis I, were repeatedly at each others' throats, turning Italy into a bloody battleground for Christians, as Ariosto was well aware. The poet did not live to see it, but one wonders what he would have made of the momentary but sinister alliance of Francis I and Suleiman against Charles V, an alliance that produced the bizarre moment in 1543 when the Ottoman fleet sacked Nice, raided the hinterland for slaves, brazenly anchored in the port of Toulon, and went on to savage the coasts of France, Spain, and Italy.[14] Given the outraged proem to canto 17 and the episode of Ruggiero in the Balkans, he might not have been wholly surprised. He had already registered the impact of similar, prophetic events in his own poetry.

No less than the Charlemagne of pleasant fiction, the new Charles of contemporary history had the Sultan at his door. Ariosto responded to the steady crescendo of Turkish triumphs in the edition of 1532, deepening the signs of his concern already present in the editions of 1516 and 1521. He responded, however, in the manner of an extraordinarily subtle poet rather than of a historian or journalist, addressing his subject not in the factual and detailed manner that some readers conceive as the only possible mode of address but in a rovingly allusive manner, creating fictional situations for his characters that mirror, with alterations, the circumstances and personages of other times. With only the Adriatic as a buffer and the Mediterranean already aflame, Italians had good cause to look with anxiety to both the east and south, and Ariosto, his own eyes fixed on something more than Carolingian mirages, ensured that they looked where he looked. In the final edition, by propelling his hero into Balkan neighborhoods wholly strange and unwonted in the chivalric tradition, he directs the attention of his courtly audience to locales that only the most ignorant and unheedful would have thought merely fanciful. Hungary, Yugoslavia, Bulgaria, and Constantinople are in Ariosto's mind as the poem moves toward its conclusion: the *placing* of his fiction is both reminder and tacit exhortation.

In Ruggiero's climactic exploit, Ariosto is not interested in recording history directly, but rather in dramatizing the impulses of the individual spirit by which history is eternally made. Insofar, therefore, as he goes eastward, Ruggiero directs his descendants' attention to a dangerous and imperiled area, one all too close to the Italian homeland he founded and one, moreover, into which the descendants might usefully project their warlike energies, in concert with their fellow Europeans. The advice seems especially valid when we reflect that the poem's dedicatee, Ippolito, was both cardinal and warrior. However, Ruggiero does precisely what Ariosto has throughout condemned the Christian princes of Europe for doing: Ruggiero needs to be rich and win territory in order to gain his bride, and so he makes war on the Christian ruler of Constantinople, aiding the Bulgarian rebels against their rightful lord and stealing those territories from the Emperor. If, therefore, he goes off in the right direction, it is only the physical, exterior, geographical direction that is right and that serves to instruct his descendants; but his moral compass is broken and his inner orientation is off. Storming out of France after being refused by Bradamante's parents, seething with rage and indignation at the poverty that keeps him from seeming a worthy candidate for her hand, and with a lust for land and honor in his heart, Ruggiero has embarked on a self-glamorizing exploit that is the very antithesis of a crusade. His mad action, by being so opposite to what is currently wanted in that particular geographical sphere, by being the last of the great egotistical deviations of the *Furioso,* points the direction in which the danger lies and suggests another manner and end for the deployment of Christian strength.

The adventure's grim outcome forms a terse commentary on its waywardness. Ruggiero's theft of a kingdom produces an overruling pride in his spirit (45.5), and that is soon his downfall. Unguardedly relaxing in an expansive mood of self-satisfaction after his conquest, he is suddenly and unexpectedly betrayed and cast swiftly down into a dark dungeon, a fool of Fortune in danger of imminent death, misery following hard on the heels of elation. Still faithless and egotistical, though very recently converted, he reverses, in falling into prison, the pattern of Matthias Corvinus, the great fighter of the infidel, and a pattern of Christian heroism. Far from being used to flatter the Estensi, Ruggiero provides a negative emblem of moral motion: a potentially good but misdirected energy that could, with rational control, be employed for better purposes, especially in an area twice troubled and devastated, and in the times of not one but two Holy Roman Emperors, two Charleses, the Carolingian and the Hapsburg. Enterprises in that eastern area, we may infer, had better be undertaken in quite another spirit, and with motives drawn from something more than glamorous self-glorification. The whole episode forms a commentary on the rapacious acquisitiveness, not only of the hero, still very much attached to self at this late stage of his career, but also, perhaps, of some famous crusading expeditions in the East in earlier history. How often had the winning of the holy places been put aside for gold and glory by diverted chevaliers?

The question arises because there is a still deeper resonance in the whole episode. In dashing off to the Balkans, Ruggiero goes to an area where other ancestors of the current family of the Estensi had latterly been engaged, perhaps dedicated less to their spiritual than their worldly profit. Ruggiero's eastern exploit cunningly alludes to, and perhaps criticizes, that of the Aragonese and Catalan adventurers with their "audacious galleys" ("audaci galee," 42.38.8) in the Near East in the fourteenth century. Here we need to recall that Alfonso, Ippolito, Isabella, and Beatrice d'Este were the children of a Neapolitan Spanish mother, Eleanora of Aragon, and that a literary heritage came with their Spanish blood. While the Este scions were engrossed in Vergil and Boiardo, they were not unaware of one of the greatest of the Spanish romances of chivalry, the *Tirant lo Blanc* of Joannot Martorell. Duke Ercole's nephew, the poet Niccolò da Correggio, even made an attempt to translate it for his favorite cousin, Isabella.[15] One of the few books saved from the bonfire of romances in *Don Quixote*, described by Cervantes as the "best book in the world," *Tirant lo Blanc* was based on the chronicler Muntaner's account of the Catalan establishment of the Duchy of Athens from 1322 to 1386, a time when the Iberians held sway over the Balkans as well. Aragonese and Catalonian adventurers had joined in this early enterprise against the Turk, and the glorious memory of that easternmost sphere of Christian expansion still circulated in the literature of the Este court in Ariosto's day. Boiardo had already found a place in the *Innamorato* for the praise of the Aragonese dynasty into which Ercole had married in 1473, and it was almost inevitable that Ariosto should go beyond his master in this respect, though with characteristic allusiveness and indirection. The Duchy of Athens, however glorious, was the product of a bit of un-Christian double-dealing: the Byzantine Emperor, hard-pressed by Turks, had been rescued by Spanish soldiers called in from afar but had then been divested of power and supplanted by those same Iberian adventurers.[16] In contrast, the long tale of Ruggiero's error and retribution, and its final exchange of self-sacrificing courtesies between Ruggiero and the Emperor's son, Leo, points to an important reconciliation of Christian East and Christian West by altering the original events to provide both an ideally harmonious conclusion and a model for the relations of Christian rulers. Indeed, the moral dignity Ariosto accords Leo speaks volumes.

The 1532 amplification of Ruggiero's adventures, crucially extending the pattern of his moral deviations into overweening ambition, pride, and despair, is true to the nature and the movement of his career in the earlier two editions, where his failures (serious enough) are those only of sensuality and love of glory. His new defects could surely have been demonstrated in other territories than the ones Ariosto deliberately chose, but he placed them allusively in one of the most imperiled areas of contemporary Europe, now, as before, a frontier of conflict with the infidel. Hence the amplification testifies also to Ariosto's awareness of European medieval history, and to his awareness of events between 1521 and 1532. The new passage is therefore many-faceted. It forms an emblematic commentary on princes of unrestrained territorial ambitions, especially when directed against co-religionists and especially in the Eastern Empire, so long a victim of outrage from the West. It also points allusively in the direction of a new crusade, in a new spirit, both the need and the occasion for which Ariosto had twice expressed forcefully, in his narrator's voice, *outside the romance-narrative* and in literal terms. On the first occasion he appears in the posture of the Christian apologist, whose chief model is Augustine, speculating that Europe's punishments are the inevitable rewards of sin:

Or Dio consente che noi siàn puniti
da populi di noi forse peggiori,
per li multiplicati et infiniti
nostri nefandi, obbobriosi errori.
Tempo verrà ch'a depredar lor liti
andremo noi, se mai saren migliori,
e che i peccati lor giungano al segno,
che l'eterna Bontà muovano a sdegno.
        (12.5)

Now God consents that we are punished by others worse, perhaps, than us, for our infinite, heaped up wickedness, our shameful errors. Yet the time will come that we go to ravage their shores, if ever we grow better, and their sins touch such a point that they move the Eternal Goodness to anger.

On the second occasion the poet touches fiercely on that very strife of French Christian with Spanish Christian that makes Europe (and particularly Italy) a shambles and lends vigor to pagans:

Se Christianissimi esser voi volete,
e voi altri Catolici nomati,
perché di Cristo gli uomini uccidete?
perché de' beni lor son dispogliati?
Perché Ierusalem non riavete,
che tolto è stato a voi da' rinegati?
Perché Constantinopoli e del mondo
la miglior parte occupa il Turco immondo?
        (12.75)

If *you* want to be "Most Christian," and you others want to be called "Catholic," why do you kill Christians, why are Christians despoiled of their goods? Why don't you repossess Jerusalem, taken from you by renegates? Why does the unclean Turk occupy Constantinople and the best part of the world?

The term *crusade* sounds ridiculous and outlandish in the context of the *Furioso* as currently interpreted and seems altogether more appropriate to the pieties of Tasso;

but this is to ignore the fact that there were crusades or calls for crusades (most of them failures) in 1444, 1448, 1463, 1480, 1486, 1501, and 1532—all through the period known as the "pagan" High Renaissance.[17] When Ariosto passionately urges warring Christians to redirect their energies to such theaters as Jerusalem, Constantinople, Africa, and Greece (17.75–77), he calls attention to areas that function importantly in his Carolingian fiction. The mention of Africa particularly should intrigue us, since Charlemagne's troubles in the *Furioso* have their root in an invasion from the northern countries of that continent, Tunisia preeminently. It should be of interest to its readers that the *Furioso* focuses on the disruption of the Carolingian empire from Bizerte, that it should have been written in Ferrara, a city with political connections to the Holy Roman Empire, and that it was successively corrected and enlarged between 1516 and 1532, the years when another Charles, fifth of that name in line of succession from Charlemagne, was Holy Roman Emperor and was likewise engaged in repelling the encroachments of infidel forces from Africa and Asia. If we miss the point, the proem to canto 17.5–6 explicitly joins two providential punishments of Christian Europe, one by medieval Moors, one by Renaissance Turks, and further identifies the two peoples as one by an ingenious "slip" on the part of the poet in claiming, when he passes from proem to narrative, that Moors *and* Turks had overrun the Empire of Charlemagne. Turks in Europe in the eighth century? Catalans with "daring galleys" who carry Angelica and Medoro home to Cathay in the time of Charlemagne? Here the careless reader undoubtedly falls subject to the taut authorial bridling of his attention. Such arresting synchronizations of history reveal a simultaneity of poetic vision encompassing as one event two separate Moslem invasions that occurred eight centuries apart, both directed at the Holy Roman Empire in two phases of its being. Bradamante and Ruggiero are another Lavinia and Aeneas living at a later, Carolingian stage of the Empire established by Trojan refugees, as their creator-poet, an imitator of the imperial poet Vergil, was living in the renovated imperial world of Charles V. In the poet's single vision, time's fragments merge into unity, and both the disasters and the arduous labors of two other imperial eras are repeated, in the invariable, cyclical ways of history, in contemporary events, during the reign of Charles V.

By such devices does Ariosto curb our fancy, but he has prepared us for this in an earlier canto. The extended praise of Charles V and of his admiral Andrea Doria at 15.19–36 keeps a salient historical fact firmly before our eyes: from 1502 on, or a matter of eight years after Boiardo's death, a Turkish Moslem power was newly establishing itself on the coast of North Africa in accordance with the second of their great objectives, noted previously. To compound the irony, this new influx was taking place even as the last descendants of the first, eighth-century, irruption of Islam into Europe were being expelled from Spain in 1492; their hardships provoked their fellow Muslims, determinedly working their way westward again, into an even more dangerous repetition of the eighth-century advance that is fictionalized in Carolingian poetry.[18] Battening on the rim of the North African states, the Turkish

pirates were a scourge that Charles V and his allies repeatedly expended their energies to destroy, all the more as they offered a temptation to the Moriscos in Spain to
act as a potential fifth column: hence the Emperor's (disastrous) attack in 1519 on
Algiers itself; and in 1535, three years after he had driven the Turks from Vienna, his
great victory at Tunis, exactly twenty-three years after Andrea Doria's 1512 expedition against the same city. Manifestly the problem was of long duration, and Ariosto
was dead at the time of Charles's triumph, but it was a culmination of events that
agitated the times in which he lived and of which he demonstrably evinced a certain
consciousness in the material of canto 15, as elsewhere. The *Satires,* for instance, have
an unforgettably impassioned portrait of an evil prelate who sets Christians together
by the ears but will not ponder how to expel the Ottoman Turks (2.211–25); and in
the *Suppositi,* Cleandro takes refuge in Ferrara precisely because the Turks have
expelled him from his native Otranto.[19] Finally, it is not surprising to find Ariosto,
at 42.20 of the *Furioso,* interrupting his tale to address directly a Genoese naval
commander, Federigo Fregoso, who had "scoured every corner of the coast of Barbary," had assailed the Turkish pirates harrying the Ligurian Riviera, and had beaten
them back to—fateful city, considering that Ariosto will send Astolfo to destroy
it—Bizerte.

Boiardo had, of course, predicted that at some indeterminate time Bizerte would
be destroyed by Orlando, and Ariosto was, in his own poem and in his own time,
fulfilling Boiardo's prediction, though in a thoroughly unexpected manner. But
history repeatedly had a way of confirming that imaginative literature had resonances for Ariosto's audiences that it simply could not have had for Boiardo's: more
than fifty years intervened between Boiardo beginning an Orlando story and
Ariosto ending one, and notions of the Empire changed drastically in that time.
Ariosto's repeated touching of this chord of Empire and Church, joined together in
government at home and crusade afar, restores something essential to the Carolingian tradition, a quality it possessed intrinsically in its early medieval beginnings
but which was dissipated in humor thereafter. In Boiardo's kind of poetry, the external world is barely glanced at; and though the poet, in one of his very rare historical
panegyrics, casually alludes to but does not mention Otranto—the Aragonese (he
says very briefly) are the sole defenders of Italy from the Turk (2.27.57)—in his own
time no fresh infusion of Islamic forces had been ready to spring from the rim of
North Africa. For Boiardo the infidel was still the stereotyped Saracen of the eighth-
century invasion, and the Holy Roman Emperor was still the sniveling graybeard of
sanctified tradition, the two-hundred-year-old Charlemagne, pathetic and babbling.
Things changed radically immediately after Boiardo's death. Now the Turks were
powerful in Tunis, Algiers, and Bizerte, and twenty-odd years after his death,
another great Charles, of the Hapsburgs, related to the Estensi by reason of their
Aragonese mother, was giving new force to the Imperial idea and extending the
Christian imperium into new worlds previously unknown. In this arduous work he
knew how to call on his relations. Isabella d'Este's son Ferrante, the child at whose

birth Ariosto was sent to congratulate the mother by her brother Ippolito, was afterward the commander-in-chief of the Emperor's forces, then his Viceroy in Sicily.[20]

There is no question that from the very first the *Furioso* began more seriously and on a higher plane of artistic projection than the *Innamorato*. But the complexities of history and the advent of Charles V to the imperial throne in 1519 reinforced and intensified the initial seriousness, the greater "art," with which Ariosto broached the Carolingian "matière." The three editions of the poem register the increasing impact of contemporary history on the continent of Europe: increasingly the *Furioso* became a poem of *European* outlook, of "wide prospect." As few other poets, Ariosto was placed fortunately in time. He works in full consciousness of both the rapid and profound developments of history, and especially of the significance of the imperial renewal under Charles V; fittingly so, considering that the Dukes of Ferrara, from Borso onward, were accorded the dignity of imperial investiture.[21] Never again could the Carolingian poem be merely the occasion for innocent laughter, nor the orientalism of its landscapes merely exotic. Throughout his poem Ariosto connects, by allusion and outright historical reference, the Italy of the Estensi to the Holy Roman Empire of Charles V, and both of them to the Roman Empire of classical antiquity; the classicism of his own poem operates to fuse the two things and asserts the continuity of a great political order over vast cycles of human life. For that reason, if for no other, he reclaims Charlemagne from the indignity of his portrayal in the romances and idealizes him as a regal and sympathetic figure, abandoned by his paladins but valiant and forceful in the defense of the Empire. In so portraying him, Ariosto gives the first indications of his own magisterial contravention of the popular tradition he redeems by his courtly, classical art. In a splendid renewal of the Vergilian posture, Ariosto adapted the Carolingian poem to the imperial idea.

I have raised the question of the historical aspect of the poem at once, and not merely to redeem it from the charge of frivolity. I do so to place it in context and to indicate its limitations, for while the world of daily reality is always on the periphery of the poet's vision, it is never allowed to usurp the place of the narrative, which is central, nor is allusion ever allowed to pass over into crude historical identification. Unlike Spenser, Ariosto had no interest whatever in overt historical allegory of the kind that produces propagandistic personifications like Sir Burbon, Belge, and Grantorto; it would be an absurdity to discover anything like historical allegory of this kind in the *Furioso*. Ariosto's method is subtler. He thought it sufficient to point, by constant juxtaposition and overlay, the similarities between the beleaguered times of Charlemagne and those of Charles V in the common threat to the civilizations they headed. The same sense of the pressure of the past on the present occurs in the *Satires,* in which, as Professor Wiggins has brilliantly stated, "Through Ariosto's imitation of Horace, gradually all of contemporary Italian society comes in for a scathing comparison with a former golden age. Cynicism in the ethical sphere, expediency in the political, and opportunism in the intellectual combine to rule out the appreciation of beauty, truth, and goodness in a society on its way to enslavement under invading armies."[22] This is some of the most intelligent criticism Ariosto has yet received, reminding us that to undertake the Horatian role at all is to show interest in something more than style; and indicating, perhaps, that the assumption of the Vergilian role is to deepen those interests in quite another kind of poetry. In the *Satires,* the Horatian poet is the repository of moral values repugnant to his society, which therefore requires instruction and cajolement in the lower and middle styles. In the *Furioso,* similarly, the Vergilian poet, on a grand canvas and in the more exalted form of a fantastic narrative, voices the concerns of his time. His dynastic archetypes are mirrors of values, never of actual individuals, and Ariosto's central concern remains the moral progress of these fictional models for the historical rulers of his own day. In representing the two prototypes as inhabitants of a world troubled by the same disruptive ambitions and lusts that their descendants inevitably suffer, he strengthens the connection implicit in their inheritance of noble blood and provides exemplars who, though imperfect and put upon to the very end of their careers, attain something like virtue in the end and aid in casting out the infection of infidel forces. Beginning in discord, ending in concord, they reveal the operation of love in the process by which the fatality that overrules their lives is brought to fruition. Love, in brief, is the force that guides them in all their errancies, Love is the lesson they learn, and it is a lengthy and difficult process.

In his narrator's role, praising the recent and contemporaneous achievements of the Estensi, of their courtiers and visitors, Ariosto sees the painful task of civilization, which Bradamante and Ruggiero in their love-story are struggling to prepare, as gloriously accomplished and fulfilled, though threatened constantly and currently needing vigilance to be maintained. Past and present are in perpetual counterpoint in the poetic process. As the celebrator of dynasty and dynastic fatality, Ariosto comes before his audience in the unmistakable guise of the epic poet and as the voice of an entire society. He assumes the continual presence of a very particular audience, and his function is, in Tillyard's language, "choric."[23] Ariosto's is the best voice of the group, and his is the best articulation of the music, but the notes were known to them all. In effect, Ariosto rewrote their music and made it polyphonic. The pleasures of the *Furioso* are almost numberless, but a chief one is that of allusion and commemoration. One example will make the point. In cantos 42 and 43 occur two *novelle,* told by a knight and by a boatman respectively, that immediately precede Bradamante's marriage to Ruggiero, and they are set, very significantly, in the confines of the future Mantua, Ferrara's near neighbor and the home of its Marchioness, Isabella d'Este Gonzaga. The two tales are a fanciful but pointed reworking of a contemporary allegorical drama on the subject of jealousy in marriage, the *Cefalo* of Niccolò da Correggio.[24] They represent not only an allusively pleasing compliment to Isabella through the imitation of an Ovidian play by her poet-cousin but also an unmistakable comment on the perils of jealousy within the wedded state. Cunningly prefixed to the marriage of the mythical founders of Ferrara as a typically indirect commentary by the poet, the two stories assert a universal truth for their descendants as well and commemorate Ariosto's tribute to a fellow-poet of his city and court.

A great work of art is local before it is universal. In reading many modern descriptions of the poem (the "*Gone with the Wind* of the Renaissance" is one of them), no one would suspect that the *Furioso* is (to put it in the simplest terms) an extended Renaissance narrative, clearly announcing itself as a romantic epic in the line of the Renaissance Vergil, conceived by a classicizing master of poetry at a court known for the Neoplatonic orientation of its arts, subtly attentive throughout to its audience's concerns, and very directly intended, in its last canto, for the eyes of scholars, critics, poets, painters, and patrons accustomed to anything but self-mirroring, self-referring art. Only after Poe can we conceive of an epic poet as a lyric miniaturist and rhapsode. Before then, by the very nature of his position, the poet inevitably creates a mirror of the society he elects to glorify, and there are some practical, determining considerations in his circumstances that are fatal to ignore, whether his patron is the conferrer of gold arm-rings or mere secretaryships. One imagines that a Renaissance poet dependent on the good will of patrons would find it difficult, perhaps suicidal, to cultivate a romantically egocentric individualism when he embarked on a poetic voyage of many years, especially when writing for so demanding a family as the Estensi. The circumstantial evidence alone should have kept us from considering the *Furioso* an iridescent bauble, for it is rare indeed that a poem gives so clear a record of the milieu in which it was written, a milieu wholly Italian in its sense of national culture, though the focus is, of course, Ferrarese throughout. Witness the tribute to the poet's great contemporaries in the art of painting at 33.2, where Leonardo, Mantegna, Giovanni Bellini, Dosso and Giambattista Dossi, Michelangelo, del Piombo, and Raphael mingle in a mixture of Florentine and Ferrarese with those of "Cador" and "Venezia e Urbino."

The reality of the poem's cultural background can be specifically determined, because Ariosto continually incorporates it into his poem, and the poem is itself the witness, in its panegyric of artists, scholars, and rulers, of the magnificence of a brilliant civilization. Ariosto knew his audience and their achievements intimately, and in a consciously celebratory gesture he gives us the names of his imagined auditors throughout his poem, a practice culminating in the extended processional of the choice and master spirits of the age. The beginning of the final canto provides the poem with a truly extraordinary moment. The passage of nineteen octaves begins with the familiar epic topos of the poet sailing home after his long literary voyage to find a crowd waiting on the shore to greet and congratulate him; among the learned and the great assembled here are a peerless collection of humanists, authors, and patrons of learning. In spite of the splendor it represents, this is the kind of passage that the impatient modern reader finds trying and all too easy to skip over, obliterating, in one swift sweep of his eyes, a multitude of great lives and minds, and a passage essential to understanding the poem. To aid in overcoming this dislike, we should try to "repristinate" the text a little by selecting and classifying.

Among the female friends whom Ariosto portrays in this posture of welcoming congratulation are two who will be immediately recognizable by students of the Renaissance: Emilia Pia, luminary at the court of Urbino, correspondent of Bembo, and wittiest of the principal speakers in Castiglione's *Courtier*; and Vittoria Colonna, Roman aristocrat, poetess, spiritual force, and intimate friend of Michelangelo; the two women may be imagined to have known something about the Neoplatonic classifications of love. Among the male figures Ariosto names we may recognize definite groups.[25] The first group includes intimates of Ariosto who were also rulers and scholars: Gianfrancesco Pico della Mirandola, lord of that territory, nephew of the philosopher, one-time student at Ferrara, and a classmate of Ariosto; and Alberto Pio, Lord of Carpi, poet, Ariosto's schoolfellow under the direction of the Augustinian monk Gregorio da Spoleto. In another group we may place two learned clerics: Cardinal Lorenzo Campeggio, canonist and papal emissary to Henry VIII in the matter of his divorce; and Cardinal Ercole Gonzaga, son of Isabella d'Este and Francesco Gonzaga, patron of learning and future president of the Council of Trent. The humanists constitute one of the most fascinating groups of all: Giovanni Lascaris, Byzantine Greek bibliophile and scholar, patronized by Lorenzo de' Medici in his search for Greek texts; Marco Musuro, pupil of Lascaris, Archbishop of Malvasia, professor of Greek at Padua, consultant to Aldus Manutius in his publication of Greek manuscripts, praised by Erasmus for his learning; Andrea Navagero, pupil of Musuro, scholar, and critic; Girolamo Vida, Bishop of Vercelli, author of the *Christiade* and the *Ars poetica*; Tommaso Inghirami ("Fedro"), Prefect of the Vatican Library; Filippo Bolognese ("Beroaldi"), Vatican Librarian; Camillo Porzio ("de Porcari"), bishop and member of the Roman Academy; Andrea Marone, poet and writer, named by the poet in *Satire II,* and author of a famous poem exhorting a new crusade against the Turk; Alessandro Guarino, nephew of the prince of humanists (Guarino Veronese), secretary to Duke Alfonso I, and professor at the Studio di Ferrara; Niccolò Maria Panizzato, teacher of rhetoric in Ferrara, perhaps one of Ariosto's professors; Gabriele Trifon, Venetian aristocrat and learned commentator of Dante and Petrarch; and Niccolò Leoniceno, doctor and scholar, courtier to Ercole I, secretary to Alfonso I, and the translator of Lucian.

In a climactic position we should place the names of two of the greatest exponents of North Italian humanism, figures with whom students of the Renaissance are increasingly familiar largely because of the attention focused on them by Erwin Panofsky and Frances Yates: Celio Calcagnini and Pierio Valeriano of Bolzano. Calcagnini (the "Celio" addressed familiarly at 46.14.8) was the most celebrated of Ferrara's humanists at the courts of both Alfonso I and Ippolito, a Canon of the Cathedral of Ferrara, later an apostolic protonotary, professor at the world-renowned Studio di Ferrara, a precursor of Copernicus, friend and correspondent of Erasmus, who met him when he passed through Ferrara in December of 1508, author himself of a Neoplatonic allegory of the *Aeneid*, benefactor of the mythographer Giraldi, and the lifelong friend of Ariosto, whose eulogy he delivered at his funeral and whose epitaph he wrote. As for the second of these notable figures, Valeriano (the "Pierio" hailed at 46.13.5) was one of the most famous polymaths of his day; friend of Leo X and of Pietro Bembo, Latin poet, educator, elected professor of eloquence by Pope Clement VII, tutor to the Pope's nephews, his fame today is based on that enormously influential textbook of pictorial symbolism, *Hieroglyphica*, an encyclopedia well known to Renaissance art historians that can be consulted with profit by students of Ariosto's iconographic imagery.

As for the family itself, we should recall Isabella d'Este, probably the most learned woman of her time and the exigent patroness of artists of the rank of Mantegna and Perugino;[26] she was one of the first auditors of the yet unfinished poem in 1507 and the recipient in 1516 of one of the first printed copies from the poet's own hand.[27] As for her brother Ippolito, to pass from the splendid to the disreputable, it was one of the ironies of history that made this inept churchman, skilled warrior, and practiced sensualist the dedicatee of the *Furioso*, but Ariosto attempted to capture even his attention by wittily prompting and cuing him on five or six occasions when his poem's matter was at its most fantastic or "realistic" and thus (characteristically) at its most radically meaningful. The passages (2.20, 10.73, 14.134, 17.17, 42.61) invariably begin with a direct appeal for his attention ("Signor") and a mildly deprecatory, suavely deferring appeal for Ippolito to cast an eye on these trifles, but we shall never know if the cardinal profited from the repetition and the grand litotes. Yet there were others on whom Ariosto could better rely, and whom he felt no embarrassment in portraying in postures of praise and welcome for his achievement: to them, he knew well, the "frutto" of his labors would be dear. Of course this may all have been an impudent plot of the "subversive" Ariosto dear to the hearts of critics who prefer a *Furioso* without apparatus as they prefer a romantic poet who holds himself aloof from his society and converts its values into subjects for irony. Undoubtedly Ariosto's audience had its lighter moments, but a whole Vergilian epic of subversion places a certain strain on the imagination; it accords not at all with the Ariosto of the letters and the *Satires*, the Ariosto of both history and literature.

These personalities formed the audience, as the proem to canto 7 maintained with some assurance, that would recognize the poem as something more than mere poetic lies. In the Lunar cantos, when all poetry is said to be lies, they were expected to keep their wits as the poet, demonstrating extraordinary brilliance and agility in the switchback convolutions of his elastic wit, repeatedly tested their capacity to maintain their equilibrium. The congregation of great names seems comically impossible, something like a vision of Miniver Cheevy's, or a stage direction from Max Beerbohm's *Savonarola* ("*Enter* Lucrezia Borgia, St. Francis of Assisi, *and* Leonardo da Vinci"), yet the fact remains that the incidence of genius and talent in Ariosto's circle is out of all proportion to one mere life. With the eyes of such an audience on it, there is no wonder that the *Furioso* is a more massively learned and recondite poem than has been hitherto acknowledged or imagined. Its author's project was to please not the "vulgo," as the jealous Trissino afterward complained, but the learned and the aristocratic. We look in vain for any of them ever to have subscribed to the superiority of style over matter, or to have asserted a doctrine of Pure Art. Of course, they knew a great deal about love. Love as the vital and universal activity—a force circulating through every stage of being, binding the macrocosm together, maintaining societies in equilibrium, harmonizing the triple potency of the human microcosm—was the constant subject of their literature and painting. Ariosto came before his audience, in the first line of his first canto, as a poet of "amori," and in his first two cantos, by immediately subordinating Angelica and Orlando to Bradamante and Ruggiero, he established at once that love was a principle of hierarchical order. Having undertaken the panegyric of a great race, he was about to dramatize the spectrum of possibilities inherent in the passion of love by manipulating, with astonishing independence, an Estean poem about a crazy lover from the previous generation. In his final canto, in so boldly anticipating his audience's praises, he manifested a justifiable pride in his own very great achievement: he had already won a reputation as a splendid Latin lyrist, and now he had acclimatized the epic as well. The sense of triumph is exhilarating and moving.

4

Neoplatonist Art

Arioosto, His Contemporaries, and His Friends

He was altogether outside the philosophy of the Renaissance, whether Ficino's or Pomponazzi's, as he was outside every philosophy.
    Benedetto Croce, *Ariosto, Shakespeare and Corneille*

Non allettava l'Ariosto la mensa dei platonici, e d'altro s'infervorava che della sapienza del Ficino.

Ariosto was not suckled at the table of the Platonists, and he was kindled by something other than the wisdom of Ficino.
    Arturo Farinelli, "Lodovico Ariosto"

In direct competition with the *Innamorato*, the *Furioso* announces itself, formally and immediately, as a poem of "loves" ("amori") against a background of war ("arme"), and Boiardo's two antiphonal actions of love and war harden into a conceptual framework. A principle of concord operates against a principle of discord: Venus set against Mars, Love against Strife or Hate. The poem begins with the disastrous Saracen rout of Charlemagne's broken forces, the retreat from Montalbano to the beleaguered capital, the light escape of unattainable Angelica into an explicitly named "selva oscura" (1.22.5, 2.68.4), and her pursuit by any number of delinquent, irascibly appetitive warriors who thereby contribute to the disaster. Forty-six cantos later it ends with the achievement of Bradamante's quest for Ruggiero and her marriage in the pacified city of Paris. In its very broadest aspect, therefore, the *Furioso* enacts a long movement to reconciliation in the restoration of hierarchical order through an intricate concatenation of disorders. Love is born out of the strife and discord of Chaos, whose warring elements it organizes, so replacing enmity with concord. And all of this takes place under the direction of Providence, which gives it a teleological thrust.

The contrast between the beginning and the ending of the poem could not be more deliberately pointed. The antithetical poles of its action are the forest of its opening and the city of its close. Between those poles an initial chaos of war and passion, violently dispersive in effect, yields finally to the homecoming of warriors in the pacification of France and the union of the progenitors of the House of Ferrara. The *Furioso* is a vast organism of profoundly complex construction set circuitously in motion toward a definite objective, and it gathers its accumulated energies as it moves to its end. Its essential meaning is in its shape: if Ariosto has his own beginning in view at his conclusion, he is conscious as well of the beginnings of the entire matter, and he describes a vast rotary movement by matching his own conclusion to the *Innamorato*'s beginning. For where Boiardo begins with Angelica arriving in Paris and setting the Christian world by the ears in her first disruptive appearance at Charlemagne's Whitsuntide feast, Ariosto terminates the vast and far-flung action 115 cantos later with Bradamante's wedding at yet another feast in the very same city. The order effected at the conclusion of the *Furioso* is inescapably suggestive of a harmony wrought out of disorder, and in its total sweep the poem's movement enacts an elaborate, cherished concept of the Renaissance, that of *discordia concors*.[1]

The Charlemagnic world is a world of disorder and strife, but with Bradamante's assumption of her quest for Ruggiero, a new love begins creatively to interpenetrate the disintegrating fabric of that disaster-ridden society, directing it ultimately to a new order and peace. In the process, the higher love of the young mother-to-be of all the Estensi wins out slowly over the centrifugal chaos that the old carnal love for Angelica inspires, and the result is a final harmony symbolized by the cessation not only of her own quest but also of all the other quests of the poem, the centripetal return of all the errant warriors, and the celebration of the wedding feast. Both exterior and interior disorders are stilled at the same time. The harmony of the macrocosm is simultaneously reflected in the harmony of the human microcosm, and the reintegration and renovation of a society is free to proceed. Indeed, once the Empire itself has again been consolidated, it extends itself, through Ruggiero and Bradamante, to a new territory in Italy. The lovers go out, "with Providence their guide," to found Ferrara, a fief whose rulers are honored by imperial investiture.

The richly Empedoclean conjunction of "arme" and "amori" in the poem's opening line is not accidental. The association of ideas implicit in those words was available to Ariosto in the central document of Florentine Neoplatonism, Ficino's *Commentary on Plato's Symposium*;[2] and on any day of his life as a courtier, he could have looked at a pictorial representation of the idea that love is more powerful than strife: one way of looking at the famous fresco of Francesco Cossa in the Schifanoia Palace in Ferrara, "The Triumph of Venus," is to see it as dramatizing the concept in the submission of a kneeling Mars to a fertile Venus.[3] We have encountered the word *harmony* previously as a deceptively romantic inheritance from Benedetto Croce, but in a context and with a meaning wholly alien to the one it had for a Neoplatonist poet of the sixteenth century. We should now adjust the perspective to ensure that we are not dealing with an anachronism. We may then venture the possibility that the purely technical and aesthetic harmony of a poem may not exist as an isolated, ineffable phenomenon; that indeed it may be the expression of a profound concern with many other kinds of harmony—cosmic, philosophic, social, moral, and artistic. "Harmonia est discordia concors" was a byword of the Renaissance.[4] In Neoplatonic mythography Harmonia is personified as a goddess; she is the daughter of Venus and Mars, the respective patrons of love and strife, and she functions as a cosmic force, the fruit of their creative reconciliation in the submission of the irascible instinct to the creativity of the higher love.[5] Harmonia is therefore the witness of the supremacy of the principle of integration to that of destruction and disintegration; and this is essentially the principle that Ariosto's energetic heroine embodies. For all its unliterary and unhistorical abstraction, then, Croce's splendid formula is essentially in accord with the values of the poem, an intuition of genius.

As an epic microcosm of love and war ("Le donne, i cavallier, l'arme, gli amori"), the *Furioso* is a poetic universe torn, like the original Chaos, by the passions of love and hate. Never is that depicted more pointedly than in canto I, when the army of Charlemagne is flying in fragments and the Saracen hordes threaten the heart of the Empire. But Ariosto moves immediately to counter this initial explosion from the center with a contrasting centripetal movement, which is long in arriving but steadily directed to the poem's end. At the very moment when total dissolution threatens, he moves, swiftly and with only the slightest precedent from Boiardo, to set a young female warrior on a divinely guided quest for her husband-to-be. When the poem opens, Bradamante is already in search of Ruggiero, and the great arc of her hunt will not touch ground until the very end. The *Furioso* is, of course, an expansive and ample poem that accords a full measure of attention to the power of disorder embodied in Discordia, an allegorical figure that Ariosto sets at the center of the action, and the body of the work is a seething cauldron of contrary movements by thousands of figures. Yet the final object of the poem is to get the pagans out of France and the paganism out of Ruggiero, to restore wholeness to the land and integrity to the hero, so that, the Empire having been secured, an offshoot of its greatness may find fruitful soil in a North Italian city. In the poem's process of ordering disorderly situations, the relationship between the landscape and the individual is metaphoric and continuous. Put briefly, Ruggiero must become worthy of his destiny; the process he undergoes is educative, though he resists to the end.

Bradamante too is bedeviled by her own contumacy and by the amusingly refractory evasions of her intended spouse, but the conclusion of the poem sees her triumphant in the achievement of her mission. Her wedding forms the climax toward which all the multifaceted action drives, and it assures the birth of a new and splendid society to spring from her loins. The young heroine asserts an undeniably vigorous presence immediately on her first irruption into the action of the first canto. In Boiardo, her intended is one of the chief heroes of the Saracen army that has brought discord into the Empire; in Ariosto's development of the story, the pressures of a tyrannizing sense of personal honor keep returning him to that mistaken fealty. In effect, Ruggiero's perpetual wavering and search for personal glory reinforce and reinvigorate the faltering pagan enterprise in France. Bradamante's task is therefore to win him—as it turns out, to *keep* winning him again and again—to the destiny to which they have together been called. Their dynastic future as Italian princes necessitates his conversion, and baptism is the end she mistakenly imagines will terminate all problems: mistakenly, because not until the very conclusion of the poem is a bridle put on the bridegroom's roving and the seal set on the peace of the Frankish empire. Ruggiero is repeatedly unfaithful in both a romantic and a theological sense:

faithless in love and an infidel in religion, and the one invariably involves the other. Yet Providence wins out at last. In Bradamante's success in bringing Ruggiero to his dynastic marriage, love wins out over strife and hate. She delivers him from paganism and bachelorhood, and she is (metaphorically only, to be sure, given her boisterous nature) the still center to whom he returns from a poem-long errancy of movement. Invariably constant herself, she makes his circle just and he ends where he began, perhaps knowing the place for the first time.

Bradamante's love is the one immutable and constant thing in the poem, as strong in her great outpouring of fidelity in a late canto (44.61–66) as it is near the beginning (7.48). Even her terrific jealousy is an intensification of her constancy to one object, one goal. Throughout she functions as the very human agent of Providence's equally unrelenting pursuit of Ruggiero. This is an aspect of the poem that needs stressing, especially in view of attempts to see the poem as centrally and essentially committed to a presentation of reality as inexorable flux and impermanence.[6] But surely this is to look at things through the eyes of Spenser's Mutability, for whom, because there is motion and change in the universe, there is nothing but motion and change. No poet is more concerned with slippery transience than Ariosto, yet all that evanescence and mutation is circumscribed by order and pattern, and it progresses inevitably toward a condition of rest. A vast homeward movement begins at the poem's end, and the banquet brings all the heroes together. Yet even here there is a final disturbance in the black appearance of Rodomonte, and the dagger-blow to the chief enemy's brain that so shockingly ends the poem's frenzied action is an assertion of a hard-won finality, for a moment at least.

The central female figure is, at one and the same time, the eventual center of the poem's repose and the source of its unwavering energy. Though he was eager to find fault with the *Furioso*'s decorum in thus reversing masculine and feminine roles, Tasso's very objection called attention to this peculiarity of Ariosto's treatment in the very act of decrying it:

But this decorum [of the male pursuing the female] is not to be found in the *Furioso*, in which Ruggiero is rather more beloved than loving, and Bradamante more loving than loved, and she pursues Ruggiero and attempts to rescue him from prison and performs all those offices and operations that would seem more proper to a Knight in order to gain the love of his lady, however much of a warrior she may be. But Ruggiero doesn't do anything to gain the love of his lady, but seems rather to despise her and hold her in little esteem, which would not perhaps be so indecorous if the poet had not feigned that from this love and this marriage should derive the Princes of Este.[7]

Whatever the validity of Tasso's objections, he does not misrepresent Bradamante's role. As a personality, she is the very opposite of the static, merely timorous, and frightened Angelica to whom, in the first canto, she is directly opposed. She is active and bustling, headstrong, willful, and passionate, and her faults are not those of deficiency. If she were symbolized by a flower, it would be the tiger lily, not the violet. Presumably she incarnates something of the energy and dedication to the family's interests of the Este women throughout history: characteristics that go along amusingly with a certain willfulness and obstinacy. Her first falling off presents her truly; there she is "animosa" and "malcauta" (2.74.1–2), a promising combination of the "spirited" but "imprudent," capable of being instructed, and generous rather than mean in her nature. If, then, Bradamante is hilarious (if also rather frightening) in her utter single-mindedness about her mission, she is also unswervingly faithful to her beloved through all kinds of vicissitudes and derelictions on his part. Again, she has none of the meaner instincts her parents seem determined to force on her, and she says herself that she is beyond Fortune in cherishing Ruggiero for himself rather than for worldly reputation or riches (44.64). The avarice that afflicts her beloved and her parents touches her not in the least.

Bradamante's hunting of Ruggiero is linked, by reflection, to Providence's unyielding pursuit of Ruggiero, and her love shares something of its single-minded intensity and, in the end, its jealousy; what her love lacks is its patience and serenity. Time tyrannizes, strong biological imperatives are at work in the story, and nothing is allowed to get in the way of the sacrifice of individual lives to the future destiny of a race. Hence, though the prophecy of Ruggiero's early death through treachery is known to both Bradamante and the hermit who finally converts him, neither of them fails to conceal that knowledge and both urge him on to his destiny. In this they master totally the sentimental magician, Atlante, whose entire project is to keep Ruggiero from Christianity, marriage, and death, and who invents, pathetically, one sensual enchantment after another to hold him aloof and remote from his heroic role, in vain hope that he will resist time, death, and destiny. Rescuing him from his first two prisons, but needing help herself in being rescued from the third, Bradamante wins out by sheer persistence. In the end her instinctive female energies cause her to overstep herself. Unknowingly but pridefully risking physical combat with her own beloved (canto 45), she must yield finally in her ambition to supremacy, and in her yielding is her final victory.

Bradamante makes the traditional submission of the comic heroine and becomes the virago gentled in marriage, the good Venus to a Mars converted from evil. In the process she becomes the exponent of a higher human love in the act of ordering itself for marriage, which is at once an end and a sign. She becomes, as well, a pattern for the spirited female descendants of her race who are called to be instructed by her story as well as delighted, and who are themselves liberally praised in its pages. Since her marriage is to have enormous historical consequences, she too must grow into the role to which destiny has called her. Necessarily, given her ardent nature, she becomes acquainted with many a passion along the way. A paradigm of her career would pass through stages of infatuated sentimentalism (cantos 2 and 4), illusion-ridden desire (canto 13), visceral longing (canto 30), jealousy and the suicidal self-dramatization of amorous frustration (canto 32), and murderous rage and frustration (cantos 35, 36, and 45). Her path is (sometimes hilariously) strewn with these steadily accumulating obstacles before she is humbled in order to be exalted. Hers is, then, an initiation into the world of a specific kind of love, the love that contemporary Neoplatonism denominated "amore umano,"[8] neither bestial nor angelic, but coasting between. Her progression through these various stages asserts the nature of love as an ordering principle operating on disorderly elements. As cosmic love orders and calms the strife of the four elements in the original Chaos, so perfected love in the *Furioso* calms the strife and harmonizes the atmosphere of its poetic microcosm. In Boiardo, Bradamante appears and falls in love; in Ariosto, she grows mightily.

For both Boiardo and Ariosto, love is plural. Boiardo requires the reader to discriminate between loves; Ariosto, his poetry being altogether more complex in its greater schematic and programmatic quality, requires the reader to discriminate among them. One of the very first things the *Furioso* does is to bring Bradamante and Angelica face to face for a first and absolutely final time (1.60). The two women are to be the objects of two different kinds of love, and it is Angelica, not Bradamante, who will be the occasion of madness in her suitor, the source of his becoming "furioso." In contrast, Bradamante's whole aim is to bring her lover to a rational, human love that will eventuate in marriage. The irony throughout is that she has to be so passionate in doing so. In excuse of her passion, the reader must note that a great weight has dropped on her woman's shoulders. In being granted, Aeneas-like, a vision of the shades of all her descendants in an underground cavern (canto 3), in scrutinizing murals mysteriously painted with their political fortunes in the far-distant future (canto 33), Bradamante assumes the immense historical burden of the dynast and a weighty knowledge she nourishes and shares with few others. Just as Aeneas had lifted the pictured shield of Vulcan, heavy with portents of the Roman future, onto his willing shoulders, alone though surrounded by many,[9] so too Bradamante is fundamentally alone and comfortless in pursuing her destiny. At issue is all her family's history; all this destiny keeps being lost by the delays and the derelictions of the yet-pagan Ruggiero, and this is precisely what lends urgency to her cause and rouses her womanly fury. Ariosto's view is not the popular one at the moment, but Bradamante is relentless in her quest and imperious in her rages because she wants to doff her armor, be domesticated, and put history into motion. Angelica will leave the poem in canto 19, well before its midpoint is reached, returning happily with Medoro to the fabulous never-never-land of distant Cathay, but Bradamante has another, harder destiny as dynast, widow, and protector of her young son, and she accepts it with full knowledge.

In his first canto, therefore, Ariosto puts before us, at a single decisive stroke, a clarification of some major issues and contrasts implicit in Boiardo but never worked out in his poem. In Ariosto the opposition between the representative loves of the two women is joined at once and is never in doubt thereafter. That is why Orlando goes down to madness and why Ruggiero marries and triumphs. Masterfully and swiftly reversing Boiardo, Ariosto accords the love drama of the Este progenitors the primary place in his poem, giving it a long and intricate development of his own invention. In the *Innamorato* the lovers meet very late, sixty-five cantos after the poem begins, only four cantos before it comes to its truncated end. Their fated union is quickly established, they are separated, and there the poem breaks off. After ten years, in Ariosto's hands, the same pair of lovers is brought forward emphatically and at once, in the very first lines. They are the intense focus of the poet's attention for the first third of the poem's length. The adventures of the other heroes are subordinated to or intermingled with their vicissitudes, and they displace Orlando and Angelica as the major center of interest and importance. Now they are lovers who must *earn* each other and their mutual destiny as dynasts.

Addressed as it is to the descendants of Bradamante and Ruggiero (and one can imagine the delight of Isabella, if not of Cardinal Ippolito), the *Furioso*'s immediate concern is with the quality of human love in its various manifestations and the varieties of experiences to which it leads. Love was the traditional great subject of Italian poetry in the Middle Ages and early Renaissance, and Vergil himself, in canto 18 of the *Purgatorio*, had read Dante a lesson on the passion, expounding a doctrine of its variety, multiplicity, and inescapability as a natural bent and craving.[10] As a truly comic artist, Ariosto treats love on a scale ranging from romantic passion to a particular kind of contemplative vision. Writing of a spectrum of "amori," he placed himself within an ancient tradition, newly revivified in the work of his famous contemporaries and friends. The treatment of love provides the chief content of his poem, and his style, in its achieved serenity and orderly progression, is the perfect mirror of its innermost meaning.

Reading Ariosto without a knowledge of contemporary Neoplatonism is equivalent to reading Shakespeare in total ignorance of the Ptolemaic universe. It can be done, but who would claim it as a triumph? The years of instruction and study Ariosto underwent in the company of some of the leading Neoplatonists of his time are casually obliterated, but at enormous cost, for it can easily be demonstrated that the experience of Neoplatonism in his young manhood was the turning point of the poet's life. The wonder is not that he became an artist in the prevailing artistic tradition, but that he should ever have been considered apart from it. The *Furioso* witnesses constantly that he fully subscribed to a dictum of Bembo's: "Perciò che di poche altre cose può avenire, o forse di non niuna, che lo intendere ciò che elle sono più ci debba esser caro, che il sapere che cosa è Amore" ("For there are few if any other things of which we should be more desirous to gather knowledge than of love").[11]

The matter can be put briefly. At twenty Ariosto is a law student who loathes the profession into which his father has forced him; he turns increasingly to Latin studies and the writing of Latin lyric poems in the Horatian manner; and he has a bent toward literature and acting.[12] At thirty he emerges startlingly as a fully formed genius wholly committed to literature, ready to apply the fruits of his Latin scholarship in a vernacular poem, and with the daring to conceive of revivifying the

Innamorato by impregnating it throughout with the spirit of Vergil and other classical poets. By 1505 the poem, its central images, values, and ideas already in place, is
known to be under way, and within little more than ten years the first *Furioso* appears
in its forty cantos. Clearly, the decade between 1494 and 1505 is crucial. Those were
the years in which, having persuaded his father of the futility of his studying law,
Ariosto gained permission to study literature at the Studio di Ferrara. Here he
encountered the philosopher Sebastiano dell'Aquila; the Augustinian friar and lecturer in humanities, Gregorio da Spoleto; and the polymath, Celio Calcagnini,
among others.[13] In those years, in the service of Ercole and then Cardinal Ippolito,
he evolved close and life-long friendships with Pietro Bembo, Mario Equicola, and
Baldassare Castiglione at the courts of Ferrara, Mantua, and Urbino. All of them
were second-generation Neoplatonists in Italy, with literary rather than philosophical gifts, but they were direct heirs, nevertheless, of Ficino and Pico. Pico was, after
all, Lord of Mirandola in the Duchy of Ferrara, and his nephew, Gianfrancesco Pico,
was the recipient of one of Ariosto's early Latin poems, mourning the departure into
France of their beloved instructor, Fra Gregorio da Spoleto.[14] It is not, then, as if
Ariosto had to go a great distance out of his way to some recondite, impossibly
exotic source for his Neoplatonic erudition. It was local, familiar, well established,
and utterly central. Even genius has roots that need exploring, and Ariosto's in his
formative years as a poet were in the Neoplatonism of his time. They became
increasingly intertwined with his Carolingian and Vergilian interests.

The Neoplatonism of Ariosto's age was a literary phenomenon largely,[15] and it
was largely concerned with a variety of loves arranged in an ascending hierarchical
order, from the most intractably material inclination of the body to the most transcendent longing of the spirit. The schematic elaborations of Platonic thought by
Ficino and Pico are general knowledge, but we may restate them briefly. Ficino
generally conceives of human love as having a two-fold direction: toward intellectual
procreation and toward bodily generation. Both are worthy and virtuous though
directed to hierarchically different ends, one moving away from the physical world
and the other operating within it. The scheme allowed no place for sensual love
aiming at personal gratification, which Ficino preferred to think of as a madness
("insania") outside any scheme of loves, and which he viewed as merely evidence of a
bodily disturbance; the notion originated in Greek medicine and is traceable down
to the time of Robert Burton. Ficino's scheme of loves remains fundamentally dual
in nature, therefore, and its "geminae Veneres" reflect the Platonic dualism of the
Venus Urania and the Venus Pandemos of the *Symposium.*

Pico expanded the scheme by equating the triple capacity for love in humans with
the three goddesses who figure in the legend of the Choice of Paris. To all three,
however, he gave the generic name of Venus. This innovation produced a hierarchy
of three loves arranged in a vertical scale, the topmost rung occupied by a Venus of
transcendent love, a middle rung occupied by a Venus of purely human love, and a
third, lowermost rung occupied by a Venus presiding over simple animal impulse.

Mythographically, they are equated with Minerva, a virgin goddess sprung from the brain of Zeus and holding sway over the works of the rational mind; with Juno, a matron consort who patronizes worldly kingdoms and acts as the bestower of treasure and power; and with Venus, an adulterous whore who aims at the gratification of the senses. Located in the brain, the will, or the loins, love has a triple aspect and is therefore divine, societal, or egocentric. The three loves determine the names of the lives over which they hold sway. The highest Venus (Minerva) presides over the contemplative life, the intermediate Venus (Juno) over the active or civil life, and the lowest Venus (Venus herself) over the feral or bestial existence. Thus in Pico we have a hierarchy of "amor divino," "amore umano," and "amor bestiale" or "amor ferino."[16] Ironically, this "new" development of the late fifteenth century is an expansion of Fulgentius's fourth-century allegorization of the myth of Paris, itself based on the three loves expounded in the final pages of the *Somnium Scipionis* of Macrobius.[17] The scheme of loves was to have enormous repercussions in the art of the generation immediately succeeding Pico's. They were the very years in which Ariosto, having left the barrenness of law, was devouring poetry and learning to practice his trade. The great fruit of his labors was a poem whose nominal "hero" goes mad for love, an action that conflates elements from both Ficino and Pico. By representing Orlando as "furioso," Ariosto characterizes his condition as one of "insania" produced by sensual love for Angelica; and by portraying him as a hairy, naked savage wandering over the face of Europe, Ariosto gives new poetic force to the concept of "amore bestiale." In dealing with the subject of love, Ariosto placed himself within an extensive artistic and literary tradition.

During his lifetime, Ariosto's closest friends and fellow artists were constantly creating works based on the ideas of their common Neoplatonist heritage. The great minds of the first generation of Neoplatonists had vanished: Ficino, Pico, and Poliziano were all dead in the decade before Ariosto began the *Furioso,* but around 1505 he was clearly at work within a specifically Neoplatonic tradition of love literature. From the last quarter of the fifteenth century onward, the philosophical love-writings of the Florentines provided the basis of numerous courtly popularizations. Whether dryly descriptive, technical compendia of the arcana of love or whether cast into the more appealing form of Platonic dialogues utilizing the resources of characterization and setting for the enhancement of their ideas, the love-treatises became widely and generally available to the courtly societies of the Renaissance, whose members were often actors in their dramas of love. It is no accident, then, that three of the most famous of these *trattati d'amore* were written by personal friends of Ariosto, two of them personages with whom he was for many years on terms of the closest intimacy. The first of these works, completed in 1495 and published in 1525, was Mario Equicola's *Libro de natura d'amore,* a voluminous, encyclopedic amplification of Pico's scheme of tripartite loves, a magisterial assortment of love lore many years in the compiling and still known in the seventeenth century to Robert Burton.[18] In literary quality, if not in importance and influence,

Equicola's work yielded, however, to Pietro Bembo's *Gli Asolani,* begun in Ferrara in 1497 and published in 1505, a date important because it cannot have been much before or after the date that Ariosto began to compose the *Furioso*.[19]

Though still quite young, Bembo had emerged as the great, undisputed literary dictator and authority on Neoplatonic love of his time, and Ariosto was bound to him by the strongest ties of affection and respect. The young Venetian was the poet's chief link to the older generation of Florentine Neoplatonists, for he had actually met Poliziano in Venice in 1491, and he had studied Greek under Lascaris in 1492. He was to be commemorated in the *Furioso* on two separate occasions, at 37.8 and 46.15, and Ariosto also addressed him in a Latin elegy and in one of his most famous *Satires,* "On Education," when entrusting him with the care of his own son, Virginio, when he sent the boy to study in Padua. But perhaps the clearest witness of Bembo's impact on Ariosto's creative imagination is registered in the *Furioso*'s debt to the *Asolani.* The direct influence of its ideas on the poem, which will emerge later, is often traceable in the very language Ariosto employs, as if in compliment to his master, throughout this work. Ironically, Ariosto has long been thought to have had the closest possible connection with the treatise: his modern biographer identifies the "Ludovico" whom Bembo entrusted with delivering the manuscript of the newly completed *Asolani,* in August of 1504, to Lucrezia Borgia d'Este, with Ludovico Ariosto himself.[20] That alone should have ensured a closer scrutiny of the treatise and the poem for ideas and techniques held in common.

A work in three books, *Gli Asolani* stands in contrast to Equicola's compilation by virtue of being an elegantly conceived piece of imaginative literature. It is a kind of dramatization, in three long monologues of Ciceronian prose separated by Petrarchan lyrical interludes, of the three loves of Neoplatonic tradition. These comprise, first, a complaint of disappointed sensual love; second, a eulogy of happy human love; third, an invocation of divine love. The setting is the hill-town of Asolo, ruled by the former queen of Cyprus, Caterina Cornaro, and the Venerean resonances are established at once through allusion. The occasion is the wedding of one of her handmaids, an event that charges the discussions of animal, human, and divine love with some significance. The work's tripartite form, finally, is the perfect mirror of its content, which traces an advance in moral and spiritual illumination in matters of love, love having here its broadest signification and encompassing all the major gradations of the passion.

With its remarkable opening paragraph, deeply Boethian in origin, commenting on life as a pilgrimage either on a stormy ocean or in a confusing place of ramifying paths, where men are either led astray or find their road by love, *Gli Asolani* is from the beginning a considerable influence on the endless voyages of the *Furioso,* which is similarly filled with error and shipwreck. However, the treatise provides an even more profoundly important precedent for the poem insofar as the three loves take on appropriate human forms and embodiments. The three loves are dramatized and incarnated in three distinct male "characters" who remain, nevertheless, emblematic rather than realistic. In the hierarchical order in which they are presented they are, first, a passionate and perturbed young lover called Perottino, the Petrarchistic rhetoric of whose lament identifies him immediately as a lover on the lowest rung of the scale; next, Gismondo, who, in contrast to Perottino's impassioned execrations of love, discourses reasonably and eloquently on the happiness of fulfilled human affection; and Lavinello, instructed by a hermit in the mysteries of divine love, who lectures him Boethianly on the universal *scala amoris* rising from vegetable and sentient to rational and divine love, and whose invocation of celestial, transcendent love ends the discussions on a lofty note.

Book 1 launches the discussion with Perottino's address, which is filled with love lore about Cupid and his portrayal in art and poetry, and with a view of love as being no more than a succession of the four perturbations of the soul, declining from joy through fear to grief, mounting through hope to joy once more, and being condemned to repeat the procedure constantly on an ever-turning wheel of Fortune. Of the three lovers only Perottino deals with love as fire and madness ("fuoco" and "furore"), and this is done in a context of egocentric, all-absorbing passion in which he, self-dramatizing and consciously delighting in the role, stands curiously apart and distanced, watching himself and watching his audience watch him in agony. Book 2, in contrast, opens with pronounced emphasis by the narrator on the life of reason and the mind, asserting the improvidence of humans in cultivating the life of the senses only and in neglecting their intellectual gifts and the cultivation of virtue. The passage functions as commentary both on Perottino's complaint in the previous book and on Gismondo's discourse that will ensue in this book, a speech that represents, in its eulogy of true love and marriage, a rational advance on the merely sensual and passionate existence of Perottino. For Gismondo invokes love as a social and civilizing process, the inborn, natural force that (to paraphrase closely) rescues men from wandering solitarily over the earth, naked, wild, and hairy, without roofs over their heads or human converse or domestic customs, and that permits them to meet together in a common life, of which the fruits are villages, the arts, laws, marriage, friendship, and large families: "It composes discord, fosters marriage, and makes our families large." This is a civic ideal later to be embodied in Ruggiero's similar journey to a "cittadinesca vita," and it is in direct opposition to the life that Orlando assumes, in yielding wholly to passion and illusory hope, joy, fear, and grief, and in wandering solitarily, like a hairy beast, over the face of Europe.

Like book 2, book 3 opens with a long passage by the narrator that "places" the previous discussion and opens the way for the third, last, and most important one. In the Neoplatonic scheme to which Bembo appeals in his narrative, neither the life of passion nor the life of reason can be an end in itself. Hence the narrator three times in a Boethian manner addresses the fundamental weakness of human capacities, preparing the way for the leap upward represented by the hermit's invocation of light from heaven to illuminate our human darkness. The opening paragraphs of book 3 harp constantly on the theme of the weakness of human *judgment* ("la debolezza de' nostri giudicii è molta," "alla debolezza de' nostri giudicii s'aggiugne la oscurità del vero," "essi vedranno essere e maggiore la oscurità nelle cose e ne' nostri giudicii minore e meno penetrevole la veduta")[21] and represent a judgment on human judgment, which Ariosto seized at once for his theme of human blindness. "Ecco il giudicio uman come spesso erra" (1.7.2) is the poet's very first authorial comment on the actors in his drama, and it intersects the otherwise complacent rehearsal of previous events in Boiardo with a lightning-like stroke asserting the new author's independence, his new breadth of vision, and his sense of control. He too, like Bembo finally, will make a leap into the heavens to contemplate ideas, but there his own artistic independence will come to the fore in a Platonism revivified by brilliant comedy. Bembo, the lesser genius, as it turned out, was altogether more orthodox and undramatic in tracing the upward movement of love to its final destination, but he was, of course, working in the more limiting form of the Platonic dialogue, and Ariosto was renovating a lively, colorful work of the imagination. The two young authors are nevertheless linked by their adherence to the triple scheme of love, capable of astonishing imaginative transformations at the hand of each. So it is, for instance, that the learned doctrine of the Neoplatonic triads of love is, in the medieval-romantic manner that Ariosto would soon adopt as his own, synopsized by Bembo in a charming little allegory of the Queen of the Fortunate Islands, demonstrating the three different ways in which she rewards the three classes of her human lovers. The hermit narrates her story to Lavinello:

Among their most esoteric memories, the ancients who were wise in sacred things held that on those islands which I have called Fortunate there was a queen of surpassing beauty, adorned with costly garments and ever young, who still remained a virgin, not wishing for a husband, but well contented to be loved and sought. And to those who loved her more she gave a greater reward; to the others one suitable to their affection. But she tested all of them as follows:

When each had come before her, as she had had them summoned one by one, she touched them with a wand and sent them off; and as soon as they had left the palace, they fell asleep and remained asleep until she had them wakened. When they returned to her presence once more, each had written on his forehead an exact description of his dreams which she instantly read.[22]

The first group, whose dreams are filled with feral visions of "hunting, fishing, horses, forests, and wild beasts," she reproves and condemns to live among the creatures of whom, thoughtless of her, they dreamed alone. The second, whose dreams are all of "trade or governing their families and communities and similar things," she rewards by appointing as merchants, citizens, and rulers in the practical work of the active or civil life. But the third group, those who dreamt only of her, she keeps with her in rounds of endless felicity, symbolic of the happiness with which the contemplative existence is crowned. The hermit himself draws the conclusion for Lavinello: "Know, in fine, that your love is not virtuous. Granted that it

is not evil like those which are mingled with bestial desires; still it falls short of
virtue because it does not draw you toward an immortal object but holds you midway between the extremes of desire where it is not safe to remain, for on a slope it is
easier to slide into the depths than to clamber to the summit."[23]

Apparently Bembo did not disdain to use a romantic allegorical method to incul-
cate familiar lessons about the tripartite nature of love, and he saw no danger in
placing, in a Christian hermit's mouth for purposes of instruction and edification, a
less than overtly Christian, apparently "trifling" narrative about the Queen of the
Faeries. Neither, it will become plain, did Ariosto disdain this kind of art in his far
more complex fiction. Ariostan legend often has it that all the allegorical readings of
the *Furioso* in the sixteenth century were the direct result of the Counter-Reformation; were, in fact, imposed readings forced on a stubbornly resisting text to save it
from censors. In fact this altogether discounts the Platonic tradition in which
Bembo and Ariosto together worked, where allegory was, in the manner of the day
and in the very nature of things, a literary device to point and set in relief the familiar
and known. Ariosto uses the triadic system of Neoplatonism to organize and to give
greater systematization to Boiardo's less coherent narrative, and readers who perceive the *Furioso* as basically structureless might, as a beginning, match in imagination an Orlando who surrenders totally to passion; a Ruggiero who initially makes a
visit to Reason and, presuming on brief acquaintance and sliding more often into the
depths than climbing to the summit, finds it "not safe" to remain there; and an
Astolfo who escapes the gravity of earth and contemplates the world and its littleness with laughing disengagement from its concerns, his "lunacy" providing
ironic counterpoint to Orlando's more worldly one. The internal complication represented by this continuous comparison and contrast of the three major heroes'
actions is Ariosto's singular contribution to his Boiardan materials, his chief means
of giving both structure and content to the narrative. In a word, the *Furioso* is not
about nothing, nor about itself or its art. In large part it is about a hierarchy of lives
in dynamic and constantly shifting interplay, with the lowest, highest, and intermediate kinds of love set into purposeful and illuminating juxtapositions, often
sharing each others' characteristics.

Bembo's discourses on love have a stunning impact on the *Furioso,* but neither his
nor Equicola's writings were the only ones that Ariosto knew. As we have seen,
Equicola's *Libro de natura d'amore* was begun in 1495 and Bembo's *Gli Asolani* in
1497, respectively one and three years after Boiardo's death, and thus intervening
between the *Innamorato* and the *Furioso*. A third work in the tradition with which
Ariosto has a certain connection was begun later, around 1508, contemporary with
the first years of the *Furioso*'s creation, and, since it was published in 1528, it appears
to attest not only the continuity but also the tenacity of a literary tradition. Baldassare Castiglione's *Il cortegiano* is perhaps the greatest and most familiar of Renaissance works on love, but it shares with Bembo's *Asolani* the combination of matter
and eloquence with graceful nonchalance and courtly atmosphere. Castiglione does

not give us the vividly distinguished trio of personalities that Bembo brought to life, but the same escalation is visible in the hierarchically ascending movement of his four dialogues. Not so remarkably, considering the stature of Bembo as an authority on love, Castiglione casts him as a major character and gives him the chief speech at the work's end, in which the ascent from sensual to spiritual love is described and invoked in one of the most remarkable pages of Renaissance prose. What is not generally known, perhaps, is that Ariosto, Bembo, and Castiglione were all present together in Urbino in 1507, at the very time that the dialogues are imagined to have taken place, and that Ariosto memorialized that wonderful conjunction of lives in his *Satires,* recalling how Giuliano de' Medici, Pope Leo's young brother,

> si riparò nella feltresca corte,
>   ove col formator del cortigiano,
> col Bembo e gli altri sacri al divo Apollo,
> facea l'essilio suo men duro e strano.
>   (3.90–93)

repaired to the court of Montefeltro, where, with the one who formed the courtier, with Bembo, and with the others consecrated to the god Apollo, he made his exile less harsh and desolate.[24]

It is of interest, finally, that the *Cortegiano*'s fourth book, in which Bembo's crucial speech on love appears, is dedicated to Ariosto's cousin Alfonso Ariosto, and that Ariosto himself praises the work at 37.8 of his own poem.

Ferrara, Mantua, and Urbino were three of the dominant city-states in Northern Italy in the sixteenth century, culturally as well as politically. They were, moreover, three courts united by intermarriage, a common way of life, and community of artistic interests. In passing from Ferrara to Mantua as the bride of Francesco Gonzaga, Isabella d'Este had become the sister-in-law of Elisabetta Gonzaga, wife of Guidobaldo da Montefeltro of Urbino; and by the marriage of her brother, Alfonso I, to the Pope's daughter, Lucrezia Borgia, Isabella had acquired another, less beloved but no less influential sister-in-law. For readers of Ariosto the cultural activities of the marchesa and the two duchesses should hold a certain interest, especially in their influence on literature. They presided over three of the most renowned courtly societies of their period, and their interests and the tenor of life in the worlds in which they moved are preserved in three influential literary works of the twenty-year period spanned by the last decade of the fifteenth century and the first decade of the sixteenth century. Each of them was the presiding spirit of a major work on Neoplatonic love that immediately preceded or exactly synchronized with the beginnings of the *Furioso.* In Mantua, Equicola's treatise was written expressly for Isabella d'Este;[25] in Ferrara, Bembo's monologues were dedicated to Lucrezia Borgia; and Castiglione's dialogues gave an immortalizing life to the gentle sway of Elisabetta Gonzaga da Montefeltro in the Urbino of 1507, the very year in which Ariosto is known to have been in attendance, as ambassador, on that brilliant court.

No reader of the *Furioso* can fail to recall the recurring praises of the three women in the poem; they and their literary celebrators had both an explicit and an implicit impact on the poetry of Ariosto, which everywhere declares its origin and orientation.

In Ariosto's circle, the impact of Neoplatonism was registered by painters as well as writers, and we may cite a few examples of contemporary masters who were also his friends and who shared with him an interest in manipulating the dual and tripartite schemes of Neoplatonic love. The twin Venuses had been, of course, the subjects of Botticelli's two famous mythological paintings, the "Birth of Venus" and the "Primavera."[26] A generation later, they reappeared in Titian's so-called "Sacred and Profane Love," latterly interpreted by Panofsky as an allegory of celestial, human, and bestial love.[27] They appeared again in Correggio's "The School of Love" and the "Venus and a Satyr," a complementary pair of paintings illustrating spiritual and carnal love, executed for Federigo Gonzaga, Isabella d'Este's son, whose tutor happened to be Mario Equicola.[28] In contrast to these explorations of the dual loves, the tripartite scheme of loves is rendered in Raphael's "Dream of Scipio," where two women offer gifts to a dreaming warrior, the one on the left offering a nosegay of perishable flowers, symbol of hedonistic vegetable existence, while the woman on the right offers both a sword and a book, symbols respectively of the mutually helpful active and contemplative lives.[29] It would be superfluous to note that, like the personalities previously mentioned in literature, both Raphael and Titian were personal friends of Ariosto, that the former painted the backdrop for a performance of Ariosto's *Suppositi* in Castel Sant'Angelo, and, in addition, included his portrait among a host of famous contemporaries in the Vatican "Parnassus";[30] or that the latter painted Ariosto's portrait, and that an engraving of the work was reproduced in the 1532 edition. What we should stress is that these relationships testify to the omnipresence and casualness of commonly held Neoplatonic ideas and images in the circles in which Ariosto moved throughout his life. More important still, they reveal how naturally artists, whether poets or painters, employed the particular imagery of Neoplatonism when addressing aristocrats in general, and rulers in particular, on the subject of the different lives and loves it was possible for a human being to achieve. The practice was Florentine in origin. The Botticelli Venuses as well as the overtly Neoplatonic "Pallas and the Centaur" were painted for Lorenzo di Pierfrancesco de' Medici, the more famous Lorenzo's second cousin, himself an actual pupil of Ficino.[31] Likewise, the Raphael depiction of Scipio's choice was addressed, very fittingly, to Scipione Borghese;[32] while the Titian twin-loves painting was a compliment to Niccolò Aurelio, a Venetian aristocrat whom Panofsky identifies as "then secretary to the Council of Ten, later Grand Chancellor of the Serenissima, and lifelong friend of Pietro Bembo."[33] Bembo himself, to make the circle complete, was the son of a friend and correspondent of Ficino, and the friend for twenty-six years of Ludovico Ariosto. As a cap on the matter, we should recall that Isabella d'Este herself was inclined to give explicit and imperious directions for Neoplatonic programs in the allegorical paintings she commissioned from artists of the rank of Perugino and Mantegna. Their respective paintings, "The Combat of Chastity and Lust" and "Minerva Expelling the Vices from the Garden of Virtue," both in the Louvre, are prime examples of the kind of painting she required,[34] and they contain elements similar to those in Ariosto's allegory of Alcina and Logistilla.

We are now prepared to see the impact of this background on the *Furioso,* not only in its content, vocabulary, and imagery, but in its structure as well. The poem's first four stanzas make its origins very clear. In rapid, decisive movements, in a summarizing pattern that constitutes his very first attempt to reorganize Boiardo's looser narrative, Ariosto outlines the three main actions of his epic and names the two main protagonists whose progress it will trace: first (in stanza 1), the all-enveloping action of the Saracen invasion of France and the assault of Agramante on the Empire; second (in stanza 2), the madness of Orlando, arising from frustrated love for Angelica; and third (in stanza 4, after a stanza of dedication to Ippolito), the exploits of Ruggiero, the destined ancestor of the family. The immediate juxtaposition of Orlando and Ruggiero, implicit in Boiardo but never realized poetically, deserves notice. Ariosto published three versions of the *Furioso*: in 1516 and 1521, a poem of forty cantos, and in 1532 the expanded version of forty-six. By deliberate manipulation of his materials, the madness of Orlando, darkly splendid, always occupied the central position: in canto 20 of the first two versions and in canto 23 of the last. In similar manner, the marriage of Ruggiero and Bradamante, an action by which the hero crowns his career and his fortunes, always formed the climax and conclusion: in canto 40 of the first two versions and in canto 46 of the third and last. Ariosto redeveloped, amplified, and closely joined two stories of lovers moving on two different planes of experience. His Orlando is subordinated to his Ruggiero at once, for now the tale of Bradamante and Ruggiero encompasses that of Orlando and Angelica, rather than the other way around, as in Boiardo. The opening stanzas therefore mark the *Furioso* immediately as a poem of two "amori" at least, and we may, for the time being, limit our attention to them.

The depiction of irrational passion and the collapse of Orlando's mind under the onslaught of fury, jealousy, and disappointed lust always marked the end of the first half of the narrative. It requires no fashionable mathematical calculation to see this, nor to see that the great climax toward which the poem moves is the marriage and triumph of Ruggiero, an earthly destiny and a mean between the two extremes. The emphasis clearly reveals that Ruggiero is to be more, much more, than Orlando, who in no way can be spoken of as the "hero" of the poem, but who serves rather as a manipulable mechanism. From the beginning, Ruggiero's story is interwoven with Orlando's by way of parallel at first and later of increasingly divergent and purposeful contrast. They move to different destinies, and at the very end, as Ruggiero prepares for the final combat with Rodomonte, Orlando's subordinate position is stressed as he helps to arm the hero and attaches the spurs to his feet

(46.109). It can hardly be fortuitous that the demented Orlando is the victim of uncontrollable passion, and that Ruggiero, after a poem-long testing under the assaults of his own nature and those of freakish Fortune, finally attempts to conquer himself and seals his adventures with a wedding, traditional symbol of achieved harmony and ordered passion.

Ariosto's Orlando is very patently the embodiment, propelled here into richly significant emblematic action, of the lowest form of love in the Neoplatonic hierarchy, and he incarnates the merely appetitive flesh-hunger with whose description the contemporaneous love-treatises are positively saturated. He is unmistakably the victim of what Ficino and Pico described as malady and bestial affection, what Boiardo suggested in calling Orlando "quella anima insana," and what Bembo less drastically dramatized in Perottino. His will crumbles and falls past the higher slopes of laughter on which Boiardo had kept him suspended, into a world of consequence, blindness of intellect, and bestiality of nature. He becomes inexorably what Perottino would become logically if, sunk into the sea of his contrarious passions of joy and grief, fear and desire, he persisted in a course of self-abandonment to the point of insanity. He is also what Raphael's Scipio would become if, breaking out of his position of arrest, he were to choose the "sinister" lady offering the flower of fleshly delight instead of the modest maiden on the right proffering the sword and book of virtue. Not without clear memories of book I of *Gli Asolani* is Orlando depicted as a tormented dreamer torn by the four perturbations of the soul on his first appearance in canto 8 of the *Furioso,* or as the thin-voiced Petrarchist of self-pitying soliloquies, singing in terror of losing Angelica's "rose." Nor was Ariosto unmindful of Bembo in the Queen of Faerie's bequest, to those who dream only of sensual blisses, of a lifetime of "hunting, fishing, horses, forest, and wild beasts." Orlando achieves precisely that image when, remorselessly following his runaway appetite, he runs bestially and terrifically mad in a forest at the midpoint of the poem; or when he confuses his faithless beloved with her own white palfrey and "rides" the poor beast to death in as savage and brutal an emblematic encounter as Renaissance poetry can provide. If, somehow, we should have mistaken or ignored all this as the play of a mind fundamentally frolicsome or meretricious, Ariosto is there with overt iconographic imagery and direct commentary, asserting that the animalistic Orlando wallows in the mud like a swine ("come porco") just before he comes upon Angelica for the last time. Immediately after Orlando's descent into madness, he will inform us with Ficinian precision of language, "Che non è in somma, amor, se non insania" (24.1.3). If all else fails, he will prompt us with his usual fine irony when the paladin, so soon to be himself berserk, haughtily addresses his rival, Ferraù, with the reverberative and philosophically evocative phrase, "Uom bestiale" (12.40.1). It seems highly improbable that Ariosto's contemporaries were as inattentive as we have become, or that they failed to match the hairy savage against the dynast who had rooted their family in Ferrara and who maintained himself, only with effort, from becoming an Orlando.

The brutish Orlando, naked and roofless, so forgetful of civilization as to make no distinction between "le cru et le cuit" (24.12.7–8), is nothing but primitive unaccommodated man, the reminder of a time, as the *Aeneid* says, when "neque mos neque cultus erat" (8.316); a time also, as Bembo said in Gismondo's speech, into which all men could slip again for lack of civilizing love. Orlando is therefore the antithesis of what Bradamante and Ruggiero are called to establish—local habitations and ordered centers of human activity. In a very real sense, he incarnates what any civilization originally labors to expel; and, unfortunately, what it is capable of reverting to at any moment in its history. Like all cities, Ferrara is an experiment in civilization, and only those who recognize how tenuous are the threads by which such order is woven can appreciate the difficulty and the magnificence of the achievement. The city gives continuity to the endeavors by which the human potential is realized, and it requires, in turn, only the madness of a single will to fracture and break them. Civilization, dependent on a concord of appetitive wills, lives perpetually on a knife-edge.

The contrast of Orlando and Ruggiero could not be more strictly drawn; it prepares us for yet another, more complex contrast between Ruggiero and another character who soars higher than he. Though both Orlando and Ruggiero are represented as lovers of the same fleshly kind in the beginning, their paths begin to draw apart thereafter, the static moral state of Orlando moving him irretrievably to madness, and the dynamism of Ruggiero taking him, progressively and by a jagged course, to his conversion, marriage, and victory. He is to emerge as the embodiment of three major facets of the active life—husband, soldier, and ruler—and as the representative of the human love of the treatises, fixed in the middle position but acknowledging the level above him. In attaining the second rung of the ladder of love, he preserves a mean between extremes, and ultimately he finds his proper sphere as the head of his wife and the future head of his people. As the antecedent of the Estensi, it is Ruggiero who is in pride of place as the true hero of the poem, and it is his love, being proper to the generality of men, that mediates in a sphere properly and particularly human. Marital love (in this case, dynastic marital love) is a chief aspect of the active life, resulting as it does not only in an order lost at the Fall and in a calming of the passions but in the propagation of scions and hence of a continuous social order as well. Tasso phrased the concept eloquently:

And therefore (most sacred matrimonie) doest not thou thinke it sufficient to separate us from rude beasts, but thou makest us resemble and to be like unto immortal creatures; for through our stock and issue, perpetuated and continued in our children by legitimate succession, the most strong Cities and most spatious kingdomes, are successively deliuered from one unto another, passing from one heire, unto the government of another.[35]

At its best, dynasty involves the stabilization and orderly transmission of political order. It provides a bulwark against change, a "momentary stay against confusion."

Renaissance Ferrara is a city of destiny, a great center of international culture to which all the great thinkers, artists, and scholars of contemporary Europe were inevitably drawn: men as various as Petrarch and Bembo, Pannonius of Hungary and John Tiptoft of England, Paracelsus and Copernicus, Erasmus and Josquin des Pres and Giaches de Wert.[36] The fact of Ferrara's greatness, its cost in human effort and discipline, is, fundamentally, what the *Furioso* celebrates, and it openly reveals the influence of the superb passage in the *Aeneid* when Evander shows Aeneas the fated site of the Capitol:

hinc ad Tarpeiam sedem et Capitolium ducit,
aurea nunc, olim silvestribus horrida dumis.
> (8.347.8)

which now is all gold, but was once wild and ragged, covered with woodland growth.

So, too, in cantos 35 and 43, Ariosto calls attention to the long and painful process by which what was once only a marshland or forest becomes, in time, an influential and powerful city, a sphere of glory and splendor. St. John is the first to take up this Vergilian note of praise while discoursing to Astolfo:

—Del re de' fiumi tra l'altiere corna
or siede umil (diceagli) e piccol borgo:
dinanzi il Po, di dietro gli soggiorna
d'alta palude un nebuloso gorgo;
che, volgendosi gli anni, la più adorna
di tutte le città d'Italia scorgo,
non pur di mura e d'ampli tetti regi,
ma di bei studi e di costumi egregi.
> (35.6)

"Between the proud branches of the king of rivers," he said, "there now sits a humble little town—before it flows the Po, behind it lies the misty whirlpool of a deep swamp—which, with the passage of the years, I perceive becoming the most beautiful of all the cities of Italy, not only for its walls and ample royal roofs, but for its humane studies and its excellent manners."

Later, Rinaldo voyages down the Po and in even more extended a passage (43.53–63), directly recalling St. John's, passes the site of Ferrara's future glory, the neglected and deserted island that is to emerge many centuries later as the famous Belvedere, the marshes that will blossom with art and science:

—Come esser può ch'ancor (seco dicea)
debban così fiorir queste paludi
de tutti i liberali e degni studi?

e crescer abbia di sì piccol borgo
ampla cittade e di sì gran bellezza?
e ciò ch'intorno è tutto stagno e gorgo,

sien lieti e pieni campi di ricchezza?
    (43.60.6–8; 61.1–4)

"How can it be," he said to himself, "that these marshes are to flower with every worthy liberal study? and how, from so small a town, so great and beautiful a city grow? and all those ponds and swamps be pleasurable fields, full of riches?"

    Ruggiero and Bradamante are working their way forward in preparation for their descendants' glory, and by no easy route. Their story connects Ariosto's double vision of the city achieved and the city yet in potency—what lies in the future in the reigns of Ercole I and Alfonso I, and the discordant world of perpetually restless motion in which the lovers move toward their destiny. Necessarily the process of civilization in which they are involved requires a subordination of certain aspects of man's nature to others, of lower affections to higher, as a reading of the *Aeneid,* the single greatest poem about the founding of a city, makes abundantly plain. Ordered love of any kind transforms the individual, but dynastic love, equipped with unusual power, extends beyond itself and becomes capable of transforming not only the individual but also the society he founds or regenerates. The process of ordering his passions is what Ariosto's dynastic hero so painfully undergoes.

    The beleaguered and burdened Ruggiero begins as a moral kinsman of the sensual Orlando, and though he at once and prudently demonstrates a willingness not to remain on that level, his falls and failures are regular, as predictable as spectacular. In struggling to become ultimately a married lover, a soldiering prince, and a Christian who, only after difficulty, comes to recognize the meaning of his conversion by a hermit, thus participating in all three lives and all three loves, this prototype of the Estensi illustrates the all-inclusive love that Ficino found characteristic of Lorenzo de' Medici, the foremost contemporary representative of the active life.[37]

    Unlike Orlando, in whom the Paris aspect predominates, Ruggiero initially makes the choice of Hercules (6.55–57) and gives an earnest at least of his essential good will and future success. Blindness of intellect and infection of his will at once cloud his perceptions and misdirect his energies. He is presented with his choice of life in the *Furioso*'s most explicitly allegorical passage, the tale of Alcina, Morgana, and Logistilla (cantos 6–10), a paradigm of psychomachia whose reverberations are heard throughout the poem's long career. But after Ruggiero's first fleshly lapse (in canto 7) with Alcina, the "puttana vecchia" of human carnality, Ariosto represents him as a man striving to avoid succumbing to passion (canto 8), temporarily and superficially undergoing the instruction of Reason herself in the person of Logistilla and her four handmaids, the Cardinal Virtues (canto 10), but falling easily into the snare of lust (canto 11), passing finally from visceral to cognitive love and promising to be baptized and to marry (canto 22), delaying his conversion through a false attachment to personal honor (cantos 25–41 passim), and undergoing thereafter (as a Christian now, and therefore in greater spiritual peril than ever before) the increasingly difficult, hierarchically arranged temptations of worldly glory, diabolic pride, and utter despair. At the end he is saved, by direct intervention of Providence, only after the most total self-sacrifice of all his ambitions and loves, only after offering, in agonized requital of a debt, to yield up even Bradamante to Leo, his rival (canto 45). The seal on this obstacle-ridden process of perfecting himself is his marriage, by which (if we may avail ourselves of Tasso's words in another context) he sets "iust lawes to humane pleasures, and a lawdable bridle to untaimed headlong desires."[38]

Ruggiero runs an increasingly difficult and thoroughly erratic course, but there is a clearly perceptible continuity in his moral career. In what may, at first glance, look like a mere jumble of difficulties, the continuity is provided by a hierarchical escalation of difficulties rising, in ever more crisis-ridden intensity, from temptations in the world of matter (Alcina) to temptations in the realm of the spirit (Agramante, the entire adventure in the East). Lust, avarice, worldly glory, wrathful fury, pride, and despair are the perturbers of Ruggiero's peace, and his laborious course is a more highly structured and more deeply serious reflection of the one that his beloved Bradamante negotiates. The fief of Ateste is won at a very high price. "Tantae molis erat," the poet seems, Vergilianly, to be saying, "Ferrariae condere gentem."

If Ariosto knew the cost involved in building and maintaining civilizations, he knew equally well and was perfectly serious about the value of poetry in persuading men to pass from beastly solitariness into the forms of civil order. Readers of the *Furioso* could turn profitably to the *Satires* (6.67–87) for an allegorical treatment of the service that poets perform in the gentling of human instinct, the bonding into societies, and the creation of cities, in the tale of the first singers, Phoebus and Amphion. This represents, of course, the old classical ideal of eloquence, Ciceronian and Horatian; and in fact Ariosto's lines are almost translations of those lines about Orpheus and Amphion in the *Ars poetica*. In the *De oratore* also, eloquence is directed to leading men out of the brutishness and savagery of life in the wild, to giving them, in social communities, laws for behavior.[39] But in poetry eloquence is evoked in its highest form by the writer of epic, who celebrates, even as he participates in, the work of civilization. The *Furioso* is the work of a law student studying Latin glosses turned poet imitating Vergilian epic. It memorializes the process of preparation necessary for undertaking to civilize a wilderness, and it does so by dramatizing at length the "civilization" of its mythic founder. Throughout, Ruggiero is in quest of a name and an identity, very much like Ferrara itself, an undistinguished expanse of dust in the Po valley until it is named and marked out by human cultivation. Neither the man nor the territory will amount to much without the shaping and the definition conferred by effort and labor. Cultivation of the wilderness, the "hyle" or "silva" of the self, is the only preparation for cultivation of the landscape, a moral art addressed to reordering the richly rooted forests of nature, forests wildly alive in both the smaller and the greater worlds.

In recording the historical process of tempering chaos, the *Furioso* enacts the process of civilization in its very own pages by building, Amphion-like, structures of song and (in reordering the *Innamorato*) by partaking itself in the ordering process implicit in its subject. It is itself an "addizione Erculea," breaking out of the bounds of an older and smaller city and enlarging and beautifying its domains. The first witness of its attempt at order is its arrangement of its major characters into perceptible patterns, thus giving shape to their otherwise confusing movements. Ariosto embraces the teeming multiplicity of Boiardo's narrative but simplifies and gives contour to all that madness by selecting and distinguishing. In no way striving for the clear unities of Vergil, irrevocably lost in the meanderings of Carolingian romance, he was nevertheless attempting, through the transformation of an older poem, to say for Ferrara and its rulers something in the nature of the Vergilian "genus unde Latinum."

5

The Vergilian Expansion

Trojan Aeneas, Trojan Ruggiero

Few readers today will believe that Ariosto's purpose was to portray a prince like Aeneas or Cyrus.
William Nelson, *The Poetry of Edmund Spenser*

. . . Ruggiero, a *pius Aeneas* who never puts a foot wrong.
Vincent Cronin, *The Flowering of the Renaissance*

A commonplace of criticism is that Ariosto classicized the chivalric romance. By 1505 he had completed a decade of intensive and fruitful apprenticeship in the study and writing of Latin poetry, and when he turned to the vernacular the result was a poem, as Pio Rajna finely put it, "Nato di padre italiano, ma di madre latina."[1] Of all classical poems, the *Aeneid* is the one most constantly laid under contribution, and the number and perfection of Ariosto's classical imitations have been the subject of an entire book.[2] Assuredly, therefore, the *Furioso* begins with a crucial decision to reweave the raveled threads Boiardo had dropped, but to interweave them throughout with finer ones drawn from Vergil. This specifically Vergilian aspect, intense and continuous, is Ariosto's original contribution to his chivalric heritage. Increasingly, as he worked at his poem for a quarter of a century, it came to have a greater and greater impact on it, and the additions of 1532 magnify and extend the Vergilian matter of the two earlier versions.

No more felicitous set of circumstances could be imagined. The *Innamorato* had been the delight of Isabella d'Este's youth, and she had constantly badgered Boiardo for the unwritten cantos.[3] Many years afterward, even Berni's usurping *Rifacimento* was dedicated to her, memorializing the poem's connection with her youth in a different world and another, more seemingly innocent time. But what renders the circumstances surrounding the creation of the *Furioso* absorbing in the extreme is the fact that now, by marriage to Federigo Gonzaga, Isabella had become the Marchioness of Mantua and mistress therefore of the very territories in which Vergil himself had been born. Italian scholars long ago produced evidence of her love of the *Aeneid,* quite as great as her love of the *Innamorato,* and not only do we know the name of the Latin tutor with whom she studied, but we also possess the letter he long after wrote to her, recalling their reading of Vergil with delight.[4] As a panegyric of the Julian emperors, and as a favorite manual of the tutors of the scions of Renaissance Italy's ruling families, the *Aeneid* recommended itself immediately as a model for a poem in praise of the Estensi, and the *Furioso* courts comparison with the Roman epic in both the larger and the smaller detail. For a Ferrarese court-poet addressing a dynastic poem to Isabella d'Este's family, then, Vergilianly to transform a poem of Boiardo's, who had already impregnated the Carolingian poem with dynastic praise, was to engage in several levels of courtly compliment.

The dominant impress of the *Aeneid* is visible in many major episodes of the *Furioso,* from beginning to end. The most obvious ones will strike every reader's eye: Bradamante's vision of her descendants in a cavern, mirroring Aeneas's pageant of the unborn Caesars in the Sybil's cavern; Melissa's mission to rescue Ruggiero from Alcina, recalling Mercury's mission to rescue Aeneas, captive to Dido; the midnight expedition of Medoro and Cloridano, based exactly on that of Nisus and Euryalus; the opposition of Beatrice and Aymon to Ruggiero's suit, modeled on that of Amata and Latinus to that of Aeneas; the final combat of Ruggiero and Rodomonte, almost translated from that of Aeneas and Turnus. Apart from these larger imitations there are numerous smaller ones, like the Harpies infesting Senapo's kingdom, near kin to those with which Aeneas does battle, or the conversion of ships into leaves, mimicking the sea-change of ships into nymphs. More elusively, the *Furioso* contains a multitude of lines and phrases that recall the Vergilian original in a particularly insistent manner. Confronted with a brimming catalog of Vergilian echoes, parallels, reminiscences, and outright translations, the reader is amply persuaded that the *Aeneid* exerted a primary influence on the *Furioso* at every stage of its composition, and that Ariosto powerfully reinforced and extended Boiardo's introduction of classicism into the romance form. The question unasked in a cataloging approach like Romizi's and still remaining to be addressed is, what finally is their cumulative effect? What is the import of Ariosto's Vergilianism, and on what conceptual basis does it rest?

The complexity and depth of Ariosto's assimilation of Vergil has never been truly investigated, and reasons for this are clear. Both earlier and current tradition appears to assume that Ariosto had the same untrammeled access to Vergil's text that the modern reader has, that for him the poem had fundamentally the same meaning that it has in the twentieth century. Consequently, Ariosto's immersion in Vergil takes the form solely of his imitation of the literal narrative; and the poet supposedly confines himself to a remodeling of the striking episode, the fine image and reverberative phrase. Rarely, if ever, in an Ariostan context is it mentioned that for Renaissance readers an intervening literary tradition of well over a thousand years had consistently represented Vergil as a teacher and seer, and his poem as a consistent allegorical representation of the course of a human life. Indisputably more learned a poet than Boiardo, Ariosto registers the impact on the *Aeneid* of an older tradition of critical interpretation not only familiar to but also practiced by his contemporaries. Even on the most literal level Aeneas's journey to a new lordship is a struggle through hardship, morally taxing, filled with deviations, and requiring a stoic endurance to accomplish. The Renaissance reading of Vergil incorporated this reading and gave it a Neoplatonic extension as a voyage through different loves and a variety of lives.[5] Hence, Ruggiero's course of moral training, a great exemplar to all his descendants, provides the fictional pattern of moral difficulties and fallings-off irremediably incident to all human life at any social level, but of greater weight in those of princes. In attempting to rival Vergil, Ariosto re-creates the epic in its intellectual and moral essence, but not at all in its structure, decor, and "furniture," which originate in Carolingian romance. The *Furioso* therefore represents a marvelous fusion of highly unlike components. Accordingly, in its deepest levels, the story of Ruggiero, the demi-Saracen descendant of Hector of Troy, reenacts the meaning and the hierarchical moral values that Neoplatonist critics had attributed to the *Aeneid* for a millennium and a half. In that tradition, figures like Servius, Fulgentius, Macrobius, Bernard Sylvestris, John of Salisbury, Dante, Petrarch, Boccaccio, Guarino Veronese, Francesco Filelfo, Maffeo Vegio, Cristoforo Landino, Celio Calcagnini, Scaliger, and Tasso all participated. Each of them altered the particular emphasis and detail, but all of them successively and unanimously transmitted the notion of the *Aeneid* as a poem of interior, spiritual journey, represented by geographical wandering through the Mediterranean and Aegean.[6]

To a modern reader, all of this frequently looks like a medieval mental derangement, though familiarity with the Stoic and Platonic elements Vergil incorporated into his poem may take some of the edge from that view. As a modern Vergilian scholar has noted, Vergil's poem, even on the most literal level, provides "many examples of thoughtless excess leading to disaster, especially excesses of inordinate affection when someone is carried too far by an exclusive love for some person or thing."[7] Still, some of the puzzlement is bound to remain. Living in an age when the rapidity of change scarcely allows a tradition to form before it is challenged and overthrown, we require a special effort to appreciate not only the existence but also the continuity of the Vergilian tradition and its appeal to so many great minds over so long a span of time. Nevertheless there is no question that Ariosto conceived of classical literature as more than a treasury of striking phrases to be imitated, as Boiardo did. We have his own poetic testimony of the moral interpretation of that literature, not only present in his Horatian poems but also incorporated directly into the *Furioso,* where its importance still goes unremarked. In canto 46, the enchantress Melissa arrives at the dynasts' wedding bringing a magic "talamo" as a present for Bradamante and Ruggiero. This nuptial pavilion is embroidered with representations of their descendants over the ages, and its central panel is given over to portraiture of the youth and education of Ariosto's patron, Cardinal Ippolito. One of the stages in his education is represented as follows:

Quivi si vede, come il fior dispensi
de' suoi primi anni in disciplina et arte.
Fusco gli è appresso, che gli occulti sensi
chiari gli espone de l'antiche carte.
—Questo schivar, questo seguir conviensi,
se immortal brami e glorioso farte,—
par che gli dica: così avea ben finti

i gesti lor chi già gli avea dipinti.
        (46.89)

Here one could see how he spent the flower of his early years in discipline and learning; Fusco stood at his side, clearly expounding the hidden meanings of the ancient writings. "This you must avoid, this you must pursue," he appeared to be saying to him: so well had the artist represented their gestures.

"Occulti sensi," "hidden meanings": precisely the kind of allegorical reading that critics repeatedly maintain is so foreign to Ariosto. The lines give clear evidence that even Ippolito, scarcely the most luminous member of his family, was touched by the allegorical interpretation of the classics universal among the literati in Ferrara, and the vulgar remark he is reported to have addressed to Ariosto on the latter's presentation of the completed poem—"Messer Ludovico, dove mai avete trovato tutte queste coglionerie?"—is less a testimony to the waywardness of the poet's fancy than to the cardinal's incapacity as a scholar. Apparently Tommaso Fusco's instruction did not, as the expression goes, "take." Certainly Ariosto proved a more assiduous student to his own preceptor, Gregorio da Spoleto, to whom he expressed his heartfelt gratitude for his classical education in a moving moment in one of his *Satires* (6.166–71). Gregorio was an Augustinian monk whose superlative teaching gifts secured his release from the cloister. As tutor to Giovanni de' Medici, later Pope Leo X, to several of the Este scions, and to Francesco Sforza, he could hardly have dealt with classical literature either as a farrago of pagan fantasy or as an objective historical document.[8] All the evidence is on the other side. Indeed, the clerical tradition was often the humanist tradition, and one of Ariosto's closest clerical friends, the great scholar Celio Calcagnini, was continuing the tradition of moral interpretation of classical literature initiated at the Studio by Guarino da Verona in the previous century. In Calcagnini's own interpretation of the *Aeneid,* the voyage of Aeneas represents an allegory of continuous ascent from the world in three separate stages. Even his alterations of the traditional pattern take place within a definable framework of Neoplatonist thought.[9]

We should attempt to dispel some of the mystery about these readings of Vergil and reveal the fundamental pattern to which they adhere and the inner consistency to which they all, in various ways, appeal. Apart from the curiosity of Petrarch's defense of the "real" Dido,[10] there was no historical criticism of the *Aeneid* in all the Middle Ages and the Renaissance. The critical tradition was firmly grounded in the concept of epic as psychomachia, and by the learned the poem was read regularly and as a matter of course as an allegory of human existence in travail and in process of perfecting itself. Thus we find Fulgentius in the sixth century asserting that the *Aeneid* illustrates the "cursum mundanae vitae," and Filelfo in the fifteenth century stating in almost the same words that it reveals "omnem aetatis humane cursum," while his friend and mentor, Guarino da Verona, guiding spirit of the classical revival under Leonello d'Este, inquires matter-of-factly, "Nonne cursum Aeneae et alle-

goricum mundanae vitae statum aperit?"[11] Since the whole purpose of the poem is
to bring the Trojan hero to the attainment of his political destiny in Italy, and since it
was inconceivable to any educated mind that that destiny could be accomplished
without previous internal preparation, the poem was read uniformly as an allegory
of spiritual travail, the protagonist girding himself morally for the assumption of an
active life of rule by a struggle to virtue, a victory over the passions. The poem is
customarily divided into two equal halves of six books each, and since man is an
ethical creature before he is a political animal, the process of individual human perfecting precedes the perfecting by right rule of society in general. Aeneas is a man
before he is a soldier and dynast. The individual's struggle to virtue is therefore
represented as taking place in the first half of the poem, the section to which the
allegorists devote the greater part by far of their considerations (John of Salisbury,
Bernard of Chartres, Dante, Filelfo, Landino),[12] though the latter half of the work,
tracing Aeneas's engagement in the military labors of the active life, is equally the
concern of others (Donatus, Fulgentius, Petrarch, Maffeo Vegio).[13] As Filelfo says,
the allegory is comprehended in the phrase with which the poem opens, the "arma"
figuring the achievement of the "virtutes bellicas et activas" of books 7 through 13
and the "virum" figuring the emphasis on the "virtutes urbanas intellectivasque" of
books 1 through 6.[14] Moreover, the first six books are frequently said to figure the
six ages of man familiar from Isidore of Seville. John of Salisbury mentions the "sex
aetatum gradus," and Filelfo almost three hundred years later specifies them (on the
old Fulgentian model) as the "infantia" that follows the shipwreck of the soul into
birth, "pueritia" that dwells loquaciously on the past (books 2 and 3), "adolescen- child-
tia" that is given over to voluptuousness (4), "iuventa" that experiences the desire   hood
for glory (5), and "aetas gravior" devoted to contemplation ("in veritatis perspicien-
tia tota versatur").[15] For Ariosto only the stages associated with voluptuousness and
glory are of consequence: Ruggiero will not live to have an "aetas gravior," and
Ariosto appears to have no trust in a life *totally* given to contemplation, especially for
a ruler.

Generally speaking, the allegorizers strike us as most outlandish when retailing
these ages of man and most nearly acceptable when representing the *Aeneid* as a
drama of advancing moral crisis and progressive growth toward a destiny. Neoplatonic motifs governing the reading of the poem over many centuries of interpretation appear again and again. Thus, Bernard of Chartres provides the familiar
Platonic description of the human body as an "arx" of the mind, a "barracks" of the
will, a "suburbs" of the loins. Similarly, John of Salisbury asserts that Aeneas mediates between irascibility and concupiscence, and comes in the end to the "arcem
beatitudinis" of Italy, where his voyage is crowned by marriage and a kingdom—the
"embrace of Lavinia" ("dulces Laviniae complexus") and the "fatal kingdom of
Italy" ("fatale regnum Italiae"). Petrarch and Filelfo both refer directly to Plato as
they rehearse the threefold division of the human body into the citadel of the intellect, barracks of the will, outskirts of the passions. In short, the organs of the brain,

heart, and loins represent the triple potency of the human body for contemplation, for active engagement in the world, and for sensual indulgence; and it is Aeneas's problem to organize their disruption in the microcosm of his body before he can govern a territory in the great world.[16]

In the *Aeneid* errancy of physical movement is interpreted as errancy of moral direction. The insistence on the hierarchical organization of the body and on the theory of the microcosm and macrocosm accounts for the steady interpretation of the hero's journey from intemperance to contemplation, and only thereafter to his virtuous career as a soldier, ruler, and husband. The figure of navigation dominant in the *Aeneid* is easily exploitable as an image of spiritual transport, and the resting-places in which Aeneas breaks his journey are susceptible of extension into the "southern" and "northern" parts of the human body. These are constants in the allegorizations for a period of well over a millennium and a half. The major difference between the medieval and the Renaissance allegorizations consists in their attitude toward Aeneas: in the former, he is an Everyman in quest of personal beatitude; in the latter, more restrictedly, he is a type of the ideal Prince. In the world of the new learning, the *Aeneid* provides a pattern of perfection-through-action that is particularly pertinent to the lives of aristocrats and rulers. All through the Renaissance, indeed, speculation on the nature and duties of civil life went hand in hand with literary criticism of the *Aeneid* as a poem not only delightful in itself but also illustrative, at its deepest levels, of the prince's need to organize and order the warring, tripartite powers of his own human microcosm.

In Ariosto's day, the longest and most elaborate and the most distinguished criticism of the *Aeneid* lay in Cristoforo Landino's *Disputationes Camaldulenses,* one of the great works of the Florentine Academy. For Ariosto, it had the added luster of having been written as a eulogy for Lorenzo de' Medici, whose son Giovanni, the future Pope, was also a pupil of Gregorio da Spoleto (and was a friend, incidentally, from whom, at his elevation, favors were later expected by the poet, which were not forthcoming).[17] The *Disputationes Camaldulenses* is cast in the form of a Platonic dialogue dealing with the relative merits of the active and contemplative lives, and it involves Lorenzo, his brother Giuliano, Leone Battista Alberti, and several others in an extended argument on the question of the "summum bonum." The title of the work, alluding to Cicero's *Tusculan Disputations,* derives from its setting at the Abbey of Camaldoli, the site of the speeches, to which the participants had made a summer's day excursion. The setting itself is clearly employed in a symbolic manner, not only suggesting the contemplative summit of human life, always present as an ideal in the minds of these famous exemplars of the active life, but also marking a Christian advance over Cicero's discussion, at his villa, of merely pagan virtue. The discourse on activity and contemplation occupies the first two books. The last two books are an "unveiling" by Alberti of the hidden sense of the *Aeneid,* a work designed, as he reveals, to illustrate the various potencies of human existence. In his reading, Aeneas achieves salvation by moving from a morally rotten Troy, doomed by Paris's lustful theft of Helen, to his true destiny in Italy. In his progress, he negotiates all three of the lives and explores all three of the loves available to humans. He experiences, first, the feral life of the passions; next, the other extreme life of the contemplative; and finally (as a mean), the active life of the will. In sum, Aeneas learns to shun the appetitive existence of lust and avarice by fleeing Thrace and Carthage and avoiding Scylla and Charybdis. He submits himself next to a cognitive, contemplative descent into the underworld, lighting his way with the golden bough of wisdom. And he emerges to pursue his battles and to exercise his virtue in the world of heroic endeavor as a future soldier and ruler.[18] In effect, then, Landino interprets the *Aeneid,* in a manner very similar to Petrarch, as an epic of the three powers of the soul and its three concomitant loves, incarnated in the single figure of Aeneas in three successive guises. He is the wayward, visceral lover of Dido; the contemplative individual in search of truth and enlightenment who descends into Hades; and the active warrior engaged in a mission to subdue his opponents, win a kingdom, marry a princess, and establish his race. The three aspects of his journey center about three women—Dido, the Sybil, and Lavinia, representing abasement in sensual passion, cultivation of inner vision, and an entrance into the duties of a virtuous life in the world. In describing a classic pattern of sensual indulgence and contemplative withdrawal, both preparatory to the final active stage of a dynast's career, the story of a Trojan exile wandering to found a particular city also shadows the greater reality of a prince in quest of beatitude.

In Landino, as in Petrarch, Aeneas's journey is immediately contrasted to that of Paris, who, having made the wrong choice among the three goddesses of wisdom, ambition, and love, is doomed to perish in the fires of Troy.[19] Aeneas's is to be a different, more laborious course, as Vergil himself had intimated by the Herculean resonances of book 8. Accordingly, led by the celestial Venus, Aeneas departs from adulterous Troy ("id est ex corporearum voluptatum ardore se expediens") in an attempt to work the "Paris" aspect out of his nature; and though his journey is not immediately distinguished by "recta navigatione" (Vergil himself calls him a "secundum Paridem"), he nevertheless comes, finally and "post multos errores," to a state of wisdom in Italy ("in Italiam ad veram sapientiam pervenit").[20] Here, of course, the geography of the Aegean and the Mediterranean functions as a metaphor for the hierarchical arrangement of the human microcosm, and as long as the hero delays in the perilous regions of Troy, Thrace, Carthage, and Scylla and Charybdis ("venereas voluptates" and "simulacrum avariciae") he is understood to be indulging the feral instincts common to all humanity, allowing the animal passions to usurp a higher place than they are rightly allowed. Regularly alternating, the concupiscible and irascible passions dominate his existence and stand in the way of his destiny. It is because he is not immediately wise (a condition "aut nunque aut raro conceditur" to humans) that Aeneas wanders from island to island of the Aegean and Mediterranean and from country to country. Thus the journey to Thrace becomes (traditionally, as we have seen from Bernard of Chartres, and with assistance from Vergil, who calls it "litus avarum") a journey into the toils of avarice ("avaritiam symbolum"); for, says Landino, when we leave the regions of pleasure and desire and have not yet contracted the habit of virtue, we fall easily into the other kind of cupidity ("in aliam cupiditatem"), that of "desire to possess," "habendi libido."[21] The Ovidian and Boethian phrase is important: lust of the flesh is succeeded by lust of the world, "concupiscentia carnis" by "libido imperandi," "voluptas" by "vanagloria."[22] Tossed between the twin cupidities of lust and avarice, which exercise their fatal attraction on his lower nature, Aeneas makes his way to Carthage and Dido, to whom he is led by an Earthly Venus. Reminded of his imperial destiny by Mercury, he sets out from Africa for Italy; his arrival in Sicily figures his achievement of a state of prudence, for the island is conceived as "Ratio," or the lower reason, as opposed to Italy itself, which is represented by the intellect. On the mainland, finally, in the cave of the Sybil, he achieves a state of mental and moral clarification, a contemplative moment of rest. At this point, Aeneas has completed his internal initiation into the private virtues and has fitted himself for his public external role. The battles for the realm of Italy in books 7 through 12 follow as a matter of course, and it is there, in practical situations, that Aeneas demonstrates outwardly what he had been at pains to learn in his inmost soul.

In accord with the Renaissance precept that we must know in order to do, that theory precedes practice and that knowledge is anterior to action, Aeneas is a contemplative, a *knowing* man, before he is a dynast and ruler. The Renaissance *Aeneid* is therefore a complex imaginative rendering of the process whereby the disorders of the microcosm are subdued, its scattered and warring powers reunited into a hierarchy and painfully restored to their prelapsarian harmony. The whole process conforms to Plato's dictum, in book 4 of the *Republic,* that virtue lies not so much in man's external actions as on the way he acts within himself, and the rationale of the Platonic allegorization of the poem lies precisely in this source. The virtuous man is master of himself, puts things in order, harmonizes the three parts of his soul, and from a plurality becomes a unity capable of performing many actions. The proposed end of the process is to procure justice for the soul, to give to each of its parts its right and due in a hierarchical scheme.[23] Harmony is the end achieved, and in this context one sees the peculiar fitness of Maffeo Vegio's book 13, celebrating Aeneas's marriage, as the proper conclusion to the poem, ending the action with an emblem of concord.

The compliment involved in Landino's representing Lorenzo de' Medici as a major participant in the debate reveals once again that the *Aeneid* is truly a handbook for princes. From its pages they could learn that the duty of rulers was to prepare for their destiny, to learn self-government before preparing to rule. Theory and practice go hand in hand. In Aeneas, in Ruggiero, we see transformed into literature the same precept of knowledge and application pictorially frozen in Pedro Berruguete's portrait of Federigo da Montefeltro of Urbino: a vigilant warrior sitting fully armed in his study while reading a book—a model of contemplation and activity joined, and a living lesson to the child-heir at his knee, holding the scepter he will one day inherit.[24]

Byron gives clear evidence of knowing the traditional pattern of life's division into stages with its attendant temptations:

Love's the first net which spreads its deadly mesh;
Ambition, avarice, vengeance, glory glue
The glittering lime-twig of our latter days,
Where still we flutter on for pence or praise.[25]

Two centuries earlier, Herbert knew the escalating impediments, in successive stages of human existence, to happiness and fulfillment: "I know the wayes of Pleasure"; "I know the wayes of Honour"; "I know the wayes of Learning";[26] impediments located in the concupiscible, irascible, and intellectual parts of the human frame. And so too, several centuries earlier still, did Ferrara's chivalric poets work in clear consciousness of the validity of the old paradigm: Boiardo furnished Ruggiero with themes of love and glory ("impeto d'amore" and "desir di laude"), and Ariosto went on to dramatize the array of temptations inherent in both and the hero's need to overcome them. Having inherited from his predecessor the barely begun story of this newcomer with a Trojan ancestry, a descent from Hector, and an Achillean adolescence spent in hiding, Ariosto independently provided him with an Aeneas-like period of long probation, a very lively exemplary moral history, borrowed largely from both the literal and the interpreted Vergil. While Boiardo supplied the impetus, Ariosto's creation of a character working out the program of providential history even in his most rampantly egocentric actions has great consequences for the Carolingian romance. It extends its scope in a way that effectively marks the poet off from every one of his predecessors and approximates his poem decisively to classical epic. The commentator who wrote that Ariosto had raised the "bassezza" ("lowness") of romance on the wing of his genius knew whereof he spoke; he was not speaking merely of style or manner.[27]

Consideration of what Ariosto and Vergil have in common reveals that the impact on the *Furioso* of Latin epic is one of powerful and relevant action and idea in concert with one of splendid rhetoric and style. The *Aeneid* and the *Furioso* have some half dozen crucial similarities in their depiction of heroes. Both poems are dedicated to the praise of a dynasty; both offer their praises through the adventures of a hero, the appointed forefather of his race and founder of a particular city. Both heroes fall victim to sensual passion; both are compared with another warrior who succumbs to lust (Paris and Orlando); both conquer a foreign land and plant Houses there, leaving a young orphaned son to carry on the struggle; both fight a titanic battle against a great enemy of towering strength, whose conquest terminates each poem. In both poems, finally, the trials and the final victory of the hero over the assaults of fortune from without, and temptation and passion from within, afford a model of conduct to his descendants, to whom the hero stands as pattern and model.

The allegorists represented the fourth period of Aeneas's life as the one in which he was most severely tried by temptations, both of lust and avarice, and Ariosto employs them selectively for his own purposes. Unlike Boiardo, he is not at all interested in Ruggiero's infancy, boyhood, or adolescence. Instead Ariosto propels his hero into his assorted adventures at the crucial period of his life, "iuventa" or youth, precisely the fiery and untamed period when (according to both John of Salisbury and Landino) passion and appetite are at their strongest, manifesting themselves in the double pull of sensuality and the desire for glory, and in sins of lust, vainglory, and avarice. Ariosto gives clear proof of his familiarity with the idea in the proem (already quoted) to canto 25, exactly the canto in which Ruggiero moves fully into the second, more worldly stage of his temptations, after his experience with Alcina is over and he is done with riding on fanciful hippogriffs.

Oh gran contrasto in giovenil pensiero,
Desir di laude et impeto d'amore!
     (1.1–2)

Oh the great struggle in youthful minds between desire for praise and the impulse to love!

By canto 25, the "impeto d'amore" no longer tempts Ruggiero to excesses of carnal passion, though it has wrought havoc enough before it ceases definitively in canto 22. In cantos 22 through 25, a graver temptation, "desir di laude," assails him. Love of personal glory and (later) love of earthly power succeed the power of sensual love, and they are more subtle and insidious. Ruggiero's egotistical sense of personal honor keeps him among the pagan heroes surrounding Agramante and pits him increasingly and painfully against Christian champions like Rinaldo, Bradamante's own brother. Later, his love of earthly power—into which he is practically driven by Bradamante's mother's greed—hurls him into combat with the armies of the Eastern Emperor and puts him at the head of a band of rebellious subjects. Love and glory are the two great themes of epic, and Ariosto gives illustration enough of the disastrous ways in which they operate on his hero's nature. In several major episodes in which Ruggiero figures importantly, the poet concentrates the essence of Aeneas's wanderings, patterning romance movement on epic movement.

In their romance transformations the twin cupidities intervene as powerfully between Ruggiero and his destiny as they do between Aeneas and his destiny in the allegorized *Aeneid.* In the very first of his great transgressions (cantos 7–10), Ruggiero's sensual delay in the embraces of Alcina functions as an exact parallel to Aeneas's delinquency with Dido in book 4. Both their voyages are overshadowed by a sense of dynastic urgency to which profane love is an impediment; and when the good enchantress, Melissa, comes to reawaken him to his forgotten purpose, her rebuke of the effeminized Ruggiero, beringed and perfumed, studiously recalls Mercury's rebuke of the dandified Aeneas: if the hero remains unmoved by the loss of his own reputation and good fortune, let him not be unmoved by the descendants he thus cuts off from life and cheats of their great destiny. This is not all. As the Trojan hero is supposed to be transported by passions of lust and avarice, so the romantic descendant of Hector and Astyanax is borne away by those very same passions, in a natural escalation of temptations. Only the physical means are different: whereas erroneous navigation is the main figure for moral misdirection in the *Aeneid,* in the *Furioso* such movement is generally represented by the plunging and soaring, the "transports," of unbridled horses and hippogriffs, appropriate enough to a chivalric poem. There is also, supremely, the difference of laughter. While Aeneas seems to grow seriously into his destiny, Ruggiero provides one comic essay after another on the perverseness of the human will in his flight from Bradamante's love and the control of Providence.

As we have just noted, Ruggiero's initial problems concern the flesh. He is, in the beginning, youthfully concupiscent. In the latter part of the poem—in the middle, and particularly in the additions of 1532—he succumbs increasingly to what Landino and Simone Fornari both called "libido imperandi," a more serious disturbance of the appetite involving a greater misdirection of the irascible powers: here Ruggiero, emerging definitively as an embodiment of Plato's "second type of man," acts out his tendency to be "haughty of soul and covetous of honor" ("*hypselophron kai philotimos*").[28] Specifically, Ruggiero's errancy concerns his explosive, increasingly self-centered sense of personal honor, in which he desires at all costs to star in martial encounters (22.56–63, 90ff.). An even greater errancy and further evidence of his desire for supremacy is his attempt to attain a kingdom by wresting it, with desperate and jealous force, from the Emperor's son, Leo. Here again the *Aeneid* makes an impact. Both Aeneas and Ruggiero have exigent and imperious mothers-in-law, Amata and Beatrice, who are not amused by valorous but poverty-stricken exiles who turn up as suitors for their daughters. Ruggiero's unhappy situation is a comic rendition of Aeneas's unhappy situation: the landless soldier desiring the daughter of stiff-necked aristocrats who want a better connection than he offers. But there is a difference in their situations as well. Aeneas moves in a straight line from lust to contemplation to a life of fruitful activity in gaining, through martial means, the kingdom that he is finally to rule and whose princess he is to marry. He proceeds to acquire a kingdom with the assurance that the gods want him to have it, that it is the will of heaven; and in the pastoral interlude of his visit to Evander, he is specifically warned against "habendi libido" by his host, explicitly urged to take Hercules as a model in humility. He receives this warning with appropriate gravity, and Vergil represents him moving toward his possession of the land with assurance and poise, apparently heedful of Evander's warning, "Aude, hospes, contemnere opes" (8.364)—"Dare, my guest, to despise riches." In action, by contrast, Ruggiero is almost never admirable as "pius Aeneas" is here and generally elsewhere, because Ariosto follows the allegorical interpretation rather than the literal surface of the *Aeneid,* and there sins of lust and avarice are repeatedly attributed to him in the first four books, sins characteristic of a certain period of life. Hence they are also attributed, though far more protractedly and with a kind of Augustinian inevitability and interconnection, to Ruggiero by Ariosto.

Ariosto can follow Vergil closely, as in the Dido-Alcina episode, or he can (more frequently) assert his independence and use his materials in a new and more complex construction. In total contrast to Aeneas, Ruggiero is driven by a lust to conquer and possess: in Boethian terms, "amor ardet habendi" (2.met.5.26). He moves from juvenile lust to contemplation on a hermit's island to a swift reversal, enacting, in his rage and disappointment of Bradamante's hand, a perversion of military might in seeking a kingdom that will merely give him titles and riches, but that, in any case, he cannot hold. His martial triumph is purely personal and momentary, motivated by the flash and outbreak of a savage mood, appeasing only the flaring assertion of his will. As a Christian, newly converted in canto 41, he is now, in canto 45, in even more perilous spiritual circumstances, for Ariosto's arrangement of the temptations differs from that of the Vergilian allegorizers. Whereas lust and avarice operate alternatively and repeatedly on Aeneas's character, Ruggiero experiences them in succession and hierarchically: for him the temptation of the world exercises a more baneful pull than that of the flesh, and it leads, climactically, to temptations of pride and despair. Ruggiero wins his kingdom, but his final problems are those of self-satisfaction and overweening pride in having triumphed. His very confidence in his own powers will cast him into a dungeon at the apparent climax of his worldly fortunes (45.5), and the experience of the terror of death and a conviction of mortality finally begin to shadow his pride of life. The recognition of death as the end of life is, or should be, the beginning of philosophy, but even here, while faithfully (for honor's sake) submitting his stubborn neck to the yoke that his promise to Leo places on him, he sinks still deeper. For Leo, who has saved Ruggiero's life, contrives a scheme whereby Ruggiero, the stronger warrior, will win the unwilling Bradamante's hand for Leo; will fight in disguise and in place of Leo, against her, with the lady herself as the prize. This is a painful test that plays profoundly upon his sense of honor, but a former weakness turns out to be an unexpected strength. The proposal is laden with ironies and dilemmas of all kinds, and for Ruggiero not to rebel or renege at this point involves the harshest trial of his ability to master himself and govern his passion. Yet the sacrifice, costing not less than everything, is one that Ruggiero, because of his sense of honor, undertakes at once without hesitation or demurral, and without revealing his interest in the situation. Though proceeding to his work in agony, his only recourse is to play his part manfully, fulfill the bargain, encounter and conquer Bradamante in battle only to yield her to another—and then think at once of suicide. All his struggles have produced only ashes; the third and lowest stage of his moral career is now upon him. Despair, a deeper version of the sin of pride, brings him a passionate longing for death to end his misery and draws him to the verge of suicide in a deep dark wood (45.84–92). The ever-threatening forest surges in once more to engulf the city-in-idea, moving to confound history, and the moment is fraught with suspense and irony.

Yet here, finally, after so long and harrowing a journey, Providence and his author-tormentor join to release him by suddenly providing a deus ex machina of information to clear up all the confusion. Indeed it seems time Ruggiero should be relieved of perturbation. He has, after all, come a long way from Boiardo's simple warrior in his experience and suffering, and in the end he demonstrates a willingness to sacrifice even his love, his only happiness in the world, to the demands of conscience and honor. In his last extremity a comic righting of confusion, apparently plucked out of nowhere, rapidly and rightly ensues. For there is a clear sense throughout that Ruggiero's will contains an element radically and perpetually averted from or recalcitrant to grace, that Providence releases him because, driven into the most trying circumstances imaginable, he is, though exhausted and weary, still ungovernable, still flailing. For all his struggles, Boiardo's *jeune sauvage* remains Ariosto's Augustinianly incorrigible *homme* more than *moyen sensuel,* in whose very victories over himself further defeats are cruelly but naturally commingled. Now, at last, his capacities as well as his limitations have clearly been established. His speech of submission is as brief and concentrated as it could possibly be—a stunned acknowledgment of his moral dependence that summarizes the poem's wisdom ("ordina l'uomo, e Dio dispone," 46.35). Hence, forbearing Providence prefers to draw music from a damaged instrument rather than cast the instrument aside and so stays his suicidal hand by a timely intervention. Ruggiero, then, does not "achieve" (much less *merit*) release either from sin or from his civic destiny: they are thrust on him freely and at a chosen moment, in wholly mysterious a fashion, and in vivid dramatization of the idea that man is saved by powers not his own. The comic poet's deus ex machina mimics the unaccountable release of Providence. Virtue is feeble, and heaven must stoop to relieve the sinner. The event provides a last striking illustration of the sovereign and irrefutable Will of Divine Providence, of what Milton called its "unsearchable dispose" of human fortunes.[29] And in this way, perhaps, Ariosto, suiting the imperfect human who seeks glory and love to a destiny in an imperfect state of life, indicates the limited nature of the active life in the world of politics and rule.

Tinged with wan, rather melancholy laughter, the rescue of Ruggiero from this final crisis arouses all kinds of questions. Why now rather than before, why to him and not to others, and, indeed, why at all? Yet even to phrase the question is to try to take on the mystery of things and be God's spies; or to miss the nature of the *Furioso,* whose form and essence are that of comedy. Questions like these are questions that the narrator perpetually forbids as issuing from a sense of purely earthly merit and logic; as well inquire into the different gifts accorded humans at birth. "On whom it will, it will; / On whom it will not, not."[30] Not all humans are rescued from self-destruction by the deliberate intrusion of Providence; neither are they all selected from the beginning for a princely destiny. The end providentially appointed for Ruggiero is known from the first, and at the conclusion it is inexorably, if unimaginably, fulfilled; paradoxically, less because Ruggiero has sought violently to bring it about than because it comes as a free gift in spite of his actions. All the space between the prophecy and the attainment is filled by the divagations of his appetitive will, humorous in its beginning errancies, decidedly less so as it hardens in its hungers. In the end, nevertheless, that very will is made matter for laughter by being recognized as only one among interconnected millions, all evolving, in concert and by some mysterious process, the design of a higher Will. The heroic furies of his last adventure get scaled down to comedy, and so Ruggiero is rescued from ever-impending tragedy.

Ever close to tragedy, Ruggiero negotiates a poem-long career of bondage in prisons, four great ones in all: Atlante's, Alcina's, Atlante's again, and finally Leo's. All the imprisonments, gilded or ghastly, are self-chosen, for his career keeps bringing him repeatedly to crossroads, and invariably he chooses the wrong fork in the path. Here again the influence of Bembo is unmistakable: "But sometimes, when a traveler who has reached a fork in the road selects the wrong way, believing that it is the right one, he will go further and further from his destination, the more he hastens to approach it."[31] For Ruggiero, the first wrong turn leads inevitably to another wrong turn and to the arrival at another and yet another crossroads opening out from the wrong branch of the one before it. In this career of choices he is invariably Paris rather than Hercules. Far, then, from being a creature who "never puts a foot wrong," he almost never puts a foot right.

Professor Murrin is instructive here, stating, "Landino's Aeneas is a hero constantly at the crossroads, choosing between opposed alternatives, often deceptive. The symbol for his situation and for the whole procedure recurs constantly in the *Camaldulensian Dialogues*: the Pythagorean Y, man choosing morally as well as intellectually."[32] So, too, for Ruggiero the road begins to fork immediately, at the very beginning of his tale; will he go left or right, will it be Reason or Passion, Logistilla or Alcina (6.60)? Influenced strongly by Landino's Vergil, this represents also the influence of Bembo superimposed on Boiardo, for in the *Asolani,* Gismondo, "having raised two of his fingers like a fork," had graphically instructed his courtly listeners in the meaning of the Y image: "The ancient philosophers divide our soul, my ladies, in two parts. In one they place reason, under whose firm guidance the soul moves along a quick and certain path; to the other they assign those perturbations which mislead the soul into the most doubtful and abandoned byways."[33] His road having forked (and Ruggiero, against Astolfo's sage advice, having chosen to be diverted from Logistilla to Alcina), it forks again at canto 22.46ff., presenting a choice between a decisive rescue and a dangerous occasion for Ruggiero's personal glory. The latter wins out. A second wrong choice having again resulted in a separation from Bradamante and a deferral of conversion, the road forks for yet a third time at 38.7, when, to satisfy the demands of personal honor, Ruggiero takes the branching road to Arles and Agramante's camp, shunning the one leading to Charlemagne's host, and to Bradamante and baptism. And, after another moral debacle, a torturingly complex final dilemma now makes the crossroads metaphorical and mental, rather than literal: will he discharge his debt of gratitude for his life to Leo, undertake to fight Bradamante and win her in combat for his rival, bringing despair and death by suicide on himself, or—but here any dereliction from the only possible choice is so unthinkable as to be immediately rejected even before it takes shape as a thought:

Ben che da fier dolor, tosto che questa
parola gli ha detta, il cor ferir si senta,
che giorno e notte e sempre lo molesta,
sempre l'affligge e sempre lo tormenta,
e vegga la sua morte manifesta;
pur non è mai per dir che se ne penta;
che prima ch'a Leon non ubbidire,
mille volte, non ch'una, è per morire.
        (45.57)

Even though he felt his heart stricken with grief as soon as he heard himself make that promise, a grief that molests him day and night, always afflicts him, always torments him, and though he sees his death clear and plain, never was he about to confess that he regretted his promise. Rather than disobey Leo, he would have died, not once but a thousand times.

Honor is still his madness, though now, by some mysterious process hidden deep in the nature of things, his addiction to its potentially good fascinations contains within itself the promise of his redemption: honor keeps him faithful to his vow, honor finally is his means of transcending his ego and allowing the claims of another to whom he is in debt for his life. This profound interconnection of weakness and strength, of blindness and insight, of advance through descent, so reminiscent of T. S. Eliot's Becket, who moves to the same triadic pattern of Flesh-World-Devil, is, essentially, Ariosto's favorite way of looking at the world and assessing its gains.[34] Each decision draws Ruggiero into the toils of another, still more difficult decision, and nowhere does Ariosto's harping on the Boethian and Bembistic blindness of human judgment find a more tribulated example. Pitched between extremities, Ruggiero constantly finds solutions that are only provisional. Still, by some mysterious process in which he appears to sink deeper and deeper into dereliction, his course is progressive rather than hopeless: Providence merely has to reach lower to seize him. At the very last, after a hard lesson in self-sacrifice and the taming of his unmastered will, Heaven suddenly takes pity, the knot is loosened, his beloved is restored, and his marriage follows. In the *Furioso,* as in the *Aeneid,* though in how remarkably different a setting and form, and by how strange an actor, the triple struggles in the flesh, the will, and the mind are all dramatized before the happy conclusion. Significantly, then, the poem ends (again like the manipulated *Aeneid*) with a marriage feast, a "banqueting together" that gives literal expression to the etymology of the word *comedy.*

Perhaps we should now recall that this romantic form of the *Aeneid* is something that Spenser also inherited, since the poem was conventionally read in its thirteen-book form throughout the sixteenth century. The version of Twyne and Phaer continues the tradition established in Britain by Caxton's *Aeneydos,* as does that of Gavin Douglas, not only in that both conclude with Maffeo Vegio's *Thirteenth Book* as a matter of course, but also because they perceive the *Aeneid* as an allegory of human striving crowned, in marriage, with symbolic fulfillment. The allegorical tradition of over a thousand years may be encapsulated by drawing two unlikely figures together, Bishop Fulgentius and John Harington. Of Aeneas's arrival at the marriage state, the sixth-century allegorist, relying on the usual fantastic etymology, writes, "Denique nunc et uxorem petit Laviniam, id est laborum viam."[35] In his commentary to his translation of Ariosto's final canto, the Elizabethan critic expresses the same idea about Ruggiero: "In the many lets that Rogero hath ear he can get Bradamant, the allegorie is continued from the beginning to the end of the whole work, to shew how hardly a man comes to a true contentment and peaceable state in this world (which is figured in the match with Bradamant) man having stil enemies bodily or ghostly to hinder or interrupt the same."[36] Vergilian epic and Ariostan and Spenserian romantic epic all come to their conclusion in marriage, all have the same conclusion in comedy. In all three, marriage has the same value of harmony achieved and concord established. After all the errors of the past, united lovers bear in their loins the promise of a new, regenerated society. Strengthened by hardship and prepared for the future, they enter at last the active life of rule, "laborum viam."

The continuity and transformations of a great idea are always fascinating. Vergil stands as the great originator for his invention of the figures of Aeneas and Lavinia, to whose union the twelfth-century romancer of the *Eneas* provided a preliminary impassioned courtship, and a fifteenth-century humanist a proper conclusion in marriage, as well as a symbolic reading of the wedding. Ripe for renewal, Aeneas and Lavinia reappear transformed into Ruggiero and Bradamante. As mere names they appear first in Strozzi, assume delightful characters in Boiardo, and (seeming to grow irrevocably older in a steadily darkening experience of the world) plunge into a prolonged and turbulently passionate existence in Ariosto. In a last phase Ruggiero and Bradamante are re-created by Spenser, who turns them into embodiments respectively of chastity and justice, Bradamante especially being splendidly revivified in Britomart with no essential alteration of her nature.

There is something unusually exciting in seeing Ruggiero, this newcomer from romance, reenacting the moral progress of the great hero of Roman epic. Two Italian civilizations are bridged by the labors of poets and scholars, demonstrating a changeful continuity of Latin civilization over a millennium and a half. In the allegorized *Aeneid,* poetic materials otherwise widely dispersed came to Ariosto assembled into a unity and with all the authority of one of the foremost Neoplatonists of the age. Landino's magisterial treatise incorporated into one extensive

treatment the debate between the active and contemplative lives, the tripartite organization of the body, the mirroring of the macrocosm by the microcosm, the evil
choice of Paris and the virtuous choice of Hercules, the concept of the Heavenly and
Earthly Venuses, and the image of life as a journey. All formed part of the criticism
and interpretation of the Roman dynastic epic Ariosto was attempting to rival, and
they were issues of unmistakable immediacy and importance to his society; quite
appropriately all found a place in the *Furioso*. From the *Aeneid*, we may say, Neoplatonic ideas flowed in on the *Furioso* as naturally as they had from the *Innamorato*.
Further, just as the *Furioso* aimed at being more than the *Innamorato*, it aimed also at
being more than the *Aeneid*. Ruggiero negotiates all three lives and loves like his
Trojan predecessor, but his "progress" (that is, his regressions), both frequent and
fatal, is arranged according to a distinctly Augustinian pattern. While he is the
natural man through the larger part of his Ariostan adventures—a pagan voluptuary
at first and afterward a misguided pagan soldier in search of honor—he is, near the
end, from canto 41 on, a baptized Christian in the throes of despair. This is an
important divergence from Vergil. It has led to repeated misinterpretation, and it
deserves some scrutiny.

Ruggiero's baptism, so long delayed, comes about as a mere by-product of an
accident at sea, and he is saved from drowning, apparently, by a complacent Providence, acceding to his importunate but conditional prayer (41.48–49). Badly frightened, he promises immediate conversion if rescued from death. As if by a miracle,
the poet says, he gains new strength and strikes out for shore, arriving on the island
of a holy hermit who first instructs, then baptizes him. The framework of the
episode is pastoral, a very different pastoral in quality from the sensual love-pastoral
of Angelica and Medoro. The "pastor" who presides here is altogether foreign to
the shepherds who complacently help the two lovers to consummate their romantic
passion.[37] He derives very clearly from Bembo's pious old hermit, who teaches
Lavinello the highest of the loves in book 3 of *Gli Asolani*.[38] Ruggiero's hermit is a
virtuous old man who happily endures the discomforts of a saintly life, dieting on
fruits from the trees and drinking pure water, as Bembo's older hermit, similarly
primitive, dines on wild berries, roots, and water. Ariosto's hermit knows Ruggiero
at once, exactly as Bembo's hermit mysteriously knows Lavinello, though he has
never seen him previously. Both hermits have been divinely forewarned about their
visitors, Ruggiero's in a vision, Bembo's in a dream; and both visitors have been
specifically directed to this pastoral instruction by the will of heaven ("non senza
volere degli idii qui sono," says Lavinello). Providence interferes fruitfully in the life
of each man, though more powerfully and violently in that of the shipwrecked
Ruggiero, who cannot escape, the hermit tells him plainly, the "lunga man" ("long
reach") of the Deity.

Bembo's description of Lavinello's education into the Christian mysteries is
charmingly straightforward and utterly untinged by laughter, but then he is dealing
with a one-dimensional "character," a docile Lavinello who is not represented in

significant action. But Ariosto has a Ruggiero on his hands; Ruggiero's past presses in on him with his known penchant for apparent docility followed by sudden, violent perversity, and so the episode of his conversion is, however true to Bembo, purely Ariostan in its deeper meaning and further irony. Ariosto can afford to be brief in detailing the process of instruction. What the hermit teaches Ruggiero is what Bembo's hermit taught Lavinello at length—the Ptolemaic order of the cosmos and the duty of man to be orderly within that order, by rising from the material to the immaterial by means of a very Boethian ladder of love.[39] Ariosto's laughter is not at all directed at this, but rather at Ruggiero's swift reception of it *in theory,* and he foresees (in a very short while) Ruggiero's utter rejection of its application *in action.* In fact, the poet's laughter begins much earlier, at the very beginning of the passage that brings Ruggiero to the hermit's island. His commentary on the hero's near-drowning (that he had made light of being baptized in clear water, and now he was being baptized in bitter sea water, 41.47) is of the kind that usually leads Ariosto's readers astray, leading away from the context to fantasies about Ariosto's personal skepticism. If Ruggiero is driven to his conversion rather than arriving at it by conviction, and if his salvation comes on him all too easily, that too is part of Ariosto's design, and the reader must enlarge the frame to account for the further complexities of the narrative. Perhaps the worst mistake is to imagine that the episode is self-contained in its irony and needs no further explanation. No more than his readers does Ariosto trust such a conversion, but he is not merely being "ironic" about conversion itself, or what it implies. He is, instead, as always and from the first, ironic about human judgment—"Ecco il giudicio uman come spesso erra"—and specifically about Ruggiero's inclination to suppose that now, by this simple gesture of a few days' visit with a hermit, all is put right, and he can expect to marry his heiress and embark on his state. But to that blindness, as to everyone else's, Ariosto opposes another sight, a "provision" that overwatches the tunnel gropings of mere mortals: and Ruggiero arrives in France, full of desire and hope, to find Bradamante's parents standing in his way with a more appealing, richer suitor for their daughter's hand. His acute sense of his own worth suffers an unexpected check, and he erupts in fury against the innocent Leo, plotting his murder and the robbery of his domains. This is scarcely the action one expects from a newly baptized Christian, but perhaps one is wrong to expect anything at all from mere submission to a sacrament in exigent circumstances. Far from requiring mere intellectual and verbal assent, Reason and Revelation both require demonstration in action; without that confirmation they remain a kind of "bookish theoric," "mere prattle without practice," conventional and unavailing "lip-wisdom." Ariosto never wearies of dramatizing this idea of human frailty. Ruggiero moves from conversion to murder as, earlier, even in pious pilgrimage to Jerusalem, amid the shrines and tabernacles, Grifone had broken from pious devotion with his companions to follow the worthless Orrigille (15.99ff.). But civilizations do not stand on the sandhill of a lover's private appetite, and Ruggiero is to be a maker of cities; so he goes on to another and harder kind of learning. In Ariosto's world there is never any cause for optimism or complacency about human nature in action. There is no cause whatever for his readers complacently to attribute such complacency to him.[40]

Ariosto does not trust Ruggiero's easy conversion to faith, as he did not previously trust (indeed, he mocked it) Ruggiero's easy conversion to reason. The very same authorial laughter and irony broke out when Ruggiero had departed from Logistilla. To date no reading of the *Furioso* recognizes that Ruggiero undergoes not merely one but *two* courses of instruction—one in reason, another in revelation—in two widely separated parts of the poem, and that they are purposefully symmetrical and strictly connected. Pointedly, both courses of instruction take place on islands, when Ruggiero is in a state of momentary repose, freed from the vertiginous flights of the hippogriff or rescued from the waves and floods of passion. Both islands present opportunities for deliberation and choice. The first episode, the first of the great seminal allegories of the *Furioso,* marking it off decisively from Boiardo's *Innamorato,* brings Ruggiero under the instruction of Logistilla and her handmaids, Fronesia, Dicilla, Sophrosina, and Andronica, the four Cardinal Virtues underlying the life of reason, all five originating in book 7 of Plato's *Republic.* The second episode brings him under the supervision of a Christian hermit, who incarnates a more transcendent set of virtues, the theological ones, and who initiates him into the mysteries of the Christian faith. Both episodes are constructed on the very same pattern: instruction, too easy assent, departure, immediate testing, and immediate fall are the exactly repeated progression in Ruggiero's two encounters with figures of moral and religious authority. He receives his instruction in the Christian mysteries with the same suspicious docility and speed with which he accepted that of Logistilla on bridling the hippogriff; and the reader well remembers the results in his swiftly attempted rape of Angelica. For Ariosto knew well (what many readers find it difficult to conceive of his knowing) that virtue has both a theoretical and a practical aspect, that both "theta" and "pi," theory and practice, are emblems on the gown of Lady Philosophy. Logistilla and the hermit provide the intellectual bases for moral conduct, one philosophical, the other transcendent and religious: the rest is up to Ruggiero to put into action, and he fails signally and dismally immediately on departing from both. In the first instance, after blithely swearing friendship forever with the figure of Reason (10.68), he succumbs instantly to lust for Angelica, the hippogriff significantly slips the bridle that Logistilla had fashioned for it, and her instruction in the art of control bears a sorry fruit. In the second instance, Ruggiero leaves the hermit's island, at once arrives in France to hear that Bradamante's parents have thwarted his plans for marriage by objecting to his poverty, and the result is his enraged, impassioned flight eastward to kill Leo and seize a crown by conquest. Disasters accumulate from that moment, and in Leo's dungeon he touches the lowest point of his fortunes to date.

Because Ruggiero is called to be a ruler, his particular and distinguishing sphere is that of human action. Yet it is precisely in action—in transposing the precepts of reason and the doctrines of faith into practical situations, into *works*—that he repeatedly fails. Peaceable and willing to lend an ear in a condition of rest, vital and dynamic but thoughtless in action, he is increasingly made aware of the gulf between the two parts of his nature, and it is a necessary and valuable lesson. A growing conviction of his unpreparedness to function properly in actual, not theoretical, situations is borne remorselessly in on him, and if he appears to be so perturbed and entangled by an external force contriving difficulties for him, it is because he has so very much to learn before the exacting rule of others is committed to his care. Ruggiero always finds it easy to slip backward into unregenerate action, evading the consequences of his instruction; yet he does not evade the omnipotent vision that presides over human blindness, of whose power the hermit is a reliable witness. Ariosto's imitation of Bembo is no secularizing satire of his friend but a great artistic deepening of the *Asolani*'s fundamental concepts about reason and revelation. The validity of neither reason nor grace is violated because *Ruggiero* rejects them; they are values that the poet asserts, as we shall see shortly, as necessities for all human action if it is not to have lamentable consequences; and another and less worldly character than Ruggiero is called on to embody the truth that reason and faith work harmoniously together.

This symmetry between an early and a late episode in Ruggiero's career helps us to see something essential about the former one, and to correct a continued misapprehension about the nature of Logistilla. The moment in which Ruggiero, so soon after waving goodbye to the lady, swoops down on the hippogriff to rape a naked Angelica is often the most misunderstood moment in the *Furioso*. In both old and recent critical mythology, this represents the sophisticated, subversive Ariosto's puncturing of the long humanist allegory he had so carefully constructed, and his turning of his irony even against his own art and learning, to say nothing of that of his contemporaries and predecessors, even unto Plato. Ariosto, we are assured, is utterly anti-allegorical and comfortingly on the side of warmth and passion.[41] This is altogether naive, the product of reading for lyrical moments; matters are never so simple in Ariosto, precisely because they are part of an extended treatment. In representing Ruggiero so suddenly, so hilariously *bouleversé* by Angelica's charms and throwing philosophy, along with his clothing, to the winds, Ariosto demonstrates the same suspicion of merely pagan humanism that writers had been demonstrating for centuries; the kind that Fielding later made the butt of his humor in the person of the schoolmaster, Mr. Square, who, though his name recalls the iconographic symbol for rational self-control over Fortune's wheel, and though he discourses eloquently on the moral values of the pagan philosophers, finds nature breaking through his Stoic crust, propelling him to an undignified appearance in wanton Molly's bed.[42] With similar rapidity, the newly converted Ruggiero ("converted" to Plato's reason, that is) frenziedly dismounts from the hippogriff and prepares to climb aboard "another mount" (10.114). Reason unaided by revelation provides only the most tenuous of holds, and Ariosto beckons to yet another journey ending on a farther shore. In this respect, a comparison with the *Aeneid* allegories will make things even clearer. Ruggiero's voyage between Alcina's palace of lust and luxury and Logistilla's fortress of self-knowledge and control is a paradigm of Aeneas's journey between Dido's Carthage and the island of Sicily, the "ratio," or lower reason. From there Aeneas moves swiftly and with linear directness to his contemplative moment in Italy, figuring "intellect." For Ruggiero both the long-protracted progress to that moment and the aftermath are troubled and agonized. The Alcina-Logistilla allegory therefore imitates Neoplatonic Vergilian allegory in giving geographical location to the rational and passionate parts of the human body, and Ariosto's island figures the chaos of the disordered microcosm, appetite and will in league and united in opposition to reason.

In Logistilla, Ariosto both pays tribute to and indicates the limitations of the power of human reason, man's highest faculty. There is no doubt about the superior status Ariosto accords Logistilla. The peaceful, Athena-like figure in a warring triad of sisters undoubtedly functions as a standard in the poem. She is all that raises men above the beasts they become in subservience to the passions her two evil sisters inspire, and she embodies the wisdom of the enlightened pagans in their praise of the life of the mind. She is especially connected with Socrates and Plato, for her palace is a place primarily of intellectual activity, where the visitor learns to scrutinize himself in her jeweled walls, *knowing himself* to his very soul ("se stesso conoscendosi") in obedience to the old precept, "gnothi sauton."[43] The very Greekness of her name is Logistilla's glory; but it is also a recognition of her limitation and lack of transcendence, an assertion of the need to look beyond her, for though she appears to operate independently, it is only by relation to the world of faith and revelation that she has any power at all. The technique of giving Greek names and attributes to worthy but imperfect beings representative of moral states is not limited to Ariosto alone. Erasmus also wrote serious comedy about Utopians who live in a state of imperfect reason, in readiness for revelation to crown it; and Spenser gave the name Medina—"meden agan," "nothing too much" or the Golden Mean—to the mistress of a house of pagan temperance where Guyon arrives much too early in his career, revealing that for a final understanding of that virtue he must look higher than to the enlightened pagans.[44] Plato in Ariosto, Aristotle in Spenser—neither represents a final resting-place for a Christian hero; both poets know enough to look beyond reason to the realm of grace that illumines the intellect.

Logistilla's ideal of control over the passions, imaged in her art of bridling the hippogriff, forms Ariosto's commentary on the limitations not only of the classical moralists but also of the classical poets, including his beloved Vergil. No Christian, for example, could be as sure of the simple power of reason as Seneca was in the *De ira*,[45] an open invitation to presumption. Christianity simply requires more; hence the richly double representation of the reasoning faculty in the *Furioso*. As a venerable thing-in-itself, man's loftiest power, reason, figured in a virtuous Logistilla, is a staid and decorous creature, besieged but steadfast. But as a thing-in-man, reason is always, in Ariosto, a volatile and flighty possession, not only in Ruggiero's case but also in the cases of Orlando and Astolfo. The poet's moon, as we shall see, is littered with the fled wits of mortals who think themselves wise, and Professor Wiggins's speculation that "Logistilla" is a pun on a mere "drop" ("stilla") of reason ("logos") is an inspired suggestion.[46] Ariosto's recognition of reason's essential power and of humankind's incapacity to use it—its tendency to drop the reins and let the horse fly to the forest or leap into the air—is a constant in his poetry. In his suspicion of what reason can accomplish he anticipates Swift, who also knew something about the lore of horses, and who had an even more deadly view of total reliance on rationality. Mere self-control is never the final step in the *Furioso,* for the simple reason that every end in the poem is shaped by a divinity, that it alone confers the power to exercise that control, and that Providence itself, through various mouthpieces, asserts itself as a sine qua non.

The *Furioso* differs radically from the *Aeneid,* as we shall see, by asserting the primacy of grace and representing the world as operating perpetually in the unblinking sight of the divine eye, in subjection to beneficent if mysterious Providence rather than, as in Vergil, to fate. This conception most clearly distinguishes Ariosto's epic from its pagan predecessor, reveals the author's attitude to the cosmos he creates in his poetry, and governs his representation of passionate humans in headlong action. Ruggiero's troubled pilgrimage will run until he can run no more, but his recurring sense of self-sufficiency, of wanting to achieve all his exploits unaided and alone, with his own strength and for his own glory, is at once one of the most risible aspects of his character and one of the most profoundly troublesome impediments in his progress to his destiny. Rebellious and impatient to the end, he is in the purview and maintenance of Providence, along with all the others, from first to last.

In so representing him, Ariosto absorbs and transcends both Vergil and Boiardo. He gives ample testimony to the belief that, while epics successively generate other epics, the latest in the line invariably extends the vision and meaning of its predecessors. The *Furioso* is not a classicizing mastodon like Petrarch's *Africa* or Trissino's *Italia liberata dai Goti,* nor mere panegyric in the simpler mode of Filelfo's *Erculeja* or Strozzi's *Borsiade.* Rather, with unerring instinct, it infuses the lively narrative traditions of Ferrara with the Neoplatonic epideictic traditions of Florence, and it lives with a triumphant life that those fastidious and wrong-headed humanists might envy. Eschewing ponderousness, it does not therefore abandon itself to folly. In the light of the *Aeneid,* the *Furioso* could not afford to be a trivial though spirited jest of nearly 40,000 lines, nor could the progenitor of the Estensi be represented complacently as a youth who likes to fly around on winged horses, dropping down occasionally for the quick rape of a naked enchantress. His story, like the Roman model on which it was based, functions as a *delightful* mirror and manual for princes. Unlike that model, it was intended for Christian princes for whom belief in Providence was an article of faith; and for profoundly influential cultural reasons, it wore a lighter demeanor. Cast in the transcendent mode of Neoplatonic comic art, it plays seriously and tells truth with a laugh.

6

A Clown's Redemption

Herculean Heroics and the Triumphs of Wit

Questi [Astolfo] che è fondamentalmente creazione del B., campione senza macchia carico di umorismo e quasi parodia cavalleresca . . . passando in seguito tra le mani dell' Ariosto perdette molto della sua peculiarità personale in vista di quel supremo armonico livellamente che è la legge del *Furioso.*

Astolfo, fundamentally the creation of Boiardo, a spotless champion bursting with humor and almost a parody of chivalry, afterward, in passing into the hands of Ariosto, lost much of his personal individuality due to that supreme harmonic leveling which is the law of the *Furioso.*
     Aldo Scaglione, *Orlando Innamorato*

This Duke of England in the Italian romances played the part of an adventurous vainglorious cavalier, eminent for courtesy and courage.
     J. A. Symonds, *The Renaissance in Italy*

Astolfo is the chief focus of the Ariostan aesthetic of *serio ludere* and *ridentem dicere verum,* and he represents as unlikely a choice as could be imagined, proof again of the originality of Ariosto's genius. In the cases of Orlando and Ruggiero, Boiardo had provided hints enough for a continuation of their lives but, in selecting Astolfo for the shockingly prominent part he gives him, Ariosto was beholden to nothing but the riches of his own educated, highly flexible imagination. Nothing in the *Furioso* is more startling than the ease with which, in Astolfo's travels, the previously earthbound Carolingian romance suddenly opens out in two directions to encompass the triple landscapes of classical epic—underworld and heavens, and the world of men between them; nothing, perhaps, but Ariosto's choice, from among the multitudinous personnel of the *Innamorato,* of *Astolfo* to negotiate the enormously expanded reaches of this new poetic world. In so choosing, the poet adds another dimension to the poem's spectrum of loves and lives.

To the modern reader, especially in English, the *Furioso*'s Astolfo is bound to appear a character like any other in the poem, to be accepted at face value. But this failure to measure him against his long past history as a stock character[1] effectively effaces the way in which Ariosto defies and devastates a romance tradition, recasting it in his own terms and elevating the merely comic or romantic into something more deeply meaningful. We look in vain for anything in his history up to and including Boiardo to support the notion that Astolfo was "eminent for courtesy and courage," or that he was "senza macchia." Braggart and coward, he is completely reoriented by Ariosto. The difficulty he always experiences in managing his "cav-

allo" in Pulci and Boiardo is given a metaphorical extension in his steady management of the hippogriff that Ruggiero, by contrast, so signally fails to control. The
converted Astolfo is truly "chivalric": the uncomplicated buffoon who once could
not sit his horse does the best job of controlling the best but most refractory "horse"
of all, the one that Neoplatonism saw figured in the flesh. Hence the *Furioso* gives us
the challenging oddity of an Astolfo who, having so often fallen from his mount and
having fallen prey to Alcina, now never once falls again, either from a horse or into
sensual abandon. In fact, he is that distinct rarity in the *Furioso,* an apparently ascetic
kind of lover, having no woman like Bradamante, Alcina, or Angelica to attract or
beguile him. In fact, after his fall to Alcina, he seems ready enough to be steadily
faithful to her sister Logistilla, the embodiment of reason.

In the case of Astolfo's first appearance (6.26–53), Ariosto makes forceful
demands on the reader's memory and understanding by recalling in detail the paladin's last appearance in the *Innamorato* at 2.13, a moment where, heedless of the
advice of his friends, he rides aboard a whale sent to entrap him by the enchantress
Alcina and is borne mysteriously away, vanishing forever from the pages of Boiardo's
poem. Over twenty cantos later, in canto 6 of the *Furioso,* he reenters the action, but
only as a voice speaking from a tree, and not a very recognizable voice at that.
Astolfo's name is very deliberately withheld for a long while, a technique of belated
identification and postponed revelation that Ariosto employs for several other
important figures when wrenching them away from their Boiardan characterizations and endowing them with very different, more symbolic characteristics of his
own invention.[2] Moreover, the arboreal voice is a grave and solemn one, identifying
itself as that of a self-accusing "volonteroso"—a heedlessly "willful" man—
imprisoned in bark for his dehumanizing passion for Alcina. The reader is forced to
cooperate in identifying him by being teased to remember Boiardo's original tale.
Illumination dawns slowly and with the force of a major surprise; and only then
does Astolfo's voice give itself a name. At the end of his account, he warns Ruggiero
from a similar destiny, though not without wise irony as to Ruggiero's chances for
avoiding disaster: Astolfo's voice takes on the authoritative irony of the poet's own
voice.

Even more importantly, Ariosto employs Astolfo's voice to introduce nothing less
than the Platonic conception of the human body, its division between reason and
passion, its various potentialities; and on Plato's division between the body's forces
he superimposes the Christian doctrine of the Fall, in which lower members rebelled
against higher. For (as Astolfo narrates it) the island to which they both have been
wafted was previously entirely under the sway of the virtuous Logistilla, but it has
suffered an insurrection in the form of civil war initiated by her two evil sisters,
Alcina and Morgana, enchantresses already linked in Boiardo to carnal lust and
worldly riches. In his slyly naive account of their misdoing, they are said to have
taken "more than a hundred" of their sister's castles from her, sending her flying
"northward" to a straitened part of the land she formerly held sway over in its

entirety, while they spread their evil dominion over the greater part of the more "southerly" territories. Everything is topsy-turvy ("sottosopra," 10.53) as a consequence of this "usurpation" (6.43), which is precisely the traditional figure Milton uses to describe the upward striving of the passions in the Fall.[3] Logistilla, though attended by an army and a navy, and surrounded by her handmaids, Andronica, Fronesia, Dicilla, and Sofrosina (transparently the four Cardinal Virtues of Plato's *Republic*), must endure perpetual attack and unceasing attempts to dislodge her. Fortunately, an isthmus—the image occurs twice ("golfo," 6.45; "stretto," 10.43)—separates the threatened "north" from the imperializing "south": the "neck" in the image of the human body in the *Timaeus,* separating the poor threatened brain from the large bodily area given over to the unruly passions.[4] This is a familiar island polity,[5] but it is one in deep trouble, and the 2:1 ratio of the forces arrayed against each other when Ruggiero, "transported" by the hippogriff, drops down on this island, is an expression of his own interior geography. This is already well prophesied in the *Innamorato:* amorous desire and lust for power already stand poised to flood over his nature, and his reason has already begun to undergo assault and to suffer diminution as a result. In warning Ruggiero to avoid his own hard case and to take the road that leads "northward" to Logistilla—the hard route to the mental life, the steep and thorny road to virtue—Astolfo becomes, in effect, the voice of chastened and repentant experience. Even more, he becomes the proponent of the Herculean rather than the Paridean choice of life, a choice figured by the three sisters in their respective patronage of pleasure (Alcina), worldly ambition (Morgana), and learning and virtue (Logistilla). Astolfo's *theomachia* between romantically disguised representatives of the contest between Venus, Juno, and Minerva renders the enduring *psychomachia* of the human soul. Ariosto's attendance at Sebastiano dell'Aquila's lectures on the *Timaeus,* mentioned to Aldus Manutius in the poet's first recorded letter, had fused with his early love of the *Innamorato* to produce an extraordinary poetic fruit.

Astolfo's narrative is a distinct rhetorical entity, a speech in a particular Socratic mode of irony inventively utilizing elements from Boiardan romance, Platonic philosophy, and Christian dogma for *delightful* instruction about the perpetual psychomachia of the human body. This is a very learned Astolfo, one who lives very much off his creator's wit and wittiness, and it is fully apparent that, no matter how simplistically the allegory it introduces has been traditionally read, Ariosto invested a good deal of learning and art in its writing. Like his creator, Astolfo appears to know that Plato's name for reason is *to logistikon,* that Fulgentius's Choice of Paris involved three goddesses, one of whom was a maiden who lived in the heights, and that the Choice of Hercules involved a crossroads. Further, he appears to recognize Logistilla's affinity to the Logistica of Colonna's *Hypnerotomachia poliphilii* and perhaps to the Minerva of the *Quadriregio* of Federigo Frezzi, whose home is also mountainous and remote. There are resemblances to Lady Reason, who descends from her tower—the head—to counsel the lover in the *Romance of the Rose* and, rebuffed, retreats sadly "upward" once more.[6] Under cover of the romantic-chivalric elements he inherits from Boiardo, Ariosto artfully infiltrates the values of humanistic allegory into his own narrative, transforming the allusively fantastic into the beguilingly recondite. The reader may indeed marvel at the curious fate that has befallen Morgana, the scheming sister of King Arthur: not only to have become a "Fata," or fay, and to have fallen into sisterly company with Alcina, an enchantress known only to Italian Carolingian tradition, but also along with her to have been subordinated to a wholly new creature, a sister quickened from the pages of Plato's *Republic.* The entire passage, which bears a distinct relation to Bembo's allegory of the Queen of the Fortunate Islands and her explication of the tripartite soul at the end of the *Asolani,* is clearly aimed at the cognoscenti of Ferrara, for whom the employment of a romantic "cover" from Boiardo would have been an additional delight. The allegory is witness to the new poet's sovereign command of an older poem as well as to the playful, cryptic style of the Platonic tradition. For, however learned the voice issuing from the vocal tree in Astolfo's name, the poet goes to considerable lengths to disguise his wisdom in a wide-eyed fabulous narrative of a distressed fairy-tale kingdom, rather like Socrates in the Platonic dialogues pretending ignorance and simple-mindedness as a stalking-horse for the menacing penetration of his intelligence.

For Astolfo this represents a signally important debut. As we shall see, the techniques expended so lavishly here to create meanings important for the poem as a whole—Reason is a not unimportant figure in a poem whose nominal hero loses his reason—will be seen to be characteristic in the depiction of Astolfo hereafter. If this new metamorphosis is meant to stun and surprise, it is not the jest of a single occasion; rather, it foreshadows a long development. The illustration of this fact necessitates the foreshortening of an extensive career. The length and complexity of Astolfo's adventures, especially in their patterned interrelation with those of Ruggiero and Orlando, will sustain more searching investigation than they have yet been accorded.[7] It appears not to have been recognized that his excursions are as programmatic in their own way as Ruggiero's. Since Astolfo voyages in two fundamentally different ways, his progresses break down into two groups, a pair of leisurely journeys. He first makes his way *around* the physical world; then, in a second phase, he surmounts and flies above it. His first journey is a horizontal circumambulation of earth, on horseback and on foot, beginning at canto 15.10 and ending in canto 22. The second journey, an aerial voyage, begins soon afterward in canto 23.9 and comes to its climax in the moon-allegory of cantos 33, 34, and 35. In this second tour he travels vertically aboard the hippogriff, descending into hell itself for a cognitive experience of vice and ascending directly thereafter to the Terrestrial Paradise and (accompanied by St. John, the "imitator di Cristo") to the moon. From that height he views the cacophonous world of human ambition (in essence it is the world of Boiardo's *Innamorato* that he looks down on and contemplates), shrunk now to a tiny, silent point.

In a world of crisscross traveling, full of deviation and error, Astolfo's is a curiously steady and undeflected progress, suggesting that the discontinuousness of the *Furioso* is a fable of critics. Even the bare sequence of Astolfo's adventures is enough to suggest that Ariosto was interested in presenting something more than a series of marvelous oriental excursions, the outward gestures of which, however, as the heir of the romantic tradition, he was studious to preserve. Thus, in contrast to the ironical "progressi" of the other errant knights, Astolfo's is the only real, uninterrupted progress in the poem, and it holds its steady way to a determined end. To illustrate briefly, Astolfo is first discovered in his arborified state of stricken but repentant sensuality (canto 6); he recovers human form with the aid of a repentant Ruggiero and symbolically reacquires his miraculous golden lance (8); he *precedes* Ruggiero in arriving at Logistilla's kingdom for instruction at her hands and those of her four handmaids (10); he departs for the East (some time *after* Ruggiero more brusquely and impatiently has left) accompanied by Andronica and Sofrosina, respectively the Fortitude and Temperance of Plato (15); he demonstrates immediately in two separate trials that he is proof against two distinctly differentiated kinds of evil, the one that works by force and the other that works by guile, when he rids the land of two monstrous oppressors, Caligorante and Orrilo, one brutish and overt, the other latent and insidious (15); he travels to Jerusalem and presses the reformed giant, Caligorante, into the service of its governor to help in building walls for the defense of the holy city (15); he sails by Venus's island of Cyprus, successfully rides out a tempest in its waters (18), and soon thereafter upholds justice by overthrowing a reign of Amazons and restoring the hierarchical order they have subverted (19); he returns to France, destroys Atlante's Palace of Illusion after prudently consulting his magic book (22), frees all the deluded prisoners (including Bradamante and Ruggiero) entrapped by their willingness to race down its corridors in pursuit of illusions, and takes the hippogriff into his possession.

At this point in canto 22, we are one canto away from the poem's center and on the verge of Orlando's madness. We are also on the threshold of a new stage in Bradamante and Ruggiero's love, for Astolfo effects their release from Atlante's bondage. Surely we are justified in seeing, in the carefully adjusted structure of these events, a connection and a contrast.

"Superata tellus / Sidera donat."[8] At the end of his initial *tour du monde,* Astolfo has accomplished, by a curiously romanticized imitation of the exercise of heroic virtue, what the enlightened pagans achieved through fortitude, justice, prudence, and temperance, though St. John will later inform him that neither bridled hippogriff nor magical horn would have availed him unless he had also the gift of grace. And since this revelation about the power of grace still awaits him, his course is now bent to the vertical instead of the merely horizontal. The second journey, begun in canto 33, is the crown of the first, though Ariosto is at pains to ensure that his readers not fall into the error of believing that Astolfo's allegiance to virtue causes him to *merit* the grace now bestowed on him. And he is especially concerned to reveal that a visit to Reason is not the terminus of the human voyage—if it were, Ruggiero would not have suffered the disastrous relapse of canto 11. Virtue is a gift from above, not a technical skill that can be learned or acquired by oneself: in the lapidary phrase of the Renaissance, "Virtus donum Dei."[9]

Once mounted on the bridled and well-controlled hippogriff, Astolfo is ready to begin his soaring to the nether and upper extremities of the universe. Thus, he relieves the blinded King Senapo from the assault of the Harpies of avarice, restoring his kingdom to wholeness (33), chases the evil birds to hell, hears a Francesca-like narrative from one of the inferno's wrathfully vicious inhabitants, blocks up the mouth of the nether world with a hedge, laves himself from head to toe in water gushing from a rock, and mounts finally to the Terrestrial Paradise. Here he is received by St. John the Evangelist, who takes him to the moon to survey the domain of mutability (34). From St. John he receives both the power to restore Orlando's lost wits and instructions on how to deploy the Emperor Senapo's Nubian armies against the city of Bizerte, capital of the Saracen invaders. Finally, in cantos 38, 39, and 40, at the climax of his long journey, he is at the head of a punitive arc of long-delayed retribution that totally outflanks the invaders of France, strikes where it is least expected, and plummets with slowly accumulated, crushing power on the head and source of all the disorders. The long meandering curve of Astolfo's attack on the infidels' African stronghold incarnates the human dream of perfect justice working to its own timetable. It also tips the scale firmly in favor of the humorous, imperturbably patient paladin rather than the ragingly furious Rodomonte, who is repeatedly poised against Astolfo as they operate simultaneously and in ignorance of each other's movements in two different theaters of action in cantos 14 through 18.[10] Hence it is the slight Astolfo, finally, and not Orlando, Rinaldo, or any other of many possible paladins, all of them strongmen and famous warriors, who is chiefly responsible for the successful ambush and destruction of the pagan capital, an action in a distant part of the world that results in the withdrawal from France of the tides of war, and in the defeat of the broken pagan forces, both by land and sea, on their own home ground. At this point the tale is developing in two directions, which are really one and complementary: the casting out of the Saracens from France, and the inexorable detachment of Ruggiero from their ranks and his movement to marriage of the dynastic couple. Astolfo's adventures close with his triumphal entry into Paris (44), a city whose pacification now makes it the fitting scene of Bradamante and Ruggiero's wedding. And there he is content to take a subordinate place.

All in all, then, Astolfo makes a long journey from being an impetuous, cowardly braggart and a bad horseman. Mild and debonair, not much renowned for physical strength, purposefully errant, and operating very much on his own, Astolfo takes the distant view and the long way around, and he knows the value of a skillful ambush from the rear. Protracted, circuitous, but purposeful and unerring, Astolfo's journeys are a perfect mirror of Ariostan narrative technique: a long uncoiling of hidden strength, by indirection finding direction out in a kind of slow hurrying[11]—Ariosto's intellectually pointed "joke" is that the immense roundabout by which Logistilla sends him home is the shortest route ("piú espedita," 15.10.8) she could devise; indeed, the road to virtue admits of no short-cuts.

Nevertheless, never content to leave his readers with the complacency of final perfections—even the dynasts' wedding gets interrupted by a final irruption of evil in Rodomonte—Ariosto is careful to keep Astolfo within the bounds of human attainments. Astolfo's discovery of some of his own wits on the moon reminds us that he is a reformed buffoon. We are warned (in one of those easily missed but deeply important Ariostan asides) that even Astolfo will succumb to frailty and foolishness at some indeterminate time outside the poem's limits (34.86). Astolfo works with strength not really his own, and this introduces the subject of his weaponry: obviously he works more effectually with books and horns than the booby Orlando in the *Innamorato,* taking over those magical devices and utilizing well the allegorical powers with which Ariosto had reinvested them. But it is his lance that most compels attention, particularly for the moment in which he reacquires it in the *Furioso.* His repossession of the magical weapon occurs when he recovers human shape after being turned into a tree, and it signalizes his loss of wildness. It is an emblem of spiritual power wielded only by those under the special protection of Providence, and (significantly) Astolfo shares it with no one but Bradamante, to whom he passes it on when he launches into the ether (23.15). No longer a merely laughable piece of romance paraphernalia with which to win comically uproarious victories, in the hands of these two characters the magical weapon allows them to win important moral victories. "Nothings that were, grown something very much,"[12] they grow, nevertheless, by special election.

All of this puts Astolfo in very select company indeed and establishes him as a very special kind of fool and madman. It also places him in a very particular kind of comedy, which it is of utmost importance to identify correctly if the *Furioso* is to be interpreted as a poem emanating from a particular time and society. The rehabilitation of Astolfo provides immediate provocation to think in terms of parody or burlesque. Demonstrably, this involves us in error; error in which the watchful poet is eager time and again to catch us. Parody and burlesque operate discontinuously, over relatively short distances. Their effect is limited to the shorter forms, and the burst of laughter declines in direct proportion to the joke, which loses its novelty with every reappearance, although it may gain the charm of the expected and familiar. This is Boiardo's sense of comedy; we need to differentiate it from Ariosto's, which operates in another sphere altogether. Ariosto aims at a subtler, more potent laughter, one directed against the reader's easy, merely provisional solutions as he reads—solutions that the insistent resumption of the Astolfo narrative repeatedly confounds. The length, curvature, pointedness, and final effect of Astolfo's pilgrimage is too prolonged for a laughter unaccompanied by the abrupt arrest of reflection or by the sudden interposition of thought. From the paladin's first appearance the poet tempts us repeatedly into unwary thoughts of satire and subversion and then traps us immediately into further meditation by a new projection of Astolfan adventures, even as we imagine that the joke is a very simple one, involving the parodying of "seriousness."

The technique is evident as soon as Astolfo appears. The paladin is introduced in the subtlest possible manner, as a nameless arboreal voice, warning Ruggiero from a similar vegetative fate. No sooner does the tree identify itself as a transformed Astolfo than the thought forms that Ariosto is having his parodic joke with the *Aeneid* or *Divine Comedy* and doing a bit of subversion of the Neoplatonizing humanists by involving Astolfo in humanistic allegory. The reader relaxes, imagining that he possesses the key to the poem's laughter and that it will proceed by blowing up gravity with explosive laughter. Thoughts similar to this reoccur when, after his farewell to Logistilla and his promise to be good friends with her forever, Ruggiero frenziedly attempts the rape of Angelica, and the hippogriff, which he was taught to bridle by the lady, flies off uncontrolledly. But Ariosto soon gives Astolfo a significant part in the Logistilla allegory, repeatedly and insistently recalling the lady's instructions on how to bridle the beast (10.65, 22.24) and reminding us that Astolfo had taken good note of her lessons (20.27). It soon becomes obvious that he has been a better student than Ruggiero. Ariosto presses in upon us immediately with a contrast between Ruggiero's derelictions and Astolfo's string of successes: as Astolfo voyages, he effects a series of linked Herculean rescues of the trapped and the oppressed, all with a very elegant, efficient outlay of mental strength. This too may seem parodic, except that now a strict contrast is forming between and among the poem's major male figures, and Astolfo is demonstrating an odd tendency to claim a central place among them. He succeeds where they ordinarily fail, and—most unusual of all—he is a transformed personality, modest, courageous, prompt to give voice to an unexampled statement of self-abnegation in the midst of danger (15.46–47). In this first round of encounters with evil, Astolfo's are the victories of intelligence rather than of sinew and muscle—an Ariostan commentary on conventional Herculeanism and traditional epic action, and also on the smash-and-bang of the Boiardan heavies.

Having given him one continuously successful journey around the earth, Ariosto soon accosts his reader with another journey, to hell and to heaven, producing an uneasy sense amid so much apparent lunacy of excogitated pattern and directed motion, a continuous line that is clearly detectable through loops and tangles of narrative. Even here, in the upper atmosphere, the hilarious lunacy of St. John, in his pride of human authorship proclaiming his own sense of human *merit*—just after the saint himself has sweetly cautioned Astolfo from attributing merit to himself—seems a final undercutting of every value the poem has established thus far, yet here precisely the irony is at its most complex and brilliant, involving the reader's capacity for misapprehension. For the poem goes on steadily from here, with even greater insistence and with darker and darker illustrations of the futility and madness of humanity's arrogation of any merit to itself at all: the career of Ruggiero is an extensive case in point. *Works* of any kind—even the poet's *opera*—are risible and unavailing.

Ariosto is a highly aggressive author in his use of laughter, being almost menacing in his technique of cajoling us into imagining he is laughing with us and then suddenly removing himself to a distance and shutting off laughter. There is a strong sense of growth and purpose in his technique, and the humor is not an end but rather a means of winning his beguiling way forward so that thought may enter: impudent *Ludere* sneaks into the castle with *Serio* well concealed in his knapsack. Ariosto gives Astolfo his own voice and perspective on human passion and makes his point about the character's credibility by refusing to name him and letting him employ his new voice for warning and prediction; and, of course, Ruggiero's immediate fall to Alcina proves the value of Astolfo's new insights into human resolution in the face of temptation. Laughter has preceded gravity and laughter is soon qualified by gravity: they co-exist, as inseparable as the two elements in an oxymoron, in a complex unity. For this kind of procedure, *mock-epic* is a description too facile by far; *serio ludere* is the very soul of comic epic.

Suavely daring, the jocular poet keeps charming us into ever deeper waters. He persists in placing Astolfo in situation after situation that requires the strict application rather than the abandonment of the mental faculties, and he repeatedly contrives fictions that tempt the reader with simpler thoughts of farce, burlesque, and parody when he should be thinking in terms of another, more prolonged and intellectual kind of comedy. How electrifying this must have been to the *Furioso*'s first readers we may only imagine, but it is surely legitimate to form a picture of their alerted surprise and knowledgeable fascination as they watched the new Astolfo emerge from the old and realized they had been manipulated from the beginning. Indeed, Ariosto had come on his audience in cunning and stealth on an even earlier occasion, in his very first stanzas. Though he enumerates three main actions in his opening (the wars in France, the madness of Orlando, the exploits of Ruggiero), no Christian hero's name is attached to the first of these, and there is, aptly enough for so subtle a poet, no indication whatever that the wars will cease only because of—of all people—*Astolfo's* crucial, roundabout attack on Bizerte. Surely, given the central part he is called on to play, Astolfo deserves a mention at the poem's beginning. But in a poem that, in externals at least, hews so closely to the tradition as to avoid taking the name of its chief hero, Ruggiero, it is hardly likely that the buffooning Astolfo would be accorded a primary place at this early juncture, or that Ariosto would show his hand at once by baldly and artlessly informing his readers, "This poem is about Orlando's love-madness, Ruggiero's growth into a dynast, and Astolfo's attack on Bizerte, ending the wars in France." To an audience that knew Astolfo only as a fiery buffoon this might have been to court derisive laughter and raise expectations of mock-epic that Ariosto never meant to fulfill. He therefore takes a very deliberate, circuitous path of gradually conveying this information of the buffoon's redemption, and only by the slow growth of understanding over a long time will the reader gain knowledge of the poet's methods and purposes, which he might not have accepted if flung at him, unsubtly, at once. Ariosto bides his time and says nothing at all about the unexampled future he has reserved for that (until now) unlikeliest of men, Astolfo, Prince of England. This knowing reticence and reserve on the poet's part is typical of his procedure throughout, and it reveals that we already, from his very first lines, come under the unsuspected domination of his irony and are totally dependent on him for our understanding and enlightenment. Ariosto takes on the attributes of all-commanding Providence, and here, in the case of Astolfo, literature and dogma run together and fuse; selection by the artist is the counterpart of election by the Deity, who has occasionally been known to choose cracked vessels for the infusion of grace. Again, the text is Pauline: "But the foolish things of the world has God chosen to put to shame the wise, and the weak things of the world has God chosen to put to shame the strong, and the base things of the world and the despised has God chosen, and the things that are not, to bring to naught the things that are" (I Corinthians 1:27–28). Picked out from a life of adorable imbecile laughter for another felicity, Astolfo is the nexus of both a moral and a literary redemption. His election to play the role of liberator to the Charlemagnic world is a startlingly literal dramatization of "The fool is chosen."

Ariosto chooses the fool to negotiate the fullest range of lives assigned to any character in his poem. When we first meet Astolfo he is imprisoned in tree bark, and he is less than human; released and restored to human shape, he participates in the rational life embodied in Logistilla and the Cardinal Virtues; voyaging to the Terrestrial Paradise and the moon, he emerges as a comic contemplator of earth's waste ambitions. As a reformed sensual lover, he has been what Orlando is and what Ruggiero has been, and in his glimpse of the immaterial world he goes beyond the best of what Ruggiero can achieve as dynast and soldier. Initially pictured as sinking lower than either, he finally races past both.

Ariosto's use of Astolfo to provide a lead for those two other warrior-lovers makes for an elaborately integrated poetic cosmos, for his adventures are first synchronized and then interwoven with theirs. The advance over Boiardo's relatively simpler art is especially apparent in the triadic design of elegant simplicity that acts as a containing framework for the richly proliferating narrative. Interlacing Neoplatonic triads now reinforce the more diffuse *entrelacement* of Carolingian romance, and by this means Ariosto efficiently sorts out Boiardo's confused thematic threads and distinguishes between and among the multiple personnel of his source. The kaleidoscopically alternated and interwoven stories of the three knights, distinguished by different destinies and personalities, provide the extensive and elaborately simple framework within which the multitudinous events of the poem are enacted, and by which the hundreds of supporting characters are enclosed and comprehended. Though this is an aspect of the poem that appears to have generally eluded notice, much of the poem's meaning reveals itself structurally in the insistent parallelism of the varying fortunes of the three. All are involved in a *peregrinatio* of one sort or another, but depending on their attitude, life is either a voyage or a series of short-sighted lurchings. Astolfo voyages, Orlando lunges in broken arcs of motion, Ruggiero tries desperately to alternate between the two.

Astolfo is ahead of Ruggiero when he first appears: he has already known passion and suffered retribution somewhere in the interval between his last appearance in the *Innamorato* and his first appearance on Alcina's island. Ariosto makes him first the advisor and then the companion of Ruggiero in the allegory; and he then inter-meshes the Alcina-Logistilla narrative of cantos 6 through 10 with the descent into darkness of Orlando, which begins in canto 8 with his desertion from Paris to chase Angelica. This group of cantos functions spatially as a kind of central depot or terminus where some important figures from the *Innamorato* are gathered together, and from which their individual courses are launched. All three are prone to the same ruinous concupiscence; they differ among themselves in that only two of them attempt resistance, and of those two one is fated for marriage and dynastic rule, the other for the contemplation of the slippery nature of crowns and power. In clear contrast to Orlando, who blots out his reason, Astolfo and Ruggiero recognize the need to submit themselves to the ministrations of reason in the person of Logistilla, and an allegory of reason is reserved for them at the very moment that Orlando is tossing Petrarchanly on his bed of passion. Nevertheless, they attend to the instruc-tion of reason in two markedly different ways. If their presence in the court of Logistilla differentiates Astolfo and Ruggiero from Orlando, a beast that wants discourse of reason, no less does it differentiate Astolfo (who demonstrates a never-failing adherence to her precepts thereafter) from Ruggiero, who is prone to desert her repeatedly after an initial, shallow vow of allegiance. Hence, Astolfo is charac-terized as a blithe, debonair figure, moving undeviatingly from triumph to triumph, while Ruggiero seems, contrastingly, a perpetually harassed young man with a knitted brow and a driving determination who is often blown up suddenly by the elations of hope and just as often cast down by depressions.[13] It takes the length of the poem to untangle all the knots in which he is bound, and he is clearly the most purely human of the lot and the poem's true hero.

At one time or another, each of the three reenacts a passage in the life of the other two, a technique by which Ariosto takes over the three hierarchical, merely *successive* loves of Bembo's *Asolani,* and propels them into *simultaneous* action by complex, reflexive interweaving of their stories—stories charged with the dynamism of vari-ous kinds of love *in process of becoming.* By canto 10, the three main proponents of the action are firmly established in their places and ready to vault into their individual careers. Progressively and increasingly they begin to draw away from each other to their particular and different destinies, and they are distinguished clearly by their individual responses to a variety of similar experiences, as well as by the rhetoric of the particular literary traditions in which their stories are cast. As the character who

achieves the highest spiritual altitude, Astolfo's role in all these actions is, by anticipation, to provide the ideal response; hence his first appearance, as a vocal tree, in the
role of ironical instructor to the naive and untried Ruggiero in canto 6. The contrast
is pointed and telling.

We should look first at the two extremes. Within the decorum of the comic
poem, Astolfo is accorded the highest of contemplative visions possible in that form,
in unmistakable contrast to Orlando, whom Providence explicitly says it has blinded
("cecato") in his mental eye as a punishment for his transgression. All this is related
to Astolfo by St. John, who makes him responsible for capturing and restoring the
mad Orlando to his sanity. The conjunction of Astolfo and Orlando is not fortuitous: as a "cugino matto" and as "Orlando furioso," the crazy cousins are representative of two distinct kinds of madness, one arising from the descent into sensual
bestiality, the other from the Platonic realization that the world of matter is a place
of shadows. Symbolic of their diversity are the gardens that they aspire to and
achieve. Orlando's dream in canto 8 is of a terrestrial paradise of sensual fulfillment,
into which he alone will be allowed to set foot, and where he alone will be allowed
to pluck Angelica's "rose." His desolation of the pastoral oasis in canto 23, when he
realizes that the rose has been plucked by Medoro, reflects the mind's capacity to
turn upon itself and make a wasteland of its disappointed fury. In contrast, Astolfo
mounts from the tranquil gardens of Logistilla in canto 10 to the Terrestrial Paradise
in canto 34. His madness is the madness of the saintly fool, and his journey constitutes an Ariostan praise of folly—the "folly" (in the world's eyes) of rising from
the world of matter into the world of the invisible. It is a journey Ariosto has made
as a poet,[14] a journey he demands of his readers in the proem to canto 7, often
mistakenly read as a dry Ariostan joke. Instead it is a proclamation of his poetic
independence from Boiardan romance: this is the very canto in which he overtly
converts Boiardo's symbols, comically emptied of their power in the *Innamorato,* to
their original moral significance.

As the mean between extremes, Ruggiero doubles the exploits of both Orlando
and Astolfo in constantly changing patterns, which leads perhaps to the sense of
kaleidoscopic movement in Ariosto's art. With regard to Orlando, the reader is first
invited to join the two warriors mentally when he witnesses Ruggiero's remarkable
doubling of Orlando's tall-tale Lucianic battle with the orc: in cantos 10 and 11, each
of them comes to the rescue of maidens about to be devoured, and Ruggiero's rescue
of Angelica only serves to link him more strongly, at this stage of his existence, to
the enchantress's chief lover. The comparison is resumed when Ruggiero in canto 11
and Orlando in canto 12 successively fall victim to Atlante's magic and become
willing inmates in his Palace of Illusion. With Ruggiero's release from bondage by
Astolfo's more potent magic, he is on the rise, whereas Orlando is ineluctably
doomed. Ruggiero's erotic pastoral is in the past, destroyed with the gardens on the
isle of Alcina, gone up in smoke with Atlante's palace. Another kind of pastoral
awaits him now, a pastoral of simple, retired holiness presided over by a hermit on an

island in canto 41, in one of the final stages of his long-delayed conversion. Ruggiero gets through the stage of sensual abandonment significantly sooner than Orlando, in whom the madness is more deeply ingrained. But Orlando's erotic pastoral is both before and behind him: in the form of his dream-vision in canto 8 and in horrible reality in canto 23, when the *locus amoenus* turns into a vision of horror, inviting his manic destruction in the noontide blaze of passion.

The contrast between Orlando and Ruggiero is essentially in terms of the labor they expend in their separate courses of action. The extended, exhausting process of learning and growing by which Ruggiero proceeds is in strict contrast to the madly comic, wildly parodic means by which Orlando is brought to his senses. As an incarnation of brute matter, Orlando can only be acted on: with a face more like a beast's ("fera") than a man's (39.45.8), compared to a bull (39.52.5) or a horse (39.54.8), he is captured, roped, tied down, plunged kicking and screaming seven times into the sea, and forced to inhale the lost wits that Astolfo has brought back to him in a phial from the moon. Yet even here his seven-fold dunking in the sea, which restores him to his humanity, is a droll parody of Ruggiero's shipwreck and agony in the very same Mediterranean waters off Africa, whence he is rescued by Providence to be converted and baptized. Both these immersions are prefigured by Astolfo's washing himself clean (just before he mounts to the heavens) of the contagion of hell-smoke in a spring that gushes from a rock: the Petrine symbol here finds a later echo in the "scoglio" where Ruggiero is rescued from being drowned. Of the three heroes, then, Orlando's is quite the most easily accomplished redemption, for it matches the ease with which he falls into one trap after another without struggle. And as the poem proceeds, less and less does Ruggiero participate in the cartoon-like, phantasmagoric world of comic Carolingian excesses, the universe of magicians, hippogriffs, and orcs. The Lucianic, Munchausenish Orlando may skewer brigands on his lance like frogs (9), kick hapless donkeys into the upper sky (29), or tear unfortunate shepherds to pieces in his fury (24), but Ruggiero moves gradually away from this world, functioning increasingly in the "more real" and more recognizable world of human action, and in European landscapes alive with contemporary relevance, those of the Mediterranean and Eastern Europe. In a word, Orlando is a simple comic mechanism, while Ruggiero is a figure evolving according to a prescribed intellectual pattern by undergoing hierarchical temptations, and in the process becoming a type and a model.

By the middle of the poem, just previous to the point at which Orlando succumbs to madness, Ruggiero has begun to draw away from his moral proximity to the paladin. Thereafter, he is increasingly compared, subtly but persistently, to Astolfo. Astolfo's longer sojourn at Logistilla's (he arrives, says the narrative playfully, "un ora prima" and departs some time afterward) is contrasted to Ruggiero's shorter and less profitable one. Ruggiero is a young man who evinces a desire to bustle about the world. The result is that, in spite of all his protestations to Logistilla, he immediately succumbs once to Angelica's nakedness in canto 10, plummeting down to rape the enchantress in a vivid parody of Perseus's rescue of Andromeda; and once to Atlante's magic in canto 11. He undergoes a lengthy imprisonment in the Palace of Illusion, being rescued only when Astolfo (who by this time has just accomplished his first instructive circuit of the world) comes to effect his liberation in canto 22. Once again there is connection and contrast.

Astolfo's course is steady and progressive, and Ruggiero's is jagged and broken, filled with regression. On occasion after occasion, Ruggiero is still toiling to achieve what Astolfo has accomplished earlier and more dexterously. If Ruggiero goes east for motives of revenge and ambition, Astolfo has preceded him in that direction, but in order to go to Jerusalem first and then to bring salvation to Charlemagne and Paris. In canto 34, Astolfo is viewing the fallacious nature of "gloriae cupido" on the moon, well before Ruggiero, in canto 44, blinded by "desir di gloria," is driven to make a last frantic grab at royal power in the Balkans. As the only two characters in the poem to have a contemplative experience, Astolfo again precedes Ruggiero in the order of time, Ruggiero only reaching his hermit's island in canto 41 and soon turning renegade even to that experience. Astolfo's saintly instructor is matched on earth by the hermit who teaches Ruggiero the same lessons about Fortune and Providence—an instruction Orlando never seeks or undergoes.

One of the most significant examples of this anticipation and doubling technique occurs in Astolfo's and Ruggiero's separate and highly suggestive encounters with a Reign of Women. In canto 19 Astolfo, sailing homeward, is driven ashore and finds himself among a band of archetypally ferocious Amazons, subjugators and killers of men, inverters of normal hierarchies (the occasion for a long novella of deliciously protracted bawdiness). The paladin enters this landscape with his usual aplomb, submits to their ludicrous but terrifying demands for a tourney (the winner must best ten men, bed ten women), and allows the whole contest its playful leisure and length. Yet at the height of the battle he asserts himself forcefully: his abrupt way with the Amazons is to rout their forces and to destroy their polity utterly by a blast of the horn that Logistilla gave him. Here he appears to have been well tutored by her handmaid, Dicilla, for, in reversing the topsy-turvy world of an inverted moral state established by vengeful women, he administers justice and provides a strict contrast to the more confused Ruggiero. Eighteen cantos later, in canto 37, Ruggiero, significantly accompanied by his Amazon sister, Marfisa, and by his increasingly headstrong wife-to-be, watches with remarkable acquiescence and complacency as they destroy the evil misogynist tyranny of Margannore in order to set up their own equally remorseless tyranny of women: one extreme succeeded by another, both productive of evil. With his own marriage only nine cantos away at this point, this is a bridegroom with much to learn about the question of mastery. And indeed the novellas of canto 42 turn significantly on the question of the relations of men and women in marriage. Told close to "home"—in the neighborhood of Mantua—the novellas form a pointed commentary on the dangers of jealousy and sensuality *within* the married state.

The comparison of Ruggiero and Astolfo affords yet another occasion for dynastic compliment. It might have been expected that the Choice of Hercules should be attached to the dynastic prototype, as it is in canto 6, that he should demonstrate an initial tendency to take the right path of virtue rather than the sinister one of evil, and that his deviation should occur only because of gentlemanly proneness to beauty rather than because of submission to loathsome, brutish vices. Yet once this Herculean motif of laborious service in the world is invoked for Ruggiero, it is referred even more powerfully to Astolfo. Part of the serious laughter of the *Furioso* originates in this: that the mythological referent for Astolfo, the former coward, is usually Hercules, and that he should be further dignified by being enveloped in a romanticized but transparent classicism. Departing from Logistilla, he is accompanied by two maidens, Andronica-Fortitude and Sofrosina-Temperance, and as they pass the Pillars of Hercules it is of some consequence that the first maiden chiefly instructs him, in a long speech in canto 15, for Hercules is one of two chief exemplars of heroic Fortitude itself, the other being Samson.[15] Like Hercules, from cantos 15 through 22 Astolfo is involved in a general cleanup of some dark and disorderly landscapes, engaged earlier by far in the work of civilization than the dynastic hero, who is, all this while, still enduring his lover's frustrations in the Palace of Illusion (cantos 11.16–22.20) and awaiting release, in good time, by an Astolfo practiced in the *laborious* exercise of virtue. No less than five of Astolfo's exploits are modeled on those of the Greek demigod. In canto 15, in a passage filled with unmistakable verbal echoes of the Hercules passage in Vergil's book 8, he subdues a fantastically re-created Cacus in the monstrous Caligorante. In the same canto he destroys an Orrilo who combines features of both Antaeus and the Hydra. In canto 19 he overthrows an Amazonian reign of women who usurp the male function of rule. In canto 23 he devastates the Stymphalides-like Harpies who have assailed a blind Phineus-like Senapo. And in canto 34 he makes a descent into hell that gives him a close-up view of the nature of evil. In effect, Astolfo takes over the good aspects of Hercules in his arduous pursuit of virtue, in contrast to Orlando, who takes over his "furens" aspect as the enraged uprooter of trees in canto 23.

Florence had long had a Herculean tradition, of which Coluccio Salutati's *De laboribus Herculis* is the finest example in literature,[16] while Baccio Bandinelli's monumental statuary at the Palazzo Vecchio's entrance (originally to have been sculpted by Michelangelo as a Fortitude) is the most bulkily prominent sermon in stone on the subject.[17] Hercules is, of course, the archetype of those who establish justice in the western world. Ridding the world of monsters and tyrants, restoring order and law, he is the prime example in classical mythology of heroic magnanimity and self-sacrifice, and as such, perhaps, he is a curiously apt precursor of the chivalric knight of romance. As the most famous champion in myth of the life of strenuous activity, he is, accordingly, preeminently suitable as a model for the ruler of a state. Considering that the Estensi for three successive generations numbered an Ercole among their rulers and scions,[18] the prominence given to that mythical figure in Ferrara's art and literature in the fifteenth and sixteenth centuries is scarcely surprising. Pietro Andrea Bassi's lovely illustrated version of the labors, *Le fatiche d'Ercole,* assumed to have been composed for the birth of Ercole I in 1431,[19] initiated this particular strain of dynastic praise, and the tradition continued long after. Lilio Gregorio Giraldi himself wrote a *Herculis vita* in tribute to Duke Ercole II,[20] and, for the same ruler, Giovambattista Giraldi Cinthio, former secretary to Ercole II, wrote his *Dell'Ercole,* a long poem in octaves celebrating the hero and (incidentally) paying tribute to Ariosto by continuing the tradition that Bradamante and Ruggiero were fountains of the race.[21] The chivalric poets, needless to say, did not scant this useful mythology. In the *Innamorato* Boiardo had played familiarly with the Herculean tradition (2.25.51–52, 2.27.55), availing himself of the boyish misfortunes of his mythical namesake to allegorize the travails of Duke Ercole I during his youth. Ariosto was, typically, more elaborately learned and more extendedly concerned with the theme. In the Herculean adventures of Astolfo, he extends and amplifies an allusive thread from Boiardo into a patterned skein of meaning, tracing the movements by which, "con piú tempo et piú fatica" (10.68.7), Astolfo surpasses Ruggiero in virtuous *labor* on earth before spurning it and directing his aspirations away from earth: "Tanto è il desir che di veder lo incalza / Ch'al cielo aspira, e la terra non stima" (34.48.5–6; "So great is the desire to see that spurs him on that he aspires to heaven and despises the earth"). Accustomed as the Estensi already were to mythical panegyric in their writers and poets, it was appropriate that the Hercules element should enter a poem so peculiarly their own as the *Furioso.* But that it came in so surprising a form, in so paradoxical a character as Astolfo, gives it a particularly Ariostan coloring. A slightly built Hercules in the tradition of thoughtful laughter and in the guise of a holy fool was an unexampled innovation; a redeemed paladin who flies off to the moon on a winged creature is an exaltation beyond any series of labors.

Finally, any comparison of Astolfo and Ruggiero must consider the contrasting pitch of their flights, for they are most firmly linked in being the only two fully human riders of that most finely imagined of all Ariosto's fabulous creatures, the winged horse.[22] In contrast to Orlando, who in a horrifyingly emblematic moment ties Angelica's dead palfrey to his foot and drags it along, Ruggiero and Astolfo are involved with another kind of horse altogether, one with a capacity for flight, and at one time or another they are astride the hippogriff and learning to control its motions, one badly, one well. This magical beast is the apotheosis of all the multiple horsy elements in the *Furioso,* unmistakably derived from the imagery of Plato in the *Phaedrus.*[23] Symbolic of the flesh that, loosed and unrestrained, conveys the soul in runaway fashion to a paradise of sensuality, or, bridled and managed, gains the upper air, its rising and falling marks the limits of the poem as ultimately vertical and symbolic in character. This is the beast for which, in a markedly iconographic moment that is twice insistently recalled (22.24, 22.27), Logistilla contrives a bridle (10.66), and whose motions she then teaches Ruggiero and Astolfo to manage and curb, lest it prove "troppo sfrenato"—"too unbridled." On two occasions both before and after her instruction, Ruggiero is abroad on the animal, and on both occasions it proves a rebellious runaway, wafting him first to Alcina's island and to delights swiftly turned to disasters; and later bearing him down to his attempted rape of Angelica.

In comparison with Astolfo, Ruggiero is the lesser horseman and the poorer student, but then, because of his role as eventual embodiment of the active life, he flies at a lower pitch and his vision is more anchored to earthly things. What he sees in his second tour aboard the hippogriff (10.69ff.) is a long succession of earthly kingdoms and warriors' encampments and armies arrayed:

> Ben che di Ruggiero fosse ogni desire
> di ritornare a Bradamante presto;
> pur, gustato il piacer ch'avea di gire
> cercando il mondo, non restò per questo,
> ch'alli Pollacchi, agli Ungari venire
> non volesse anco, alli Germani, e al resto
> di quella boreale orrida terra:
> e venne al fin ne l'ultima Inghilterra . . .
>
> Dove ne' prati alla città vicini
> vide adunati uomini d'arme e fanti,
> ch'a suon di trombe e a suon di tamburini
> venian, partiti a belle schiere.
>   (10.72, 74.1–4)

Even though Ruggiero desired to return quickly to Bradamante, nevertheless, having tasted the pleasure of going in search of the world, he was not so satisfied that he did not wish to travel among the Poles and Hungarians as well, and the Germans and the rest of those off-putting northern countries: and he came at last to distant England . . . where in the fields surrounding the city of London he saw armed knights and foot-soldiers being drawn into orderly troops to the bray of trumpets and the roll of drums.

This is a foretaste of what will later, more grievously still, withhold him from Bradamante: the temptations of honor and glory, symbolized by his fixation with eagle-emblems and his desire to rule kingdoms. One point is especially notable. Since Ruggiero, from on high, can so clearly distinguish men and their heraldic devices—men of a particularly martial occupation, devices to which he has and will have a certain obsessive attachment—he is clearly not very far above the earth. This is essentially a vision of the *vita activa* in motion, exactly appropriate to his role as warrior and dynast. Still, considering the scale of possibilities, it is quite limited and earthbound in comparison with contemplative withdrawal. No longer tossed by refractory mounts (as so often before), Astolfo will fly at a much higher pitch, one at which, by comparison, *all* earth's glories, military and political as well as erotic, are utterly effaced, and earth itself is reduced to a pinprick in the heavens, risibly tiny.

Quivi ebbe Astolfo doppia maraviglia:
che quel paese appresso era sí grande,
il quale a un picciol tondo rasimiglia
a noi che lo miriam da queste bande;
e ch'aguzzar conviengli ambe le ciglia,
s'indi la terra e'l mar ch'intorno spande
discerner vuol; che non avendo luce,
l'imagin lor poco altra si conduce.
        (34.71)

Here Astolfo had two surprises: close up, that place (the moon) was very big, which, to us,
seems but a little sphere when we look at it from down here; while, if he wanted to descry
the earth and the sea that surrounds it, he had to narrow both his eyes: for, not having any
light of their own, their features are not visible at any distance.

In the end, the final test is one of vision. How and what these lovers *see* provides a
clear index to the moral altitude of their loves and a means to differentiate and to
distinguish them on a vertical scale of attachments. Not for nothing does Atlante, in
his first flight, graze the earth ("rade la terra") and soar to the stars ("s'alza ne le
stelle") at both 2.52 and 4.6.[24]

7

The Laughter of Lucian

Astolfo as Christian Menippus

The vertical dimension characteristic of epic fiction, transcending the world of human action and lending it intelligibility, has been effectively collapsed and eliminated from the *Furioso*.
> David Quint, *Origin and Originality in Renaissance*
> *Literature: Versions of the Sources*

A diffuse and episodic poem . . .
> J. M. Steadman, *The Lamb and the Elephant:*
> *Ideal Imitation and the Context of*
> *Renaissance Allegory*

Orlando is distinctly earthbound; Ruggiero flies at a middling pitch; Astolfo flies at the highest level of all. But the comic epic observes its own decorum, and in the *Furioso* the highest level to be touched is only the moon. For one thing, this accords well with a poem of lunacy. For another, poetry in a language already in possession of the *Divina commedia* will scarcely attempt to penetrate the heaven of heavens for a second time,[1] and Ariosto has a real sense of how,

> salendo lo intelletto in suso
> per veder Dio, non de' parerci strano
> se talor cade giù cieco e confuso.
> (*Satire* 6.46–48)

when the intellect ascends on high to see God, we must not think it strange if sometimes it falls down blind and bewildered.

Recognizing limitations is evidence of sanity, but while stopping at the moon indicates prudence in avoiding an encounter with Dante in his own space, Ariosto invokes other authorities for very particular resonances. The moon is the threshold of the permanent, uncorrupted, immaterial world of the Ptolemaic universe. In that paradoxical borderland, earth inevitably appears as a tiny pinprick in the heavens, the diminished tilting-ground of minuscule earthlings. What Astolfo laughingly sees from the moon, the sheer inconsequentiality of earth, is what not only Dante but also a select company of contemplators saw before him: Pompey in Lucan's *Pharsalia*, Scipio in Macrobius's *Somnium*, Arcita in Boccaccio's *Teseida*.[2] A long tradition of what has been termed "disembodied laughter"[3] stretches before him, and Astolfo, though still wearing his body, slips in among his betters. Wrapped in an aura of excellent good humor, his sense of fun intact, constantly amazed at

166

finding himself—of all people, and still in the flesh!—in the heavens, he comes under the tutelage of St. John, doyen of contemplatives. Conversion and enlightenment do not eradicate but rather redirect the essential elements of his nature, and his humor, preserved but purified, is in the best traditions of Christianity, furthest from puritan contagion.

Bembo is the poet's most proximate literary connection to a great tradition, and Ariosto engaged his witty friend in wittier rivalry. What Astolfo learns in his lunar sojourn is an imaginative, very witty renovation of the mental altitude enjoined on Lavinello in plangently Ciceronian prose by the Platonizing hermit of the *Asolani*:

And those things [says the instructor] which other men love so much down here and to secure which we so often see the whole world thrown into confusion, the very streams run red with human blood, and even the ocean on occasion, as this wretched age of ours has often known and still knows, for that matter—empires and crowns and lordships, I mean—: these are no more sought by one of our celestial lovers than he who can have water from a pure wellspring, when he is thirsty will seek that of some turbid, marshy rivulet.[4]

Ariosto's world, like Bembo's, is one with two tiers of reality.

An Astolfo enskyed and squinting to see an all but vanished earth is a paladin both literarily and spiritually promoted. This necessitates careful critical handling. The "location" of the episode—generically, structurally, tonally—is all-important; possibly more than any other, it suffers from being wrenched from its context and utilized as an entity in itself, a procedure in which it is often made to subserve fashionable but wholly unhistorical critical functions.[5] What Astolfo hears and sees, the particular mode of his hearing and seeing and what comes of them—in other words, the function of the lunar visit and its relation to the overall design of the *Furioso*—is the subject of the following pages. The focus throughout is on the paladin's central role, on the thematic and structural continuity of a series of episodes in which he is cast as protagonist, and on Ariosto's relation to a Neoplatonic tradition of philosophic laughter.

Considering the modality first, in contrast to all those solemn antecedents who scrutinized the little earth, Astolfo sees in a very particular and determining way: the way of Lucian of Samosata, irradiated with a coruscating Menippean wit. As a comic contemplator and observer in this mode, he has nothing at all to do with the Dantean religious-contemplative mode that Fornari appears to attribute to him and that provoked Rajna to his raucous horse-laugh about an inappropriate mysticism.[6] Modern scholars have traced the vogue for Lucian in fifteenth-century Italy to Guarino da Verona's rediscovery and translation of the Syrian satirist in Constantinople between 1403 and 1408, just previous to his arrival in Ferrara to initiate his great educational program at the Studio.[7] Numerous translations thereafter attest to the Renaissance infatuation with the satirist, among them those of Pope Pius II, Maffeo Vegio, Leo Battista Alberti, Niccolò Leoniceno, and Boiardo himself.[8] In that light, Ariosto's Lucianism represents a characteristic alertness to exploitable contemporary literature, as well as an attempt to extend Boiardo's more tentative classicism into Carolingian romance.

We should distinguish between two kinds of Lucianism in Ariosto. He introduces a Lucianic atmosphere in Orlando's fight with the orc-monster (11.35ff.), but for Astolfo's more serious "lunacy" he invokes another Lucianism altogether, a more "philosophic" one, brilliant with intellectual fireworks and impregnated with paradox suited to the wise fool: this is the Lucian of the dialogues rather than the *True History.* And here another distinction is necessary. Modern readers value Lucian as witty skeptic and relativist, but in fifteenth-century Italy he was prized particularly for verbal elegance and moral seriousness, and it was for that combination of virtues that he appealed to Erasmus, Thomas More, and their exact contemporary, Ariosto.[9] Laughter and weight were the combined Lucianic qualities all three sought to match: ironic distance from human madness and involved concern for its impact on life. The distanced philosophic view from the moon is one of Lucian's characteristic devices, allowing him a transcendent perspective on mindless human possessiveness, and it provides the great exemplar for the moon-allegory of the *Furioso.* Two brilliant passages from a pair of relevant dialogues are especially important for the passage in which Astolfo contemplates the world below him. In the first dialogue, the *Icaromenippus,* Lucian's mouthpiece, Menippus, borne to the moon by eagle and vulture feathers attached to his body (parodies of Plato's white-and-black horses of the soul), wonderingly describes the busy anthill of mortality to a friend, which includes warring Getans, migratory Scythians, farming Egyptians, trading Phoenicians: "Suppose you collected a large number of singers, or rather of massed choirs, and told each member of them to forget about harmony and concentrate on singing his own tune, what would you expect it to sound like, with every performer trying to execute a solo of his own, and shout down the man next to him?" The friend responds that it would be a "pretty nasty noise"—and the metaphor of discord, so central in Ariosto as to be personified in the figure of Discordia herself, is soon continued and elaborated: "It's not just that people sing out of tune, but that they all sing *different* tunes, each with its own rhythm and its own meaning." But what especially provokes Menippus's wonderment is humanity's perpetual squabbling for land, the pride of ownership,

when the whole of Greece appeared from up there to be about four inches across, of which Attica doubtless represented only a tiny fraction! . . . I thought of all the Argives and Spartans who died in a single day for a bit of land no broader than a bean. It was also amusing to see how proud people were to possess, say, eight gold rings and four golden bowls—when the whole of Mount Pangaeus, gold-mines and all, was about the size of a millet-seed.[10]

Here the appetitive, incomprehensible Many are telescoped and comprehended in the glance of the One, and the contrary madnesses, purely by being seen as universal, emerge as comic in the purer air of heaven.

For comparison with the *Furioso,* the view from above is even more splendidly illustrated in the second dialogue, *Charon Sees Life,* in which a bemused Charon and Hermes look down from the heights of Pelion piled on Ossa and wonderingly contemplate a world of multiform activity and interlocking, discordant ambitions, a world in travail with "hopes and fears." At Hermes's direction, Charon observes a "complicated muddle" of humans involved in navigation, warfare, litigation, money-making, and begging and suddenly inquires, "But what are those dim shapes flying round them?"—which causes Hermes to identify them as two of the most powerful forces in the *Furioso*:

HERMES: Hopes and fears, Charon—stupidities, pleasure, accumulative instincts, rages, hatreds, and things like that. At ground level you have stupidity, which is a fundamental part of their make-up—in fact it's quite inseparable from human nature, and so are hatred, rage, jealousy, ignorance, bewilderment, and avarice. But hopes and fears tend to fly at a rather higher altitude. Fears dive on to their targets and knock them out, sometimes even causing a permanent stoop, but hopes hover overhead, and just as a person thinks he's going to catch them, they shoot up into the air and leave him with his mouth hanging open. You've probably seen Tantalus having much the same sort of trouble with his water down below. And now, if you strain your eyes a bit, you'll be able to see the Fates up there in the sky, working away at a spindle, from which human beings are suspended by fine threads. Can you see the threads I mean, coming down like strands of cobweb on to each individual?
CHARON [*after gazing intently for a moment*]: Oh yes, now I can see them—incredibly thin, and mostly tangled up with one another.
HERMES: Of course they are, skipper, for [*pointing to each in turn*] this chap here is destined to be killed by that fellow over there, and that fellow by another fellow. And this chap's going to inherit the estate of someone with a shorter thread than his, and another chap's going to inherit it from him. So no wonder the threads are all tangled up.[11]

The answer, "Hopes and fears, Charon," is ultimately Platonic in its conception of the futility of the chase after shadowy, mutable materiality. This Lucianic laughter at the numberless avenues that human desire can take (and the numberless interceptions death can contrive for its expectations) provides Ariosto with a notable, beloved precedent. "Speme" and "timore" form two of the Stoic perturbations of the soul (along with joy and grief) that agitate his creatures' hearts and lead them forever into the chase, most particularly in the mad pursuits of Atlante's empty Palace of Illusion, which are positively alive with the hope of possession and the fear of loss. Finding the satirist's genius cordial to his own, Ariosto applies Lucian's perspective on Scythian, Greek, Egyptian, and Cilician madness directly to the no less egregious turmoil of the Carolingian world, and he gives us his vision through the eyes of Astolfo, who sees, transfigured in the moon's rubbish, the fruit of all the "voluptas carnalis" and "avaritia mundi" that spur his peers to pursue them. Like Menippus, who significantly has Empedocles for his guide, Astolfo sees the fruits of love and strife; hence those "empty plans that have no rest," those "tears and sighs of lovers," those "vain desires," memorably universalizing the condition of the topsy-turvy Carolingian world. They come in bizarre Ariostan forms, but they are not totally unfamiliar. They are comic variants of images we have noted in numerous museum pictures, the broken things under the chariot of the Triumph of Time, the melancholy leavings and spilth of shattered glasses and insect-depredated bouquets in many a *Vanitas* picture of the Dutch moralists.[12] Implicitly, all the desired and hunted things of the *Innamorato* and *Furioso* are in this lunar dustbin—the beauty of women, fabulous armor, kingdoms, and power; "implicitly" because all these earthly prizes are here in an emblematic guise, as Platonic types of their true nature in the light of eternity, presented with withering laughter in their essential decadence, and giving the "ubi sunt" formula an astonishing response. At this point the poet's posture and tone more than ever suggest a Boethian withdrawal into a Minerva's tower of wisdom to watch the furious scavenging for booty below.[13]

If we know the *Innamorato,* the pathetic remnants Astolfo sees are easily recognizable as the transfigured objects of all the hunts and chases begun in Boiardo. In the melancholy music of Ariosto's lunar stanzas, the regularly alternated lusts, ambitions, and rages of the Boiardan world are magnified into those of all human history, elevated into a universal emblem of eternal human cupidity. The panoramas of romance, surcharged with comically wasteful, endlessly laborious pursuits of nothing are, finally, an image of the wild forest of the world itself. Passing in review all the forms of human felicity, Ariosto utilizes one astonishing figure after another for the plunder and detritus of the ages, his imagery crystallizing into clear comic allegory.[14] Angelica's and Alcina's beauty is represented by that bird-lime (anticipated by Petrarch's verb, "invescato");[15] Agramante's and Ruggiero's ambitious desire for kingdoms is figured in that heap of tumid bladders (linked certainly to St. Paul's "Pride puffeth up"); gold and silver hooks figure the futile gifts of greedy givers, as exploded crickets[16] do the empty verses of flattering poets, as eagles' talons do authority misused, as windy bellows do princely favors and courtly praises. Preserved on the moon from the remorseless attrition of time, these ludicrous remnants are perfect immutable ideas of nullity, imperishable forms of illusion, for, in finding heavenly correspondences for earthly objects, Ariosto is turning to excellent poetic account the doctrine of correspondences he learned from the solemn Bembo, if from nowhere else:

The [upper] world contains all that we have in this, but things as much more excellent than these as the heavenly are better than the earthly here.[17]

Astolfo is the only character in the *Furioso* who has illustrated for him the absurdity of unaided human effort, who is granted a vision of the fruit of man's works, stripped to their essence and deprived of worldly gloss. In contemplating all these witnesses of desire and power in their ridiculous lunar transmutations, he looks on an apparent triumph of time from the perspective of timelessness. It is only at this point that he perceives as shadows all the objects his fellow Christians and pagan adversaries exercise themselves fanatically and fruitlessly to grasp in the world below. What he perceives, in its very essence, is loss: loss of power and glory, loss of time and effort, loss finally of the self in a futile expense of the spirit is exemplified again and again in that valley of lost things. Twice and with heavy emphasis as he instructs Astolfo, St. John employs the verb "perdere":

ciò che si perde o per nostro diffetto,
o per colpa di tempo o di Fortuna:
ciò che si perde qui, la si raguna.
        (34.73.6–8)

whatever is lost here, either by our inadvertence, or by Time or Fortune—whatever is lost here, is gathered and heaped up there.

ciò che in somma qua giú perdesti mai,
là su salendo ritrovar potrai.
        (34.75.7–8)

whatever, in sum, you ever lost down here, by voyaging up there you can find once again.

And this is where the lunar episode begins to illuminate several earlier, very important areas of the poem. The moon is the locus in which Ariosto most forcefully recalls losses perpetually suffered by deluded and frustrated seekers in the reaches of his sublunary world. Loss due to human folly, capriciousness, and miscalculation—the loss of helmets, enchantresses, wits, kingdoms, and territories—is the great recurring theme of the *Furioso,* and the sheer slipperiness of the frantically desired but ever-vanishing Angelica is at once its most potent symbol and its chief comic wonder. The enchantress has only to fly past and her pursuers and their wits take flight as well: double flight, double loss, of the enchantress as well as of reason, which is "apt to exhale" ("atto a esalar," 34.83). The almost formulaic pattern of furious hunt and sudden loss represents Ariosto's elevation of two or three brief moments in Boiardo to the level of symbolic action, as it perhaps raises the equestrian Angelica to a kind of "Fortuna a cavallo."[18] In the *Innamorato,* Angelica, provided with her magic ring, twice displays a wonderful talent for vanishing from pursuers: first from Ferraù, who wildly searches the thick woods for her; and later on from Orlando, who goes "errando" on the same hopeless mission. The symbolic overtones of this repeated action in the particularly suggestive locales of dark woods and forests are reinforced by the similar language linking both disappointed searchers. Ferraù is the very picture of baffled desire: "Non se arresta correre e cercare; / Ma quel che cerca non può lui trovare" (1.2.16; "Not for a moment did he stop running and searching, but what he went in search of, he did not find"). Orlando similarly loses both himself and his prey in a wood: "Errando andò per quella in sino al dì, / Ma ciò ch'el va cercando non trovò" (2.18.53; "There he went wandering till break of day; but what he went in search of, did not find").

In Boiardo, to seek is not always to find. In Ariosto, the seeking is attended with greater gravity; it may indeed be to lose even more, to be, ultimately and in the punningly pertinent phrase from *A Midsummer Night's Dream,* "wood within this wood,"[19] as Orlando chiefly learns in a dark forest at the poem's midpoint. The sudden disappearance, the shocking loss, the seeking and not finding of some intensely desired thing (and the losing of oneself into the bargain because of the mad nature of the hunt)—all these are among the most memorably dramatized actions in the *Furioso.*

In Astolfo's company, we are above the world of the poem, in a space where the controlling poet has been from the very beginning. The lunar elevation not only allows us to glimpse the thickets and copses of the *Innamorato,* filled with strange vanishings, but it also allows us mentally to unify and integrate the multiple narratives of the *Furioso,* especially some crucial earlier episodes in which Astolfo has taken a central role. In essence, it focuses and concentrates the major ideas of the poem. For if, in the midst of the lunar waste of canto 34, the wise narrator philosophically informs us that the moon is full of lost wits of people mistakenly reputed wise here below, and that most of us lose our wits in the manifold ways of the world, he has also told us previously (in the proem to canto 24, in a reflective gesture immediately following Orlando's mad-scene) that the world is like a great forest, a "gran selva," in which all those who venture must necessarily lose their way: one here, one there, one and all ultimately lose their direction in mazes of erring desire. The root of all these Ariostan forests is deep in the locus classicus on the forest of human madness with its multiple byways and alleys in Horace's *Satires.* Ten cantos apart, the two passages on the loss of wits create one overarching harmony, and the reader's faculty of memory must stretch to bridge the distance between them. This is the voice of the poet discoursing, on the earlier occasion, on the ways that humans lose their wits:

e se ben come Orlando ognun non smania,
suo furor mostra a qualch'altro segnale.
E quale è di pazzia segno piú espresso
che, per altri voler, perder se stesso?

Varii gli effetti son, ma la pazzia
è tutt'una pero, che li fa uscire.
Gli è come una gran selva, ove la via
conviene a forza, a chi vi va, fallire . . .
chi su, chi giú, chi qua, chi là travia.
        (24.1.5–8, 2.1–4, 8)

And even if everyone does not go crazy in the same way as Orlando, nevertheless he reveals his madness by some other sign. For what clearer indication of madness is there than, by wanting another, to lose yourself? The effects are various, but the madness that produces them is single and one. It is like a great forest in which whoever enters must necessarily lose his way: . . . one here, one there, one deeper, one more shallowly: all lose their way.

More extendedly (and ironically) Ariosto elaborates the ways to madness in this discourse ten cantos later in the midst of Astolfo's visit to the moon.

Altri in amar lo perde, altri in onori,
altri in cercar, scorrendo il mar, richezze;
altri ne le speranze de' signori,
altri dietro alle magiche sciocchezze;
altri in gemme, altri in opre di pittori,
et altri in altro che piú d'altro aprezze.
Di sofisti e d'astrologhi raccolto,
e di poeti ancor ve n'era molto.
　　　(34.85)

Some lose their wits in love, some in chasing honors, some, scouring the sea, in seeking riches; others, in expectations placed in their lords, others on the trail of follies in magic; others in jewels, others in paintings, others still in other things that are prized by other men; here, of sophists', and astrologers' wits, and of poets' as well, there was a great heap.

The passage is utterly central. When he writes in this vein and adopts this particular rhetorical mode, Ariosto is most essentially a poet of love in its widest sense, most clearly a Lucianist and Platonist concerned with the infinite ramifications of human desire. The staggering variety of appetite is a constantly reappearing concern in Ariosto's poetry, especially in his imitations of Horace where, in the very language of the *Furioso*, he was later to write, "Degli uomini son varii l'appetiti" (*Satires* 3.52). Boiardo too knew from Horace that every man's desire is different, but whereas "Il voler di ciascun molto è diverso" is but a single line in the *Innamorato* (2.13.1.1), Ariosto gives it a complex, poem-long elaboration in the *Furioso*. Accordingly, the poem is shot through with the rhetoric of the classical moralists, who cast their vision over a universal space and scan the theater of the world in all its mad variety of hunger, its sheer laughable irrationality.

For authors in this tradition, and for Boethius especially, the act of scanning the panoramas of existence ("hanc vitae scaenam") for the multiple forms of human desire resolves itself rhetorically into a lively catalog of "huic," "hunc," "ille," and "alius," revealing the wide scope of the author's contemplative gaze as it darts into far-flung arenas of human activity, differentiating and demonstrating the myriad forms of desire.[20] Similarly, in the *Asolani* Bembo domesticates the Boethian model in the love-treatise, with further unmistakable impact on the *Furioso*. "But Love," says one of Bembo's speakers,

is never satisfied to hold us merely by one hook or lash us with one whip; nay, just as all the other passions are born of desires, so from the first desire which springs up in us a thousand others are derived as from a great river, and in lovers these are as various as they are numberless. For although they all, in general, tend to one conclusion, yet because their objects are diverse and diverse the fortunes of lovers, each undoubtedly desires in a different way.

This is where Bembo proceeds to illustrate the many desires of men, using the familiar rhetoric just noted in Boethius: "Sono alcuni . . . alcuni altri . . . altri . . ."[21] Demonstrably, then, Ariosto's forests, alive with unproductive, unrewarded desire, dominated by the twinned verbs "cercare" and "perdere," have a recognizable background in a certain kind of literature. They derive first and foremost from Platonism's multiform *hyle* or *sylva,* and they accumulate rich echoes of Horace, Boethius, Boiardo, and Bembo, in whom the tradition is encapsulated within Ariosto's own generation. Ariosto's genius repeatedly fuses the different sonorities of multiple, disparate sources into a totally new and harmonious unity of his own, which is distinctively "Ariostan." In the particular instance of canto 34 and its vision of human follies working at cross-purposes and with tunnel vision, the effect of Ariosto's creative fusion of Horace and Lucian is altogether electrifying in its thrust and force. For Ariosto superimposes on the Horatian forest image,[22] in a great unparalleled imaginative leap, a wholly innovative Icaromenippean expansion, whereby the mad chases in the "selva oscura" are ironically subsumed under the witty garbage dumps of the lunar landscape. He forges the crucial link between the Horatian madness in the forests of earth and the Lucianic lunacy of the moon, directly relating the evaporation of men's wits in sylvan worldly hunts to the stores and stocks of fled intellects on the lunar surface. Yoking the Roman and Syrian satirists, he notes that the various enchantments of the wild wood of the world make all men appetitive and acquisitive; and in the process (he now adds with triumphant originality) their intellects, volatile as always, fly off to that eternal symbol of change, the moon, where a new Menippus in the form of Astolfo arrives to find them. Angelica may vanish to reappear again and again, but men's wits, perpetually sacrificed to her alluring passage, evaporate and exhale forever: so fragile is human reason, so needful of armies and navies the shrunken and perpetually assaulted kingdom of Logistilla. For it is reason essentially that most suffers diminution and loss in the forest.

These connected, interacting passages on the varied passions that agitate mankind attest to a recurring and incremental concern in the *Furioso.* The richness and splendor of the moon episode of canto 34 hardly exist in splendid isolation; the episode elaborates the reflective Horatian passage ten cantos earlier, which it directly recalls. But—moving even further backward—both the proem on forest-madness in canto 24 and the exploration of lunar madness in canto 34 have been fully anticipated on a much earlier occasion, in the Palace of Illusion in canto 12. Attentive to Ariosto's patterns of rhetoric and to the power of his peculiar poetic rhythms ("altri . . . altri . . . altri . . ."), we cannot fail to match this insistence on the varied ways of losing oneself in the world with his splendid realization of that idea in the confining palace constructed by the magician Atlante, who presides masterfully over a variety of concupiscent desires embodied in the prisoners Ruggiero, Orlando, Ferraù, Brandimart, Gradasso, Sacripant, and many others, all of whom are desirers imported from the pages of the *Innamorato.*

The episode of the Palace of Illusion extends over many cantos, from canto 11 to canto 22.[23] Beginning with Ruggiero's entrapment in its frustrating confines when he *fearfully* sees "Bradamante" borne off by a mysterious captor, the episode of the Palace of Illusion gathers momentum when Orlando, in a forest, *fearfully* chases after a mysterious rapist bearing off "Angelica" and threatening to plunder her "rose" and so to deprive the paladin of his rights to her virginity[24]—here, as we have seen before, Orlando runs a parallel course with Ruggiero. Falling victim to the enchanter's illusions, which are in reality a manifestation of his own previously expressed sensual fears about being supplanted in Angelica's affections, Orlando pursues the figment of his beloved into the palace only to find that she has suddenly vanished into thin air (12.8ff.). Darting back and forth in the silent corridors ("Corre di qua, corre di là"), he passes in succession, unseeing and unseen—for appetite is egocentric and monopolistic, and this is clearly not a place of cognition—all his fellow prisoners as they blindly scramble up and down ("alto e basso") in pursuits as vain as his own for things they have sought for and lost. Common inmates in a house of increasingly frustrated desire, all of them are invisible to each other, all are entrapped by the outward projection of their own particular obsessions, all are furiously enraged at the concealed maker of that palace, whom they blame for their error and their several losses of damsels, horses, swords, and helmets:

Tutti cercando il van, tutti gli danno
colpa di furto alcun che lor fatt'abbia:
del destrier che gli ha tolto, altri è in affanno;
ch'abbia perduta altri la donna, arrabbia;
altri d'altro l'accusa: e cosí stanno,
che non si san partir di quella gabbia;
e vi son molti, a questo inganno presi,
stati le settimane intiere e i mesi.
    (12.12)

All are in search of him, each accuses him of a theft: one is aggrieved for the horse he has taken, another is enraged for the lady he has lost. Others accuse him of other things: and there they remain, for they know no way out of that cage; and there were many there, captivated by this deception, who remained for weeks and months entire.

In reality the captives are themselves the agents who have constructed their prison. Atlante is merely their surrogate, one they all have in common, who is representative of the part of their human nature they find convenient to blame, as if it were some external force.

Here, certainly, Atlante emerges unmistakably in his guise of Amor, presiding over the desiring faculty in its most comprehensive sense. Because that faculty is so often left unsatisfied and deluded of its object, ignoring reality and imagining things that are not, Amor is the constant focus of bitter reproaches, and the traditional "Complaint against Love" is the frequent result. The *Furioso* is rife with such complaints, not only here but also in the Orlando-narrator's lament of unrequited love in the proem to canto 2, in the laments of many characters in the narrative proper, and throughout the narratives of characters in the novellas.[25] Further, when Ariosto represents all the inmates failing utterly to recognize one another's presences in their common prison, while all of them simultaneously imagine the thing they desire most in the nonexistent phantoms of the place, he is brilliantly dramatizing exactly what he had said about the nature of Amor as early as the first canto: "Quel che l'uom vede, Amor gli fa invisibile, / e l'invisibil fa vedere Amore" (1.56; "What a man sees, Love can make invisible, and what is invisible Love can make a man see"). In the rush and bustle of this magical house of attraction and frustration, of swift hope and swifter despair, the poet's gestures are imitative. He has borrowed both his tone and his metaphor of the cage of love from one of his favorite poems, Petrarch's *Trionfi,* one section of which, the *Trionfo della Morte,* supplied the model for his earliest vernacular poem: not only do Atlante's prisoners re-enact Petrarch's "Un lungo error in cieco laberinto," but the magician's "gabbia" is modeled directly on the "gabbia" of the *Trionfo d'Amore,* into which Amor leads the wretched captives tied to his chariot.[26] All their time indoors is given a vivid illustration in the *Trionfo d'Amore's* last verses, which (exactly as in Atlante's Palace) depict a furious activity of uncertain happinesses and certain griefs ("confusion turbida e mischia / di certe doglie e d'allegrezze incerte") in an outwardly smiling mansion whose very steps, Petrarch says, are strewn with slippery hopes ("lubrico sperar"). So too, in the *Furioso,* the palace stands open and smiling in a broad meadow, but once within the prisoner, self-caught however much he turns his accusations outward against "Amore" for deceiving him, spends weeks and even months beguiled by momentary apparitions of beatitude, which, chased with wild expenditure of energy up and down the stairs, inexorably vanish and breed only chagrin. No better illustration has ever been given of Vergil's "carcere caeco" (*Aen.* 6.733–34) with its incessant quadruple perturbations of joy and grief, hope and fear.

All these caged Ariostan birds are lovers, but "love" here has the widest possible application, indicating attachment to objects as well as to persons. It is employed, that is, in the wide philosophical sense in which Boethius and Bembo use it. There is a more comprehensive denomination for this great variety of obsessive hungers experienced by the self-blinded prisoners: its name is cupidity, a single though broad track in the wood of error, and sensual or romantic love is only one of its components. Little wonder, then, that Atlante, the mansion's creator, is said to be a "mago," makes red seem yellow, and aims his enchantment at the eye primarily (4.20). This is most certainly not Boiardo's "mago," who is simple by comparison. Ariosto's three long descriptions of the magician and his powers insistently strive to focus a metamorphosed Atlante in the reader's imagination before his first appearance in the *Furioso's* action. Thereafter he is insistently equipped with the attributes, and he imitates the actions, of Petrarch's "Amor" in the first and second sections of the *Trionfi,* even to running up with a chain to bind the apparently blinded Bradamante, who bests him and binds him instead, as Laura does Amor.[27] The corruption of the visual sense is the basis of both erotic and other material cravings, and Atlante is the chief master in all the *Furioso* of this deception and confounding of human sight. He incarnates something present in every human psyche, and, on two occasions before he appears as the master of the Palace of Illusion—in a Pyrenean steel castle given over to ease and indolence (canto 4), and on Alcina's island of consummated sensual loves (cantos 6, 7, 8)—he has demonstrated an extraordinary ability to divert the poem's soldiers from a life of activity to one of sensual abandonment. Now, as Atlante emerges as the creator of the Palace of Illusion, Ariosto clearly points the magician's triple, linked stratagems, ensuring that the reader notes the linked progression:

Dopo il castel d'acciar, che nulla giova,
E dopo Alcina, Atlante ancor fa pruova.
   (12.21)

After the steel castle, which didn't work, and after Alcina, Atlante is still preparing stratagems.

Atlante's power is decisively terminated in canto 22 by Astolfo's arrival at the palace and his swift undoing of the magician's illusions. Having just returned from his first, or Herculean, labor-filled circumambulation of the globe, he achieves a singular triumph in refusing to fall victim to the trap that has proved unavoidable for everyone else. Astolfo's sight, doubtless aided by having looked, like Ruggiero, into Logistilla's lucent walls and "knowing himself" ("se stesso conoscendosi," 10.59.8), is not blinkered by desire, and by consulting his magic book he sees prudently and immediately into the heart of the problem to be resolved. How unlike the stupid Orlando of the *Innamorato*! Hence he undoes the charm that holds the inmates captive: the palace dissolves in a trice and goes up in smoke, and the magician vanishes, his power broken. His disappearance exactly coincides with Ruggiero's *recognition* of Bradamante when the scales of illusion fall from their eyes and the hero *knows* his beloved in her true being for the very first time. Platonic verbs of knowledge and cognition emphasize the meaning insistently:

guardò Ruggiero, e fu a *conoscer* presto
quel che fin qui gli avea nascoso Atlante:
fatto avea Atlante che fin a quell'ora
tra lor non s'eran *conosciuti* ancora.

Ruggiero riguarda Bradamante, et ella
riguarda lui con alta maraviglia,
che tanti dí l'abbia offuscato quella
illusion sí l'animo e le ciglia . . .

Molto lor duol che per incantamenti,
mentre che fur negli errabondi tetti,

tra lor non s'eran mai *riconosciuti,*
e tanti lieti giorni eran perduti.
    (22.31.5–8, 32.1–4, 33.5–8; italics mine)

Ruggiero looked and was quick to *recognize* what Atlante had hidden from him till this
day; Atlante it was who had contrived that they should not *know* each other till that hour.
Ruggiero looks at Bradamante and she at him with deep wonder that for so many days that
illusion had so clouded both her soul and her eyes . . . much it grieved them that, because
of enchantments, while they were inmates in that house of erroneous chases, they had
never *recognized* each other and had lost so many happy days.

In vowing at last to wed and to be converted (though in terms that are comically
ambiguous; that is, he would put his head in fire for love of her, not to mention
water), Ruggiero now passes from a sentimental to a more cognitive kind of love,
and the poem moves to yet another, even more difficult stage in the lovers' careers.
By the end of canto 22, the temptations of sensuality are being superseded by those
of power, honor, and fame, and, by canto 25, alleging the damage his honor would
suffer, he is writing Bradamante excuses for deferring both baptism and marriage.
Formerly, it appears, Atlante had had lecherous Alcina at his command to engage
Ruggiero's heart; now, her sisterly co-ruler, Morgana, patroness of worldly honors
and riches, is beginning to show her power.

Astolfo's arrival on the moon *to see* allows us a very distinct perspective on the
narratives in which he has been functioning as an insightful and effective liberator on
the earth below. It reveals, as well, the cumulative growth of a set of characteristic
Ariostan ideas. The lunar episode forms, in fact, the aggregate of three or four
previous parts of the poem. Reading backward, the lunar visit of canto 34 recalls the
Horace-influenced forest proem of canto 24, crowns the anticipatory allegory of
baffled chases in Atlante's empty palace in canto 12, and projects a powerful echo
from on high to the Logistilla allegory of cantos 4 through 10. For, as the text says
plainly enough, it is love for Logistilla that leads man stoically to cast out the perturbations of hope and fear, "speme" and "timore," to which Atlante's captives are
nevertheless so thoroughly devoted:

Il suo amore ha dagli altri differenza:
speme o timor negli altri il cor ti lima;
in questo il desiderio piú non chiede,
e contento riman come la vede.
    (10.46.5–8)

She inspires a different kind of love: in other loves hope and fear erode the heart; in hers,
desire seeks no further and remains content with the sight of her.

Assuredly, Ariosto could be expected to know something about the power of
reason to control the perturbations of hope and fear in the soul, perturbations by
which the soul submits itself to the power of fortune. Bembo in the *Asolani* had had

a good deal to say about the matter, though not as much as Petrarch, who had written an entire book on the subject,[28] and certainly Ariosto himself was in a position to know that Isabella d'Este's motto was "Nec spe nec metu," and that it was emblazoned all over the ceiling of her Studiolo in the Gonzaga castle in Mantua.[29] He could also be expected to know the great commonplace about Reason and the four Cardinal Virtues that support her and testify to her existence in humans, namely, that they are pagan in origin and therefore limited in effect. As the figure of the reasoning faculty, Logistilla is obviously not the highest ideal to which the poem rises, though she is a guard against the wiles of Atlante, and she keeps men from becoming engaged in the Palace of Illusion, from losing themselves in the forest of desire, and from having their wits evaporate into phials or jugs on the moon. Orlando's fragility of reason assures us of Logistilla's fragility of control in the reason of all humans. She shadows a high ideal, and her sober gardens, contrasted to the riotous ones of Alcina, are contrasted also with the Edenic gardens of the Terrestrial Paradise, of which they are a paler reflection. Though Logistilla's hold on man is tenuous (witness Ruggiero, who meets her once, vows eternal friendship, and immediately falls into dereliction), she has connections upward, and Astolfo resolutely pursues them. Without Logistilla, Orlando goes mad, tossed between the two perturbations of hope and fear in the central canto 23. Without Logistilla, his fellow warriors, in submission to Atlante in canto 12, not only lose their wits but also, figuratively, chase illusions down empty corridors of desire, increasingly and simultaneously heaping the moon with deposits of evaporated reason and accumulations of ashen treasure. Lunatic action, resultant madness, and displacement to the moon have an inexorable connection, Luna never lacking for earthly renewals of her chief resource of lunacy.

The reader of the *Furioso,* too often encouraged by romantic and neo-romantic criticism to think of it as a diffuse and discontinuous narrative to be read and interpreted in segments unrelated to each other, may profit from an attempt to see far more continuity and intellectual and moral content in the passages under discussion. The lunar fantasy of canto 34 constitutes the third of three linked allegories, mutually dependent and mutually illuminating narratives, each with its particular tonal richness and each serving as a nodal nerve center of the poem's cumulative action and meaning. The episodes we have just considered are models of calculated rhetoric adapted to different narrative strategies, gradually combining to form an organic whole. The first of the three, the Alcina-Logistilla allegory, with its transparently Platonic opposition of reason and passion and its dense, highly conventional iconography drawn from Petrarch, Boccaccio, and Poliziano, immediately establishes the poem's values and represents Ariosto at his most traditional, both in concept and in image. Here he means at once to be understood, even at the risk of a bit of old-fashioned representation of virtue and vice in opposition. The second episode, the Palace of Illusion, moves a step beyond, domesticating the orthodox idea of the chase after shadows in a cunning and most originally imagined palace of empty rooms and corridors filled with figments; perhaps only a Renaissance courtier constantly fed with "expectations vain" could have conceived it, but the particular instance rises to the level of universal resonance in its picture of perpetually aroused and perpetually baffled hope. Finally, the Limbo of Lunar Vanities, with its melancholy laughter and inspired imagery of transmutation, is quite possibly the high-water mark of Ariosto's poetry and perhaps of the Italian Renaissance, a concentrate of all its values and techniques. In an art poised between Democritean laughter and Heraclitan tears, the poet employs a brilliant iconography of bladders, bellows, talons, hooks, shackles, heaps of rotten flowers, and broken phials—relics picturing the obsessions by which mortality is perpetually trammeled in its sublunary existence. Cupidinous Alcina and Atlante contrive to defeat the reason embodied in Logistilla, and as an inevitable consequence the moon is heaped high with the wit of lunatics.

Here, finally, we should note the central fact toward which this discussion has been working. Only one character links all three narratives by appearing as a chief actor in each in turn. Astolfo is a converted sensualist in the Alcina allegory, the liberator of all the deluded captives in Atlante's Palace of Illusion, and the comic visionary of the voyage to the moon. More importantly, his lunar vision of earthly madness links him decisively to the omniscient narrator whose ironic voice echoes through the empty halls of the Palace of Illusion and comments on the deluded inmates; or more philosophically informs the proem to canto 23; or, in canto 39, grows muted and brooding while contemplating, even in death, the various minds of men. Here the Lucianic contemplation of the varieties of human desire changes significantly, in the harrowing description of the alternate ways in which, on being driven back to Africa, the sailors of Agramante's fleet try to escape their deaths when Astolfo's navy assaults and vanquishes them. Avid as they are for life, their desire to survive only drives them more certainly to death, and even in life's last moments, a rooted passion causes them to enact scenes of horrifying barbarism and savagery as they maim and slaughter to save their own lives (39.84–86).

Astolfo sees what his poet-creator sees. In the penetration of his steep downward gaze on earth, the redeemed buffoon is linked unmistakably to the wise director of the story by language and gesture. Nor is it the first time that the voice of the one has taken on the ironically shaded tones of the other. For if on his very first appearance in the guise of a reformed vegetable we detected in the myrtle-Astolfo's wry challenge to Ruggiero a certain suave "Ariostan" irony about human nature— "Perhaps *you* will find a way to avoid an evil that a thousand before you have not discovered" (6.53)—then this further similarity of their voices in heaven should reinforce the sense of tonal likeness heard previously. They are both, inevitably, serious jesters. At the conjunction of the boundaries of time and no-time, Astolfo is introduced, with complex comic gestures, to those Boethian conceptions of time, causality, fortune, and Providence that have been the poet's from the beginning of his tale. The climax of his journey reveals nakedly the laws by which the poem has been operating throughout and (even after a wildly ironic and paradoxically outrageous speech by the Apostle) by which it continues to operate serenely thereafter.

The moon is the second stopping place in Astolfo's voyage of instruction and represents a secondary, or visual, stage in his illumination. It is prepared for by a crucial first stage, his arrival at the Terrestrial Paradise and his greeting there by St. John, who is to guide him later to the lunar circle. Astolfo's (and the reader's) illumination takes a double form, a favorite Ariostan form of instruction. The knight later has confirmed for him in a vision what has previously been imparted to him in an address, *seeing* on the moon what he has *heard* previously from St. John in the Terrestrial Paradise. What he hears in those heavenly gardens is a small but centrally important sermon delivered in the language and imagery of romance by a magus figure in scarlet and white, but touched throughout with an aura of unmistakable Augustinian doctrine, in which Ariosto humorously adopts the cautionary voice of a gentle old pastor:

"O baron, che per voler divino
sei nel terrestre paradiso asceso;
come che ne la causa del camino,
né il fin del tuo desir da te sia inteso,
pur credi che non senza alto misterio
venuto sei da l'artico emisperio.

"Per imparar come soccorrer dei
Carlo, e la sante fé tor di periglio,
venuto meco a consigliar ti sei
per cosí lunga via, senza consiglio.
Né a tuo saper, né a tua virtú vorrei
ch'esser qui giunto attribuissi, o figlio;
che né il tuo corno, né il cavallo alato
ti valea, se da Dio non t'era dato."
                (34.55–56)

"O baron, who by God's will have ascended to the Terrestrial Paradise: as both the cause of your journey and the object of your desire are not understood by you, nevertheless believe that not without high intervention have you come here from the northern hemisphere. Unawares in your long journey have you come to me to seek counsel on how to succor Charles and rescue the Holy Faith from danger. Neither to your intelligence nor to your virtue do I wish you to attribute your arrival, my son; for neither your horn nor your winged steed would have availed you, if they were not bequeathed by God."

Here, in its highest manifestation, is the profoundly witty mustard-seed effect of much of Ariosto's poetry: vast, ramifying proliferation from an apparently inconsiderable source, an effect reinforced, of course, by elevating one of the "small things" of Carolingian romance, Astolfo himself, into so grand a literary and theological atmosphere. Immediately after this moment, Ariosto says, St. John took Astolfo "by the hand and told him many things worthy to be kept silent." The artful dismissal of these Christian profundities is litotes raised to a transcendent level.

So, in exactly the same fashion, had Logistilla's instruction of Astolfo—presumably she teaches him the voluminous wisdom of the enlightened pagans!—been wittily condensed into "instructions that would take too much time to tell" (15.13). There is, in fact, no need to rehearse those truths communicated to Astolfo: they form the major intellectual substance of the entire poem. St. John's few lines of benevolent deprecation of human pride and self-sufficiency reflect the core of the *Furioso's* meaning and enshrine the poet's favorite doctrine of human limitation, both in blind vision and in crippled action. Astolfo has arrived at this height to learn ("imparar") and to believe ("credi") because he has previously been acting without having fully understood ("inteso"): by grace, and by grace alone, he has risen to that altitude, and not intelligence nor will nor virtue suffices to draw him there. Only the mysterious election of Providence has been at work in all his movements, just as (he only now learns) Orlando, in all the days of his errancy, has been submitted to the same ineluctable power. The theme of the darkness of human intelligence and the lameness of human action is put into the mouth of a mystic, the very type of contemplation, and his paternal mild charm of phrasing gives, oddly, a litotes-like edge to this wisdom. Yet the romantic phrasing does not conceal its closeness to the Boethian "Sed tu quamuis causam tantae dispositionis ignores, tamen quoniam bonus mundum rector temperat, recte fieri cuncta ne dubites" ("But although thou beest ignorant of the causes why things be so disposed, yet because the world hath a governor, doubt not but all things are well done").[30]

The burden of St. John's little discourse is that the human will, however improvident, adjusts itself inevitably to the divine will. This divine will extends and presides over the whole universe, not merely a part, and its order is not to be gainsaid or limited by perversity on the part of creatures: least of all (later on) by St. John's lunatic fit of pride in authorship! Only when in accord with "il voler divino" is the "voglia" or "brama" or "desiderio" or "appetito" of humans fruitful, for of and by itself it can achieve nothing whatever. Indeed, the bent will of humankind, all unknowing, in its very crookedness fulfills divine ordination's serenely undeflected purposes. St. John's human vanity will momentarily get in the way of his saintly orthodoxy and sanity, but that will not for a moment dissipate the power of Providence or alter the way the poem inexorably proceeds. And in so proceeding, comic epic reveals itself as the true obverse of "serious" epic, for who would have thought to hear, in an Italian Carolingian poem, an anticipation of

Man shall not quite be lost, but saved who will;
Yet not of will in him, but grace in me
Freely vouchsafed . . .
By me upheld, that he may know how frail
His fall'n condition is, and to me owe
All his deliverance, and to none but me.[31]

This assertion of the total dependence of the human will on the divine will, of humanity's *meriting* nothing in the way of grace from heaven, is one of the radical ideas of the *Furioso,* twinned inevitably with its focus on human folly, and it permeates many of its major strands and forms a great part of its intellectual substance. Long afterward, one canto from the end, in one of those belated comments he delights in tucking away like a leaf in a forest, Ariosto is his wonted ironic self about Ruggiero's refusing the magical golden lance that wins every battle (45.65), which is a blindness about his own powers that once before led him to disown his magical shield; it is a blindness, moreover, that is preceded by Astolfo's and Bradamante's blindness about their power:

Anzi Astolfo e la donna, che portata
l'aveano poi, credean che non l'incanto,
ma la propria possanza fosse stata,
che dato loro in giostra avesse il vanto;
e che con ogni altra asta ch'incontrata
fosse de lor, farebbono altretanto.
            (45.66.1–6)

Indeed Astolfo and the lady, both of whom had borne the lance, believed that not magic but their own proper powers had availed to give them the victory in battle; and that they would have achieved as much with any other lance they might have picked up.

Ariosto's world is divided, essentially, into Christians and Saracens. But the Christians are Christians of a peculiar and distinctive stripe, generally Pelagians, confident of their own worth, drivingly sure of their own ends and ambitions, certain it was their own virtue and courage that were *rewarded* by triumphs (as St. John crazily claims he was *rewarded* for writing about Christ). Providence and the poet seek, nevertheless, amply and repeatedly to persuade them to another, humbler point of view, largely without success. The poet does not fail to post his warnings. Only one character in all the *Furioso* gets the matter doctrinally right, and that character is Ariosto's rehabilitated Charlemagne: imploring heaven's help for a Paris about to fall to the Saracen hordes, the Emperor knows that "i meriti nostri" are not capable of satisfying humanity's debt by an ounce, that the gift of grace ("di tua grazia il dono") is the absolute essential in moving men's depraved existences ("nostra vita sconcia") to good (14.72). Though the humbling of unaided human action is initiated here and finds climactic, authoritative utterance in the Terrestrial Paradise, it has previously been voiced on occasion after occasion when the destinies of its four major characters are directly concerned. Appropriately enough, the first revelation of heaven's purposes is made to Bradamante when, having fallen by a combination of her own willfulness and the murderous malevolence of Pinabello into a cavern where she is cruelly left to die, she finds herself instead in the tomb of Merlin, ironically the place where she first learns of her great destiny and the centuries-long life of her family. Melissa, the benign enchantress and tutelary spirit of her House, first greets her with the following words: "O generosa Bradamante, /

Non giunta qui senza *voler divino*" (3.9.1–2; "O great-hearted Bradamante, you have not arrived here without *God's will*"; italics throughout this section are mine). Her statement about the divine will is echoed and amplified immediately by Merlin's voice speaking from his tomb:

Acciò dunque il *voler del ciel* si metta
In effetto per te, che di Ruggiero
T'ha per moglier fin da principio eletta,
Segue animosamente il tuo sentiero.
        (3.19.1–4)

To the end, therefore, that *heaven's will,* which has chosen you from the beginning of time to be Ruggiero's wife, shall be put into effect, follow your path with courage.

Likewise St. John, many cantos later, informs Astolfo that there is nothing fortuitous in Ferrara's rise to greatness in the future, that it is part of divine ordination:

Tanta esaltazione e cosi presta,
non fortuita o d'aventura casca;
ma *l'ha ordinata il ciel.*
        (35.7.1–3)

So great, so swift an exaltation is not fortuitous, does not befall by chance: *heaven has ordained it.*

How ironic then that the action that precipitates this vast panorama of human history finds its germ in Pinabello's hatred and his desire to kill Bradamante. The cry of triumph he utters when he watches her plunge to what he imagines is the death he has contrived for her—"Qui fosser teco insieme / tutti li tuoi, ch'io ne spegnessi il seme!" (2.75.7–8; "Would that all your family were here with you, that I might exterminate the seed!")—is undermined in the most ironic way, for Bradamante's "seed" and all her family's history is truly "with her" at the moment, potential in her love, and she is shortly to see them in a pageant of the yet unborn.[32] The irony is rendered immediately clear by an authorial comment on Pinabello's wish, and especially by his use of the verb of volition: "Non come *volse* Pinabello avenne / de l'innocente giovane la sorte" (2.76.1–2; "Not as Pinabello *willed* did the innocent young woman's fate befall"). Mysteriously, his crooked will, aiming at evil, serves the benevolent "voler" of heaven. The heroine's own willfulness is redirected into a worthier course of action; in urging her to proceed "animosamente," Providence utilizes those very qualities in her character ("animosa e malcauta") that, unaccompanied by judgment, conspired in her fall. In the strange outcome of the opening action the reader is reminded forcibly of the *sentences* of the poem's initial stanzas: "Ecco il giudicio uman come spesso erra"; "Contrari ai voti poi furo i successi." And again that very element of contrariness confounding itself, finding itself opposed by a greater Will and becoming part of a larger plan, returns us to Milton, this time to Satan:

But contrary unweeting he fulfilled
The purposed counsel preordained and fixed
Of the Most High.
          (*Paradise Regained* 1.126–28)

The subject of human meritlessness is raised early and amusingly when Brada-mante, recovering from her stunning fall into Merlin's cavern, is apprised of Merlin and Melissa's expectation of her arrival and voices a question dangerously loaded with echoes of the Annunciation: "Di che merito son io, / ch'antiveggian profeti il venir mio?" (3.13.7–8; "Of what merit am I, that prophets foresee my coming?"). This intimates a strong sense of self-importance in Bradamante's words and actions as her concern for her "merito" peeps coyly through her self-deprecation—in passing we should note how deeply Ariosto has re-created Boiardo's Bradamante. The answer the poet is at pains smilingly but resoundingly to return to her odd question is, "None whatever." She is chosen, informed, educated, set on her course, guided, and perpetually rescued by a Providence that has to keep at her constantly lest, unsustained and left to her own inclinations to pride and rage, she fall by the way-side. In this tendency to deviation she is surpassed only by her betrothed, and the assertion of divine power is made with even greater force to Ruggiero as well on another, equally memorable occasion when he has pursued his own ends, deferred Heaven's ends as usual, and fled again to his pagan master. Something like St. John's mild sermon to Astolfo is voiced with greater urgency and passion by the hermit to the perversely willful dynast, barely escaped from drowning on his intended return to Africa: "Vedi che Dio, c'ha lunga man, ti giunge / quando tu gli pensasti esser piu lunge" (41.53.7–8; "See how God, who has a long reach, confronts you at the moment when you thought yourself furthest from Him"). This is an emphatic statement. Its appearance and its force are attributable to the depths of Ruggiero's ignorance and rebelliousness, which try Heaven's patience; and it directly confronts one of Ruggiero's profoundly revealing earlier outbursts that is wild with unre-strained pride in human energy and rife with petulance and scorn for external inter-ference in his personal quest for fame and glory:

Disse Ruggier:—Non riguardiamo a questo:
facciàn nui quel che si può far per nui;
abbia chi regge il ciel cura del resto,
o la Fortuna, se non tocca a lui.
          (22.57)

Ruggiero said, "Let's not worry about that. Let's do ourselves what we can do by our-selves, and let whoever governs the heavens take care of the rest, or let Fortune do it if it doesn't concern him."

Here Ariosto gives us the voice of the authentic pagan, who separates human endeavor from that of the divine and presumptuously allots them individual compartments of activity while affecting impatiently not to know or care if the government of the universe is in divine hands or in those of some alternative power like Fortune. But if Ruggiero is irascibly uncertain about Providence on this earlier occasion, here, in canto 41, rescued from drowning, he has his uncaring uncertainty about divine order forcefully clarified. The "Gran Motor" has tracked him down his nights and down his days and is most present (as the hermit says clearly) when Ruggiero fled furthest. Finally Ariosto ensures that this future governor of a people learns something essential about the government of the universe: the jerk on the bridle confirms unwithstandable power.

The three revelations to Astolfo, to Bradamante, and to Ruggiero are the only moments in the poem when a *direct* revelation of the "voler divino" is made to any of the poem's characters, though all of them without exception operate unequivocally under its power. Astolfo learns in heaven that Orlando especially is being punished by the divine will (34.66.3), but, in an authorial aside at canto 40.30 the reader has been apprised long before that the *will* of God ("Fu *volontà* di Dio") causes even the winds to blow against him, withholding and restraining him that he might accomplish his rescue of Olimpia at an appointed time. Similarly, Rinaldo's providential return from England with auxiliary forces at the very moment when Paris is on the verge of falling to Rodomonte occurs by the *will* of heaven ("Dio *volse* . . . che Rinaldo giunse," 16.29). Humanity accomplishes nothing unaided, and a deeply skeptical Ariosto supplies no reason whatever for complacency about human conduct or the lasting glory of human achievements. Orlando reduces himself to a lustful beast until he is seized by the hand of Providence and literally forced to reinhale his humanity in a rebirth of his existence. Over a long-protracted, event-ridden, and tumultuous period of trial, Ruggiero manages to learn a single lesson: the lesson of the intricate concatenation of his evil impulses and the depth and obduracy of his inclination to wrong-doing, from which only Providence rescues him. And Astolfo is a fool redeemed astonishingly by grace, preserving, even as he operates as a force for good, all the scatter-brained light-headedness and vanity of his former state of folly—planning a tour to heaven as if it were yet another round of sight-seeing (23.12), or finding the fruits of the Tree of Knowledge so tasty that Adam and Eve can be excused for plucking them (34.60). Divine volition is all, and humanity's willfulness is laughable in the extreme. Nevertheless the essential paradox remains of the necessary but minuscule place of human *voglia* in the vast scheme of divine *voler*.

In clear reminiscence of Lucian's comical vision of the Fates at their confused work with the tangled threads of human life, Astolfo's tour of the ultramundane world in canto 34 terminates with a vision of old women weaving and sorting various lengths of thread, and of Time casting them, to sink or float, into the stream of Lethe. This introduces a canto (35) whose opening movement (3–30) generally attracts the attention of modern readers for Ariosto's self-reflexive gesture of scrutinizing his own epic epideictic art. And since no less a personage than St. John, virtually breathing self-importance as a "scrittore," is made the voice of a bulgingly opulent skepticism (no hero, heroine, or patron of antiquity was really as virtuous as portrayed; authors trim their verses according to the gifts they receive; St. John himself praised Christ and *merited* the reward he got, which was nothing less than his salvation) the way lies clear to fantasies about the *Furioso* self-destructing in mid-career. In fact, for all its fashionable modernity, this reading merely returns us to an Ariosto-as-solipsistic-genius, familiar in the old romantic criticism of DeSanctis and Croce.

Several kinds of objections could be registered against a reading that accords such disproportionate importance to a segment of twenty-three octaves, a passage that is so obviously meant, in the showy brilliance of its convoluted paradoxes and its massively impudent reaching for effect, as a tour de force on the poet's part. In the first place, a reading that makes St. John's abrupt polemic an open declaration of the poet's aesthetic principles is patently "off," if only because it ignores the poet's persona, which is prominently reintroduced in the canto's first two stanzas as if in warning of what is to follow: here is the witless Orlando-persona back once more, dreamingly wondering who will retrieve his lost intelligence from the moon, and finding his paradise in his mistress's eyes, her face, her alabaster breasts. *Caveat auditor.* Perhaps the lover-writer is a liar for saying that poetry lies. After all, the moon is a paradoxical place, and Ariosto may be constructing a series of Chinese boxes of irony. Again, such a reading ignores the importance of the *locus*. The poet, his reader, and his characters are standing on very shifty ground. They are on the borderline between the changeful and the changeless, lunacy is in the air, and St. John, so sensible (doctrinally speaking) in the previous canto, and so true to the issues of the poem both up to this poetic moment and long after this poetic moment, suddenly enacts a lightning-like change when the thought crosses his mind that he too is to be numbered among writers: "fui scrittore anch'io." The alteration in his wits is provoked solely by his writer's pride—Ariosto's joke about authorial vanity, most probably not excluding his own. This introduces yet another consideration. By thrusting his own sense of merit into his declaration, St. John is running directly counter to what he has said about merit to Astolfo in the previous canto, and what Ariosto repeatedly makes one of the central issues of his poem—humanity's deep sense of its own worth in the face of repeated illustrations of its ravaged and imperfect natural inclinations. Here is hilarity indeed, of a deliberative rather than trifling kind, and even St. John (once human himself) is enwrapped in its complexity. Finally, the complexity is augmented by open allusion to a source as obvious as it is generally overlooked. In Boethius's *Consolation,* exactly as in Ariosto's canto 35, the distanced view of the earth as an inconsequential pinprick in the vast heavens is the immediate occasion for an attack on the absurd desire for fame by which writers are often motivated (2.pros.7). At the Este court, Boethian irony about human endeavors sub specie aeternitatis probably did not pass unnoticed, even by Cardinal Ippolito; and Ariosto's turning irony on his poetry as well as on his patron's exalted station probably did not lessen the cardinal's chagrin.

To imagine, then, that this is a "confessional" bit of composition in which the author confides his most private misgivings about the nature of his art, and thereby undermines or sabotages his own epic, is seriously to undo one of Ariosto's best and most considered bits of comedy, one in which he clearly courted the understanding and the intellectual cooperation of his audience. It also indicates a tactless sensibility and a refusal to let the poem operate on its own terms. The brilliant craziness of canto 35 exists not in and for itself, nor as a merely isolable poetic phenomenon according to which to interpret the other forty-five cantos of the poem—the tail wagging the dog—but as part and parcel of a poem-long context: the whole of Ruggiero's near-tragic story of error and punishment is yet to come. Issues developed and dramatized at length in the *Furioso* as a whole provide the context for canto 35, not the other way around. Manifestly the poem has for its subject vastly more than writing commenting on writing.

Though Ariosto occasionally borrows Lucian's ironic voice, his is a very particular use of Lucian for his own purposes, one in which the concept of Fate with its clumsily tangled strings is adapted to his own conception of Providence. Like More and Erasmus, he obviously rejoiced in the satirist's skeptical scrutiny of human folly, but just as obviously he ignores another aspect of Lucian's art, mockery of the synod of gods and cynicism about all philosophical systems. In contrast to his model, Ariosto looks up as well as down, considering the source of order against the sources of disorder. Where Lucian is concerned solely with life on earth, under the gaze of a confused and harried Zeus who is not really in control of the Fates and is all too human himself in his desire and his rage, Ariosto sees life on earth in dependent counterpoint with supernal direction: Fortune is the shadow of Providence, in no way a competitor. The endless folly of man is a delightful endpoint for Lucian; for Ariosto, even madness is subsumed under a divine organizing principle and has its uses in achieving a total design. The poet's stance is philosophic rather than merely satiric, asserting an ultimate power overarching the tumults of earthly confusion, even if often dark and inscrutable itself. Lucian may mock wayward Zeus, shrewish Hera, seductive Aphrodite, and perpetually adolescent Apollo—an unruly many incapable of functioning as one—but to his own deity Ariosto repeatedly attributes something like a sense of humor as well as a mysterious kind of benevolence as "Gran Motor" and "Superno Amore." More than that, the "All-Mover" has a definite end in mind and will not stay forever to watch it impeded.

Ariosto's distinctive perspective becomes clearest when viewed against what he superadds to Boiardo's wholly sublunary world, which is, like Lucian's, perpetually open-ended and delighting in confusion. The Count of Mirandola had been content with the addition of rivalry to rivalry in exuberant and teemingly fertile comic increment. The story of Orlando's stupidities could conceivably go on forever, and the *Innamorato*'s world of disputatious desiring has a fascination for its creator that manifests itself in a tumultuous roll-call of drolly repetitive magnificence. Hence, he gives us Gradasso of Sericana, invading France for the sole purpose of capturing Orlando's sword, Durindana, and Rinaldo's steed, Bayard; and Agricane of Tartaria, invading Cathay to possess the enchantress Angelica; and Ferraù of Spain, bent on possessing both Angelica and Orlando's magical helmet; and Sacripante of Circassia, lusting after both Angelica and Ruggiero's steed, Frontino; and Marsilio of Spain and Rodomonte of Algiers, both striving to conquer the whole of France; and, finally, Mandricardo of Tartaria, burning unquenchably first for the sword Durindana and then for Doralice, Rodomonte's betrothed. In Boiardo, all these actions are serial and repetitive, new desiring agents being constantly imported to swell the ranks of the old, as when Mandricardo, a very late arrival, steps in to take the place of his father Agricane, killed much earlier for his pains. Battles are inconsequential in Boiardo, rivalries without issue, for that would be to invite conclusions, both narrative and philosophical. In Ariosto, by contrast, Orlando goes conclusively insane, Ruggiero makes his way *through* a host of obstacles to his destiny as dynast, Agramante is defeated, and Charlemagne emerges victorious. Actions are seen as possessing a certain gravity, and they point to resolutions and endings. In the pages of the *Furioso* the logic of action and incalculable consequence, often over great distances of space and time, produces compelling ironic effects of the most profound kind. A piercing attention to causality is one of the chief distinguishing features of the poem and reveals an inescapable overall direction in all its movement, a direction to resolution. Hence the real difference between the *Innamorato* and the *Furioso* might be said to be the difference between complication and complexity.

The focus for Ariosto's final resolution of Boiardo's "storie isparte," his open-ended narratives, is in cantos 27 through 33, immediately before Astolfo's lunar visit. Providence, through the agency of Discordia, has already set afoot one part of its offensive against its enemies; with the arrival of Astolfo in the Terrestrial Paradise it has begun to employ the second of its armaments. The first part of the plan takes the form of allowing the disintegration of the Saracen forces through egotistical erosion from within. This is a favorite Ariostan idea, and he gives it a complex dramatization. In Agramante's army, now on the verge of final victory over Charlemagne, one warrior after another suddenly recognizes a horse, an ensign, a talisman, a sword that once was his or to which he once laid a claim, and which is now infuriatingly in the possession of one or another of his co-religionists. Canto 27 forms a climax of the complicated, disruptive quarrels that originated so long ago in the *Innamorato* and were suspended without issue for the whole of its length. In Ariosto, in the overheated, compressed atmosphere of Agramante's camp, heightened desires now begin to converge crazily on the same few objects, involving the allies in a vortex of contrary challenges and counterclaims of proprietorship. The discord in the hunger itself is the reason for its own undoing, and the universal wolf of appetite at last eats up himself. With intense insight into the nature and folly of human craving, the poet represents a Lucianic discord growing from the slightest, most innocent-seeming and inconsequential beginnings, remorselessly compounding, like a Rossinian crescendo, in a chain of linked causality, and erupting finally in explosive and disastrous consequences for all involved. The end result is the collapse of the Saracen enterprise from within as its heroes turn on one another, and the withdrawal of the weakened forces from Paris to Arles, and thence back to Bizerte, which they find ablaze—the work of Astolfo at the end of his journey, the second prong of the assault supervised by Providence and confided to Astolfo by St. John. And perhaps the reduction to ashes of that city, home of pride and presumption, has been prefigured in the vision of lunar detritus already accorded the paladin.

There is a finely domesticated Lucianic wit at work amid all the welter of desire in these cantos of dissolution, although all the chaos is at the service of Providence. Here is the very soul and essence of tangled chains of desire in the four-way quarrel of Agramante's warriors, and Ariosto, clearly mindful of Lucian's knotty threads of desire in *Charon Sees Life,* calls them "questi intrichi," "these tangles" (27.94.6). Thrusting obsessively at the same desiderata, the courses of these appetitive soldiers are doomed to collide, and the threads of their Fates will be ineluctably (in Lucian's apt phrase) "tangled up with one another" in a nexus of apparently accidental happenings. However, Ariosto superadds something to Lucian, something essentially Boethian, when the drawing of lots to determine who will fight whom to win swords, ensigns, and horses, among other things, is said to involve putting themselves at the "arbitrio de l'instabil Dea" (27.45.6). One and all, the poet makes clear, they hunt the goods of Fortune; and Fortune, constant only to her own mutability, mischievously ensures that those possessions, all through the poem, take leave of their owners and pass giddily from hand to hand with no fidelity whatever to their temporary proprietors. Swords, horses, helmets, in company with that other desideratum, Angelica, are in constant motion; and her airy slippage from Orlando and Rinaldo to Sacripante and Ruggiero and Medoro finds an exact parallel in the crazy progress to which the madly desired emblems of warfare are progressively submitted. This infidelity of desired objects provokes angry surprise, yet Fortune herself had long ago given warning, "Opes honores ceteraque talium mei sunt iuris. Dominam famulae cognoscunt; mecum veniunt, me abeunte discedunt."[33] Giving dramatic life to the axiom in moving mindlessly about from owner to temporary owner, these objects of desire in Ariosto appear to live almost with a willful life of their own; and in the poet's highly patterned, remorselessly recurrent rotation of property, the eternal cranking of the goddess's wheel is unmistakably audible. For Fortune—as "Vergil" (who had it from Boethius) told Dante, who must somehow have imparted the secret to Ariosto—has been "ordained by Providence as a general minister and guide over worldly splendors, to preside over the changeful passing from time to time of vain possessions from people to people, in a manner beyond the power of human reason to conceive":

. . . agli splendor mondani
ordinò general ministra e duce,

che permutasse a tempo li ben vani,
    di gente in gente, e d'uno in altro sangue,
    oltre la difension de' senni umani.
        (*Inferno* 7.77–81)[34]

There is one revealing instance of the chained progress, tortuous and insinuating, of these fugitive goods in the *Furioso* to which no critical attention has yet been drawn. Near the poem's end, Orlando's faithful friend and companion, Brandimarte, is killed with Orlando's sword, wielded savagely by Gradasso (41.100–2). The long, protracted process by which the weapon comes into the pagan's possession to be used with such terrible purpose, its inexorable progress from hand to hand, snakes through the narrative in the most insidious manner, forming a commentary on the real role of "accident" in Ariosto's narrative. For in one of the poem's centrally significant actions, at canto 24.4, at the very climax of his madness, the truant Orlando himself flings the sword away when divesting himself of his armor, piece by piece, to run naked in the forest, mad in his sensual disappointment. Armor, chain mail, helmet, shield, breastplate—all are hurled away with furious abandon. This passion-laden act of denial and dereliction at the poem's center catapults both the paladin himself and his weapon into the vortices of fatality, as Ariosto with great deliberateness and intensity dramatizes a central passage on "hope and fear" in a lyric of Boethius:

At quisquis trepidus pauet uel optat,
    Quod non sit stabilis suique iuris,
Abiecit clipeum locoque motus
    Nectit qua ualeat trahi catenam.
        (*Cons. Phil.* 1.met.4.5–8)

But he whom hope or terror takes, / Being a slave, his shield forsakes, / And leaves his place, and doth provide / A chain wherewith his hands are tied.

The Elizabethan translation is not exact: the derelict warrior "fastens the chain by which he will be *dragged* [*trahi*]." Moreover, Orlando fastens the chain not only for himself but also for others whom he loves and by whom he is loved, who, in their innocence, are inexorably dragged along with him. Now the glittering prize, neutral in itself, begins to be endowed with the malignity and menace of the human wills that wield it, and the apparently casual peregrinations of an inanimate object like a weapon begin to take on a life of their own. Zerbino comes upon the abandoned sword at canto 24.50 and piously collects the discarded armor into a trophy, surmounting it with an inscription attesting to Orlando's ownership and warning all others away. Defying the warning, at 24.58 Mandricardo rashly seizes the sword and immediately employs it to slay the protesting Zerbino. Here the sword becomes the magnet of desire, drawing its pursuers ever more deeply into the currents of conflict and remorselessly to their doom and to the doom of innocent others. At 27.54 the Tartar prince's possession of the prize is contested by the jealous Gradasso. The ultimate result of his importunate claim is a clash that ends in Mandricardo's death at 30.17. At 30.74 the sword itself is ceded to the triumphant Gradasso, who uses it to kill Brandimarte at 41.100, and who, as a direct result, inevitably procures his own death: he is killed at once, with swift vengeance, by Orlando himself. The circle is finally complete. To the original act of Orlando's self-spoliation we may trace the deaths of two friends by circuitous and unimaginable means, and also of two pagans whose desires bring about their ends.

Ariosto's universe, it appears, is not relativist nor disjointed but positively haunted by responsibility, and the mesh of action and remotest consequence finds its ultimate root in some ascertainable action of the human will, however distant or dim. Here again the influence of Vergil, concealed but potent, is at work in Ariosto's mistrust of mere possessions. This is something he shares with the major Vergilian critic of his age, as well as with Vergil himself, for as Michael Murrin has recently asserted:

As a literary critic, Landino remains faithful to his text, for the *Aeneid* dramatizes an ascetic quite as rigorous as that of the Florentine. Value loci in the poem are always internal, and anyone who turns to outside objects dies. The glitter of a helmet kills Euryalus, a gilded belt is enough for Turnus . . . and Camilla, momentarily distracted by the finery of Chloreus, dies in her hour of glory. All external things are finally either rejected or lost in the *Aeneid,* and Vergil's setting perfectly mirrors this dynamism of negation.[35]

Like a Vergil newly come to life in romantic shape, Ariosto, exactly like his Roman master, deals in the glittering currency of romance, in pieces of armor and martial finery, but the idea embodied in his narrative is a universal one, whether, as students of history, we contemplate the ineluctable fluctuation of treasures and kingdoms or in our own lives marvel at the vagaries of high finance or the mysterious transition through alien hands of the coin in our pockets, "slave to thousands." The whole extended narrative of Orlando's sword is alive with the stern, devastating irony of a Boethian idea: "Crede fortunis hominum caducis, / Bonis crede fugacibus" (*Cons. Phil.* 2.met.3.15–16; "Trust, trust if you dare, in the fugitive fortunes of men; trust in fleeting treasures indeed"). For the Saracens, the blind materialism of their trust in things ensures their defeat and expulsion; Agramante loses not only his kingdom but also his life, Ruggiero snatches at a crown and finds himself in a dungeon, and the poem moves by carefully plotted stages to its inevitable conclusion of defeat on one side, and victory and marriage on the other.

What St. John's instruction of Astolfo asserts, both in and through its mad comedy and bizarre wittiness, is the providential nature of the universe as Ariosto has conceived it. In the lunar heights, the statement about divine order is deliberately, through a kind of daring litotes in casting the saint as a magus of old romance,

made to seem simplistic and pietistic, but in the doings on earth the poet has dramatized the concept at length and with utmost complexity, according vivid imaginative life to a central Platonic-Boethian idea that evil ineluctably operates to its own
confusion, that matter is shadow and earthly strength is illusion. In the case of the
provocative meanderings of Orlando's discarded sword, a deliberate, deeply submerged, intricately woven, and extensively continued pattern emerges from the
welter of overwhelming narrative detail, and it testifies to a poetic strategy that
works in long and cumulatively meaningful, rather than brief and ephemeral, terms.
This pattern beguiles the reader by inviting him to think of the poem's happenings
as "accidents" rather than as a pattern growing according to a complex order. As the
example of Orlando's sword serves to prove, the *Furioso* does not yield its meaning
to the casual reader: "Fortune," the reader thinks; "Providence," returns the poet
after a long while, "of which my artistic design attempts to be the mirror." Only
removal to an altitude makes the statement ring true.

A Boethian context clarifies immeasurably those constantly recurring outcries
about Fortune that rise up in the *Furioso*'s narrative from the first canto onward,
outcries finally put in perspective by St. John and by the narrator in his great meditation on Fortune's frustrating power in the proem to canto 41. Sacripante begins the
cursing at 1.44 ("fortuna crudel, fortuna ingrata"), Angelica plaintively accuses the
Great Mover of setting all the Fates against her (8.39), and Gradasso at 30.69 has
learned nothing new, venting the same sense of frustration at Fortune's power to
which he so heavily contributes. Here the mental ceiling is very low and the motto
might be taken from Juvenal: "multum numen habes si sit prudentia: nos te, / nos
facimus, Fortuna, deam caeloque locamus."[36] The richness of the poem's poetry
springs from the way in which Ariosto has imagined and reimagined variations on a
perpetually fertile pattern of events. Two or more antagonistic wills bent on con-
verging courses of action collide and meet in conflict, resulting in some third,
unforeseen eventuality, which is accompanied by the loss to all of the cause of their
strife and the creation of some new and ever more expansive pattern, difficult of
comprehension but steadily growing. Though cursing Fortune repeatedly, each
character is on a deliberately chosen course of his own when the two courses inter-
sect. Each comes to that disastrous moment by a willed motion of his own, and the
result is a Boethian "inprouisus inopinatus concursus"[37] in which Ariosto repeatedly
delights. The unforeseen, unimagined coincidence is precisely the "running
together" of two quite separate motivations, and the barren result is implicit,
"plaited into" the very nature of things. A reverberative Boethian line from the
Furioso's first canto distills the future action: "Si messero ad arbitrio di fortuna"
(1.23.5; "They put themselves into the governance of Fortune"). All the while,
however, the movement to fruition of individual wills is at the disposition of a higher
order than Fortune's, which steals quietly on them unawares and utilizes even their
furies for the production of order. The concatenation of appetites weaves, according
to Lucian, merely a tangled web of Fate, but in Ariosto the threads of the skein and

their ultimate pattern are in the hands and the mind of the Weaver. The shuttles and bobbins have no sense of the whole, though they are the necessary means by which the fabric is woven. This finds early demonstration in Rinaldo's rabid horseback chase after Angelica, a hunt that leads him hurtling back to Paris to kill his rival, Orlando—and in his arrival just in time to suffer a check. Beleaguered Charlemagne missions him to Britain to request auxiliary forces, and he is equipped and shipped in a trice, all his mad energies diverted suddenly to a better purpose and to a larger scheme, which becomes evident only in his timely return to Paris in canto 16. Weighty, grave issues are born from apparently nugatory, fortuitous actions, and the poet begins to weave the raveled threads of his world together, the pattern enlarging slowly but inexorably as he works.

The textile metaphor has a philosophical base in Neoplatonic and Stoic thought and is crucial to the *Furioso* in ways that could still be better understood.[38] In manipulating his Boiardan heritage from his new lunar altitude, Ariosto plays a Lucianic conception of the unskillful weaving of the Fates against a Boethian conception of the intricate weavings of Providence as it elicits order, though not without a certain tragic cost, from human disorder. What previously seemed only the satirist's "tangle" (*"epiploke"*) is ultimately revealed as the philosopher's "web" (*"series"*). Lucian's three Fates are witnesses of bewildering multiplicity; helpless themselves, they can only watch the snarled lives hanging from their ever more jumbled threads, which are incredibly thin and mostly tangled up (*"epipeplegmenon"*) with one another. But in Boethius those multiplicities yield to the single vision of Providence, in whose sight humans are not mere puppets dangled from knotty strings but beings endowed with wills of their own, however needful of direction in their growth toward a place in the fabric. The operative text is a very familiar one from the *Consolation of Philosophy.* In its assertion of a discernible pattern designed and woven by a Mind into all human action, it preserves the original weaving metaphor of Lucian but employs it for wholly contrasting purposes and so prepares the way for Ariosto. This is how Lady Philosophy links the human craftsman to the divine Artificer and discourses tellingly on the multiplicity of Fate and on the unity of Providence:[39]

They are different, but the one depends on the other. The order of Fate is derived from the simplicity of Providence. A craftsman anticipates in his mind the plan of the thing he is going to make, and then sets in motion the execution of the work and carries out in time the construction of what he has seen all at one moment present to his mind's eye. In the same way God in his Providence constructs a single fixed plan of all that is to happen, while it is by means of Fate that all that He has planned is realized in its many individual details in the course of time. So, whether the work of Fate is done with the help of divine spirits or Providence, or whether the chain of Fate is woven [*fatalis series texitur*] by the soul of the universe, or by the obedience of all nature, by the celestial motions of the stars, or by the power of the angels, by the various skills of other spirits, or by some of these, or by all of them, one thing is certainly clear: the simple and unchanging plan of events is Providence, and Fate is the ever-changing web [*mobilem nexum*], the disposition in and through time of all the events which God has planned in His simplicity. (4.6)

In its central textile metaphor, this passage is essential to an understanding of the *Furioso*, whose own ever-changing "web" presents an ever-recurring series of "accidents" locked purposefully into a great design. In the ultimate simplicity of his role as Weaver, Ariosto is to the baffling multiplicity of his creatures' actions as the unity of Providence is to the tangled multiplicities of Fate in a sublunary world of ever-shifting motion. The perpetual crisscross of historical events represented as occurring simultaneously in the eye of Providence is simultaneous in the poet's imagination as well. The shaped and directed work of art—what Ariosto (perhaps with Petrarch also in mind)[40] calls the "tela grande," the "great web" of the *Furioso* itself—is formed from an enormous mesh of human wills ("voglie") crossing constantly in appetitive wanderings. Vehicles of the poem's movement, the poem's many actors move in and out of sight on impulse-ridden courses, and the threads of the various actions they carry along with them dive in and out of sight over long periods of time in the total fabric, but the horizontal weft is strung on the poet's fixed vertical warp. Propelled into action by an incandescence of will, their motion conforms not only to the larger pattern ineluctably established by the divine will ("voler divino") but also to the author's governing patterns and sense of form, the witness of his rationality paradoxically asserting itself in a poem on madness itself. For if, as Boethius says, "Providence is the very Divine reason itself" ("Prouidentia est ipsa illa diuina ratio"),[41] then the poet's extended shaping process is the earthly mirror of that heavenly reason, similarly maintaining a vast cosmos in order and losing sight of nothing. The chain of his narrative fatalities is itself chained to a sense of the macrocosm's darkly transcendent order.

Through a redeemed clown's adventures, then, a jestingly purposive Ariosto finally and explicitly reveals the perspective from which he has been operating throughout his poem from his first canto onward. Looking with his eyes, the reader is finally asked to see the vertical line of eternity intersecting the horizontal stream of time and to see the poem's parts falling into a complex shape, much as removal to a viewpoint is essential to perceive the shape of a pointillist painting. As a poet working simultaneously in Carolingian and Neoplatonic traditions of art, Ariosto achieves significant distance from the world of matter, as he achieves an even greater distance from his chosen "Matière."

Conclusion

Divine Providence and Poetic Provision

Where Boiardo achieves a genuine elevation, through pathos and noble sentiment . . .
Ariosto deliberately cheapens his emotional values, depending on disillusion and irony for
a sophistication which negates the heroic. His is the technique of the "debunker," who
recognizes in human motivation only the most practical and selfish considerations.
    Josephine Waters Bennett, "Genre, Milieu, and the 'Epic Romance'"

A part of him goes to sleep whenever he fulfills his duty of homage—the passages in praise
of his patrons may be skipped without regret.
    Guido Waldman, Introduction to his translation of *Orlando Furioso*

One of the *Furioso*'s most pointed contrasts involves the different ways in which
Orlando, Ruggiero, and Astolfo submit to the notion of providential control over
human affairs. The first operates in utter unawareness of its power; the second reacts
with choleric impatience, struggling vainly to be free of an intolerable restraint on
his flaringly assertive sense of freedom in action; the third, blithe and good-
humored, acquiesces mildly in the divine will with which he finds himself so sur-
prisingly to have been in accord in his past adventures. Essentially these are mirrors
of the varying responses readers will make to Ariosto's assertion of control over the
vast universe he creates and governs. The history of criticism shows that those
responses are collectively rather more Orlando- and Ruggiero-like than Astolfan.
Ariosto has all but ensured that they should be, and it is even vital to the poem's
nature that this should be so. This goes to the heart of a central problem. Whether
we think of the *Furioso* as a vast randomness of pieces and patches or as a cosmos of
intricate and elaborate design depends very much on the picture we form of the
narrator. Is he wholly, partly, or not at all in control of his work? Fixing the narrator
is no simple affair: as there is no one chief figure in the *Furioso* but rather a triad of
warriors acting out the various potentials of love, so too the figure of the author is
distributed hierarchically among a triad of figures who mirror aspects of the fictional heroes. We may fittingly conclude this study with a closer look at the poetic
mind that harmonizes its diversities and orders its multiplicities.

    Ariosto immediately tempts us to think in terms of a charming but intellectually
rather unbuttoned compositor of love-stories.[1] The guise in which he first comes
before us (1.2) is that of an Orlando-like unsuccessful lover, one who protests love's
erosion of his wits, laments his incapacity to complete the work in hand, and on
occasion after occasion voices excuses for the "slips" in love of those brave youths,
Orlando and Ruggiero, for whom he feels an all too revealing sympathy. To this
figure, elegant but apparently incapable of long meditations or extended projections, we are inclined to attribute the capricious leaping about from character to
character, episode to episode, that begins to characterize the *Furioso* from canto 2

onward, when the poem begins to fragment, several separate narratives confusingly crowding on one another's heels in that one canto alone.[2] But this attractive portrait of an easily diverted romantic incompetent is soon qualified by, and forced to co-exist with, another more dignified one in the invocation to canto 3, when the author steps forward in a second guise to introduce the dynastic theme associated with Bradamante. Here now is the Vergilian celebrator of Estean splendor, energetic rather than languishing, imploring Apollo for inspiration to complete his work of building and "sculpting" a verbal monument worthy of the great race he glorifies. The courtly celebrator then puts in regular appearances, memorializing the achievements of a great family at the head of a brilliant civilization in the valley of the Po. Because he too is involved in the process of civilization, as an architect of verbal structures, he is obviously associated with Ruggiero in his Vergilian aspect of dynast and founder.

In terms of the poem's values, the Vergilian persona represents an advance over the persona of the Rueful Lover, but, as the last chapter attempted to demonstrate, the *Furioso* gives constant evidence of yet a third voice that, positioned in the heights and Astolfan in its abstraction from worldly phenomena, subsumes and presides over both these others. The fact that this figure is concealed rather than overtly depicted or characterized, that he is a voice and that his presence has to be deduced from his ironic manipulations, makes his participation more notable and confers on his subtle workings a disturbing power. In his supervision of the immensities of the *Furioso*'s poetic universe, he is the comic surrogate for Providence in the world of epic poetry,[3] mimicking its Boethian action of "omnia certo fine gubernans." Plot declares the "plotting" of Providence.

The *Furioso* has both the philosophical outlook and the complex form of comedy, revealing human action perpetually enveloped in the action-diminishing shadow of utter omnipotence. Like chronicle history, which also mingles elements of history and comedy, often represents the growth of apparent nonentities to a life of rule, and similarly disperses a multitude of actors into many apparently independent arenas of action, the *Furioso* asserts man's ignorance of the whole and his dependence on a higher power for illumination and guidance.[4] Divine Providence is the manifestation of this power in the poem, and the poet associates his art with its beneficent control of the universe's complexities by his playful imitation of its function in his smaller cosmos of art. The complexities of the *Furioso*'s plot are greater by far than the effects of any one creature's actions; hence the drama is fundamentally played out over the heads of the participating agents and is vastly larger than any one of them, thrusting ahead on his own single, rather blinkered course, can perceive or imagine. This makes for a certain disjunction between teller and tale, the renowned Ariostan aloofness, and this is especially apparent in the narrative of the dynastic pair, over whom the power of divine foresight particularly presides. With each crisis in their lives, the obstacles are raised a little higher, dilemmas become a little more complex, and two quite normal young people, Boiardo's charming adolescents, with their usual complement of passions and problems, are forced to overleap them to prove their mettle. To no one's surprise, they stumble often. At times this repeated conviction of inadequacy produces a sense of sulking, aggrieved annoyance, a wish to let down the burden; and Ariosto generously fosters a sense throughout that it is hard enough to be young and passionate, but that to be harassed by dynastic fatality is something of an imposition. Nevertheless, not for an instant does he relax his relentless pressure, revealing, perhaps, that he knew a good deal about what life holds in store for those who are called to govern. In the intellectually most compelling of his three aspects, the artist knowingly casts himself as the poetic instrument of the remorseless will that runs the world. Providence is the force he represents as perpetually raising the stakes and defining the problems, testing the limits of human weakness and refining its virtues. At the end, perhaps by merely enduring, the dynasts have successfully negotiated a difficult course, responding to Providence as it interposes every possible impediment to their headstrong waywardness. Ariosto begins the process immediately, in canto 2, with Providence curbing a willful Bradamante and causing her a painful but fortunate fall, and he continues it to the very end, as Ruggiero is pressed to the limits of his moral strength. After forty-six cantos, Providence finally has its way and the Estensi are launched into history, though not without bruises: the interaction of divine and human wills, essentially comical, is also a painful engagement.

Though Ruggiero is Ariosto's chief focus for his dark view of human nature, long ago wounded, limping when unsupported, flightless unless imped, the hero is by no means the single focus of this supernal attention or the target, in his blind drive to sad fruitions, of the poet's distanced irony. However it runs counter to the prevailing simplistic view of the poem's action, the truth of the matter is that *all* the main actions of the poem—Bradamante's quest for Ruggiero, Ruggiero's journey to rule and marriage, Orlando's aberrancy and descent into madness, the process by which Astolfo negotiates his way to Bizerte, the mission of Discord to the pagans to wreak their destruction, the irresistible process by which the Saracens fail in their enterprise and, defeated from within as much as from without, lose their own kingdom into the bargain—are said explicitly to be under the scrutiny of Providence, as they are under the scrutiny of the poet weaving his web. It is precisely this emphasis on an overruling power, a corrective to simple human blindness, that gives the *Furioso* its epic dimension, differentiating it from the *Innamorato* and transforming it into something greater than romance. Yet there are ways in which Ariosto must be distinguished from all writers of epic before and after. His poem is unique in at least two ways. First, the poet, participating in his poem as an actual persona, boldly and overtly asserts his power over his own literary creation. Second, the poet tacitly asserts his own likeness, in its highest form, to Providence in his timeless perspective and disposition of human affairs. By this device he gives notice that an apparent chaos is constructed according to an extraordinarily complex design.

Unfailingly the poem presents the crazy many-mindedness of the universe operating under the beneficent moral supervision to which, in the manner befitting a poem Neoplatonically conceived, the names given are "Il Gran Motor" (3.44.5, 8.39.5; "The Great Mover"), "Il Sempiterno Amante" (14.74.5; "The Eternal Lover"), "Bontà Ineffabile" (17.5.8; "Ineffable Goodness"), and "Superna Bontà" (45.41.5; "Supernal Goodness"). Throughout, the poem's moral optimism allows events and personages their length and leisure, however abandoned the course on which they appear to be set. Nevertheless they are always inevitably circumscribed and in view of a higher vision, and their limitations provoke benevolent laughter as well as correction. Consequently, Discordia herself, the freakishly concentrated emblem of all that is wrong in this fantastic world, is a ripely humorous creation. Repeatedly represented as being at the service of Providence in cantos 14, 18, 24, 26, and 27, her crazy dress and fuddled manner reveal her as an incompetent working at cross-purposes, a denizen of the world of the unharmonized Many. She is a fit instrument to be at the service of the One and to descend into the warring multi-plicities of the world to stir up trouble. Readers of a puritan cast of mind will not enjoy it, but there is a supreme truth embodied in the Archangel Michael's use of a crucifix to smite her when she stupidly muddles her errand (17.38), which is to embroil the pagans and let them undo themselves. Given the Christian outlook, what better instrument to break her head? Even inevitable Discord is brought into the framework, given a job, and put in her place. In two senses, she is a subject, for Providence as well as for Art.

Nineteenth-century critics seized on something essential in Ariosto when they declared Art to be one of his most profound concerns. Nevertheless, denying him an organizing mind and unwilling or unable to recognize his profound attachment to Neoplatonic ideas, they failed to perceive that he conceived of his art theoretically, as an imitation in poetry of Divine Art, in much the same way as his friend and contemporary, Castiglione.[5] This conception of Art as the mirror of the ordered multiplicity of the macrocosm and the microcosm profoundly energizes the com-plexities of his narrative mode, which is a labyrinth filled with recurring illustra-tions of human blindness in proposing and acting—blindness not only of the characters caught in its meshes but also of the reader groping his way forward through a narrative filled with deviations and detours. In the *Furioso*, Providence is to the universe what the poet is to his poem; its will is absolute, though it chooses to work through the wills of erring mortals. In the actual universe, Providence func-tions as a master ironist, sees all the separate but interrelated activities of creation at a glance, and knows their beginning and ending in an eternal present. In the *Furioso* likewise, hot-headed humans propose and propose, but it is Providence, working mysteriously through the concatenated tangle of their contrarily striving wills, that finally and quite simply disposes. There is matter enough for wonder here. A poem with a vision of irrational passion and human madness at its exact center everywhere asserts the rational direction of the macrocosm under the eye of Providence.

Ariosto's conception of Providence's relation to the macrocosm determines his conception of his own relation to his poem. The basis for both resides in a universally familiar text of Plato, the *Timaeus,* almost the sole work by which Platonic philosophy was conveyed to the west in the Dark and Middle Ages,[6] and (as we have noted previously) one that Ariosto encountered in early youth at the Studio. Its central tenet, that the deity is an artificer, a supreme artist, has as inevitable corollary that human art is a mimicry of Divine Art.[7] Accordingly, therefore, the Neoplatonic artist shares several important attributes of the Godhead, the very least of which is his capacity to punish, for if Providence can call up tempests to punish the incorrigible, Ariosto is amusingly aware that he can only hurl an inkwell at his offenders, creatures of his own imagination and (so he feigns) vessels of willfulness prone to perversity.[8] This wittily establishes the human artist's limits, providing the comic obverse of a central Christian idea. But more important than punishment is the artist's timeless perspective, the absoluteness of his will in the confines of his own creation, and his serenity in the face of constant human misdoing as his action unfolds. In those three interrelated aspects of Boethian Providence, Ariosto asserts the "divine" patterning implicit in the microcosm of his human art, fusing the *Timaeus* and the *Consolation.*

The "divine analogy" in the *Furioso* is a subject for analysis not only because it provides an incidental, often amusing facet of the poet's art, but also because it is his chief means of unifying the complexities of his narrative, and also because it allows him to establish connections between the authorial frame of reference and the narrative he tells. Ariosto postulates a complex series of relationships: the presiding Deity, manifesting Himself providentially in His attributes of timelessness, omniscience, and benevolent omnipotence, is to the errant characters in the story as the poet (in his persona of Platonic visionary) is to the readers of the tale—readers who are trapped in time and proceed laboriously canto by canto, limited in their knowledge and fallacious in their projections, and requiring to be curbed often in the (assumed) perversity of their appetites and wills in the act of reading.

For Plato the Divine Artist resides in an atemporal state to which the attribution of the verbs "was" and "shall be" is wholly inapplicable. He resides in an eternal present and simply and very bafflingly *is.* The timelessness in which the Divine Artist resides (and, by analogy, the timelessness that the human artist perpetually mimics by giving form to mutable experience) is a concept distilled as an essence in the *Furioso*'s very individual handling of *entrelacement.* Interlace is a technique of interweaving actions interrupted constantly at crucial points and keeping the whole in constant, continually suspended motion until the very end, when all the parts fall finally together and cohere in a totality of pattern. Authorial interception of the reader is by its very nature built into his narrative method, but Ariosto differs from his predecessors by employing it with very conscious purpose and more than usual cunning, simply by maintaining a dialogue with his readers on the subject of human blindness, repeatedly calling attention to his sovereign control over the times and places of his narrative (most of all when ironically "forgetting" them), and inculcating a sense of powerlessness in his audience. He was, of course, committed to a certain complexity of presentation by the very nature of his inheritance from Boiardo, for *entrelacement* is almost inevitably a feature of any narrative that combines Arthurian with Carolingian materials, plurality with centrality. *Entrelacement* is the technically complex narrative counterpart of a romantic material dealing with multiple characters and multiple adventures set contemporaneously afoot and requiring to be managed simultaneously. Accordingly, the *Innamorato* is full of segmented action, interrupting itself repeatedly and with delight to dash after warriors and enchantresses at opposite ends of the world, as if in authorial imitation of the characters' mad chases after whatever object or person crosses their view. Nevertheless, Boiardo has a relatively uncomplicated end in mind with the suspension of any narrative moment; his multiple stories are interlinked, but they never interlock, and no single vision operates to reconcile their diversity into one organic whole.

Though he inherits the basic narrative mode from Boiardo, Ariosto holds himself more distinctively aloof, operates at an even greater artistic distance, and his alert governance of his cantos conveys the sense of a master hand of tremendous power stirring an enormous centrifuge. The poet playfully assumes the part of the "Gran Motor," communicating motion to his characters and constantly wafting them into ever more distant adventures, then suddenly, without warning and even in the midst of the projected arc, magisterially stopping them dead in their tracks until they are needed again. Purely by being human, they are completely unaware of how matters are proceeding elsewhere in the wildernesses, cities, airs, and seas of the globe, though repercussions of distant events will have an impact on all their lives: the greater the multiplication of personnel and spheres of activity, the greater the emphasis on human ignorance, the less availing any single human will in the tangle, the more comic the proceedings. Movements by individuals emerge as discrete and limited, yet they unite ultimately in time to form an overarching pattern vouchsafed to no one individual. These movements represent an unfolding in time of a timeless idea. The idea is the property of Providence and the poet, and it manifests itself in a plan of history and a plan of art in an epic poem of history.

In the course of reading, the reader seizes on as many "finalities" as he can, but each proves to be an *horizon chimérique*. For, on his confused and complicated way to The End in canto 46, the reader too is moved about and shunted off into sidetracks on innumerable occasions, in striking illustration of the power of the artist's will in his own cosmos. This practice reaches a pitch of uncommon intensity in canto 18, where on no less than seven successive occasions the author provides a devastating demonstration of his technical power in his whirlwind interceptions of his reader's attention. These are roadblocks against which the reader's anticipation and curiosity come rushing to gratification, seven times to be turned off into the beguiling alleys of still other adventures, themselves all too soon truncated and leading to still others, all of them opening out in a very determined prolongation and interconnection of actions and lives. Here, if anywhere, the reader feels the force of contravention in the poet's personality wresting him from his repose in any one incident and wrenching him onward to others. This enforces reconsiderations—glances backward and perhaps upward. It becomes necessary to read as if one were flying overhead as well as rambling through the pleasant places beneath. Global, not merely local, vision is required, and the meaning increasingly must be found in the whole, not simply in the part. What looks like mere "horizontal" succession, the product of indecisive, jumpy imagination, is really vertical in organization.

From our perspective as limited intellects trapped in space and time, having perforce to read the poem "horizontally," turning a page at a time, the *Furioso*'s narratives appear merely to interlink. But from the narrator's perspective, the narratives interlock in great arcs of time and space, from beginning to end. He sees a unity, not just contiguous territories viewed two or three at a time at very most. Ariosto's *entrelacement* takes in the entire poem: it operates at an altitude where, from the beginning, all the interwoven narratives are a potency directed to a final Act, and where the poem itself is a great Becoming. From that perspective, individual narratives are continually fusing into a single highly patterned fabric on a loom of considerable vastness.

Ariosto's imitation of divine omniscience, with its concomitants of timelessness and omnipotence, is at the heart of his manipulation of the *Innamorato*. In a manner wholly unlike Boiardo, who constantly flattered his audience by casting them in idealized postures in an unchanging Maytime world, Ariosto all but equates his readers with the blind, passion-ridden characters of his tale, and no less than his paladins and viragoes do they fall victim to his fine irony and sudden, disturbing illuminations. To assert, therefore, that Ariosto's interlacing patterns of action "create suspense" and "heighten interest" is to circulate on the lower slopes only of a very high mountain and to leave wrapped in clouds an aspect that distinguishes him totally from Boiardo. The greatest and most important effect of his *entrelacement* is to confound the linear progression of time, the time by which both actors and readers, in common mortality, are similarly enchained; and also to press in on us with the radical unpredictability of life, in which we know what we are but know not what we shall be—and be very soon indeed, the poet implies with a certain suave menace. More instant than his predecessor, more insistent and unshakable as a narrator, he labors to make his narrative mirror our experience of life as a series of apparently accidental, meaningless fragments. By contriving confusions, misfootings, a sense of directionlessness, the poet suggests how easy it is to lose sight of the plan and settle for pieces.

Ariosto presents the universe of his poem as a series of images in a broken mirror. Yet it was whole once, before "the Fall" that evicted Logistilla, made her a fugitive "northward," and brought lunacy into the world. The mirror has been shattered by human passion, and in his darkened intellect the reader can perceive it only in pieces. On the other hand, the poet's art presents the possibility at least of reflecting a whole and unshattered reality, or of arranging phenomena into the reflection of an idea; and the reader, by cooperating laboriously in the process of reading, can mentally rearrange an apparent disorder into the forms of order. Events in the *Furioso* are therefore distributed to its readers in an order that is not the one they expect or desire: another fallacy of human intention. As we have already seen, *in his proems* Ariosto simultaneously manipulates ancient classical, medieval Carolingian, and contemporary Renaissance historical times, fusing them into one essence by the power of his poetic art. In an even more marvelous innovation, *within the fictional Carolingian world itself,* he deliberately confounds the past, present, and future of his creatures' lives, revealing them in future states of being well before they have progressed to that point in actual time. What he increasingly demands is an extension of vision, spatial and temporal, to encompass the ever-forming, ever-expanding pattern.

Ariosto points subtly but remorselessly to this obscurity of vision, this failure of reading. Hence the easily overlooked occasion, at canto 19.42, which pictures Angelica and Medoro, happy in their mutual love, descending to the sea to embark for Cathay and unexpectedly encountering a naked, hairy savage who starts up with threatening suddenness, interrupting their passage. There the poet abruptly leaves them, without explanation, frozen in terror: he has other concerns to pursue. Nevertheless, by an astonishing proleptic movement dramatizing timelessness, he has stunningly extended the present into a still mysterious future known only to the artist who governs the action. Here he reminds his readers how totally ignorant they are, how dependent they are on his guidance as he quickly, calmly retreats into the present again to another thread of the story, leaving his characters suspended in mid-career, and his audience likewise immersed in ignorance of what is to come. It is all too like life, the past forgotten and the future indistinct. For when, four long cantos off, in canto 23, the naked Yahoo flashingly glimpsed in that terrifying moment in canto 19 is revealed as the jealous, enraged Orlando *in process* of becoming "furioso," *in process* of *becoming* that bestial creature, the reader is coerced into a retrospective scrutiny of events and should begin to reappraise his sense of having fully understood the poetic territory through which he has recently passed.

The case of Orlando seen as a beast in the divine eye before he is a beast in reality reveals a curiously unnoted aspect of the *Furioso*'s art and meaning. Repeatedly we see the effect before the cause, a revelation of both the Deity's and the artist's freedom from the tyranny of sequence in time. Ariosto never *states* that he presides timelessly over the universe of his poetry like the Godhead of the *Timaeus* or the *Consolation*; he *dramatizes* the notion in the form his poetry takes, in the disarranged arrangement of his materials. The meaning declares and proclaims itself silently, to be intuited by the reader in a mental flash, producing an almost forcible heightening of his mental perspective, one more unsettling and perhaps even more menacing for being tacit and requiring immediate apprehension of an undeclared reality. Orlando provides but one instance of this kind of demonstrated power, by which the reader is silently compelled to scrutinize the possibilities and meanings implicit in action and to bend a keener eye on the process of cause and result. Yet another striking instance of poetic control of timelessness occurs in the hurtling flash-forward at 22.4 when Zerbino comes upon the corpse of Pinabello, whom only later in the same canto, at 22.97, do we see *in process* of being hunted down and killed by Bradamante for his attempt to murder her earlier in canto 2. Deferral has not passed over into oblivion, as the poet reminds the careless, forgetful, or skeptical reader: justice has a long arm, the artist a correspondingly long memory and a long vision. Another instance of the length of both the poet's and Providence's reach is apparent in the most fortune-ridden passage of all, the encounter of Angelica and Medoro. At 12.65 Angelica, fleeing pursuit as usual, stumbles on the body of a young soldier lying wounded in the forest, and the poet freezes her in a posture of surprise, wafting us from the scene without identifying him. Only much later, at 18.165, is the young Medoro represented *in process* of setting out on that very midnight expedition during which he is wounded and nearly killed, but which puts him so unexpectedly in the way of Angelica and a throne in Cathay. Irony is of the essence here, as it is in all the similar passages we have referred to, but it seems time to identify the irony as something more than mere romantic or modern irony. It is divine irony, and its source and nearest equivalent is in the lyric poetry of Boethius, asserting the timelessness of the Deity:

Quae sint, quae fuerint ueniantque
Uno mentis cernit in ictu.
        (*Cons. Phil.* 5.met.2.11–12)

He at one time doth see / What are, and what have been, / And what shall after be.

The blinding blur produced by this welter of thousands of distinct lives, each a miracle of egotism, all apparently unconnected to the others, is bound to be every reader's first experience of the poem. Yet Ariosto's authorial raids into the future, pregnant with reserved knowledge and marvelously juxtaposing "quae sint" with "quae fuerint" and especially with "quae veniant," should be disturbing to a reader's complacency in accepting the poet's confession, in his Rueful Lover's guise, of mental weakness and inability to recall his story. Ariosto's pose as an ignorant incompetent who provokes others to examine their mental positions is a variant on the pose of Socrates in the Platonic dialogues: only at our peril do we take him at his word. The sense of a curtain let down in curtailment of human vision is what gives Ariosto's poem its particular and very distinct ethos. It is a creation in which something is always out of sight, an art of distant repercussions of proximate events, tragic as well as merely comic or ironic. The shadow of a privity or an incalculable mystery at the heart of creation—both God's and the poet's—is always on us. As we read, blinded by the onrush of characters and events, crippled with poor memories and an inability to forecast the future, something has happened in full view, the significance of which we have failed to remark in passing. Something concurrent has happened out of sight that will be recounted at some future time. But all of it is certain, at some distant, unforeseen hour, to have a wholly unsuspected impact on the action in view at any given moment. The reader who enters the world of the *Furioso* is hurried on a journey in which he must either learn something about the laws of the territory or pass through without much improvement to his sight. Fundamentally, the poet demands two pieces of baggage: reason (which he will do all he can to diminish in its pride) and memory (which he will often accuse of deficiency and challenge to sharpen its powers of connection). In essence, he places severe demands on the inner eye to pierce the murk of the incident-crowded past, with a view to instructing by connecting, prophesying, and perhaps learning warily to foresee. At the very least he counsels a kind of humility.

An existential Ariosto is the creation of the modern period. Like Boethius, like Bembo, he makes the point repeatedly not that the universe is wholly unintelligible and without plan but that man's darkened intellect and innate adherence to passion render divine purposes incomprehensible; and no one could accuse him of not sufficiently delineating that passion and its effects. For Ariosto, man is blind, Providence an all-seeing Eye, and the discrepancy makes for frequent laughter but also (toward the end especially) for a certain grim outlook on the processes of history, which is decidedly not progressive. In a pointless universe, Ariosto's diligence in instructing and illuminating would be similarly pointless, but with every weapon in his considerable arsenal he warns, instructs, admonishes, and curbs throughout. By no means is his ironic art a thing of splendid trickery and flashy entrapment. Its very essence resides in the vitality and the complexity it accords to a Boethian commonplace, the errors of human intelligence ("ingenii error humani"),[9] a concept Ariosto found brilliantly reinforced not only in occasional phrases throughout the *Asolani* ("la sciocca e bamba oppenione degli uomini," "quanto è leggiera e folle la falsa e misera credenza de' mortali")[10] but also in a passage of concentrated Platonic and Boethian wisdom spoken by the hermit to Lavinello:

Tanto è largo e cupo il pelago della divina providenza, o figliuolo, che la nostra umanità, in esso mettendosi, né termine alcuno vi truova, né in mezzo può fermarsi; perciò che vela di mortale ingegno tanto oltre non porta e fune di nostro giudicio, per molto che ella vi si stenda, non basta a pigliar fondo; in maniera che bene si veggono molte cose tutto dì avenire, volute e ordinate dallei, ma come elle avengano o a che fine, noi non sappiamo.

So wide and deep, my son, is the ocean of God's providence that our humanity can find no limit when setting forth upon it and cannot rest midway; for the sail of our mortal wit cannot carry us to its bounds, and the rope of our judgment, however lengthy, cannot reach to its bottom, so that though many things are seen to happen every day in accordance with its wish and plan, we do not know why or how they happen.[11]

This view has its effect, both implicitly and explicitly, throughout the *Furioso*. If, in reading the poem, our knowledge comes only late and retrospectively after authorial ambushes of our normal expectations, the cause is in a residual human

blindness that overlooks the repeated previous warnings of the poet and ignores the
laws of the universe he so carefully constructs. The persona who asserts his control
has begun to operate very early indeed, in the poem's first stanzas in fact. There is a
caution in the way he repeatedly arrests us in the course of his headlong opening
narrative, restraining and tempering our unbridled absorption in sheer story with
sententious utterances that cut across the *brio* of the action with a grave and solemn
lento of their own. If anything, Ariosto is an *arresting* poet. His confident interposition and call for attention occur twice in the space of nine stanzas filled with factual
rehearsal of events in Boiardo, and even as we try to absorb the facts we are intercepted by warnings to interpretation: "Ecco il giudicio uman come spesso erra!"
(1.7.2; "Behold how frequently human judgment errs!"); "Contrari ai voti poi furo
i successi" (1.9.5; "Events turned out contrary to their prayers").[12] Both the prose
and the poetry of the *Asolani* harp repeatedly on this human blindness and the veil of
darkness over all earthly things ("il velo della mondana caliggini")—the last phrase,
of course, exactly translating the Boethian "mortalium rerum nube caligantia."[13]
No wonder that Ariosto, in the proem to canto 7, calls for readers with sharpened
sight, readers who have traveled out of the encumbering world of mortal things.
The world and its palpable but deceptive "realities" evaporate like air—or like
Angelica—from the grasp. Hence the narrator's repeated exclamations on the subject of his characters' blindness in acting, believing, hoping, proposing, and
judging:

Oh sommo Dio, come i giudicii umani
spesso offuscati son da un nembo oscuro!
        (10.15.1–2)

Oh highest God, how often are human judgments veiled by a dark cloud!

O degli uomini inferma e instabil mente!
come sian presti a variar disegno!
        (29.1.1–2)

Oh infirm and unstable minds of men, how quick they are to change their plans!

Oh fallace degli uomini credenza!
        (41.23.1)

Oh fallacious hope of mortals!

If nothing else, and if only because they are Boiardan desirers, set newly and more
intensely in motion, Ariosto's characters are proposers of happiness—"fallace credenza." Wonderfully narrowed intelligences, marvelously single-minded wills,
they know what they want, and they launch course after course to achieve it. The
world they inhabit is a world of mad projections, dramatizations of the human will
acting in all its rich perversity of intent. Yet something always escapes, and the

vaulting projections fall flat. Ariosto adopts a brilliant combination of Vergilian, Lucianic, and Boethian tonalities when contemplating these limits of human understanding; and here not only the poem's major characters but even the poem's nonentities, characters of a single appearance who make up part of its epical swarm and are no more than a name, participate in this theme of the baffling and overturning of the proud constructions of the human mind. In evolving this strain of thought, the *Furioso* elaborates a persistent note struck (sometimes with a grimly comic irony not immediately associated with Vergil) in the grave music of the *Aeneid*:

nescia mens hominum fati sortisque futurae
et servare modum rebus sublata secundis!
       (10.501–2)

How blind are men to fate and futurity, and how little they know how to preserve moderation at the proud moment of success!

The *Furioso* wears a totally different look, comes in completely different a narrative form, is populated by stranger incarnations, and moves in more fantastic geographies than does the *Aeneid*. Yet the *Furioso* absorbs and transcends the essence of the *Aeneid*, particularly (in books 9 and 10) in its sense of high energies vitiated by human blindness in proposing actions without a sense of futurity. Ariosto makes it a universal condition. Hence, in imitation of the death in Vergil of the seer Rhamnes, who could not prophesy his own destruction, of the improvident gamesters Lamyrus, Lamus, and drunken Serranus, and of boastful Anxur, who anticipates, in his blindness, great length of years ("longos promiserat annos"), Ariosto gives us the death of Moschino, a drunkard who shuns water like poison, yet finds his death in a moat (14.124); the death of Alphaeus, the physician, wizard, and astrologer, who had prophesied his death at a great age on the bosom of his wife, but whose end comes upon him in the form of Cloridano and Medoro's stealthy nocturnal attack as he lies sleeping (18.174); and the death of Malindo and Ardalic of Flanders, given honors and promised lands by Charlemagne, but now, because of this same murderous outbreak by moonlight, forever prevented from enjoying them (18.180). Truly,

   non potria negli uomini il destino,
se del futuro ognun fosse indovino.
       (18.177.7–8)

Fate would have no power over men, if everyone were able to forecast the future.

Touching the chord with increasing frequency, repeatedly revealing the ambush of human calculations and cravings by some unimaginable conjunction of things or persons, Ariosto modulates at the end into a Boethian and Pauline irony about human proposals in the face of the multiple confusions of the world. In the story of Ruggiero's dereliction in following Agramante to Africa, the governing text is reminiscent of Romans 11:33: "How unsearchable are His judgments and how inscrutable are His ways." Here another, greater intelligence presides over setbacks, revealing itself at work behind the scenes and witnessing a sovereign, very leisurely order in process of evolving, and intimating a design of its own that no human vision, no matter how acute or broad, can wholly penetrate: here the disjunction between the poet's provision and the Deity's Providence widens into a dark laughter and a confession of infirmity on the part of the human artist. The thematic strand is at its darkest and most mysterious in the death of the entire crew that bears Ruggiero, faithless to Bradamante, faithful to Agramante, back to rejoin his beaten pagan lord (canto 41). Beset by a terrifying tempest, fearful of sinking, and enticed to their deaths by their very will to life, the sailors one and all throw themselves into the waves, where they perish miserably. The ship itself—"O fallace degli uomini credenza!"—by what seems a cruel and inexplicable irony, unmanned and apparently undirected, rides out the storm with suddenly recovered seaworthiness and comes to rest, finally and with almost insolent buoyancy, on the shores of North Africa; Orlando, walking on the shore, has *already* in the previous canto (40.60–61) seen the ship's approach, and now, at 41.24, he recovers his horse and sword from the hold and tardily prepares to avenge Charlemagne. Here on the shores of North Africa Ariosto contrives the penultimate convergence (initiated in the Palace of Illusion) of the three main figures: the animalistic Orlando arriving by swimming like an otter, Ruggiero by shipwreck and by the forcible propulsion of Providence, and Astolfo, as always, by leisurely, roundabout journeying, in a triumphal procession that strikes Bizerte into ruin. A curious universe indeed: with strange confluences, perhaps not without a broad and dark design. Here Ruggiero seems the focus of an action not merely capricious but also curiously *directed* to him by a Power accustomed to patient cajoling but, growing more importunate, willing to terrify to gain Its ends and to be cruel only to be kind, and devastating Its path to an unshared love. This dramatizes the concept of a jealous and omnipotent God, and Ariosto humorously catches something of the Deity's Old Testament manner in his own sovereign disposing of characters and events, and his catching errancies up short, as when he deliberately leaves Ruggiero thrashing a while in the overwhelming ocean to pursue other narrative concerns (41.22). Like the Creator, the poet has power to punish.

Truly, Divine Providence is, as Bembo had said, a "pelago," a bottomless gulf of mysterious purpose beyond human wit to conceive. It is that very wit, source of man's pride in his elevated state, that is humbled in the encounter with the universe. The universe is not totally unpatterned, or crazily patterned, but rather darkly patterned. Things interlock in unimaginable ways, and the margins of the plan are always out of sight. When, as in Ruggiero's case, the laughing universe turns unexpectedly grim and the "voler divino" becomes more inscrutable, the poem asks the question that most tormented Bembo's master, Boethius: "Premit insontes / Debita sceleri noxia poena" (*Cons. Phil.* I.met.5.29–30; "Why should punishments

/ Due to the guilty, light on innocents?"). The question is tormenting precisely because the universe so often does give teasing evidence of design. The annihilation of a crowd of men involved only tangentially with Ruggiero, for whom Providence raises the storm as punishment and warning, and who swims free to his baptism on an island, is Ariosto's deepest meditation on a darkly inscrutable interposition in human affairs, his most serious "O altitudo." Yet here too he asserts the reality of a world decidedly fallen, subject to concatenating Fortune and stained in its deepest nature. Here "speme" and "timore" put in more somber appearances than in Orlando's hope and fear for the loss of Angelica. And as if to confirm the stark Pauline and Augustinian focus of the episode, the drenched and desperate Ruggiero, swept suddenly ashore by the tides of the deep, is greeted by the hermit with that astonishing address, "Saul, Saul, why do you persecute my Faith?" A will in flight has been curbed by another Will, here nakedly revealing its absolute power.

Volition, overpowering reason, gives the *Furioso* its matchless energy and provides the drive for its movement. On foot and wing, sailing, and especially on horseback, every one of its participants is in ceaseless motion, forging links in an interminable chain of longing to be elsewhere and in possession of a distant desire. Precisely because of the *Furioso*'s recurring concern with repining restlessness and passionate willfulness does it move with such astounding rapidity to the thunder of hoofbeats in forests. As Ficino said, "Ambae vires nominantur equi propter motum" ("Both powers [of the soul] are called horses because of their motion").[14] The galloping movement, *laxis habenis,* is the movement of desire, "not" (most often) "in itself desirable." As a poem of loves ("amori") the *Furioso* is a poem of many motions, for love itself is philosophically defined as a motion of the will toward enjoyment and rest in an object.

Ultimately, Ariosto's characters find their way to what they love and seek by two kinds of movement only. The rarer movement, indeed the singular one, reveals the contained and regulated motion of the spirit that is the basis of love rightly understood; it occurs habitually in only one character, jaunty and amiably crazy, and is said to be a temporary condition (for the duration of the poem, that is) even in him (34.86). The second kind of motion is the predominant motion of the poem, violent and headlong, and it is figured in the constantly recurring image of men and women (Ferraù, Rinaldo, Ruggiero, Orlando, Gabrina, Doralice, and many others) carried swiftly and clatteringly away by an impetus of passion. Nevertheless, all the myriad unbridled motions of the *Furioso* succumb to the sudden restraints of a headlong narrative, an artistic technique that imitates and so testifies to a more effective set of reins in the government of the universe itself, the bridle of Nemesis.[15]

Perhaps the most striking illustration of those two kinds of movement, counterpointing the strength that goes willingly in rhythm with the providential universe and the strength that willfully and vainly pits itself against it, having to be dragged, occurs in a series of cantos where the assault on Paris is finally begun. The figures in question are, of course, Rodomonte and Astolfo, who are completely unconscious of each other as they work to utterly contrary purposes in widely separated corners of the world. One, activated by fury and heroic egotism, cuts a wide swath of destruction among innocent victims of all kinds, and the other, apparently almost randomly, pursues a tourist's course in the Near East and rids the world of monsters and tyrants. Throughout cantos 15, 16, 17, and 18, the poet cuts rapidly from one to the other in a series of compelling poetic maneuvers, displaying his technical powers at their highest in his management of the *entrelacement,* asserting a global control over the actions of his universe, and forcing his reader to shuttle back and forth in disorienting movements and at a whiplash pace. The focus here is on Rodomonte. Selected by Ariosto for a role as the deadliest opponent of Christianity, superseding all others, Rodomonte is a character invented by Boiardo and filled to bursting with an infectious vivacity and youthful bravado that is one of the best, most characteristic things in the *Innamorato.* It is astonishing then to find these attractive boyish qualities totally suppressed in the *Furioso.* When Ariosto finally unleashes him in canto 14, thirsting for the destruction of Paris, Rodomonte is driven by passion and hatred extraordinary for their violence and out of all proportion to the already energetic Boiardan original. The *Furioso*'s Rodomonte is, typically, several things:[16] a figure formed from the superimposition on a Boiardan base of a classical model. For Rodomonte is a revivified Turnus, ardent and unappeasable; and although Ariosto preserves him as a character from Boiardan romance, with a faithless Doralice of his own, he independently enwraps him in the "atrox" and "horrens" aspects of the great Rutulian warrior, the rival of Aeneas. The prolonged episode that begins when Rodomonte bounds over the moat of Paris and ravages the city from end to end (14.108) marks one of Ariosto's great Vergilian moments. This studious imitation refers pointedly to a crucial happening in Vergil's book 8, the siege of the Trojan encampment, when Turnus, set loose within Aeneas's provisional timber walls on the Tiber—Rome in embryo—ranges in inflamed fury among the sparse defenders whose leader is temporarily away. Rodomonte and Turnus are two invaders joined in wreaking havoc, one in an offshoot of Empire being planted by Aeneas, the other in the long-established Empire's fictional center of Paris. They are exactly similar also in their common mode of escape from the forces finally closing in on them, by a climactic plunge into a river, the Tiber in one case, the Seine in the other. The site of Empire shifts from Rome to France to Germany, but the idea of Empire remains alive: transition framed by continuity.

   Ariosto deepens the diabolic resonances that Boiardo, representing Rodomonte as a descendant of Nimrod, had written into his portrait. On his first appearance in the *Furioso,* Rodomonte is ever more closely enwrapped in rhetoric and imagery that are overtly Satanic and serpentine, both in the glancing identification of a comic messenger (16.86–87) and in the poet's own heroic simile, borrowed from Vergil, of a magnificent serpent (17.11). Even here laughter prevails. The page who arrives, breathless, pale, and panicky, to tell Charlemagne of Rodomonte's irruption into the city knows that this is big news. It is his moment of glory as a messenger and he gives it his loquacious all:

"—Ahimè! signor, ahimè!" replica molto,
prima ch'abbia a dir altro incominciato:
"Oggi il romano Imperio, oggi è sepolto;
—oggi ha il suo popul Cristo abandonato:
il demonio dal cielo è piovuto oggi,
perché in questa città più non s'alloggi.

"Satanasso (perch'altri esser non puote)
strugge e ruina la città infelice.
Volgiti e mira le fumose ruote
de la rovente fiamma predatrice;
ascolta il pianto che nel ciel percuote;
e faccian fede a quel che'l servo dice.
Un solo è quel ch'a ferro e a fuoco strugge
la bella terra, e inanzi ognun gli fugge."
        (16.86.3–8, 87.1–8)

"Alas, my lord, alas," he exclaimed over and over again, before he got to the heart of his
tale. "Today the Roman Empire, today it is buried; today Christ has abandoned his people; today the devil has rained down from heaven to make this city uninhabitable forever
after. Satan—for it can be no other than he—destroys and ruins this unhappy city. Turn
and see the smoke wheeling up from the roving, ravening flame. Listen to the cries that
strike the very heavens and testify to what your servant says. One only is he who destroys
the sweet earth with fire and sword, and everyone flees before him."

Two separate and distinct meanings, wedded for a moment, play richly over and
against each other: the one of the hyperexcited and officiously garrulous page, and
the graver one of which it is merely the comic shadow. Trust Ariosto to announce
satanic presence in hyperbole that has the effect of litotes. The nameless underling,
proud of his proximity to great events and rising volubly to the occasion, speaks
better than he knows. For when Rodomonte appears he fully justifies his heralding,
triumphantly evil in his splendid, reptilian energy:

Sta su la porta il re d'Algier, lucente
di chiaro acciar che'l capo gli arma e'l busto,
come uscito di tenebre serpente,
poi c'ha lasciato ogni squalor vetusto,
del nuove scoglio altiero, e che si sente
ringiovenito e piú che mai robusto:
tre lingue vibra, et ha negli occhi foco:
dovunque passa, ogn'animal dà loco.
        (17.11)

The King of Algiers stands in the gate, shining in the bright steel that armed his head and
trunk, like a serpent issued from darkness after he sloughs off his ancient coat: proud of his
new scales, feeling his youth revivified and more than ever strong. Three tongues he
vibrates, fire flashes from his eyes; wherever he passes, every other animal gives way.

There is more here than meets the eye: more than a snake rejoicing in a new outward accoutrement, more than a Vergilian heroic simile acquiring a new life and energy.[17] Amid sulfurous fumes rising from the defenders' ditches around Paris, unmistakable overtones of another older assault play over the surface of Rodomonte's protracted attack on the capital city with its representatives of all Christian nations, and the invasion of Paris assumes symbolic significance as an attack on the center of the Church and Empire militant. Indeed, Rodomonte's deep penetration of that city is the closest the poem brings us to the utter annihilation of both institutions.

At this point in the *Furioso,* expansive Hate has all but expelled the power of Love, restricted now to its narrowest compass. But this is precisely the point at which the poem's centripetal energies begin to assert themselves, and the centrifuge begins to whirl in the contrary direction. At this very moment Providence compassionately begins to employ Discordia in the ranks of the enemy (14.75). This is a slight comic beginning that will swell to tremendous conclusions as evil erodes from within. That is not all: far off in his own comical-magical world, Astolfo again *at this very moment*—and surely the tight, close interweaving of these contrasted actions compels attention—is subduing wrong-doers and making his leisurely but steady way to Jerusalem, where "il superno Amore / Lavò col proprio sangue il nostro errore" (15.94.7–8; "divine Love first washed away our error with His own blood"). Interestingly, Astolfo arrives Herculeanly, by taking the difficult *right* branch of a forking road (15.93). Rodomonte's furious energy and mindless exertion of force finds an unexpected check in the complex narrative arrangement, which "places" his impulse to destruction and empties it of power even as it exerts itself to its utmost. From a stance of timelessness, Ariosto's synoptic poetic vision accomplishes that Lucianic spatial diminution of "heroic" evil that Milton's Satan also undergoes, when he is first seen close-up in all his epic fearsomeness and then is swiftly and telescopically reduced to a speck in the purview of Providence.

At base, and in ways that diminish to utter invisibility the emaciated pieties of its post-Tridentine commentators, the *Furioso* is concerned to assert a complex, mysteriously responsible moral universe. Apparently Charlemagne's babbling messenger was doubly wrong: Christ has indeed not "abandoned his people." For it is no accident that on his way eastward, at the very moment when the siege of Charlemagnic Paris is in progress, Astolfo should be hearing, from the mouth of Andronica-Fortitude who accompanies him, the blazon of yet another Holy Roman Emperor, the Aragonese kinsman of the Estensi, Charles V,[18] and of the vast extension of his future empire into the New World. At the very moment, therefore, when the "romano Imperio" of the eighth century is apparently being "buried" under the assault of Rodomonte, Providence not only protects it by unleashing Discord and sending Astolfo on the first stage of his retributive journey, but also has already provided for the extension of both Empire and Church in times far off and in a New World yet unknown to geographers. Human blindness is again convicted of error, and perhaps also the casual reader.

Here the poetic intellect controlling the mesh of narrative threads is at its most formidable in its sense of economy and design. The blazon spoken by Andronica-Fortitude to an Astolfo soon to undertake a series of romantically transformed Herculean labors praises Charles in Herculean terms, clearly recalling the Emperor's adoption of the device of the Pillars of Hercules, columns set by the demigod at the entrance to the Mediterranean as a sign to mark the limits of his labors, a sign challenged by Charles V in his device of "Plus ultra," affirming the extension of his own power beyond the inner sea and into the Americas.[19] Hercules, the mythical patron of the cardinal virtue of fortitude, or of patience under stress, finds new avatars in the Hapsburgian Hercules of history and in the romantic-chivalric Hercules of Astolfo. The whole episode turns on the virtue incarnated by Logistilla's handmaiden, Andronica, and it is to Astolfo, finally, that Ariosto entrusts a spoken dramatization of the very essence of that virtue (15.46–48), making him its exemplar, immediately before his battle with Caligorante, Ariosto's version of Hercules's antagonist, Cacus.

In Rodomonte's devastation of Paris in cantos 14 through 18, Ariosto combines romance, epic, and history in fruitful, unprecedented ways. The narrative manipulation is extraordinarily complex and skillful, the patterning at its densest and weightiest. In the foreground is a romantic fiction, a Boiardan *narratio fabulosa,* retailing a wholly unhistorical Saracen attack on Charlemagne's Paris, which was, of course, never his capital. Beyond that, by a process of close imitation and steady allusion to the Latin original, the reader is asked to see *through* the romantic fiction to its ancient Vergilian model, Turnus's heroic attack on Aeneas's fragile encampment on the Tiber, matrix of Empire. Beyond that even, because Ariosto remembered the Vergilian interpreters' association of Turnus with the devil,[20] and because he darkens and brutalizes Turnus's energy in Rodomonte, depriving him of heroic qualities in his blood-lust against women and children, we see through to the primal attack on human felicity in Eden, when Christendom, if we may so put it, was a commonwealth of two, an epitome of "the whole included race." Finally, interwoven with Rodomonte's assault in a stunning example of the deep resonances of Ariostan *entrelacement* is the story of Astolfo's journey to the East and the prophecy of the triumph of the Hapsburgian Holy Roman Empire in the sixteenth century. The *Furioso* therefore combines allusions to the Holy Roman Empire in three moments of mortal peril—Roman, Carolingian, and contemporaneous—and it affirms the providential nature of the ancient institution, so often delivered before and (it is clearly implied) though now in the sixteenth century again being threatened in the Mediterranean by Moslems, again being delivered and indeed expanded afar into the New World. In effect, Ariosto recapitulates the entire history of the poetry associated with and springing from the Empire: the *Aeneid,* the Neoplatonically interpreted *Aeneid* of the intervening Christian centuries, and the Carolingian popular poems. And he now deftly inserts into that mainstream his own recreation of Vergil with elements borrowed from all three.

Purely as poetry, the episode is a rich concretion of disparate elements in which structural manipulations and density of content are truly remarkable. We may wish to prescind from a disquieting Catholic and Imperial triumphalism heralding the transfer of old hatreds westward into the New World. For the critic to record it as an element of the *Furioso*'s art is to do no more than record a thematic reality and then to stand aloof from its religious and political enthusiasm, as he may wish to stand aloof from *The Faerie Queene*'s as well. That said, it is obvious that, for Ariosto at least, the line of descent from Augustus to Charlemagne to Charles V is a compelling notion, witnessing providential protection of the most venerable political institution in the life of Europe, one to which the Estensi, through kinship, could claim a connection. What Ariosto thought about Charles V as a man remains unknown. As an agent of history at the head of an empire that tried to give coherence to European life, he acquired another value altogether, and the poet makes it plain that the construction and maintenance of a social order is no trivial affair: at the very end of his career, for the edition of 1532, he lavished all the resources of his art on this passage of praise. Unless, then, we imagine that in honoring the poet with the title of laureate in Bologna in 1532, Charles was putting a severe strain on that famous Hapsburg phlegm and concealing his distaste for a writer of comic verses and mock-epic fantasies merely, we must acknowledge that the encounter of Emperor and poet brought together the embodiment of the Roman Imperial idea and one of its subtlest poetic celebrators in the sixteenth century.

Here, then, by way of conclusion, is an epitome of Ariosto's art as we have examined it at length in various aspects in the preceding chapters, an art social and historical in its deepest impulses, and creating from the rich fusion of Boiardo, Vergil, Plato, and Lucian a new and altogether inimitable Carolingian poem, the kind of work that by an act of perfecting effectively terminates a tradition. Ariosto wrote with eyes unblinkered by phenomena and with a courtier's deep attention to the difficulty of creating and maintaining civilizations. In a comic, comprehensive, and idealizing romantic epic, he placed himself within a rich continuum of culture, and his poem preserves the manifold energies of a society long scattered into dust.

Notes

Notes for Introduction

1. The standard work on the editions of *Orlando Furioso* is G. Agnelli and G. Ravegnani, *Annali delle edizioni ariostee*, 2 vols. (Bologna, 1933). But since various editions unlisted there are mentioned by Allan Gilbert in his English translation of the poem (2 vols. [New York: Vanni, 1954], 1:xi), and also by Rensselaer W. Lee in *Names on Trees: Ariosto into Art* (Princeton University Press, 1977), pp. 91–92, n. 37, the number of sixteenth-century editions given by Agnelli and Ravegnani (154) is clearly too low. Gilbert estimates as many as 200 printings, with 200,000 copies in print by 1601.

2. The standard account of the *Furioso*'s impact on French culture is by A. Cioranescu, *L'Arioste en France des origines à la fin du XVIIIe siècle*, 2 vols. (Paris, 1939); for an equally voluminous treatment of its fortunes in Spain, see Maxime Chevalier, *L'Arioste en Espagne, 1530–1650* (Bordeaux: Institut d'études iberiques et ibero-américaines de l'Université de Bordeaux, 1966); for influence in England see Mario Praz, *The Flaming Heart* (Garden City, N.Y.: Doubleday, 1958), pp. 289–307; A. Benedetti, *L'Orlando Furioso nella vita intelletuale del popolo inglese* (Florence, 1914); and, more recently, A. Sammut, *La fortuna dell'Ariosto nell'Inghilterra elisabettiana* (Milan: Vita e pensiero [Publicazioni dell'Università Cattolica del Sacro Cuore], 1971). There is an especially rich bibliography on the *Furioso*'s impact on art; see, for instance, Lee, *Names on Trees*; the article by G. Rouchès, "L'Interprétation du 'Roland furieux' et de la 'Jerusalem delivrée' dans les arts plastiques," *Etudes Italiennes* 2 (1920): 129–40 and 193–212; and U. Bellochi and B. Fava, *L'interpretazione grafica dell' "Orlando Furioso"* (Reggio Emilia: Banca di Credito Popolare e Cooperativo, 1961). See also the bibliography at the end of Remo Ceserani's fascinating "Ludovico Ariosto e la cultura figurativa del suo tempo," in *Studies in the Italian Renaissance: Essays in Memory of Arnolfo B. Ferruolo*, ed. G. P. Biasin, A. N. Mancini, and N. J. Perella (Naples: Società Napoletana Editrice, 1985), pp. 145-66. For interpretations by particular artists, see E. Mongan, P. Hofer, and J. Seznec, *Fragonard: Drawings for Ariosto* (New York: Pantheon Books, 1945); *Doré's Illustrations for Ariosto's "Orlando Furioso": A Selection of Two Hundred and Eight Illustrations* (New York: Dover, 1980); and R. Palluchini, *Gli affreschi di Giambattista e Giandomenico Tiepolo alla Villa Valmarana di Vicenza* (Bergamo: Instituto Italiano d'Arti Grafiche, 1945).

3. The Vivaldi dates from 1727, the three Handel operas from 1733 and 1735, the Haydn from 1782, revealing a continuous interest in the *Furioso*'s plot as a mine for pastiche and travesty. Earlier musicalizations of the *Furioso*, centering on the Alcina-Ruggiero allegory, include Francesca Caccini's *La liberazione di Ruggiero dall'isola d'Alcina* (Florence, 1625), which was (according to information supplied to me by Professor Raymond Waddington) performed as recently as the spring of 1983 by the music department of the University of California at Davis; and Giovambattista Lully's part in the three-day fête of plays, cavalcades, and dances entitled *Les plaisirs de l'île enchantée* (Versailles, 1664), in which Louis XIV assumed the part of Ruggiero: see the fascinating commentary in Victor-L. Tapié, *The Age of Grandeur: Baroque Art and Architecture*, trans. A. Ross Williamson (New York: Praeger, 1961), pp. 106–9. There is still, unfortunately, no orderly, extended account of the *Furioso*'s impact on European musical culture over the centuries comparable to any of those available for the plastic arts, yet its influence in that area is surely as voluminous and persistent. See Elise B. Jorgens's "Orlando Metamorphosed: Handel's Operas after Ariosto," *Parnassus* (Fall/Winter 1982): 45–74, and Reinhard Strohm's "Comic Traditions in Handel's *Orlando*," in his *Essays on Handel and Italian Opera* (Cambridge University Press, 1985), pp. 249–67.

4. For Voltaire's affinity for the poem, see Giosuè Carducci, "L'Ariosto e il Voltaire," in *Edizione nazionale delle opere*, ed. Nicola Zanichelli, 30 vols. (Bologna, 1935–1940), 14:117–35. For Charles James Fox's dictum, "For God's sake, learn Italian as fast as you can in order to read Ariosto," see *The Continental Renaissance, 1500–1600*, ed. A. J. Krailsheimer (Harmondsworth: Penguin, 1971), p. 111.

5. Quoted in Giuseppe Fatini, *Bibliografia della critica Ariostea, 1510–1956* (Florence: Felice LeMonnier, 1958), pp. 15-16, entry no. 57. For an essential Ariosto bibliography covering more recent years, see Guido Baldassari, "Tendenze e prospettive della critica Ariostesca nell'ultimo trentennio (1946-1973)," *La Rassegna della Letteratura Italiana* 89 (1975): 183–201. More recently, Robert J.

Rodini and Salvatore Di Maria have put all Ariostans in their debt with their excellent and comprehensive updating, *Ludovico Ariosto: An Annotated Bibliography of Criticism, 1956–1980* (Columbia: University of Missouri Press, 1984). Here I wish to record my gratitude to Professor Rodini for his kindness in allowing me to see his "Selected Bibliography of Ariosto Criticism, 1980–1985," forthcoming in *MLN* in a special edition devoted to Ariosto.

6. See the delicious frontispiece of *Fragonard: Drawings for Ariosto,* representing Love and Folly as two *putti* perched on Ariosto's desk as he sits, laurel-crowned and chin on hand, meditating his verses. The original is in the Besançon Musée des Beaux Arts.

7. In "Life of Milton," in *Lives of the English Poets: Samuel Johnson's Literary Criticism,* ed. R. D. Stock (Lincoln: University of Nebraska Press, 1974), p. 221.

8. Chapters in books include Thomas M. Greene's *The Descent from Heaven: A Study in Epic Continuity* (New Haven: Yale University Press, 1963); Robert M. Durling's *The Figure of the Poet in Renaissance Epic* (Cambridge: Harvard University Press, 1965); and A. B. Giamatti's *The Earthly Paradise and the Renaissance Epic* (Princeton University Press, 1966). In addition, see the stimulating article by D. S. Carne-Ross, "The One and the Many: A Reading of *Orlando Furioso,* cantos 1 and 8," *Arion* 5 (1966): 195–234, and a rather curious one in which the same author finds something akin to artistic failure in the *Furioso*'s ending with celebrations of religious, social, and political values: "The One and the Many: A Reading of the *Orlando Furioso,*" *Arion* n.s. 3, no. 2 (1976): 146–219. For an earlier and equally important Italian contribution, see G. De Blasi, "L'Ariosto e le passioni," *GSLI* 129 (1952): 318–62, and 130 (1953): 178–203. For a curious critical throwback, banal and uncertain in its perceptions, see A. Fichter's skeletal treatment of the *Furioso* in *Poets Historical: Dynastic Epic in the Renaissance* (New Haven: Yale University Press, 1982), which "adapts" my thesis title "The Dynastic Romance" (Princeton, 1964). Peter De Sa Wiggins has translated Ariosto's Horatian poems—*The Satires of Ludovico Ariosto: A Renaissance Autobiography* (Athens: Ohio University Press, 1976)—and equipped them with an uncommonly intelligent commentary, essential for the illumination of the *Furioso*; the same author has recently demonstrated the multiplicity of Ariosto's vision in shaping characters in a full-length study, *Figures in Ariosto's Tapestry: Character and Design in the "Orlando Furioso"* (Baltimore: Johns Hopkins University Press, 1986). C. P. Brand's *Ludovico Ariosto: A Preface to "Orlando Furioso"* (University of Edinburgh Press, 1974) remains the most readable general introduction in English to the poet and his works.

9. See a treatment of this progressive movement from Pulci to Boiardo to Ariosto in my "Redemptive Laughter: Comedy in the Italian Romances," in *Versions of Medieval Comedy,* ed. Paul G. Ruggiers (Norman: University of Oklahoma Press, 1977), pp. 227-48. There is no comprehensive study of the Arthurian and Carolingian romance traditions in Italy before Pulci. In addition to the standard works—Roger Loomis, *The Development of Arthurian Romance* (London: Hutchinson, 1963); E. G. Gardner, *The Arthurian Legend in Italian Literature* (London, 1903); Enrico Carrara, *Da Rolando a Morgante* (Turin, 1932)—there is an extensive and detailed account of the penetration and diffusion in Italy of these chivalric materials in the introduction (pp. ix-lxxv) to Nicola Zingarelli's edition of *Orlando Furioso* (Milan, 1934), which is equipped with the most substantial index of characters and historical personages in Ariosto criticism.

10. See my article entitled "Shaping the Ore: Image and Design in Canto I of *Orlando Furioso,*" forthcoming in the special Ariosto edition of *MLN.*

11. For an example of Ariosto's transformation of a Boiardan character, see my article entitled "The Flight of Ariosto's Hippogriff: Genesis, Elaboration, and Function," in *Ficino and Renaissance Neoplatonism,* ed. Konrad Eisenbichler and Olga Zorzi Pugliese, University of Toronto Italian Studies, 1 (Ottawa: Dovehouse Editions, 1986), pp. 87–99.

12. Various works illuminate the social and cultural background of the *Furioso*: the remarkable nine-part monograph by Alessandro Luzio and Rudolfo Renier, "La coltura et le relazioni letterarie di Isabella d'Este Gonzaga," *GSLI* 33–40 (1899–1902); Giosuè Carducci's monograph, "La gioventù di Ludovico Ariosto e la poesia latina in Ferrara," in *Edizione nazionale delle opere,* 13:119–374;

Giulio Bertoni's *La Biblioteca Estense e la cultura ferrarese ai tempi del duca Ercole I* (Turin, 1903), and his *L'Orlando Furioso e la Rinascenza a Ferrara* (Modena, 1919); and Domenico Fava's *La Biblioteca Estense nel suo sviluppo storico* (Modena, 1925).

13. It circulated instead in a Tuscanized, much altered version. See *Orlando Innamorato composto dal signor Matteo Maria Boiardo Conte di Scandiano . . . e rifatto da Francesco Berni,* 2 vols. (Venice, 1799). William Stewart Rose made a prose abridgment of this work in his *The "Orlando Innamorato" Translated into Prose from the Italian [Version] of Francesco Berni and Interspersed with Extracts in the Same Stanza as the Original* (Edinburgh, 1823). The original *Innamorato* was reprinted only in the nineteenth century, by Sir Antonio Panizzi, Principal Librarian of the British Museum. See his *Orlando Innamorato di Bojardo; Orlando Furioso di Ariosto: With an Essay on the Romantic Narrative Poetry of the Italians,* 9 vols. (London, 1830–1834).

14. For a good account of these cultural shifts and their impact on the poem's interpretation, see Antonio Piromalli's *Ariosto,* La Nuova Critica series (Padua: R.A.D.A.R, 1969), esp. pp. 7–27: "Dai contemporanei ai romantici."

15. The documents are collected in *Apologia del S. Torquato Tasso, in difesa della sua Gierusalemme Liberata. Con alcune altre opere, parte in accusa, parte in difesa dell'Orlando Furioso dell'Ariosto, della Gierusalemme istessa, e dell'Amadigi del Tasso padre* (Mantua, 1585). The standard work on the controversy is Bernard Weinberg's *A History of Literary Criticism in the Italian Renaissance,* 2 vols. (University of Chicago Press, 1960): for the Ariosto-Tasso debate, see esp. 2:954–1073. See also Baxter Hathaway, "Tasso's Magic Realism," in *The Age of Criticism: The Late Renaissance in Italy* (Ithaca: Cornell University Press, 1962), pp. 390–96.

16. See Piromalli, *Ariosto,* p. 9.

17. Awareness of the problem of the Ariosto-Boiardo relationship dates from the first criticism of the *Furioso*. In modern times, a slowly forming awareness of the problem surfaces again after Panizzi's great edition of the two *Orlandos* in the early nineteenth century, and then only fitfully. In *Le fonti dell'Orlando Furioso* (1876; 2d ed. 1900; rpt., Florence: Sansoni, 1975), Pio Rajna apologized for gliding over matters that needed to be accorded a "more ample" treatment (p. 35, n. 1). Nevertheless, Rajna's method of accumulating parallels and sources at the expense of evaluating Ariosto's use of them drew its own critical fire: see Francesco d'Ovidio, *Saggi critici* (Naples, 1879), pp. 150–68. Afterward, it is difficult to think of any work dealing with either Ariosto or Boiardo that does not touch in some way on the relation of the one to the other. But it is equally difficult to think of any work that specifically isolates that relationship as a problem to be dealt with centrally, intensively, and comprehensively. Of older works on the subject in English, E. W. Edwards's *The "Orlando Furioso" and Its Predecessors* (Cambridge, 1924) remains a graceful appreciation, but it is a slight performance, now badly outdated. Among older works in Italian, there are Enrico Carrara's *I due Orlandi* (Turin, 1935), a study on general rather than specific lines, and Luigi Costanzo's *Ariosto contro Boiardo: pazzia pagana e pazzia christiana* (Naples: Federico & Ardia, 1967), a brief pamphlet, while Angelandrea Zottoli's work has a misleading title; *Dal Bojardo all'Ariosto* (Milan, 1934) consists, in fact, of four separate essays on unrelated aspects of the two poets' art.

Essential to the study of Ariosto are several recent articles that proceed on an altogether different level of literary sophistication. All share the virtue of locating the problem in the decade of fracture intervening between the *Innamorato* and the *Furioso,* and of presenting the resumption of Boiardo's Orlando materials as a matter of deliberate and serious artistic choice. Carlo Dionisotti's "Fortuna e Sfortuna del Boiardo nel Cinquecento," in *Il Boiardo e la critica contemporanea,* Atti del convegno di studi su Matteo Maria Boiardo, Scandiano-Reggio Emilia, 25–27 April 1969, ed. G. Anceschi (Florence: Leo S. Olschki, 1970), pp. 221–41, reveals how Ariosto flew in the face of an antichivalric, pro-historical bias operating at the turn of the century; Rosanna Alhaique Pettinelli's "Tra il Boiardo e l'Ariosto: Il Cieco da Ferrara e Niccolò degli Agostini," *La Rassegna della Letteratura Italiana* 79 (1975): 232–78, gives extensive consideration to important chivalric material intervening between Boiardo's breaking-off and Ariosto's beginning; Giovanni Ponte's "Boiardo e Ariosto," in the same issue (pp. 169–82), speaks of a "willed contest" ("voluta gara") evident in the *Furioso* between itself and the *Innamorato*; and Antonio Franceschetti's "Appunti sull'Ariosto lettore dell'*Innamorato*," in *Atti del convegno internazionale dei Lincei per Ludovico Ariosto* (Rome: Accademia Nazionale dei Lincei, 1975), pp. 103–17, attacks the problem squarely, affirming the necessity of a "conoscenza approfondita" and "confronto diretto" with Boiardo. More recently we have had another brief glance at the problem from a modernist point of view by Andrea Di Tommaso, "Boiardo/Ariosto: Textual Relations and Poetic Integrity," *Stanford Italian Review* 4 (1984): 73–91. I think it is fair to refer to the first paragraph of my doctoral thesis, "The Dynastic Romance," which pointed out the necessity of beginning with Boiardo, though (needless to say) I had no idea at that early date where my researches were to lead me.

18. The best and most comprehensive study of the *Innamorato* is Antonio Franceschetti's *L'Orlando Innamorato e le sue componenti tematiche e strutturali* (Florence: Leo S. Olschki, 1975). For an extensive bibliography on Boiardo see *Orlando Innamorato*, ed. Giuseppe Anceschi, 2 vols. (Milan: Garzanti, 1978), pp. xxxvi–xliv. See also *Annali d'Italianistica* 1 (1983): pp. 159–73, for further bibliography by M. Bregoli-Rousseau; the issue contains interesting articles on Boiardo by M. Murrin and A. Franceschetti.

19. For a suggestive article on this subject, see C. P. Brand, "Ariosto's Continuation of the *Orlando Innamorato*," in *Cultural Aspects of the Italian Renaissance: Essays in Honor of Paul Oskar Kristeller*, ed. Cecil H. Clough (New York: Zambelli, 1976), pp. 377–85.

20. All references to the *Innamorato* are taken from the edition by Aldo Scaglione, *Orlando Innamorato, amorum libri* (Turin: UTET, 1963); all translations from the poem are my own. Here it should be noted that I use Ariosto's versions of the characters' names to avoid complication: Ruggiero, Bradamante, Rinaldo, Ferraù, etc., rather than Rogero, Brandiamente, Ranaldo, Feraguto, as they appear in Boiardo.

21. All references to the poem are to *Orlando Furioso*, ed. Santorre Debenedetti and Cesare Segre (Bologna: Commissione per i testi di lingua, 1960). All translations from the Italian text are my own. The recent text by Emilio Bigi (2 vols. [Milan: Rusconi, 1982]) has a noteworthy introduction.

22. I except the novelle, which (because the *Furioso*'s simultaneities are the despair of the critic) require a separate study that will illuminate their individual nature and assess their relation to the narrative scheme of the *Furioso* as a whole. C. P. Brand's remarks on these tales, in his previously mentioned study, are well worth pondering.

23. The most trenchant criticism of this formula is by Durling, *Figure of the Poet*, pp. 250–51, n. 5. Another is in the review by Prue Shaw, "Seeing Dante Whole," *TLS*, 2 May 1980, p. 501.

24. The standard biography, including the relevant contemporary documents, is Michele Catalano's *Vita di Ludovico Ariosto*, 2 vols. (Geneva, 1930).

25. In *The King of Court Poets: A Study of the Work, Life and Times of Lodovico Ariosto* (London, 1906), p. 37, E. G. Gardner notes (p. 32) that Alberto Pio's mother was Caterina Pico, sister of Giovanni Pico della Mirandola (see also Gardner's third genealogical chart, "The House of Pio," following p. 368). The Latin text of Ariosto's letter, freed of Gardner's curious translation *à l'antique,* may be found in the *Lettere di Ludovico Ariosto*, ed. A. Stella (Verona: Mondadori, 1965), p. 3: an Italian translation is given on p. 419, where Stella identifies the Aldine text Alberto Pio brought back from Venice ("un volume in cui sono raccolti scritti di filosifi accademici" in Stella's translation), as one containing an "Iamblichus de mysteriis Aegyptoriorum," published in 1498.

26. An excellent introduction to the man, his works, and his influence may be found in the introduction to the *Prose e rime di Pietro Bembo*, ed. Carlo Dionisotti (1960; 2d ed., Turin: UTET, 1966), pp. 9–56.

27. Brand, *Ludovico Ariosto*, p. 59. In contrast, for an assertion of Ariosto's role in diffusing Ficinian Neoplatonism in Ferrara in his student days, and for an assertion that the impact of Neo-

platonism on the *Furioso* has been insufficiently assessed, see Gennaro Savarese, "Ariosto al bivio tra Marsilio Ficino e 'adescatrici galliche,'" in *Filologia moderna,* Annali dell'Instituto di Filologia Moderna all'Università di Roma (1978), pp. 21–39; and also Eduardo Saccone, *Il "soggetto" del "Furioso" e altri saggi tra Quattro e Cinquecento* (Naples: Liguori, 1974), "Third Appendix," pp. 157–60.

28. For my earlier outline of the successive stages of Ruggiero's moral career, see my article, "Redemptive Laughter," pp. 244–45.

29. For a different view see Greene, *Descent from Heaven,* p. 125, and, more recently, Elizabeth A. Chesney's *The Countervoyage of Rabelais and Ariosto: A Comparative Reading of Two Renaissance Mock Epics* (Durham: Duke University Press, 1982).

30. Standard works on the life and the activities of the great humanist are Remigio Sabbadini's *La scuola e gli studi di Guarino Guarini Veronese* (Catania, 1896) and *La vita di Guarino Veronese* (Genoa, 1891), and Giulio Bertoni's *Guarino da Verona fra letterati e cortigiani a Ferrara, 1429–1460* (Ginevra, 1921). A good brief account in English is "Guarino da Verona, 1374-1450," in William Harrison Woodward's *Studies in Education during the Age of the Renaissance, 1400–1600* (New York: Columbia University Press, 1967), pp. 26–47.

Notes for Chapter 1: "Furore" and "Dismisura"

1. For an earlier consideration of this aspect of the *Innamorato,* see Robert M. Durling, *The Figure of the Poet in Renaissance Epic* (Cambridge: Harvard University Press, 1965), pp. 91–111.

2. For the kinds of appealingly archaic *dolce stil novo* poetry these proems of Boiardo deliberately recall, see poems nos. 14 and 23 by Guido Guinizelli and Guido Cavalcanti respectively, in *The Oxford Book of Italian Verse,* ed. St. John Lucas, 2d ed., rev. C. Dionisotti (Oxford: Clarendon, 1952). The Cavalcanti poem is printed and translated in *The Penguin Book of Italian Verse,* ed. George R. Kay (Harmondsworth: Penguin, 1958), p. 55.

3. See the *Oxford Book of Italian Verse,* poems nos. 138–40, and for translations of two of these see the *Penguin Book of Italian Verse,* pp. 148 and 152–54.

4. For an encyclopedic treatment of the tradition, there is no better source of information available to the reader than the "Love-Melancholy" section of the "Third Partition" of Robert Burton's *The Anatomy of Melancholy,* especially as Burton draws his knowledge from a vast variety of classical, medieval, and Renaissance authorities on the malady of love, and knows well the humanists among whom Ariosto moved and whom he himself mentions as his friends. The best modern treatment on the subject is by D. W. Robertson, Jr., who surveys the medieval tradition of love-writings, tracing it back to the Greek medical tradition and coming forward to Chaucer: see chapter 5 ("Some Medieval Doctrines of Love") of *A Preface to Chaucer* (Princeton University Press, 1960), pp. 391–503. Maurice Valency's *In Praise of Love: An Introduction to the Love-Poetry of the Renaissance* (1958; rpt., New York: Octagon, 1975) is a valuable survey of the tradition and has an extensive bibliography on the subject. Older works that provide interesting insights into love-malady are J. L. Lowes, "The Loveres Maladye of Hereos," *MP* 11 (1914): 491–546, and L. Babb, *The Elizabethan Malady* (East Lansing: Michigan State University Press, 1951).

5. Ovid, *Metamorphoses,* 7.20–21, lines occurring in the midst of a famous psychomachia in which Medea's better and worse instincts battle for supremacy.

6. See chapter 16, "Medea, Queen of Colchis," in the translation of Boccaccio's *De claris mulieribus: Concerning Famous Women,* by Guido A. Guarino (New Brunswick: Rutgers University Press, 1963), pp. 35–37.

7. See poems nos. 135 ("Qual più diversa et nova") and 72 ("Gentil mia Donna, i'veggio") of the *Rime sparse,* especially the lines in which Petrarch represents himself as limping tardily after good and running swiftly after evil ("S'al ben veloce et al contrario tardo"). All references to Petrarch's poetry are taken from Robert M. Durling's text and translations, *Petrarch's Lyric Poems* (Cambridge: Harvard University Press, 1976). The root of Petrarch's protestations is probably as much to be

sought in St. Paul as in Ovid; see the Epistle to the Romans: "For I do not understand what I do, for it is not what I wish that I do, but what I hate, that I do" (7:15).

8. The *canzone* ("I' vo pensando et nel penser m'assale") concludes with the line, "et veggio 'l meglio et al peggior m'appiglio."

9. *Consolation,* 3.met.5.1–4. All references to Boethius are taken from the Loeb edition of *The Consolation of Philosophy,* tr. "I. T.," rev. H. F. Stewart (Cambridge: Harvard University Press, 1968).

10. The figure of Temperance on Orcagna's Tabernacle in Or San Michele in Florence (1355–1359) is illustrated in K. Steinweg, *Andrea Orcagna* (Munich, 1929), plate 17, p. 19. The Raphael fresco of Temperance in the Stanza della Segnatura in the Vatican is illustrated in *The Complete Work of Raphael* (New York: Reynal, 1969), fig. 131, p. 114 (the Cardinal Virtues wall, depicting Temperance with her sister virtues, holding out her bridle in the typanum over the door); and see also fig. 133, p. 116, for an enlargement of the figure of Temperance alone. For the Veronese fresco, where a masculine figure embodying "Virtù" has passed a bridle through the mouth of a seated female figure representing "il Vizio," see plate 6 of Robertson's *Preface to Chaucer.* For a late sixteenth-century example of Temperance, see the splendid, life-sized piece of marble statuary by Giovanni Caccini now in the New York Metropolitan Museum of Art, executed in Florence between 1583 and 1584 and described by Olga Raggio in "The Metropolitan Marbles," *Art News* 67 (Summer 1969): 45–47. For non-Italian examples, see R. Tuve, *Allegorical Imagery* (Princeton University Press, 1966), fig. 17, p. 75, for a "bizarre set of cardinal virtues" dating from 1470: among them, a seated Temperance who, in addition to the bridle through her mouth, holds eyeglasses for clear-sightedness, turns a windmill with her foot (for regularity), and wears a clock on her head, illustrative of measured motion. See, finally, for a climax of sorts, the "Temperantia" of Bruegel, which has affinities with the one just mentioned, in H. Arthur Klein, *Graphic Worlds of Peter Bruegel the Elder* (New York: Dover, 1963), p. 245.

11. See sonnet 49 of *Astrophil and Stella,* in *The Poems of Sir Philip Sidney,* ed. William A. Ringler (Oxford: Clarendon, 1962), p. 189. Other relevant "horse" sonnets, equating the mount and the desire of the rider, are the Shakespearean pair, nos. 51 and 52: see *The Sonnets, The Complete Pelican Shakespeare,* gen. ed. Alfred Harbage (Baltimore, Md., rev. ed. 1969; rpt., Harmondsworth: Penguin, 1970). Also highly pertinent here is Erwin Panofsky's chapter, "Blind Cupid," in his *Studies in Iconology: Humanistic Themes in the Art of the Renaissance* (1939; rpt., New York: Harper and Row, 1972), pp. 116ff.

12. See the "Discorso di M. Lodovico dolce sopra il *Furioso,*" *Orlando Furioso* (Venice, 1542), sig. ij: "dimostrava chiaramente la via d'impazzire" ("he demonstrated clearly the way to losing his mind" [translation mine]).

13. "Every day we see a thousand, and those perhaps who are held to be the most trustworthy and the wisest, who when they turn to love, go plainly mad." Cf. the proem at 9.1 of the *Furioso:* "Che non può far d'un cor ch'abbia suggetto / questo crudele e traditore Amore, poi ch'ad Orlando può levar del petto / la tanta fé che debbe al suo signore? / Già savio e pieno fu d'ogni rispetto, e de la santa Chiesa difensore: / or per un vano amor, poco del zio, / e di sé poco e men cura di Dio." The speaker here is, of course, the scatter-brained lover, the persona who sympathizes with Orlando. The Bembo quotation is from the *Gli Asolani,* in *Prose e rime di Pietro Bembo,* ed. Carlo Dionisotti (Turin: UTET, 1966), p. 347. All references to the *Asolani* are to this edition. The English translation of Bembo is from *Gli Asolani,* tr. Rudolf B. Gottfried, Indiana University Publications, Humanities Series No. 31 (Bloomington: Indiana University Press, 1954), p. 39. All translations of Bembo are taken from this version.

14. "Allegoria universale sopra tutta l'opera dell'Ariosto," in *Orlando Furioso di M. Lodovico Ariosto nuovamente adornato di figure di rame da Girolama Porro Padovano* (Venice, 1584), p. 8. Bononome notes Boiardo's insertion of "facole teatrali senza senso" ("showy fables without meaning") in the *Innamorato* and declares that they were afterward "trasportate nella favola d'Alcina a significatione de' concetti morali" ("transported into the fable of Alcina to signify moral con-

cepts"). For a richly suggestive modern essay on the connection between the marvelous and the allegorical, see Morton M. Bloomfield, "Episodic Motivation and Marvels in Epic and Romance," in his *Essays and Explorations: Studies in Ideas, Language, and Literature* (Cambridge: Harvard University Press, 1970), pp. 97–128.

15. See the fascinating chapter, "Falerina's Garden," in Michael Murrin's *The Allegorical Epic: Essays in Its Rise and Decline* (University of Chicago Press, 1980), pp. 53–85: as Murrin notes at once, Boiardo's is a totally discontinuous kind of allegory; his poetry may on rare occasions manifest interior patterns and complications, but they are not of the kind that radiate into the main body of the narrative and reinforce meanings, as in Ariosto.

16. See Pio Rajna, *Le fonti dell'Orlando Furioso* (1876; 2d ed. 1900; rpt., Florence: Sansoni, 1975), p. 173.

17. For an emblem of "Occasio," see Andrea Alciati, *Emblematum liber* (Augsberg, 1531), A8, and Machiavelli's poem, "L'Occasione," in the *Oxford Book of Italian Verse*, p. 168. Exactly as in Boiardo, she is followed by Penitence.

18. A fivefold arrangement of temptations repeated at the end of 3.2 of the *Consolation* as "divitias," "dignitates," "regna," "gloriam," and "voluptates," treated individually and with remarkably pointed order in the prose sections of 3.3, 4, 5, 6, and 7, and finally recapitulated in 3.8 and 9.

19. See *Macrobius' Commentary on the Dream of Scipio,* ed. William Harris Stahl (New York: Columbia University Press, 1952), pp. 69–77.

20. For a richly detailed pictorial representation of their opposition, see plate 16 in *The Riverside Shakespeare,* ed. G. Blakemore Evans (Boston: Houghton Mifflin, 1974), which reproduces the title page from Robert Record's "The Castle of Knowledge" (1556), showing Urania, or Heavenly Wisdom, standing firmly on a solid square block, indicative of her relationship to the "Sphaera Fati" or Divine Providence, and holding the compasses (associated with rational knowledge) in the light of the sun, symbolic of rational knowledge; and, opposite her, a blinded Fortune, mounted uneasily on a wheel, standing in the changeable light of the moon, indicated by the inscription "Sphaera Fortunae." For a more sophisticated continental treatment, see Jean Fouquet's "Debate of Virtue and Fortune" (circa 1460), in André Chastel's *The Myth of the Renaissance, 1420–1520,* tr. Stuart Gilbert (Geneva: Skira, 1969), p. 69.

21. See chapter 31 ("On the Whale, that is, the Aspidoceleon") in *Physiologus,* tr. Michael J. Curley (Austin: University of Texas Press, 1979), pp. 45–46. See also *Paradise Lost,* 1.192–209, in *The Complete Poetical Works of John Milton,* ed. Douglas Bush (Boston: Houghton Mifflin, 1965), pp. 216–17; all references are to this edition.

22. See *Gerusalemme Liberata* (10.66), ed. Marziano Guglielminetti, 2 vols. (Milan: Garzanti, 1982) for Armida represented as a fisherwoman; Andrea Alciati, *Emblemi* (Padua, 1626), 65ᵛ, portrays a woman fishing as an example of "Meretrix," or a whore ensnaring lovers; Shakespeare's Cleopatra is also cunningly and unflatteringly represented as an angler in 2.5.10-15; and Donne's "The Bait" effects a piscatorial transformation of the pastoral seduction scene in Marlowe's "The Passionate Shepherd to His Love," emphasizing the cynicism behind the pastoral and depriving it of all sentiment: see my *Pastoral* (1971; rpt., London: Methuen, 1978), pp. 27–30.

23. See his "Canzone d'amore," 4.3, 6. For the influence of Cavalcanti's song on later love literature, see the "Seventh Speech" of Ficino's *Commentary on Plato's Symposium,* ed. and tr. Sears Jayne, University of Missouri Studies, 19 (Columbia: University of Missouri, 1944), pp. 216–17. All references to Ficino are to this work.

24. See no. 134 of the *Rime* ("Pace non trovo"), translated by Wyatt as "I find no peace." "Peace" is, of course, the final word of the Petrarchan sequence: "ch'accolga'l mio spirto ultimo in pace" (no. 366). In view of what is said in the text about the proximity of love and wrath, Robert Burton's comment is highly relevant: "These concupiscible and irascible appetites are as the two twists of a rope, mutually mixed one with the other, and both twining around the heart: both good, as Austin

holds, *lib.* 14, *cap.* 9, *de Civ. Dei,* 'if they be moderate; both pernicious if they be exorbitant' "—
"exorbitant" having the value for Burton of "dismisurato" for Boiardo. Burton continues, "This
concupiscible appetite, howsoever it may seem to carry with it a show of pleasure and delight, and
our concupiscences most part affect us with content and a pleasing object, yet, if they be in extremes,
they rack and wring us on the other side. A true saying it is, 'Desire hath no rest,' is infinite in itself,
endless, and, as one calls it, a perpetual rack, or horse-mill, according to Austin, still going round as
in a ring" (Pt. I, Sec. 2, Mem. 3, Subs. II ["Causes of Melancholy"], *The Anatomy of Melancholy,* ed.
Holbrook Jackson [New York: Vintage, 1977], p. 280).

25. See Giulio Bertoni, *La Biblioteca Estense e la cultura ferrarese ai tempi del duca Ercole I* (Turin,
1903), p. 249. One of Ariosto's allegorizers, Tommaso Porcacchi, has an illuminating comment on
the allegorical nature of the fountains: "questa fintione è simile à quell'altra, ch'assegna due strali à
Cupido: l'uno d'oro, che induce amore; & l'altro di piombo, che partorisce odio" ("this fiction is
gold, which induces love, and the other of love, which produces hate"): see *Orlando Furioso* (Venice,
1577), sig. A5ᵛ. The "fiction" is the same one operating in the *Roman de la Rose,* with the difference
that there the number of arrows is increased to ten, five arousing and five dispelling love: see the
translation by Harry W. Robbins, *The Romance of the Rose,* ed. Charles W. Dunn (New York:
Dutton, 1962), pp. 19–20. Cupid is therefore associated with either arrows or fountains, which
alternatively arouse and extinguish the passion of love. The fountains occur in Petrarch (*Rime,*
135.76–79), Boiardo, and Tasso (*Gerusalemme Liberata,* 15.55–66), and can be traced to Claudian's
"Epithalamium of Honorius and Maria": "Here spring two with the first, poison with the second,
and in these streams 'tis said that Cupid dips his arrows" (see *Works,* tr. Maurice Platnauer [London,
1922]). In Shakespeare's *A Midsummer Night's Dream* we find neither arrows nor fountains but
flowers with opposite virtues: the white and purple flower that Cupid hits with his arrow at
2.1.165ff., and "Dian's bud" (4.1.72), which has power to remove the charm inflicted by "Cupid's
flower." Behind all these fictions, of course, lies the Platonic myth of Reason, capable of invoking
the aid of the irascible power to curb that of the concupiscible—which brings in the image of horses
to join arrows, fountains, and flowers.

26. *Gerusalemme Liberata,* 15.55ff., and *The Faerie Queene,* 2.12.60–75. For an illuminating comparative study of the two passages, see Robert M. Durling, "The Bower of Bliss and Armida's
Palace," *Comparative Literature* 6 (1953): 335–47.

27. Ariosto refers to the fountains briefly, almost in passing and as an afterthought (at 1.78 of the
Furioso: "e non sono lontane").

28. Here Ariosto clearly follows Ficino's remedy for unrequited love: "Therefore, the unrequited
lover lives nowhere; he is completely dead. Moreover, he never comes back to life unless indignation
revives him" (*Commentary on Plato's Symposium,* p. 144).

29. See Simone Fornari, *Spositione sopra l'Orlando Furioso,* 2 vols. (Florence, 1549–1550), 2:334.

30. See the important article by Ettore Paratore, "L'*Orlando Innamorato* e l'*Eneide,*" in *Il Boiardo e
la critica contemporanea,* Atti del convegno di studi su Matteo Maria Boiardo, Scandiano-Reggio
Emilia, 25–27 April 1969, ed. G. Anceschi (Florence: Leo S. Olschki, 1970), pp. 347–75, which
shows how thoroughly Boiardo's imagination was permeated with phrases and expressions from the
Latin poem. My emphasis on the Vergilian resonances in Boiardo differs from Paratore's in that I am
concerned to trace the interpenetration of classical and romantic (or chivalric) diction in the
Innamorato, and particularly the way in which Boiardo found chivalric equivalents—often demotic
and rendered comic through insistence and repetition—for the stately vocabulary of Latin epic. My
point here and elsewhere in this chapter is that an underlying risibility often, though not of course
always, underlies Boiardo's classicism.

31. See *A Vergil Concordance,* comp. Henrietta Holm Warwick (Minneapolis: University of Min-
nesota Press, 1975), pp. 433–35.

32. For these isolated lines, see *Purgatorio,* 17.97–99; "Canzone d'amore," 4.43–44; *Rime sparse,*
no. 65 ("Lasso, che mal accorto fui da prima") and no. 35 ("Solo e pensoso i più deserti campi").

33. *Asolani*, pp. 345, 355, 350, of the Italian text. All of this emphasis on the mean is provisional, of course, for while the state of being "fuor di misura" is throughout represented as being morally dangerous in the extreme (see, e.g., pp. 347 and 365 of the Italian text), the hermit of book 3 will give a vertical direction to this simple horizontal view and advise Lavinello that his love is not good if it does not draw him upward to an immortal object but merely holds him "nel mezzo dell'una e dell'altra qualità di disio, dove il dimorare non è sano" (pp. 495–96).

34. For virtue as having an aesthetic as well as a moral dimension, see Ficino, *Commentary on Plato's Symposium*, ed. and trans. Sears Jayne, University of Missouri Studies, 19 (Columbia: University of Missouri, 1944), p. 130: "love seeks only what is temperate, moderate, and decorous. Pleasures and sensations which are so impetuous and irrational that they jar the mind from its stability and unbalance a man, love does not only not desire, but hates and shuns, because these sensations, being so intemperate, are the opposites of beauty." The greater decorum of Ariosto's art, as much Horatian as Platonic, may result from precisely such an awareness, and from his substitution of more recognizably human physiognomies, less drastically violent puppetry of action, for Boiardo's essentially hectic and spastic creations. Needless to say, we are speaking here of a Platonic, rather than an Aristotelian, decorum. In Ariosto's case, the latter is anachronistic.

Notes for Chapter 2: "Con atto umano"

1. See the standard biography of the poet by Giulio Reichenbach, *Matteo Maria Boiardo* (Bologna, 1929), p. 141; also Giulio Bertoni, *Nuovi studi su Matteo Maria Boiardo* (Bologna, 1904), p. 105. The Vergilian phrase from the *Eclogues* (10.69) that Boiardo shares with Chaucer's prioress says much about his classical inclinations.

2. For these relationships, see the genealogical chart in E. G. Gardner, *Dukes and Poets in Ferrara* (New York, n.d.), p. 254.

3. For a good treatment of the importance of the tradition in the work of Boccaccio, see Robert Hollander, *Boccaccio's Two Venuses* (New York: Columbia University Press, 1977). The Augustinian foundation of the two loves that underlies the Neoplatonic expansion into a triadic scheme of loves has been repeatedly explored by D. W. Robertson, Jr., particularly in his *A Preface to Chaucer* (Princeton University Press, 1960). The Augustinian bent of Ariosto's Neoplatonism was briefly but crucially noted by Robert M. Durling in *The Figure of the Poet in Renaissance Epic* (Cambridge: Harvard University Press, 1965): "For Ariosto's view of the darkness of human life—'Questa assai più oscura che serena / Vita mortal, tutta d'invidia piena' (4.1)—is, like Petrarch's hard-won *contemptus mundi,* ultimately Augustinian" (p. 174).

4. Remnants of this Vergilianizing poem are reprinted in Bertoni, *Nuovi studi*, pp. 232–35. Tito Vespasiano Strozzi's classicizing influence had still another fortunate issue; he was the first to translate Horace into a vernacular tongue, thus providing the impetus to Ariosto to write his *Satires*. Interestingly, even today, in the heart of Ferrara, Via Tito Strozzi symbolically connects Via M. M. Boiardo with the parallel Via Ariosto, where at no. 67 the greater successor to these two kinsmen built his house and deepened their art.

5. See the translation, by John A. Yunck, *Eneas: A Twelfth-Century French Romance* (New York: Columbia University Press, 1974).

6. See Anna Cox Brinton, *Maphaeus Vegius and His Thirteenth Book of the "Aeneid": A Chapter on Virgil in the Renaissance* (Stanford, 1930). Brinton prints the text of the "editio princeps" with the English translation of Thomas Twyne (1584) and follows it with the text of the Scottish translation of book 13 by Bishop Gavin Douglas.

7. Translated by Helen M. Mustard and Charles E. Passage (New York: Vintage, 1961), p. 442. For another view, see E. H. Wilkins, "The Naming of Rodomonte," *MLN* 70 (1955): 596–600.

8. For this emergence of the theme of courtesy, and for Ariosto's later extension of it in the concluding cantos of the *Furioso,* in the Leo-Ruggiero episode, see the fine essay by David Marsh,

"Ruggiero and Leone: Revision and Resolution in Ariosto's *Orlando Furioso*," *MLN* 96, 1 (1981): 144–51, though he misses the bewitching humor in Boiardo's portrait of the lovers.

9. See Andrea da Barberino's *Aspramonte,* ed. Luigi Cavalli (Naples: Rossi, 1972), bk. 1, chs. 30–44 (pp. 62–76). The last chapter of this late fourteenth-century or early fifteenth-century work terminates with Andrea giving alternate versions of Galaciella's fate: (1) she was burned alive for having betrayed her people; (2) she was sent off in a boat to Africa where she was imprisoned and delivered of two children, one male, one female. Both Boiardo and Ariosto chose to follow the second version, calling the two children Ruggiero and Marfisa (later the Amazon warrior). See Andrea's *I reali di Francia,* ed. Giuseppe Vandelli and Giovanni Gambarini (Bari: Laterza, 1947), bk. 6, ch. 71 (pp. 564–68), for a prodigious list of pedigrees of famous heroes to which Andrea ultimately attached Ruggiero, providing the impetus to Boiardo to follow him. The name "Roger" had, of course, long been venerated in southern Italy for the illustrious Norman kings of Sicily, and Boiardo's revival of the name may have been occasioned, by way of compliment, by the presence in Ferrara of a daughter of the King of Naples, the Duchess Eleanora of Aragon.

10. For Ariosto's remanipulation of Boiardo's Atlante and for the Petrarchan emphasis, see my article, "The Flight of Ariosto's Hippogriff: Genesis, Elaboration, and Function," in *Ficino and Renaissance Neoplatonism,* ed. Konrad Eisenbichler and Olga Zorzi Pugliese, University of Toronto Italian Studies, 1 (Ottawa: Dovehouse Editions, 1986), p. 93. The complaints registered by the narrator and by Pinabello and other disappointed lovers are exactly the same as those voiced against Amor in traditional love poetry and in the *Furioso*'s novelle. See, for example, Isabella's complaint against Love himself in 13.4: "Colpa d'Amor: ch'io non saprei di cui / dolermi più che de la sua nequizia; / che dolcemente nei principii applaude, / e tesse di nascosto inganno e fraude" ("This is Love's fault: for I wouldn't know against whom to complain more than against his iniquity; sweetly he applauds us at the start, but he contrives traps and deceptions out of sight"). See also 13.20 for Isabella's complaint that love undoes all our rational purposes: "stempre / ogni nostro disego irrazionale." All of this is a perfect example of what Atlante does in the Palace of Illusion. Moreover, the first account of Atlante's depredations occurs in canto 2, which begins with the narrator's complaint, "Ingiustissimo Amor."

11. For the tradition, see Donald R. Howard, *The Three Temptations: Medieval Man in Search of the World* (Princeton University Press, 1966).

12. See notes 16 and 17 in my article referred to in note 10 above.

13. For Bradamante's description of passionate love as an irrational flight, see 32.21: "Ma di che debbo lamentarmi, ahi lassa, / fuor che del mio desire irrazionale? / ch'alto mi leva, e sì ne l'aria passa, / ch'arriva in parte ove s'abbrucia l'ale" ("But against what can I complain, alas, except my own irrational desire, which lifts me on high and passes through the air to the point where its wings are burned").

14. See *Gli Asolani,* in *Prose e rime di Pietro Bembo,* ed. Carlo Dionisotti (Turin: UTET, 1966), p. 354.

15. Boiardo was not exactly idle during this decade: in 1480 he was elected "Capitano" (Governor) of Modena, a post he occupied until 1483; in 1487 he was elected "Capitano" of Reggio, and he spent the rest of his life in that city.

16. For a view of the *Innamorato*'s structure essentially similar to the one expressed in these paragraphs, see Antonio Franceschetti's penetrating article, "Struttura e compiutezze dell'*Orlando Innamorato,*" in *Il Boiardo e la critica contemporanea,* ed. G. Anceschi (Florence: Leo S. Olschki, 1970), pp. 281–94. See also Aldo Scaglione, Boiardo's editor, *Orlando Innamorato, amorum libri* (Turin: UTET, 1963): "La trama del racconto non risulta unitaria, anche perché non si può prevedere la conclusione. E evidente uno stacco fra primo e secondo libro, mentre il terzo introduce imprese e favole tutto nuove" (1:21). At the end, as well as at the very beginning of his poem, it appears certain Boiardo was being true to his cherished and richly productive but perhaps also ultimately self-defeating aesthetic of constantly providing "cose dilettose e nove."

17. Torn between his father-in-law, the king of Naples, and his son-in-law, Ludovico il Moro, the ally of the French king now descending on Naples, Duke Ercole tried to maintain a balance between the two by allowing passage of the Milanese and French troops through his domains although he offered no further help. The last picture we have of the poet is in his official capacity, attempting vainly to control the destructive belligerence of an army passing through territories he administered and leaving behind the immemorial tokens of their passing. For a desolating picture of a harried and weary poet in his last days see Reichenbach, *Matteo Maria Boiardo,* pp. 236–40.

Notes for Chapter 3: Homage to the House

1. Yates has strikingly apt and resonant things to say about *Orlando Furioso* in relation to its time in various essays in *Astraea: The Imperial Theme in the Sixteenth Century* (Harmondsworth: Penguin, 1977), passim, but particularly with regard to the *renovatio imperii* of Charles V. Reynolds is at pains throughout her introduction to the two volumes of her translation of *Orlando Furioso* (2 vols. [Harmondsworth: Penguin, 1975 and 1977]) to establish the poem's contact with reality, but her pages on "Reality and Fantasy" (2:20–21) are especially worthwhile and reinforce the fine perception of Carlo Dionisotti that the *Furioso* (in contrast with the *Orlando Innamorato* which, on contact with historical reality—that is, the French wars of 1494—simply breaks apart) proceeds on a path in its fantastic soaring in order that "non perde mai d'occhio quanto avviene nel mondo" (*Prose e rime di Pietro Bembo* [Turin: UTET, 1966], p. 21). Though much of it is concerned with Ariosto's *Cinque canti,* Giorgio Padoan's "L'*Orlando Furioso* e la crisi del Rinascimento," in *Ariosto 1974 in America,* Atti del Congresso Ariostesco—December 1974, Casa Italiana della Columbus University, ed. Aldo Scaglione (Ravenna: Longo, 1976), pp. 1–29, is important for its assertion of the relevance of the Italian political scene between 1509 and 1515 to the composition of the *Furioso.*

2. See *Lettere di Ludovico Ariosto,* ed. A. Stella (Verona: Mondadori, 1965).

3. Ariosto was on diplomatic missions for the Duke of Ferrara in both instances: in the first, to offer condolences to Lorenzo de' Medici, Duke of Urbino, for his wife's death in childbirth, an occasion that soon turned into a double tragedy with the death within days of the father as well (Peter De Sa Wiggins, *The Satires of Ludovico Ariosto: A Renaissance Autobiography* [Athens: Ohio University Press, 1976], p. 55; E. G. Gardner, *The King of Court Poets: A Study of the Work, Life, and Times of Ludovico Ariosto* [London, 1906], pp. 100–41); in the second instance, to attempt to placate Pope Julius II, infuriated by the diplomatic dealings of the rulers of Ferrara (Wiggins, *Satires,* p. 23, n. 14; Gardner, *Dukes and Poets in Ferrara* [New York, n.d.], p. 78). The remote and solipsistic fantasist created by romantic criticism is a being to be found in neither the *Satires* nor the letters.

4. The historical proems (apart from those purely philosophical, moral, or epideictic) include those prefixed to the following cantos: 14, 15, 17, 33, 34, 36, 40, 42, 45, and 46.

5. The matter is rehearsed in the first *Satire,* a remarkable document founded on an actual event in Ariosto's life as well as being an assertion of his values, in which he assumes the Horatian persona to assert the importance in human existence of internal independence and freedom (see Wiggins, *Satires,* pp. 3–24). For Corvinus as a figure linked securely with the West and as a chief force in naturalizing Italian art in Hungary, see the absorbing and beautifully illustrated study by Jan Białostocki, *The Art of the Renaissance in Eastern Europe* (Ithaca: Cornell University Press, 1976).

6. The link to Spain and Naples, forged first by Leonello's marriage to Maria, daughter of Alfonso the Magnanimous, was strengthened through Duke Ercole's marriage into the House of Aragon in Naples; to Hungary through the marriage of the Duchess Eleanora's sister Beatrice to King Matthias Corvinus; to Milan through her namesake, their daughter Beatrice's, marriage to Ludovico il Moro; to Mantua through Beatrice's elder sister Isabella's marriage into the Gonzaga family; to Rome through the marriage of their eldest son, Alfonso I, to Lucrezia Borgia; and to Urbino through Isabella's husband, whose sister Elisabetta was Duchess of Urbino. The dukes of Ferrara held the territory in fief from the Papacy, which, it has been already noted, reclaimed it at the

end of the sixteenth century on the failure of the legitimate male line of the house, though they continued to hold Modena and Reggio from the Empire. Hence Modena was the city to which the Estensi, surviving in an illegitimate line, removed themselves on being forced to quit Ferrara in 1598.

7. See Geoffrey Barraclough, *The Crucible of Europe: The Ninth and Tenth Centuries in European History* (Berkeley: University of California Press, 1976), pp. 98–100.

8. Quoted in Werner L. Gundersheimer, *Ferrara: The Style of a Renaissance Despotism* (Princeton University Press, 1973), p. 19, n. 9. As the author notes, "He also takes Ariosto to task for propagating the myth," and in the interests of truth the author introduces his own view of the Germanic origins of the family in chapter 10 of his *Antichità Estensi ed Italiane*. Apparently the "sickness" is not limited to vile "feudal" or capitalist societies alone: the headline of an article in the *New York Times* (Sunday, 28 March 1976, p. 11) advises, "Two Soviet Literary Journals Debate Whether Achilles was a Forebear of the Russians."

9. See Stanford Shaw, *History of the Ottoman Empire and Modern Turkey*, 2 vols. (Cambridge University Press, 1976), 1:55-58, 87–111. Chapters 3 and 4 are of utmost importance to the understanding of the international scene in Ariosto's time and his exclamations against the Hapsburg-Valois dissension that bled the energies of Christian Europe and even opened the way for opportunistic Christian-Turkish alliances. Needless to say, Fernand Braudel's *The Mediterranean and the Mediterranean World in the Age of Philip II*, 2 vols. (New York: Harper & Row, 1972-1973) is crucial, especially his chapter on "Empires" (2:657-703).

10. For a recent treatment of the impact on Europe of this disastrous battle on the Danube, see the chapter "Nicopolis" in Barbara W. Tuchman's *A Distant Mirror: The Calamitous Fourteenth Century* (New York: Knopf, 1978), pp. 538–63.

11. Shaw, *History of the Ottoman Empire*, 1:69–70.

12. Ibid., 1:96–98. See also, for the career of the Turkish pirate Hayruddin ("Barbarossa"), the popular account by Ernle Bradford, *The Sultan's Admiral: The Life of Barbarossa* (New York: Harcourt, Brace & World, 1968), and chapters 1–3 in John B. Wolf's *The Barbary Coast: Algiers under the Turks, 1500–1830* (New York: Norton, 1979), pp. 1–54.

13. See Shaw, *History of the Ottoman Empire*, 1:91–94, for the campaigns of 1526, 1527–1529, and 1532, precisely the years in which Ariosto was readying for the press the third edition of the *Furioso*, with its striking additions, notably the disastrous adventures of Ruggiero in eastern Europe, adventures in which he manifests the same blind pride in personal glory that often appeared to be motivating the headstrong brothers-in-law, Francis I and Charles V.

14. Shaw, *History of the Ottoman Empire*, 1:102–3.

15. Isabella d'Este is known to have procured a copy of the book (first published in Valencia in 1490) in its republication in Barcelona in 1497, and to have been so delighted with it as to persuade her cousin, the poet Niccolò da Correggio, to attempt a translation: see Alessandro Luzio and Rudolfo Renier, "Niccolò da Correggio," *GSLI* 22 (1893): 70. A delightful modern translation has recently appeared: *Tirant lo Blanc*, tr. David H. Rosenthal (New York: Schocken, 1984). From this work Ariosto drew the tale of Ginevra and Ariodante for canto 5 of the *Furioso*, a novella which is at the base not only of Spenser's tale of Phedon in book 2 of *The Faerie Queene* but also of Shakespeare's *Much Ado about Nothing*. For the importance of Muntaner's work to the dynastic theme of the *Furioso*, see the highly suggestive article by Ezio Levi, "L'*Orlando Furioso* come epopea nuziale," *Archivum Romanicum* 17 (1933): 459–96.

16. For a standard history of these Spanish attempts to establish an empire in the East, see J. Lee Shneidman, *The Rise of the Aragonese-Catalan Empire, 1200–1350*, 2 vols. (New York University Press, 1970), 2:347ff.; also, a bit more briefly but less fascinatingly, William C. Atkinson, *A History of Spain and Portugal* (1960; rpt., Harmondsworth: Penguin, 1970), p. 96.

17. See Shaw, *History of the Ottoman Empire*, 1:51, 53, 54, 71, 71, 75, and 93. In *The Aragonese Arch at Naples, 1443–1475* (New Haven: Yale University Press, 1973), George L. Hersey notes (p. 12) that the Spanish conqueror of Naples, Alfonso V, the Magnanimous, planned a push to the East by an

alliance with Scanderbeg in Albania and, in 1455, a crusade against the Turks; Levi, "L'*Orlando Furioso*," notes that Alfonso's son and successor, Ferrante I, father of the Duchess Eleanora of Ferrara, may have deliberately resumed the orientalizing policy of his father by marrying his daughter Beatrice to King Matthias Corvinus of Hungary (pp. 481–82).

18. See Shaw, *History of the Ottoman Empire*: "When Granada fell to the Spaniards in 1492 and the Muslim states in North Africa began to face the possibility of Christian invasions, the pressure for Ottoman intervention increased in the face of numerous appeals for help. Problems in the East still prevented Bayazit from sending assistance. But many of the Ottoman sea gazis, called pirates in the West, began to move to help their Muslim brothers while securing easy pickings from the Christians. Also, as the Ottoman fleet was built up, many of these 'pirates' were drawn into Ottoman service, and under their influence it was not long before the Ottomans were ready to use their new naval power to begin operations in the West" (1:76).

19. Ariosto mentions his own dramatic creation, the aged lover, Cleandro, in his first satire: see Wiggins, *Satires*, p. 17.

20. For Ferrante, third son of Isabella and the Marquis Francesco II of Mantua, a son named for Isabella's grandfather, King Ferrante of Naples, and for her own brother, immured for life in Ferrara, see Eric Cochrane, *Florence in the Forgotten Centuries, 1527–1800* (1973; rpt., University of Chicago Press, 1974), p. 3. Cochrane notes also (p. 50) his later position as Governor of Milan for Spain. See also, for his vice-regal role in Sicily, the index of *Orlando Furioso*, ed. Nicola Zingarelli (Milan, 1934), p. 549. Lauro Martines, in *Power and Imagination: City-States in Renaissance Italy* (New York: Knopf, 1979), adds that he served Charles V in Spain from 1524 to 1527 (where his role would not have remained, we may be sure, unknown to Ariosto, who had been sent by Cardinal Ippolito to congratulate his sister Isabella on the child's birth), and that in 1530 he was general of the imperial armies that laid siege to Florence (p. 222).

21. In this regard, it should be noted that Ariosto had several important imperial contacts of his own in the latter part of his life. As Wiggins notes, "He participated in the reception held in Modena in 1529 for Charles V, where Duke Alfonso was forced for the security of Ferrara to use all the diplomatic skill at his command to win the Emperor's favor. In 1531, the poet was in the Duke's entourage when he entered Bologna to be reinvested by Charles in the Duchies of Modena, Reggio, and Ferrara. Again, in 1532, Ariosto found himself in the Emperor's presence when Alfonso went to Mantua where the Emperor and Clement VII were busy forming a league against France. On this occasion, Charles gave Ariosto an honorary diploma naming him poet laureate" (*Satires*, p. 173). After his death, as we know from document no. 626 (31 October 1533) in Michele Catalano's collection of materials relevant to his life (*Vita di Ludovico Ariosto*, 2 vols. [Geneva, 1930], 2:343), Charles V restricted to Ariosto's heirs the rights to publication of *Orlando Furioso*.

22. Wiggins, *Satires*, p. xxii.

23. E. M. W. Tillyard, *The English Epic and Its Background* (London, 1954; 2d ed. New York: Oxford University Press, 1966), pp. 12–13.

24. On this play and Ariosto's adaptation, see the important article by Irving Lavin, "Cephalus and Procris: Transformations of an Ovidian Myth," *JWCI* 17 (1954): 260–87.

25. The biographical information in these paragraphs is often a mosaic gathered variously from several sources: from Panizzi, a pioneer in identifying these forgotten personalities; from Luzio and Renier; from Gardner, who appears to have profited often from the researches of those two scholars; from Catalano; from Zingarelli's indispensable index to his edition of the *Furioso*; from Emilio Zanette's *Personaggi e momenti nella vita di L. Ariosto* (Milan: Pan Editrice, 1970); and from Wiggins, *Satires*. The names (Calcagnini, Valeriano) that crop up constantly in Ariosto's life as his familiars and friends are those that are often discussed as learned antiquaries and mythographers by art historians like Erwin Panofsky, Jean Seznec, or Edgar Wind to elucidate the art, particularly the Neoplatonic art, of the period; they furnish many of the fascinating connections in this group, and it is odd to see that Ariosto's name is almost never mentioned in connection with them.

26. For paintings directly commissioned by Isabella, see J. Seznec, *Fragonard: Drawings for Ariosto* (New York: Pantheon Books, 1945), p. 109. With regard to Perugino's "Battle of Love and Chastity," see Carlo Castellaneta, *L'opera completa del Perugino* (Milan: Rizzoli, 1969), who notes (p. 107) the "copious correspondence" that passed between Isabella and the artist about the content of the painting and its expression in images. She was, in any event, dissatisfied with the result. Two other works examine Isabella's relations with the world of art: Clifford M. Brown and Anna Maria Lorenzoni's *Isabella d'Este and Lorenzo da Paria: Documents for the History of Art and Culture in Renaissance Mantua* (Geneva: Librairie Droz, 1982); and Egon Verheyen's *The Paintings in the "Studiolo" of Isabella d'Este at Mantua* (New York University Press, 1971).

27. See Catalano, *Vita,* 1:287, and Gardner, *King of Court Poets,* pp. 51–52.

Notes for Chapter 4: Neoplatonist Art

1. For a discussion of the concept of *discordia concors,* the idea of universal order achieved by the countermovements exerted by opposed principles of love and strife, embodied mythologically in the figures of Venus and Mars, see Edgar Wind, *Pagan Mysteries in the Renaissance,* rev. ed. (New York: Norton, 1968), pp. 86ff. Wind's note 18 (p. 87) is especially relevant to the *Furioso*: quoting Plutarch's *Moralia,* where the fable of Mars and Venus is allegorized as Empedoclean Strife and Love, from whose union the goddess Harmonia was born, Wind notes that Celio Calcagnini, Ariosto's lifelong friend and whose epitaph the great humanist wrote, paraphrased the Plutarchan passage in his own essay, "De concordia." Once again, the availability of such notions to Ariosto is beyond question. In addition, the reader should consult E. H. Gombrich, *Symbolic Images: Studies in the Art of the Renaissance* (London: Phaidon, 1972), pp. 82–84, for another discusson of *discordia concors,* which is relevant for the connection of the concept and the "Parnassus" of Andrea Mantegna, commissioned from the artist by Isabella d'Este herself.

2. In the "First Speech," Orpheus is said to have "placed Love in the heart of Chaos itself" (p. 125); shortly afterward, we find the same phrase repeated: "Out of a chaos was made a world" (p. 129).

3. See André Chastel's *The Myth of the Renaissance, 1420-1520,* tr. Stuart Gilbert (Geneva: Skira, 1969), pp. 82–83, for reproductions of two frescoes in the Palazzo Schifanoia by Francesco del Cossa (circa 1436–1478). The frescoes themselves, still in place after many vicissitudes, date from circa 1470, four years before Ariosto's birth; the fresco for the month of April depicts a throned Venus being reconciled to a shackled Mars.

4. Wind, *Pagan Mysteries,* p. 86.

5. For an expression in poetry of this concept of the amicable reconciliation of Mars to a beneficent Venus, see one of Boiardo's most beautiful proems in the *Innamorato,* 3.19.1–3.

6. See D. S. Carne-Ross, "In Quest of Mutability," *TLS,* 31 October 1975, pp. 1303–4, reviewing volume 1 of the translation of *Orlando Furioso* by Barbara Reynolds. For a similar view, expressed in an earlier review of Robert McNulty's edition of Harington's Ariosto, see the anonymous article, "Ariosto Approached," *TLS,* 6 October 1972, in which the poem's "life-line" is said to be "not the God-directed loves of Bradamante and Ruggiero but Orlando's ill-starred passion for Angelica" (oddly, since the latter comes to an end when the poem has twenty-three more cantos to run) and in which Ariosto is said to create a "fluid discontinuous world where the only constant is perpetual change." Further, "the *Furioso* is a poem in praise of mutability. It looks for no permanence beyond the flux, yearns for the certainties of no farther shore" and "celebrates the vagaries of impenitent process" (pp. 1195–96).

7. *Apologia del S. Torquato Tasso in difesa della sua Gierusalemme Liberata, a gli Accademici della Crusca* (Ferrara, 1586), p. 132: "Ma questa conveneuolezza non si ritrova nel Furioso, nel quale Ruggiero è amato più, che amante, & Bradamante ama più, che non è amata, & segue Ruggiero, & cerca di trarlo di prigione, & fa tutti quegli uffici, & quelle operationi, che parebbono più tosto

conveneuoli, a Cavalliero, per acquistar l'amore della sua donna, quantunque ella fosse guerriera; la dove Ruggiero non fa cosa alcuna per guadagnarsi quello di Bradamante, ma quasi par che la disprezzi, & ne faccia poca stima, il che non sarebbe peravventura tanto sconvenevole, se il poeta non fingesse, che da questo amore, & da questo matrimonio dovesse derivare i Principi d'Este" (the translation in the text is my own).

8. See Flaminio Nobili, *Il trattato dell'amore humano* (Rome, 1895), a work for which Tasso himself provided the notes.

9. *Aeneid,* 8.729–31. All references to the Latin text are taken from the Loeb edition, tr. H. Rushton Fairclough, 2 vols. (London: Heinemann, 1954). All English translations from the *Aeneid* are taken from the Penguin translation by W. F. Jackson Knight (1956; rpt., Harmondsworth: Penguin, 1973).

10. Relevant to Ariosto's depiction of ceaseless motion in quest of desired objects are lines 31 through 33 of canto 18 of the *Purgatorio,* in which Dante defines desire as "moto spiritale," "a movement of the spirit which never rests until the object of its love makes it rejoice." All references to *The Divine Comedy* are to the Temple Classics edition, 3 vols. (London: Dent, 1941).

11. This is the hermit's instruction of the lover Lavinello in the higher love in book 3 of Bembo's *Gli Asolani,* in *Prose e rime di Pietro Bembo,* ed. Carlo Dionisotti (Turin: UTET, 1966), p. 482, and tr. Rudolf B. Gottfried, Indiana University Publications Humanities Series No. 31 (Bloomington: Indiana University Press, 1954), p. 173.

12. See Peter De Sa Wiggins, *The Satires of Ludovico Ariosto: A Renaissance Autobiography* (Athens: Ohio University Press, 1976), pp. 160–61. *Satire VI,* addressed to Bembo, narrates the barrenness of law study as Ariosto experienced it in his youth. See Carducci for the Latin lyrics of his apprenticeship. For Ariosto's part in the revival of classical theatrical entertainment at the court of Ercole I (again under the aegis of the Strozzi family), see E. G. Gardner, *The King of Court Poets: A Study of the Work, Life, and Times of Ludovico Ariosto* (London, 1906), pp. 25–26.

13. Gardner notes (*King of Court Poets,* p. 37, n. 1) that the documentary records on the presence of Sebastiano dell'Aquila as reader in law and medicine at the Studio, the University of Ferrara, apparently run from January 1495 to August 1502; see also, for this personality, Giulio Bertoni, *La Biblioteca Estense e la cultura ferrarese ai tempi del duca Ercole I* (Turin, 1903), p. 189. Ariosto studied philosophy with him from 1497 to 1498 (see Michele Catalano, *Vita di Ludovico Ariosto, 2 vols.* [Geneva, 1930], 1:103), a period that coincided exactly with Bembo's arrival in Ferrara in 1497, the year in which he set about composing the Neoplatonic *Asolani* (ed. Dionisotti, p. 20). The biographical facts we possess about Gregorio da Spoleto will occupy us in a later chapter; for Calcagnini, who was in the Cardinal Ippolito's service contemporaneously with Ariosto (and followed him, as Ariosto did not, to Hungary), and who held the chair of rhetoric for nearly thirty years at the Studio di Ferrara, see Alessandro Luzio and Rodolfo Renier, "La coltura et le relazione letterarie di Isabella d'Este Gonzaga," *GSLI* 35 (1900): 240–44.

14. See the entry "Pio" (for Alberto Pio, Lord of Carpi, Ariosto's fellow student while studying with Gregorio da Spoleto) in the index to Nicola Zingarelli's edition of *Orlando Furioso* (Milan, 1934), p. 579.

15. For critical works on the popular diffusion of Neoplatonism, see Nesca Robb, *The Neoplatonism of the Italian Renaissance* (London, 1935), and John Charles Nelson, *Renaissance Theory of Love: The Context of Giordano Bruno's "Eroici Furori"* (New York: Columbia University Press, 1958). Giuseppe Zonta collected some of the chief Neoplatonic literary treatises in *Trattati d'amore del cinquecento* (Bari, 1914).

16. For a clear graphic visualization of Pico's alteration of Ficino's hierarchy of two loves into his own hierarchy of three, see Erwin Panofsky, *Studies in Iconology: Humanistic Themes in the Art of the Renaissance* (Oxford, 1939; rpt., New York: Harper & Row: 1972), p. 145.

17. See *Fabii Planciades Fulgentii opera,* ed. Rudolf Helm (Stuttgart: Teubner, 1970), pp. 36–37, for the "Fabula de iudicio Paridis" in bk. 2, ch. 1 of the *Mitologiarum libri tres;* and for Macrobius, ch. 17

of *The Commentary on the Dream of Scipio,* pp. 244–46. Wind, *Pagan Mysteries,* p. 78, gives a variety of sources for the tripartite scale of life and love.

18. I have used the copy of Mario Equicola's work in the Houghton Library, Harvard University: *Di natura d'amore* (Venice, 1561), ed. Thomaso Porcacchi, otherwise known as one of the allegorists of the *Furioso* in *Le bellezze del Furioso*. For Equicola, Isabella's Latin teacher and later her secretary, see Panofsky, *Studies in Iconology,* p. 146, n. 58; and for Robert Burton's reference to him as an authority in love matters, see pt. 3 ("Love-Melancholy"), sec. 1 of *Anatomy of Melancholy,* ed. Holbrook Jackson (New York: Vintage, 1977), p. 4.

19. See *Prosa e rime di Pietro Bembo,* ed. Dionisotti, p. 19.

20. See Catalano, *Vita,* 1:463, for the letter from Bembo to Lucrezia, repeatedly mentioning "nostro Lodovico," who will convey the manuscript to her. See also Wiggins, *Satires,* p. 148: "It is believed that Ariosto was privy from the start to the infatuation Bembo felt for Lucrezia Borgia, the dedicatee of the *Asolani,* and that he, personally, in the author's absence, was entrusted with conveying to Lucrezia a copy of the manuscript as soon as the work was completed."

21. *Asolani,* ed. Dionisotti, p. 457.

22. *Asolani,* tr. Gottfried, pp. 184–85.

23. Ibid., p. 186.

24. The whole introduction to *Satire III* (Wiggins, *Satires,* pp. 51–52) is relevant here, as are his highly informative notes (pp. 76–81).

25. See Rudolfo Renier, "Per la cronologia et la composizione del *Libro de natura d'amore,*" *GSLI* 14 (1889): 212-33, which notes that Equicola was Isabella's first preceptor and then her secretary (pp. 214–15) and that, while there is evidence that the book on love was not originally planned with Isabella in mind, as it progressed it increasingly became her book and was finally dedicated to her. Other materials relevant to Isabella's relationship to Equicola are in Luzio and Renier's "La coltura et le relazione letterarie d'Isabella d'Este Gonzaga," *GSLI* 34 (1899): 1–21.

26. See "Botticelli's Mythologies," in Gombrich, *Symbolic Images,* pp. 31–81.

27. See Erwin Panofsky, *Problems in Titian, Mostly Iconographic* (New York University Press, 1969), pp. 110–19.

28. See Cecil Gould, *The School of Love and Correggio's Mythologies* (London: National Gallery Publications [1970]), pp. 7–8. The "School of Love" represents Mercury, god of wisdom, educating Cupid, who is engaged in the symbolic act of reading a book under the mild eye of his tutor; the "Venus and a Satyr" is, *tout court,* a scene of incipient rape. The paintings were executed for Isabella's son, Duke Federigo II of Mantua, as a gift for Charles V. Alberto Bevilacqua, *L'opera completa del Correggio* (Milan: Rizzoli, 1970), p. 107, provides the information that the "Education," as he prefers to call it, is a "pendant" to the "Venus and a Satyr," and that for a time they were the property of Charles I of England. The "School" remained in England when the King's collection was broken up and sold by Cromwell; the "Venus" was removed to France and is now in the Louvre. In his later study, *The Paintings of Correggio* (London: Faber & Faber, 1976), p. 127, Gould mentions the Louvre allegories ("Allegory of Virtue" and "Allegory of Vice") as "being allegories of a learned kind, painted at the request, and indeed to the specifications of, Isabella d'Este, who had a well-known taste for such things, and among whose possessions these paintings were first recorded in the inventory of 1542."

29. Wind, *Pagan Mysteries,* p. 81.

30. Wiggins, *Satires,* p. 54; see also the entry "Rafael" in Zingarelli's edition of *Orlando Furioso,* p. 581.

31. See Gombrich, *Symbolic Images,* pp. 33 and 70.

32. Wind, *Pagan Mysteries,* p. 81.

33. Panofsky, *Problems in Titian,* p. 110.

34. See Jean Seznec, *The Survival of the Pagan Gods* (1953; Princeton University Press, 1972), p. 109.

35. *Of Marriage and Wiving,* tr. R[obert] T[ofte] (London, 1599), sig. L. Robert Tofte is also the Elizabethan translator of Boiardo's first three cantos.

36. See Bertoni, *La Biblioteca Estense,* pp. 115–16, for scholars journeying from France, Germany, Hungary, and Greece to study with Guarino in Ferrara; and, for musicians from northern Europe who repeatedly found favor at the court of Ferrara, see Domenico Fava, *La Biblioteca Estense nel suo sviluppo storico* (Modena, 1925), pp. 160–61.

37. Wind, *Pagan Mysteries,* p. 82.

38. Tasso, *Of Marriage and Wiving,* sig. K³.

39. See Horace, *Ars poetica,* pp. 391ff., in the Loeb edition of *Satires, Epistles and Ars poetica,* tr. H. Rushton Fairclough (London, 1932). All further references to Horace are to this edition. See also Cicero, *De oratore,* in the Loeb edition, tr. E. W. Sutton (London: Heinemann, 1948). Both passages must inevitably have been in Ariosto's mind as he wrote his striking paraphrase of the Horatian passage in his own *Satires* (see Wiggins, *Satires,* p. 27).

Notes for Chapter 5: The Vergilian Expansion

1. Pio Rajna, *Le fonti dell'Orlando Furioso* (1876; 2d ed. 1900; rpt., Florence: Sansoni, 1975), p. 39.

2. See Augusto Romizi, *Le fonti latine del Furioso* (Turin, 1896), pp. 44–95, for an extended catalog of Ariosto's echoes or translations of Vergil. For an excellent account of the Vergilian reminiscences permeating the *Innamorato,* see Ettore Paratore, "L'*Orlando Innamorato* e l'*Eneide,*" in *Il Boiardo e la critica contemporanea,* ed. G. Anceschi (Florence: Leo S. Olschki, 1970), pp. 347–75.

3. See Alessandro Luzio, "Isabella d'Este e l'*Orlando Innamorato,*" *GSLI* 2 (1883): 163.

4. See Giulio Bertoni, *L'Orlando Furioso e la Rinascenza a Ferrara* (Modena, 1919), p. 82. The tutor was Jacopo Galliani. For the names of various preceptors (preponderantly clerics) of the Estensi scions in the period with which we are concerned, see Giulio Bertoni's *La Biblioteca Estense e cultura ferrarese ai tempi del duca Ercole I* (Turin, 1903), p. 96, and also his article entitled "I maestri degli Estensi nel quattrocento," *Archivum Romanicum* 1 (1917): 58–72. The education of Ercole's children was, as Bertoni asserts (*La Biblioteca Estense,* p. 69), largely Latin in orientation, a cultivation of the Latin classics being the peculiar hallmark of Ercole's own cultural activities, one in which he involved Boiardo, who translated many classical works for him, and one which distinguishes him from his brother Borso, whose culture tended to be French- and romance-oriented.

5. See the penetrating discussion of Cristoforo Landino's *Disputationes Camaldulenses* in the chapter, "Landino's Vergil," in Michael Murrin's *The Allegorical Epic: Essays in Its Rise and Decline* (University of Chicago Press, 1980), pp. 27–50.

6. In Italian there exist the older studies by Dominico Comparetti, *Virgilio nel medio evo,* 2 vols. (Turin, 1896), marred by a simplistic conception of allegory as a "dialectical hallucination," and Vladimiro Zabughin's still valuable *Vergilio nel rinascimento italiano da Dante a Torquato Tasso,* 2 vols. (Bologna, 1921). Vergilian allegory has recently been studied extensively, though not exhaustively, by D. C. Allen in his chapter, "Undermeanings in Virgil's *Aeneid,*" in his *Mysteriously Meant: The Rediscovery of Pagan Symbolism and Allegorical Interpretation in the Renaissance* (Baltimore: Johns Hopkins University Press, 1970), pp. 135–62. There are many valuable insights also in Merritt Y. Hughes's *Virgil and Spenser* (Berkeley, 1929), as in his "Vergilian Allegory and 'The Faerie Queene,'" *PMLA* 44 (1929): 696–705.

7. See the introduction to the Penguin translation of the *Aeneid* by W. F. Jackson Knight, (1956; rpt., Harmondsworth: Penguin, 1973), p. 14.

8. For biographical information on Gregorio da Spoleto, see E. G. Gardner, *The King of Court Poets: A Study of the Work, Life, and Times of Ludovico Ariosto* (London, 1906), p. 31. Gregorio had been prior of the convent of Sant'Agostino in Siena, lecturer at the Studio di Siena in 1459, had left the cloister to teach and had taken up residence in Rinaldo d'Este's palace in Ferrara, only a few paces from the Ariosto home, as the tutor of several young Estensi princes. Rinaldo's palace was known as the "Paradiso," and now functions, in part, as the library of the University of Ferrara, to which, by decree of Napoleon Bonaparte, Ariosto's remains were transported in the nineteenth century and

where he now lies entombed (see Robert J. Rodini and Salvatore Di Maria, *Ludovico Ariosto: An Annotated Bibliography of Criticism, 1956–1980* [Columbia: University of Missouri Press, 1984], entry 173). In his *Personaggi e momenti nella vita di L. Ariosto* (Milan: Pan Editrice, 1970), Emilio Zanette adds some interesting details: Gregorio's full name was Gregorio Ellio di Andrea d'Angelo, nicknamed "Elladio," that is, son of Hellas (Ariosto himself testifies that he was a master of Greek as well as Latin); he arrived in Ferrara in 1492 from Florence, where he had been the instructor of Giovanni de' Medici, son of Lorenzo and the future Pope Leo X. Gregorio was abruptly summoned to France in 1499 to serve in the employ of Francesco Sforza, but Ariosto paid him the tribute of recalling him as one of the major influences on his life twenty years later. See Peter De Sa Wiggins, *The Satires of Ludovico Ariosto: A Renaissance Autobiography* (Athens: Ohio University Press, 1976), pp. 167–68, n. 30, for commentary on his appearance in the *Satires*.

9. See his *Lectiones antiquae,* 2 vols. (Lyon, 1560), 2:555-59, in which he discusses the allegorical interpretation of ancient poetry; and see also 2:429 for his criticism of Landino, a passage in which he argues that Troy does not represent youth or the body, from which Aeneas flees, but rather the world, from which the hero rises on a three-scale Neoplatonic ladder. (The notion of Troy as the body derives, of course, from the Vergilian commentary of Bernard of Chartres, to be discussed shortly.)

10. See *Boccaccio on Poetry,* tr. Charles G. Osgood (1930; rpt., New York: Library of Liberal Arts, 1956), p. 173, n. 27.

11. See Fabius Placiades Fulgentius, *De Vergiliana continentia* (circa 520), in *Mythologici latini* (Heidelberg, 1599), p. 239; Francesco Filelfo, *Epistolae* [Venice, 1488], sig. aiii^v; and Guarino Veronese, *Epistolario,* ed. Remigio Sabbadini, 2 vols. (Venice, 1916), 2:526. The Filelfo letter dates from 1427 and is addressed to his fellow humanist, Ciriaco d'Ancona; the Guarino letter addresses Giovanni da Prato.

12. See John of Salisbury, *Policraticus* (8.24), in *Opera omnia,* 4, ed. J. A. Giles (Oxford, 1848); Bernard of Chartres, *Commentum super sex libros Eneidos Virgilii,* ed. Guilielmus Riedel (Greifswald, 1924); Dante, *Convito* (4.24 and 26), and *De vulgari eloquentia* (2.4); Filelfo, the aforementioned "Letter to Ciriaco d'Ancona"; and Cristoforo Landino in the *Disputationes Camaldulenses* (Venice, 1500): copy in the Houghton Library, Harvard University. The work by Bernard Sylvestris has lately attracted the notice of modern editors and translators: see *The Commentary on the First Six Books of the "Aeneid" of Vergil Commonly Attributed to Bernardus Sylvestris,* ed. Julian Ward Jones and Elizabeth Frances Jones (Lincoln: University of Nebraska Press, 1972); and *The Commentary on the First Six Books of Virgil's "Aeneid" by Bernardus Silvestris,* tr. Earl G. Schreike and Thomas G. Maresca (Lincoln: University of Nebraska Press, 1979).

13. Comparetti notes the fantastic elaboration of the *Aeneid* by Donatus (circa 333); Fulgentius sees Aeneas moving through life from the first moment of birth, represented by a "shipwreck into flesh"—a Platonic conception: see Marvell's lyric poem, "A Dialogue between the Soul and Body," in which Soul complains (ll. 27–30) of being "Constrain'd not only to indure / Diseases, but, whats worse, the Cure; / And ready oft the Port to gain / Am shipwrackt into Health again"—to his maturest attainment of virtue. Petrarch in the long detailed allegory of the *Aeneid* in his collection of letters called the *Seniles* (4.5: "To Federico Aretino") again looks at Aeneas's career as a whole, and Maffeo Vegio crowns the hero's career, not only by a marriage but also by an apotheosis in which he is lifted to the stars (at the end of Vegio's book 13) and is also said, in the allegory of the *Aeneid* in 1.5 of Vegio's devotional work, *De perseverantia religionis* (1448), to have found heavenly salvation. All four do the rarer thing in Vergilian allegory, which is not to stop at the end of the contemplative descent of book 6 but to acknowledge that Aeneas's course of instruction has a practical, active end in the world itself. By capping Vergil's epic with a thirteenth book in which marriage, both as a formal ceremony involving a social bond and as a symbolic achievement of interior harmony, is celebrated, Vegio provided a climax toward which the tradition had been moving for centuries: his lovers are graver and more mature than the giddy, love-wracked Aeneas and Lavinia that the twelfth-

century poet of the *Eneas* envisioned, but that is the Latin humanist decorum at work, supplanting the witty imaginings of the French courtly romancer.

14. Filelfo, *Epistolae,* sig. aiii.

15. Salisbury, *Policraticus,* 4.371; Filelfo, *Epistolae,* sig. aiii^v.

16. In all these allegories, the derivation from the Chalcidian allegorization of Plato is clear in the equation of parts of the exterior landscape with the internal moral dispositions of the human micro-cosm: the "south" (Carthage and Thrace) standing for the location of passion in the loins, the "north" (Italy) standing for the placing of reason in the citadel of the brain. See *Petrarch's Secret, or The Soul's Conflict with Passion: Three Dialogues between Himself and St. Augustine,* tr. William H. Draper (London, 1911), pp. 39–42, 100–2, for St. Augustine's use of this kind of Vergilian allegory to instruct the wayward "Petrarch."

17. See Wiggins, *Satires,* pp. 62–69.

18. "Est enim triplex hominum recte & ex ratione viventium ordo" (Landino, *Disputationes Camaldulenses,* sig. hii^v).

19. Ibid., sig. g^v.

20. Ibid., sig. g^v.

21. Ibid., sig. g^{iv}: "Quid cum a uoluptate discessimus atque non dum uerae uirtutis habitum contraximus, facile ex illa in aliam cupiditatem incidimus: insurgitque habendi libido. . . ."

22. "Amor sceleratus habendi" (Ovid, *Metamorphoses,* 1.131); "Amor ardet habendi" (Boethius, *Consolation* 2.met.5.26); and see the Vergilian "innatus amor habendi" (*Georgics,* 4.177), as well as Vegio's *Thirteenth Book* for a striking recall: "O fragilis damnosa superbia sceptri! / O furor, O nimium dominandi innata cupido" (ll. 145–46). All quotations from Ovid's *Metamorphoses* are from the Loeb edition, tr. Frank Justus Miller, 2 vols. (1916; rpt., London: Heinemann, 1951).

23. See *The Republic of Plato,* tr. Francis MacDonald Cornford (1945; rpt., New York: Oxford University Press, 1963), 14 (4.442–43) (pp. 141–42): "But in reality justice . . . is not a matter of external behaviour, but of the inward self and of attending to all that is, in the fullest sense, a man's proper concern. The just man does not allow the several elements in his soul to usurp one another's functions; he is indeed one who sets his house in order, by self-mastery and discipline coming to be at peace with himself, and bringing into tune those three parts, like the terms in the proportion of a musical scale, the highest and lowest notes and the mean between them, with all the intermediate intervals. Only when he has linked these parts together in well-tempered harmony and has made himself one man instead of many, will he be ready to go about whatever he may have to do."

24. See fig. 3 in *The Book of the Courtier,* tr. Charles S. Singleton (Garden City, N.Y.: Anchor, 1959).

25. See canto 5.22.5–8 of *Don Juan,* ed. T. G. Steffan, E. Steffan, and W. W. Pratt (1973; rpt., Harmondsworth: Penguin, 1977), p. 224.

26. In his lyric entitled "The Pearl.Matth.13."

27. This is the phrase employed by the Venetian publisher Gabriele Giolito in his "Dedication" of the 1542 edition of *Orlando Furioso* to the Dauphin of France.

28. See Landino, *Disputationes Camaldulenses* (sig. Kii^v), where the phrase is applied to the passion that Juno inspires in Aeneas, hoping thereby to bind him to Dido and keep him from Italy; and Simone Fornari's *Spositione sopra l'Orlando Furioso,* 2 vols. (Florence, 1549–1550), 2:19. Plato's second type of man ("deuteron andra") is defined at 8.550 of *The Republic,* ed. Paul Shorey, 2 vols. (London and Cambridge, Mass., 1930), 2:261.

29. For this apt phrase, see *Samson Agonistes,* l. 1746.

30. This paraphrases slightly and utilizes in another sense than the original one the reverberative line from *Measure for Measure* (1.2.118–19), ed. R. C. Bald (Baltimore: Penguin, 1973).

31. *Gli Asolani,* tr. Rudolf B. Gottfried, Indiana University Publications Humanities Series No. 31 (Bloomington: Indiana University Press, 1954), p. 96.

32. Murrin, *The Allegorical Epic,* p. 46. In her chapter on Ariosto in *Inescapable Romance: Studies in*

the Poetics of a Mode (Princeton University Press, 1979), Patricia A. Parker notes the same tendency to "erring" in the romance narrator of the *Furioso*.

33. *Asolani,* tr. Gottfried, p. 97.

34. Here I have in mind the way in which Eliot's Becket, expecting only three tempters, is presented instead with four, and of the highly patterned way in which the initial temptation of the flesh, easily repulsed by him, leads inevitably to more difficult, interlinked temptations of worldly power, and finally to the most deeply rooted, unsuspected one of spiritual pride, with its desire to die. For the radical interconnection of great sin with greater sin, see Augustine, *Confessions,* tr. R. S. Pine-Coffin (1961; rpt., Harmondsworth: Penguin, 1966), bk. 10, pp. 207–52.

35. "At last he asks for Lavinia's hand in marriage, that is, for the life of labors," meaning the active life: see Fulgentius, *De Vergiliana continentia,* ed. Van Steveren, p. 763. Here marriage becomes the seal on the assumption of the civil and active life, at once a social reality and a metaphor for the achievement of harmony.

36. *Orlando Furioso* (London, 1607), p. 382: I silently correct a misspelling and ignore Harington's italicization. See my unpublished dissertation, "The Dynastic Romance" (Princeton, 1964), p. 299, for another use of this same Harington quotation, connecting it to the allegorizers of the *Furioso.* The emphasis in my study (pp. 9–12) on dynastic marriage as the fitting conclusion to both Vergilian and romantic epic has been reiterated in A. Fichter, *Poets Historical: Dynastic Epic in the Renaissance* (New Haven: Yale University Press, 1982), pp. 15-16, who employs the same quotation in the same context.

37. See my *Pastoral* (1971; rpt., London: Methuen, 1978), pp. 65–68, for an earlier statement of the typically Ariostan suspicion of pastoral retreat.

38. See *Gli Asolani,* in *Prose e rime di Pietro Bembo,* ed. Carlo Dionisotti (Turin: UTET, 1966), pp. 478ff., and tr. Gottfried, pp. 169ff.

39. Cf. Boethius, *The Consolation of Philosophy,* tr. "I. T.," rev. H. F. Stewart (Cambridge: Harvard University Press, 1968), pp. 302–3, and *Asolani,* ed. Dionisotti, pp. 496–98, and tr. Gottfried, pp. 187–88.

40. See, for instance, the comments on Ariosto in the article "How Good is Tasso?" *TLS,* 14 December 1962, pp. 965–66.

41. See, for an egregious older example, Luigi Rosso, *L'Orlando Furioso* (Pisa: Nistri-Lischi, 1956), p. 114. Though pitched on an altogether higher level of critical sophistication, Daniel Javitch's "Rescuing Ovid from the Allegorizers: The Liberation of Angelica, *Furioso,* X," in *Ariosto 1974 in America,* Atti del Congresso Ariostesco—December 1974, Casa Italiana della Columbus University, ed. Aldo Scaglione (Ravenna: Longo, 1976), makes the similar mistake of supposing that Ariosto constructs his allegory to mock the literary mode rather than his wayward character and his characteristically easy solutions to profoundly difficult problems. In both cases, the continuation of the allegorical mode in Astolfo's narrative is completely ignored. The same tendency to empty the poem of content and to make of it only a self-referring artifact is apparent in William J. Kennedy's "Ariosto's Ironic Allegory," *MLN* 88, 1 (1973): 44–67, as well as in his *Rhetorical Norms in Renaissance Literature* (New Haven: Yale University Press, 1978), pp. 135–51.

42. See *Tom Jones,* 3.3 and 5.5.

43. For this second of three Delphic precepts ("Nothing too much," "Know thyself," "Be"), see Pico della Mirandola, *Oration on the Dignity of Man,* tr. Charles Glenn Wallis (1940; rpt., Indianapolis: Bobbs Merrill, 1965), pp. 14–15. Since Pico died in 1494, when Ariosto was a young student of twenty and a familiar companion of members of his family, his ignorance of one of the philosopher's most famous texts is scarcely credible.

44. Alma, the Soul, is of course the Christian counterpart, the transcendence, really, of the Mean embodied in Medina. She gives a vertical spiritual dimension to what (so to speak) is a merely "horizontal" balance between opposing deficiencies and excesses in the classical authors.

45. "Nature has given us an adequate equipment in reason; we need no other implements. This is

the weapon she has bestowed; it is strong, enduring, obedient, not double-edged or capable of being turned against its owner. Reason is all-sufficient in itself, serving not merely for counsel, but for action as well": see *Moral Essays*, tr. John W. Basore, 2 vols. (Cambridge: Harvard University Press, 1953), 1:151.

46. Wiggins, *Satires*, p. xxviii.

Notes for Chapter 6: A Clown's Redemption

1. See Giuseppe Guido Ferrero, "Astolfo (storia di un personaggio)," *Convivium*, n.s. 29 (1961): 513–30: an absolutely essential article in which the author summarizes the growth of Astolfo into a stock character, taking the development up to Boiardo only. Nicola Zingarelli's "Introduction" accords Astolfo's adventures and equipment some highly intelligent attention without discovering a pattern in them (pp. xlix-l); Emilio Zanette's chapter entitled "Astolfo," in his *Conversazioni sull'Orlando Furioso* (Pisa: Nistri-Lischi, 1958), notes the new characterization in Ariosto without showing how it came to be created or what part it plays in the total design of the *Furioso*. A more modern treatment is Mario Santoro's "L'Astolfo Ariostesco: *homo fortunatus*," in his *Letture Ariostesche* (Naples: Liguori, 1973), pp. 135–214, where Astolfo is said to act "sine ratione," a reading undermined by 14.10–15, 22.24 and 27–28. For other criticism of this formula, see Peter De Sa Wiggins, "Ariosto's Rinaldo: *Homo Prudens* or 'Gran Pedone'?" *Forum Italicum* 16 (1982): 33–59.

2. Apart from Astolfo, Bradamante acts in significant fashion in canto 1 before her sex and name are revealed; Atlante is given three separate descriptions and two epiphanies, establishing him as an Ariostanly transformed character before his identity is revealed (see my article, "The Flight of Ariosto's Hippogriff: Genesis, Elaboration, and Function," in *Ficino and Renaissance Neoplatonism*, ed. Konrad Eisenbichler and Olga Zorzi Pugliese, University of Toronto Italian Studies, 1 [Ottawa: Dovehouse Editions, 1986], pp. 90–94); Melissa performs her office of providential *care*—the poet puns twice on "cura" (7.39, 42)—before he "remembers" to give her a name derived from "melein," "to care for" (7.66). "Sdegno" or "Indignation" functions allegorically through dress and action in canto 42, effecting the rescue of Rinaldo, before he identifies himself (42.64).

3. *Paradise Lost*, 9.1127–31, in *Complete Poetical Works*, pp. 396–97: "understanding rul'd not, and the will / Heard not her lore, both in subjection now / To sensual appetite, who from beneath / Usurping over sovran reason claimed / Superior sway."

4. See *Timaeus*, tr. H. D. P. Lee (Harmondsworth: Penguin, 1965): "And since they shrank from polluting the divine element with these mortal feelings more than was absolutely necessary, they [the subordinate gods] located the mortal element in a separate part of the body, and constructed the neck as a kind of isthmus and boundary between head and breast to keep them apart" (p. 95), so defending the intellectual faculties from the appetitive functions.

5. For popular and learned versions of the island-body in seventeenth-century English literature, see Richard Bernard, *The Isle of Man or, The Legall Proceeding in Man-Shire against Sinne* (1626), and Phineas Fletcher's *The Purple Island, or The Isle of Man* (1633). In the latter, the Platonic tripartite kingdom is represented in its ideal state and functioning harmoniously, as opposed to Ariosto's more dynamic picture of the body in disorder, its elements battling.

6. For Logistica, who sends Poliphilo to make his choice among Theodoxia, Cosmodoxia, and Erotrophos—variants of Athena, Juno, and Venus in the Choice of Paris, and of Logistilla, Morgana, and Alcina in Ariosto—see bk. 1, ch. 10 of *Hypnerotomachia: The Strife of Love in a Dreame* (London, 1592); for Frezzi's Minerva and her attendants, see *Quadriregio*, ed. Enrico Filippini (Bari, 1914), bk. 1, ch. 12. For Ariosto and Frezzi, see Pio Rajna, *Le fonti dell'Orlando Furioso* (1876; 2d ed. 1900; rpt., Florence: Sansoni, 1975), p. 176, and Giulio Bertoni, *La Biblioteca Estense e cultura ferrarese ai tempi del duca Ercole I* (Turin, 1903), p. 115. For Lady Reason, see the translation by Harry W. Robbins, *The Romance of the Rose*, ed. Charles W. Dunn (New York: Dutton, 1962), p. 94.

7. Marianne Shapiro, in "From Atlas to Atlante," *Comparative Literature* 35 (1983): 328, notes

how "Ruggiero and Orlando often double one another's plot-functions as they pass through similar adventures," but she neglects the similar function of Astolfo.

8. Boethius, *Consolation,* 4.met.7.34–35.

9. See Vincent Cronin, *The Flowering of the Renaissance* (New York: Dutton, 1969), p. 187: "Virtus Dei donum" was the device borne by the sonnets of Gaspara Stampa.

10. An important issue treated recently by Peter De Sa Wiggins, in *Figures in Ariosto's Tapestry: Character and Design in the "Orlando Furioso"* (Baltimore: Johns Hopkins University Press, 1986), pp. 146–49, where he notes, "As if to stress the futility of Rodomonte's efforts in Paris, Ariosto interlaces their description with the panorama of Astolfo's fabulous travels through the Orient and Grifone's adventures in Damascus." Chapter 8 of the present study will develop the contrast between Rodomonte and Astolfo.

11. "Festina lente" was the motto employed by Aldus Manutius in his dolphin-anchor device; since he was the recipient of Ariosto's first recorded letter, we may take it as evidence that the poet employed the paradoxical phrase with as much consciousness as he brought to his use of the similar paradoxes and oxymorons "wise folly" and "laughing seriousness."

12. Browning's phrase about the participants in the action of *The Ring and the Book,* 1.1086.

13. Possibly this difference in temperament represents Ariosto's dramatization of Castiglione's differentiation between serene temperance and embattled continence, previously stated by Landino in his allegory of the *Aeneid:* see Castiglione, *The Courtier,* pp. 301–2; Cristoforo Landino, *Disputationes Camaldulenses* (Venice, 1500), sig. giiiv.

14. Ariosto voices the sense of earthly and unearthly madnesses in the Horatian *Satires* in his reply to friends who urge him to seek preferment and gain: "Ma chi fu mai sì saggio o mai sì santo / che di esser senza macchia di pazzia / o poca o molta, dar si possa vanto? // Ogniun tenga la sua, questa è la mia / se a perder s'ha la libertà, non stimo / il più ricco capel che in Roma sia" (2.148–53; "But who was ever so wise or so holy that he could boast of being unstained by insanity, in some degree? To each man his own madness. This is mine. I value not the richest hat in Rome if freedom must be lost to gain it").

15. For the traditional depiction of the cardinal virtue of Fortitude, see illustration 167 ("Strength") in Cesare Ripa, *Baroque and Rococo Pictorial Imagery: The 1758–1760 Hertel Edition of Ripa's "Iconologia," with Two Hundred Engraved Illustrations,* ed. Edward A. Maser (New York: Dover, 1971). Fortitude is depicted as a robust woman equipped with various attributes appropriate to both Hercules and Samson, respectively classical and Old Testament exemplars of the virtue: the lion-skin and the columns are appropriate to both (the columns of the Temple of Baal, the columns of the Pillars of Hercules), and in this edition of the *Iconologia,* Herculean symbols are represented solely but suggestively by the base of a column. The editor of this edition utilizes Ariosto's friend Piero Valeriano to explicate some of the engraving's details, so the use of this figure in a discussion of Ariosto seems not inappropriate.

16. Ed. B. L. Ullman, 2 vols. (Zurich: Thesaurus Mundi, 1947).

17. See Eva Borsook, *The Companion Guide to Florence* (1966; rpt., London: Collins, 1973), p. 49.

18. See the second genealogical chart, "The House of Este," in E. G. Gardner, *The King of Court Poets: A Study of the Work, Life, and Times of Ludovico Ariosto* (London, 1906): Ercole I (1431–1505) was the second Duke of Ferrara and Modena; his grandson, Ercole II (1508–1559), son of Alfonso I, was the fourth Duke of Ferrara and Modena; and the generation between them was represented by Ercole di Sigismondo, a nephew of Ercole I.

19. See *The Labors of Hercules by Pietro Andrea di Bassi,* tr. W. Kenneth Thompson (Barre, Mass.: Imprint Society, 1971). Thompson suggests (p. 9) that the MS (now in the Houghton Library, Harvard University) was composed before 1435, for the marquis Niccolò III d'Este, perhaps in celebration of the birth of his son Ercole in 1431. For biographical information on Bassi, see *GSLI* 83 (1924): 258–320. In *The Allegorical Epic: Essays in Its Rise and Decline* (University of Chicago Press, 1980), pp. 70–72 particularly, Michael Murrin discusses his commentary on Boccaccio's *Teseida,* published (like the work on Hercules) in 1475 at Ferrara.

20. See his *Operum . . . tomi duo* (Basle, 1580). Jean Seznec, in his *The Survival of the Pagan Gods* (1953; Princeton University Press, 1972), pp. 230 and 232, notes that Celio Calcagnini was a benefactor of Giraldi the mythographer, whose *De deis gentium varia et multiplex historia* was dedicated to Duke Ercole II of Ferrara—another instance of the circle of acquaintances in which Ariosto habitually moved.

21. This work, published in Modena in 1557, represents Jove, in canto 9, discoursing to Pallas Athena on the glory of the descendants of Hercules, among whom are the Estensi. The canto portrays a long procession of Este rulers, climaxing in Ercole II, whose ancestors are Bradamante, daughter of Leone and Beatrice, and Ruggiero, "da la famiglia / D'Hettore" (p. 111).

22. The only other rider of the hippogriff, Atlante, functions as an allegorical representation of Amor, independently equipped by Ariosto with the conventional attributes of the figure for the cupidinous appetite: see the classic essay, "Blind Cupid," in Erwin Panofsky's *Studies in Iconology: Humanistic Themes in the Art of the Renaissance* (Oxford, 1939; rpt., New York: Harper & Row, 1972), pp. 95–128, and the illustrations following, esp. 90 and 91.

23. Crucial here is Michael J. B. Allen's *Marsilio Ficino and the Phaedran Charioteer* (Berkeley: University of California Press, 1981); and see Ariosto's friend, Mario Equicola, *Di natura d'amore* (Venice, 1561), pp. 80–81, for the absorption into courtly Neoplatonism of the Platonic lore concerning the black and white horses of "cupidità" and "ira."

24. A commonplace in Renaissance poetry, from Sidney's "Leave me, O love, that reachest but to dust," to Constable's "When others hooded with blind loue doe flye / Lowe on the ground with buzzard Cupids wings / A heauenly loue from loue of loue thee brings / And makes thy Muse to mount aboue the skie": see *The Poems of Henry Constable* (Liverpool University Press, 1960), "Sonet 5," p. 141, ll. 1–4.

Notes for Chapter 7: The Laughter of Lucian

1. For commentary on Ariosto vis-à-vis the *Commedia*, see Patricia A. Parker, *Inescapable Romance: Studies in the Poetics of a Mode* (Princeton University Press, 1979), pp. 16–53, and Emilio Zanette, *Conversazioni sull'Orlando Furioso* (Pisa: Nistri-Lischi, 1958), pp. 275–88.

2. See *Pharsalia*, 6.507ff.; *Somnium*, 3–5; *Paradiso*, 22.127ff.; *Teseida*, 11.1ff.; and (for Arcita's successor), *Troilus and Criseyde*, 5.1807–27. The tradition of laughing contemplation of earth's littleness is traced by C. S. Lewis in *The Discarded Image* (1964; rpt., Cambridge University Press, 1967), pp. 22–23: the account does not encompass Lucian of Samosata, and (needless to say) Astolfo cast in the role of any kind of contemplator whatever makes no appearance in these pages.

3. John Steadman, *Disembodied Laughter: Troilus and the Apotheosis Tradition* (Berkeley: University of California Press, 1973); see also Marjorie Hope Nicolson, *Voyages to the Moon* (New York: Columbia University Press, 1960), in which Astolfo is accorded a brief paragraph of recognition (pp. 20–21).

4. *Gli Asolani*, in *Prose e rime di Pietro Bembo*, ed. Carlo Dionisotti (Turin: UTET, 1966), pp. 502–3, tr. Rudolf B. Gottfried, Indiana University Publications Humanities Series No. 31 (Bloomington: Indiana University Press, 1954), p. 193.

5. David Quint, "Astolfo's Voyage to the Moon," *Yale Italian Studies* 1 (1977): 398–408, raises false genre expectations; the *Furioso* (in which Dantean illuminations are sought and not found) again becomes a romantic self-referring artifact.

6. See Pio Rajna, *Le fonti dell'Orlando Furioso* (1876; 2d ed. 1900; rpt., Florence: Sansoni, 1975), p. 174, n. 2. Simone Fornari analyzes Astolfo's adventures in cantos 8, 15, 33, and 34. See *Spositione sopra l'Orlando Furioso*, 2 vols. (Florence, 1549–1550), 2:152, 206–22, 223–75. Fornari's treatment is limited by its leaden inattention to nuance (the paradoxical juncture of "serio" and "ludere" is totally wasted on him, and he understands only the former). He deals with Astolfo's role in a limited rather than a comprehensive way, failing to see how his adventures play against those of Ruggiero and

Orlando, or how the texture of the poetry distinguishes his adventures from theirs. His value, ultimately, resides in his directing us to Ariosto's nearest literary models. Robert McNulty, raising the same objections as Rajna, would be on better ground if his translation of Fornari's passage were not marred by an egregious mistranslation in which he totally mistakes the sense: he has exacerbated the problem by saying that Fornari presents Astolfo soaring into the heavens as the type of the poet ("In Astolfo . . . is demonstrated figuratively the poet"), whereas Fornari's sense is very different: "In Astolfo, who gives Bradamante his horse and his arms to make himself lighter for his flight through the air, the poet figuratively instructs us [c'insegna figuratamente . . . il Poeta] that those who wish to acquire prudence must lighten themselves of earthly encumbrances." See *Ludovico Ariosto's "Orlando Furioso" Translated into English Heroical Verse by Sir John Harington* (Oxford: Clarendon, 1972), p. xxviii.

7. See C. R. Thompson, *The Translations of Lucian by Erasmus and St. Thomas More* (Ithaca: private, 1940), pp. 4–5, and also Christopher Robinson, *Lucian and His Influence in Europe* (London: Duckworth, 1979), pp. 81–95. Two early examples of Lucian's influence on Renaissance painting are found in Botticelli's "The Calumny of Appelles" and his "Mars and Venus," both founded on episodes in the satirist of Samosata: see L. D. and Helen S. Ettlinger, *Botticelli* (New York: Oxford University Press, 1977), pp. 141, 144–45.

8. Thompson, *Translations of Lucian*, p. 5. Boiardo was the author of a dramatic version of Lucian's *Timon*; see two recent essays, the first by Marcello Aurigemma, "Il *Timone* di M. M. Boiardo," and the second by Lienhard Bergel, "I due *Timone*: Boiardo e Shakespeare," both in *Il Boiardo e la critica contemporanea*, ed. G. Anceschi (Florence: Leo S. Olschki, 1970), pp. 29–60 and 73–80 respectively.

9. Thompson, *Translations of Lucian*, p. 84, provides a strong statement of Lucian's value in fifteenth-century Italy as a kind of Horatian or Senecan moralist. Dolan says, "Those who are impervious to [Erasmus's] learning will certainly fail to see the basis of his effort to expose human foibles in terms of Menippean satire. The *ridendo dicere verum* employed by Erasmus have exposed his works to the accusation of skepticism, but on the other hand it had the happy effect of bringing the entire drama of human existence under his scrutinizing eye": see *The Essential Erasmus*, sel. and tr. John P. Dolan (New York: Mentor, 1964), pp. 94–96. Perhaps for this reason alone Ariosto merits a place among those "praisers of folly" that Walter Kaiser, in *Praisers of Folly: Erasmus, Rabelais, Shakespeare* (Cambridge: Harvard University Press, 1963), grouped together and treated so intelligently. Interestingly, though there is no record of a meeting between the authors of the *Praise of Folly* and *Orlando Furioso*, two of the central works on madness in the Renaissance, one was indeed not only possible but also probable. Erasmus is known to have passed through Ferrara in December 1508 and to have made the acquaintance not only of the great Calcagnini, with whom he afterward corresponded, but also of Niccolò Leoniceno of Vicenza (1428–1524), the distinguished Latin and Greek scholar and physician, who for sixty years was a teacher at the Studio di Ferrara and was, like Guarino da Verona (and Erasmus himself), a translator of Lucian. Dionisotti (*Prose e rime*, p. 20) informs us that Bembo studied with him in Ferrara, deepening his philosophic studies by attending Leoniceno's lectures. At the time of Erasmus's visit in 1508, Richard Pace, Erasmus's English friend, was on a diplomatic mission in the city and studying with Leoniceno himself. Seventeen years after this visit we find Erasmus mentioning Leoniceno in a letter to Calcagnini and being apprised, also in 1525, of the death of the ninety-two-year-old scholar: see *The Correspondence of Erasmus*, tr. R. A. B. Myers and D. F. S. Thomson, annotated by Wallace K. Ferguson, 2 vols. (University of Toronto Press, 1975): 2:154; and also F. M. Nichols, *Epistles of Erasmus*, 2 vols. (London, 1907), 1:451–52. For Ariosto's tributes to Calcagnini, see *Orlando Furioso*, 42.90, 46.14; for the one to Leoniceno, see 46.14.

10. For these aboundingly vivid renderings, see Lucian, *Satirical Sketches*, tr. Paul Turner (Harmondsworth: Penguin, 1961), pp. 122–23.

11. Lucian, *Satirical Sketches*, pp. 89–91.

12. See, for instance, plates 7 ("The Triumph of Death") and 9 ("The Triumph of Time") in D.

D. Carnicelli, *Lord Morley's "Tryumphes of Fraunces Petrarcke": The First English Translation of the "Trionfi"* (Cambridge: Harvard University Press, 1971); and also "The Triumph of Time," laying waste to all human effort, by Brueghel, in H. Arthur Klein, *Graphic Worlds of Peter Brueghel the Elder* (New York: Dover, 1963), pp. 175–77. See R. H. Ruchs, *Dutch Painting* (New York: Oxford University Press, 1978), pp. 40-54, for the notion of man as a mere bubble ("homo bulla") and for the special emphasis given by the school of Leiden, a university town, to intellectually difficult paintings and to allegorical still lifes, requiring to be "read" for symbolism.

13. "At nos desuper inridemus vilissima rerum quaeque rapient securi totius furiosi tumulti" (*Consolation*, 1.pros.3). Note the emphasis on "furiosi."

14. For Ariosto's reliance on the brilliantly bizarre imagery of one of L. B. Alberti's *Intercenali*, the "Somnium," see the essay "Leon Battista Alberti e Ludovico Ariosto," in Cesare Segre's *Esperienze ariostesche* (Pisa: Nistri-Lischi, 1966), pp. 85–95.

15. See *Petrarch's Lyric Poems*, no. 34 of the *Rime*, l. 8; and also, for the image of bird-lime, see nos. 40, 99, 105, 142, 165, and 211.

16. Chirping insects are a wholly traditional figure for poets: see D. C. Allen, "Richard Lovelace: The Grasse-Hopper," rpt. in *Seventeenth-Century English Poetry: Modern Essays in Criticism*, ed. William R. Keast (New York: Oxford University Press, 1962), pp. 280–89.

17. *Asolani*, tr. Gottfried, p. 189.

18. See Edgar Wind, *Pagan Mysteries in the Renaissance*, rev. ed. (New York: Norton, 1968), p. 147, n. 124, for this highly suggestive emblem. Wind notes that a "Fortuna a cavallo" is listed by Vincenzo Cartari in his *Imagini de i dei degli antichi* as a "Renaissance symbol of fugacious fortune," highly apt for Angelica, since she also capriciously elevates Medoro to a throne.

19. 2.1.192: sometimes given as "wode within this wood," with no diminution whatever of the pun's force in equating being lost in a forest with the state of being mad. At the root of the pun stands the old identification of the body and the material stuff of which it is composed, with its attached lusts and desires, with a wood or forest (*sylva* in Latin, *hyle* in Greek).

20. See *Consolation*, 2.pros.4: "Huic census exuberat . . . expertus exhorruet."

21. The passage beginning "But Love . . ." is taken from Gottfried's translation, pp. 45–46; the one beginning "Percio che sì come nell'entrar d'alcun bosco" ("For just as at the entrance of some forest") is from Dionisotti's edition, p. 354. Both the Bembo and Ariosto passages have their closest roots in Ficino: "We all love continuously in some way, but almost all of us love wrongly, and the more we love, the worse. And if one in a hundred thousand loves rightly, because his is not the common practice, no one follows his example. We fall into this great error, unfortunately for us, because we boldly start out upon *the difficult journey of love* before we know its destination or how to travel the perilous path of the journey. The farther we go, the farther we stray to our great undoing; and *losing our way in this dark forest* is more serious than on other journeys because we travel there in larger numbers and more often" (italics mine). See the letter, "Marsilio Ficino to Bernardo del Nero and Antonio Manetti," in *Commentary on Plato's Symposium*, ed. and trans. Sears Jayne, University of Missouri Studies, 19 (Columbia: University of Missouri, 1944), p. 238. With these three passages from Ficino, Bembo, and Ariosto, compare Boiardo, 3.7.13, discussed earlier in Chapter 2.

22. "Nunc accipe, quare / desipiant omnes aeque ac tu, qui tibi nomen / insano posuere. velut silvis, ubi passim / palantis error certo de tramite pellit, / ille sinistrorum, hic dextrorsum abit, unus utrique / error, sed variis illudit partibus": *Satire II*, 3.46–51, in the Loeb edition of *Satires, Epistles, and Ars poetica*, tr. H. Rushton Fairclough (London, 1932), pp. 156–67. The importance of the passage was demonstrated by Robert Durling in *The Figure of the Poet in Renaissance Epic* (Cambridge: Harvard University Press), pp. 165–66.

23. This crucial episode has regularly been perceived as emblematic but never really related to the other narrative peaks with which it forms an extended poetic sequence: see Robert J. Rodini and Salvatore Di Maria, *Ludovico Ariosto: An Annotated Bibliography of Criticism, 1956–1980* (Columbia, University of Missouri Press, 1984), entry nos. 72, 160, 728, 741, and 906.

24. See Orlando's fearful lament, 8.76–78.

25. For various other readings of this figure, see Marianne Shapiro, in "From Atlas to Atlante," *Comparative Literature* 35 (1983), which relates him to Atlas in Petrarch's *Africa*; Valerie M. Wise, "Ruggiero and the Hippogriff: The Ambiguities of Vision," *Quaderni d'Italianistica: Rivista di Letteratura Italiana* 2 (1981): 39–53; and David Quint, "The Figure of Atlante: Ariosto and Boiardo's Poem," *MLN* 94 (1979): 77–91, which, in its writerly preoccupations, allegorizes the magician as Boiardo in disguise, struggling with Ariosto for control of the poem; of far greater value is Quint's assertion of Ariosto's determination for closure (p. 84).

26. With the Ariostan "gabbia" compare Petrarch's lover-figure: "In così tenebrosa e stretta gabbia / rinchiusi fummo" (*cap* 4, 157–58): see *I Trionfi*, ed. Paolo Lecaldano (Milan: Rizzoli, 1956), pp. 40–41. All references are to this edition.

27. See *Trionfo della Pudicizia*, ll. 118–26.

28. *De remediis utriusque fortunae,* which details at crushing length the dangers of both good and bad fortune.

29. See *Le Studiolo d'Isabelle d'Este,* catalogue by Sylvie Béguin, et al. (Paris: Editions des Musées Nationaux, 1975), illustration no. 17, for a fragment of the Studiolo ceiling and a note that Isabella devised the phrase herself, adopting it in 1504 as a device signifying intellectual balance and a spirit armed against hope and disquiet.

30. *Consolation,* 4.pros.5.

31. *Paradise Lost,* 3.174ff.: the Father in dialogue with the Son.

32. For the notion of good wrought out of evil in Bradamante's fall as contrived by Pinabello, see my unpublished thesis, "The Dynastic Romance" (Princeton, 1964), p. 102. For the intervention of Providence in Bradamante's career, the curbing of "voglia" or human willfulness by "voler divino," and the ironic comic effects it produces in the *Furioso,* see p. 247 of my article entitled "Redemptive Laughter: Comedy in the Italian Romances," in *Versions of Medieval Comedy,* ed. Paul G. Ruggiers (Norman: University of Oklahoma Press, 1977), in which I announced the present study under a different title. For echoes of the ironic interaction of human and divine wills, see A. Fichter, *Poets Historical: Dynastic Epic in the Renaissance* (New Haven: Yale University Press, 1982), p. 85. William J. Kennedy, in *Rhetorical Norms in Renaissance Literature* (New Haven: Yale University Press, 1978), pp. 138–40, has some valuable insights on the way in which Ariosto allows "voler" and "poter" to play against each other.

33. *Consolation,* 2.pros.2: "Riches, honours, and the rest of that sort belong to me. They acknowledge me for their mistress, and themselves for my servants, they come with me, and when I go away they likewise depart."

34. "For worldly splendours, He ordained a general minister and guide, to change betimes the vain possessions, from people to people, and from one kindred to another, beyond the hindrance of human wisdom." For a charming eighteenth-century vulgarization of the idea, see Joseph Addison's *Tatler* essay (no. 249), "The Adventures of a Shilling," the tale of a coin's picaresque passage through many kinds of pockets, prefixed with the telling Vergilian motto: "Per varios Casus, per tot Discrimina Rerum, / Tendimus" (*Aen.* 1.204–5).

35. Michael Murrin, *The Allegorical Epic: Essays in Its Rise and Decline* (University of Chicago Press, 1980), p. 48.

36. *Satire X,* ll. 365–66: "Thou wouldst have no divinity, O Fortune, if we had but wisdom; it is we that make a goddess of thee and place thee in the skies"; see *Juvenal and Perseus,* tr. G. G. Ramsay (London, 1928).

37. An "unexpected and not foreseen" concourse of things running together: *Consolation,* 5.pros.1.

38. In addition to Boethius, see Marcus Aurelius: "Whatever may happen to you was prepared for you in advance from the beginning of time. In the woven tapestry of causation, the thread of your being had been intertwined from all time with that particular incident": see *Meditations,* tr. Maxwell Staniforth (1964; rpt., Harmondsworth: Penguin, 1974), p. 152.

39. In this one instance I use, for the sake of its greater clarity and fidelity to the metaphors of a notoriously difficult passage, the translation by V. E. Watts (Harmondsworth: Penguin, 1969), pp. 135–36.

40. See Petrarch, "La tela novella ch'io ordisco" (*Rime sparse*, no. 40.2); cf. *Orlando Furioso*, 2.30.5-6 ("varie fila a varie tele / Uopo mi son, che tutte ordire intendo") and 13.81.1-2 ("Di molte fila esser bisogno parme / a condur la gran tela ch'io lavoro"). And for yet other uses of the weaving metaphor, see Dante, *De monarchia*, 3.16.

41. *Consolation*, 4.pros.6.

Notes for Conclusion

1. For a statement of the dual nature of the persona in *Orlando Furioso*, see my "The Dynastic Romance" (Princeton, 1964), pp. 101–2, my "Redemptive Laughter: Comedy in the Italian Romances," in *Versions of Medieval Comedy*, ed. Paul G. Ruggiers (Norman: University of Oklahoma Press, 1977), pp. 247–48; cf. A. Fichter's *Poets Historical: Dynastic Epic in the Renaissance* (New Haven: Yale University Press, 1982), pp. 73 and 84. For an apt designation of these two aspects of the persona as "Vergilian" and "Ovidian," see William J. Kennedy, in *Rhetorical Norms in Renaissance Literature* (New Haven: Yale University Press, 1978), pp. 137–38. In his *A Preface to Chaucer* (Princeton University Press, 1960), pp. 277–78 and 280–82, D. W. Robertson first noted this creation of a conversationally adept persona, traceable, like the one in Ariosto, to Ovidian poetry of the twelfth century, and one all too likely to be confused with the actual poet.

2. Thus, Rinaldo chases after Angelica, only to have his hot pursuit intercepted by Charlemagne in Paris and diverted so that he might seek aid in England—the beginning of the first great geographical leap outward (2.1–30); at once the poet shifts to Bradamante in her pursuit of the vanished Ruggiero and her encounter with Pinabello, which creates the beginning of an arc of narrative not concluded until canto 19 (2.30–76).

3. For the importance of Providence to the workings of the *Orlando Furioso*, see Tasso (no friendly witness) in *Discourses on the Heroic Poem*, tr. Mariella Cavalchini and Irene Samuel (Oxford: Clarendon, 1973), pp. 16–17. Ariosto's association of his art with providential control was a concept first brought clearly to notice by Robert Durling in a superlative chapter on Ariosto in *The Figure of the Poet in Renaissance Epic* (Cambridge: Harvard University Press, 1965), pp. 112–81, and I am indebted to him for these extensions of his argument. For a more recent restatement of his critical position, see Robert J. Rodini and Salvatore Di Maria, *Ludovico Ariosto: An Annotated Bibliography of Criticism, 1956–1980* (Columbia: University of Missouri Press, 1984), entry 289.

4. I have in mind the allusive, provocative remarks E. M. W. Tillyard prefaced to *The English Epic and Its Background* (London, 1954; 2d ed. New York: Oxford University Press, 1966), p. v, indicating the connections that had formed in his mind between the epic and the history play. Compare the way an epic hero like Ruggiero conceives of his place in the world and of his ability to direct events to his own satisfaction, and the very similar way the hero of a chronicle play conceives of himself as a disposing center of the action, unaware of the ironies involved (Prince Hal, for instance).

5. For this concept of human art mimicking the order, utility, and beauty of God's art in both the macrocosm and the microcosm, see Bembo's speech in Castiglione's *Courtier*: "Behold the constitution of this great fabric of the world. . . . Think now how man is constituted, who may be called a little world. . . . Leave nature, and come to art" (pp. 343–44).

6. Both the *Meno* and the *Phaedo* had been translated into Latin by Aristippus at the court of Frederick II of Hohenstaufen (circa 1156) at Palermo, Sicily, but these versions had not passed into universal currency and remained little known: see Vincent Cronin, *The Florentine Renaissance* (New York: Dutton, 1967), p. 287.

7. Durling, *Figure of the Poet*, pp. 123ff.; and see also E. H. Wilkins, *A History of Italian Literature* (Cambridge: Harvard University Press, 1954), pp. 148–49, citing Landino's "Preface" to his edition

of *The Divina Commedia* (Florence, 1481): "The latter part of the preface contains an impassioned discussion of the nature and origin of poetry, considered supreme among the arts, as being directly inspired by God, who is Himself the supreme poet, the world being his poem." For the world as God's *epic* poem particularly see Tasso, *Discourses*, pp. 77–78.

8. "To hurl an inkwell" is spoken figuratively: Ariosto has power to punish the offending Rodomonte by the power of his pen and ink (29.2); it is also that he may not remain "captive" in the poet's pen that Astolfo shouts and gestures to his creator to be released from the narrative limbo to which he has long been consigned by the poet's lordly *entrelacement* (15.9).

9. *Consolation* 1.pros.4.125: "the error of human judgment."

10. *Gli Asolani*, tr. Rudolph B. Gottfried, Indiana University Publications Humanities Series No. 31 (Bloomington: Indiana University Press, 1954), p. 410: "the foolish, stupid opinion of men."

11. *Asolani*, tr. Gottfried, p. 171, ed. Carlo Dionisotti, in *Prose e rime di Pietro Bembo* (Turin: UTET, 1966), p. 481.

12. See the oddly reminiscent way in which Milton, who definitely had Ariosto in mind in book 1 ("Things unattempted yet in prose or rhyme," "Cose non dette in prosa mai né in rima"), in book 2 puns twice on this word with regard to Satan's doomed struggles to win out over superior power: Satan is "by success untaught" (2.9), and the timorous Belial speaks of an "ominous conjecture on the whole success" (2.123). In the first instance especially, the word "success," usually nothing more than "outcome," seems definitely to verge on a more modern signification.

13. See Boethius, *Consolation* 1.pros.2.15–16.

14. See chapter 7 of the *Commentary on Plato's "Phaedrus,"* in *Opera*, 2 vols. (Paris, 1641), 2:326. Highly relevant also is the *Commentary on the "Symposium"* ("Seventh Speech," ch. 14), with its Platonic imagery of the various steeds of the soul (pp. 231–33).

15. See A. Bartlett Giamatti's "*Sfrenatura*: Release and Restraint in *Orlando Furioso*," in *Ariosto 1974 in America*, Atti del Congresso Ariostesco—December 1974, Casa Italiana della Columbus University, ed. Aldo Scaglione (Ravenna: Longo, 1976), pp. 31–39. Albrecht Dürer's engraving, "Nemesis" ("The Larger Fortune"), called "Temperanza" by Vasari in recognition of her appearance as a sky-striding deity, is prominently equipped with a bridle suggesting powerful restraint: see Erwin Panofsky, *The Life and Art of Albrecht Dürer* (1943; rpt., Princeton University Press, 1955), fig. 115, and pp. 80–82. Also relevant is an emblem in Achille Bocchi's intriguingly titled *Symbolicarum quaestionum, de universo genere, quas serio ludebat, libri quinque* (Bologna, 1574), symb. 67: Nemesis with her bridle and square, and the accompanying poem explaining that she is "Dea / Severa, vindexque, aspera / Titanicae superbiae." Edgar Wind, *Pagan Mysteries in the Renaissance*, rev. ed. (New York: Norton, 1968), p. 72, n. 68, makes another interesting connection, or series of connections, between friends of Ariosto and the mythographic and emblematic tradition stemming from the middle and late Quattrocento. Wind notes the "close association" of Bocchi with Ariosto's schoolmate, Alberto Pio, "who, like Gyraldus's patron, Gianfrancesco Pico, was a nephew and literary executor of Giovanni Pico della Mirandola." A further link is provided in the same note by a reference to "Bocchi's friendship with Valeriano," whom Ariosto called "Pierio" in his stanzas in praise of his friends at the opening of the *Furioso*'s last canto. For the creator's love as bridle of the world, see *Consolation*, 2.met.8.1–18; 3.met.2.1–8; 4.met.1.19–22; 4.met.6.34–35. For the same image of Love bridling the universe, see Ficino, *Commentary on Plato's Symposium*, ed. and tr. Sears Jayne, University of Missouri Studies, 19 (Columbia: University of Missouri, 1944), p. 150. As Sears Jayne notes, Ficino alters the metaphor of the Orphic Hymn to Eros, which gives a nautical (rather than chivalric) value to the operation of love, making it hold the "helm" of the world rather than the "reins" of the world to establish its stable governance. For helm and rudder imagery in guiding the frame of the universe, see *Consolation*, 3.pros.12.38-42. The combination of the two modes of transportation, by horseback and shipboard, is, of course, of the utmost importance to the literary forms of epic, romance, and allegory. In Ariosto, ships and horses are interchangeable metaphorically: see 4.50 and 23.16.

16. See the discussion of this complex figure in Peter De Sa Wiggins, "The *Furioso*'s Third Protagonist," *MLN* 98 (1983): 30-54, and his *Figures in Ariosto's Tapestry: Character and Design in the "Orlando Furioso"*, passim. My own interpretation would add one or two other dimensions to a character fascinatingly shown to be multifaceted.

17. For this simile, imitating the description of Pyrrhus at *Aeneid* 2.469-75, see Kristen Olson Murtaugh, *Ariosto and the Classical Simile* (Cambridge: Harvard University Press, 1980), pp. 93-96. The discussion misses the strong diabolic undercurrents Ariosto develops from Vergil out of hints in Boiardo.

18. The following composite chart will clarify the relationships of the Estensi and the Hapsburg emperor:

The House of Aragon in Spain and in Italy

Ferdinand I of Antequera m. Eleanor of Alburquerque

SPAIN		ITALY
Juan II of Aragon		Alfonso Magnanimous, King of Aragon, later of Naples and Sicily
Ferdinand II of Aragon m. Isabella of Castile		Ferrante (Ferdinand I) of Naples and Sicily
Juana the Mad m. Maximilian the Fair		Eleanora of Aragon m. Duke Ercole d'Este of Ferrara
Charles V, Holy Roman Emperor		Isabella Beatrice Alfonso Cardinal Ippolito Ferrante

19. The association of Turnus and the devil ("id est, diabolus") was made by the famous fifteenth-century humanist, Maffeo Vegio, long a familiar figure at the court of Ferrara. Previous to that time, Turnus appears to have been associated merely with the inflamed senses ("furibundus sensus"), as in Bernard Sylvestris. The identification of the champion of the Italian tribes and chief opponent of Aeneas and the archenemy of mankind occurs in an allegorical reading of the *Aeneid* contained in 1.5 of Vegio's *De perseverantia religionis*: see Anna Cox Brinton, *Mapheius Vegius and His Thirteenth Book of the Aeneid* (Stanford, 1930), p. 28. Another strand in the complex of Turnus-Satan-Nembroth-Rodomonte may have been forged by Landino, interpreting Dante. In his notes to canto 31 of the *Inferno,* Landino says of the builder of Babel (whose arms Boiardo's Rodomonte inherits and wears): "Costui veramente si può dire, che tal fosse tra gli huomini, quale era stato Lucifero tra gli Angeli" ("Of him it may truly be said that he was among men what Lucifer was among the angels"). See *Dante con l'espositioni di Christoforo Landino et d'Alessandro Velutello sopra la sua Comedia dell Inferno, del Purgatorio, & del Paradiso* (Venice, 1578), p. 150r, col. 1. Ariosto's characterization of Rodomonte is very carefully layered. It begins with his transformation of a romance type inherited from Boiardo, a transformtation involving superimposing a classical Vergilian characterization on a Boiardan model, and then simultaneously evoking the allegorical, biblical resonances attached to that classical image in traditional humanistic interpretations. Both Boiardo and Ariosto found the association of Saracens with devils in popular Carolingian literature: see W. W. Comfort, "The Saracens in Italian Epic Poetry," *PMLA* 59 (1944): 882-910. Since both Turnus and the Saracens were associated with diabolical forces, it was inevitable that Rodomonte would partake of a Luciferean nature. Boiardo first (through his dragon-skin armor) connected him to the dragon of Revelation, and Ariosto reinforced that precedent by evoking a Vergilian heroic simile to intensify the biblical echo. Finally, it should be noted that David P. Harding, in *The Club of Hercules: Studies in the Classical Background of*

"Paradise Lost" (Urbana: University of Illinois Press, 1962), p. 50, recalls that on several occasions Milton allusively associates Turnus, Aeneas's opponent in Italy, with Satan himself. At the very end of book 4, Milton skillfully rewrites the last line of the *Aeneid*, in which Turnus's indignant spirit flees murmuring "sub umbras": "The Fiend looked up and knew / His mounted scale aloft: nor more; but fled / Murmuring, and with him fled the shades of night." As Harding rightly says, "Turnus . . . stands in the same relationship to Aeneas as Satan to the Fallen Adam. Just as Aeneas embodies the Roman *virtus* and *pietas* which Virgil would set up in the place of the discredited military virtues of an earlier age, so the Fallen Adam comes eventually to exemplify the Christian ideal of conduct which for Milton constitutes the only heroism" (pp. 50–51). So too, it might be said, that opposition is prefigured by that between Ruggiero and Rodomonte at the very end of the *Furioso,* which also, it may be recalled, terminates with Ariosto's fine rewriting of Vergil's last lines about the death of Turnus. Lastly, see John M. Steadman, "A Milton-Ariosto Parallel: Satan and Rodomonte (*Paradise Lost,* IV, 181)," *Zeitschrift für Romanische Philologie* 77 (1961): 514–16.

20. See Roy Strong, *Splendor at Court: Renaissance Spectacle and the Theater of Power* (Boston: Houghton Mifflin, 1973), pp. 79–119.

Index